More Real Than Reality

Black Mermaid in the Fifteenth-Century Restoration of the Chancel Arch at Clonfert, County Galway

More Real Than Reality

The Fantastic in Irish Literature and the Arts

Edited by
Donald E. Morse and Csilla Bertha

*Contributions to the Study of
Science Fiction and Fantasy, Number 45
MARSHALL B. TYMN, Series Editor*

GREENWOOD PRESS
New York • Westport, Connecticut • London

Library of Congress Cataloging-in-Publication Data

More real than reality : the fantastic in Irish literature and the
  arts / edited by Donald E. Morse and Csilla Bertha.
      p.   cm.—(Contributions to the study of science fiction and
fantasy, ISSN 0193-6875 ; no. 45)
  Includes bibliographical references and index.
  ISBN 0-313-26612-3 (alk. paper)
    1. English literature—Irish authors—History and criticism.
2. Fantastic literature, English—History and criticism.
3. Ireland—Intellectual life. 4. Ireland in literature.
5. Fantasy in art. 6. Art, Irish.   I. Morse, Donald E., 1936-
II. Bertha, Csilla.   III. Series.
PR8722.F35M6 1991
  823'.0876609—dc20   90-47537

British Library Cataloguing in Publication Data is available.

Library of Congress Catalog Card Number: 90-47537
ISBN: 0-313-26612-3
ISSN: 0193-6875

First published in 1991

Greenwood Press, 88 Post Road West, Westport, CT 06881
An imprint of Greenwood Publishing Group, Inc.

Printed in the United States of America

The paper used in this book complies with the
Permanent Paper Standard issued by the National
Information Standards Organization (Z39.48-1984).

10 9 8 7 6 5 4 3 2 1

70758

For Wolfgang and Hannelore Zach
who first brought us together to discuss things Irish.
". . . my glory was I had such friends"   W. B. Yeats

Contents

Illustrations

Acknowledgments

It is a pleasure to acknowledge the many people who helped bring this volume into being. We would like to thank especially Wolfgang and Hannelore Zach, to whom we dedicate this book for their many efforts to bring scholars from the East and West together to discuss Irish literature; including the memorable International Association for the Study of Anglo-Irish Literature international conference of 1984 in Graz, Austria, where for the first time Eastern European Irish scholars were invited to participate. We also wish to thank Heinz Kosok, Wuppertal University, Christopher Murray, University College-Dublin, and Dean Andrew Carpenter, University College-Dublin for their early encouragement and help. Our universities have been unusually generous in providing moral and material support: Oakland University, Rochester, Michigan, especially Professor Robert Eberwein, Chair of the Department of English; Tanárképzö Föiskola, Eger, Hungary; and Lajos Kossuth University in Debrecen, Hungary, as was the American Embassy in Budapest at crucial moments. The early and ongoing enthusiasm of our editors, Marshall Tymn and Marilyn Brownstein, has sustained us even over long distances. Finally, we owe a huge debt to Robert Collins whose generosity helped bring the book finally into being.

An earlier version of the introductory essay was presented as the opening plenary lecture at the 1989 International Conference of IASAIL in Debrecen, Hungary; an earlier version of "Myth and the Fantastic: The Example of W. B. Yeats's Plays" was given at the Eighth International Conference on the Fantastic in the Arts in Houston. Much of the material in the essays on Tom Murphy and Samuel Beckett was developed from lectures given at Hungarian, Austrian, and West German universities in 1988 and 1989. We wish to thank the organizers of these conferences and our hosts for the lectures for giving us such fine occasions to think aloud about issues so central to the discussion of the fantastic in literature and the arts: in Austria: Wolfgang Zach, Graz University; in Germany: Joseph Swann, Wuppertal University; and in Hungary: Aladár Sarbu, Lóránd Eötvös University, Budapest; László Budai and Lehel Vadon, Tanárképzö Föiskola, Eger; and István Pálffy, Lajos Kossuth University, Debrecen.

More Real Than Reality

Donald E. Morse

"More Real Than Reality": An Introduction to the Fantastic in Irish Literature and the Arts

L ong ago the Irish discovered one of the great secrets of the human mind, that "ultimately, meaning is not a rational matter" (Hume 196) and set out to exploit their discovery. The result was a rich explosion in art, literature, and religion. For many readers, the Irish and the fantastic are synonymous. Certainly from the ancient texts and medieval illuminated manuscripts to twentieth-century poetry, painting, drama, stories, and novels, Irish writers and artists have always found the fantastic congenial and, even, necessary for their art. Early on they realized that "there is an elegant efficiency to fantasies" (Hume 191) that enables a writer to express ideas, emotions, and insights not available through mimesis. Thus for the Irish, the road to insight often lay not through literalism, rationalism, or logic but through the marvelous and the fantastic.

"Critically, fantasy is all but uncharted territory," asserts Kathryn Hume, in the introduction to her excellent study, *Fantasy and Mimesis: Responses to Reality in Western Literature* (xv). True, but the one island that all critics appear to agree exists in that uncharted territory is the one labeled "the impossible." For whatever else it may be – and there is a good deal of controversy about exactly what constitutes the fantastic – virtually all critics agree that it occurs when we encounter the impossible.[1] Thus, for example, at the end of Tom MacIntyre's novel, *The Charollais* (1969), when the huge heroic bull takes off into the empyrean propelled by his vigorously twisting gonads, we know we are in the fantastic wind-up of a fantastic novel and not in the more mundane reality of a Farm and Food column in the *Irish Times*. A flying bull is clearly an impossible event in our everyday world and may, therefore, be properly labeled "fantastic." The same is true for the many fantastic devices in Sean O'Casey's late plays, such as the horn playing statue of Saint Tremolo, the giant Cock who creates winds that blow the pants off people, and the incessant drum playing of Father Ned, as Jürgen Kamm so convincingly demonstrates in "The Uses of the Fantastic in the Later Plays of Sean O'Casey."

But, as our notion of what we consider fantastic depends upon our belief in what is possible or impossible, so these categories themselves shift in turn depending upon the times, society, or culture in which we find ourselves. There is a real sense, for instance, in which the situation in Northern Ireland in the late 1980s "would appear as pure fantasy to earlier times" (Landow 107).[2] In the 1960s most people for very good reasons were optimistic about a peaceful solution to the Northern Ireland question. Looking back on the 1960s from the vantage point of twenty years later, F. X. Martin, co-author of the best-selling survey of Irish history, *The Course of Irish History* (1967 and 1982), reflects that optimism: "All was then changing, and mostly for the better" (2). Most predictions made at that time were for more and better contacts between the Republic and Northern Ireland (F. X. Martin 2-3), yet in the early 1960s Seamus Heaney warned: "that kind of thing could start again" (41). Heaney's poem, "Docker," goes so much against the commonly held assumptions of the day about what was possible or impossible that it has about it the ring of prophecy.

What we call "fantastic" also depends upon our personal beliefs. To cite a well-known example from Irish letters: in the last years of the nineteenth century W. B. Yeats and Æ (George Russell) came to believe that the "external world" was undergoing a major change in that the ancient gods were returning to Ireland (A. Martin 110-111). These gods, which they saw as having been a living reality in the past, would—both men believed—at any moment manifest themselves in the present thereby compelling belief in what was considered purely fantastic. Their millennial beliefs proved too optimistic, however, and the history of most of Ireland from the beginning of the twentieth century to today is that of the destruction of the habitat of these gods as well as that of the Little People. The "enchanted Green Lands" at Rosses Point where Yeats "brought his faery-obsessed friend, Æ" (Cahill 180) are now lined with upscale bungalows whose owners in all probability do not put out saucers of milk at night for the Little People; nor does the newly laid tarmac provide a congenial surface over which they can ride their fairy horses. Thus in our headlong pursuit of material pleasure and gain we continue to scrape the earth free of its magic—exactly the reverse of what Yeats and Æ believed would occur. Today both the Little People and the ancient gods remain remote in time and place, and both today are considered fantastic in Ireland except in those few older rural, agrarian, and usually isolated places where such belief persists—places where the natural and the supernatural keep close and frequent company. Dermot Mac Manus describes the relationship between these worlds while lamenting the "lost knowledge" of the faerie kingdoms:

> In Ireland the world of the Shee (Sidhe), that is, of the faeries and of all those spirits which are elemental and have never been human, was called the Middle Kingdom, a satisfactory and expressive term. In ancient times, and almost up to this very age, this world of "faerie" has been as much an accepted reality to the country people as has the normal material world around them. But today

[1959], though belief still remains widespread, the old knowledge of the organization, of the ordered hierarchy of the classes and castes that compose the spirit world has almost disappeared. (15-16)

With its disappearance has gone as well a rich literary tradition of which Maureen Murphy ("Siren or Victim: The Mermaid in Irish Legend and Poetry") and Vernon Hyles ("Lord Dunsany: The Geography of the Gods") write; for, as Augustine Martin observes: "this concern with the unseen world gave rise to a great body of writing—poetry, drama and fiction—which employed the methods of fable and fantasy to express its peculiar idea of life and reality" (110). What remained of this ancient rich tradition is now mostly a literary convention, rather than a living body of belief.[3] Such an attitude sharply contrasts with that of John Millington Synge who worked hard to capture the genuine folk quality of the stories and tales he retold or used on the stage, without ever condescending to either his subject or audience, as pointed out by both Toni O'Brien Johnson, "Interrogating Boundaries: Fantasy in the Plays of J. M. Synge," and Anthony Roche, "Ghosts in Irish Drama." At worst, there are the caricatures to be found in virtually every Irish souvenir shop where the once-powerful Little People are reduced to cute pins to decorate blouses, or to plaster statues to adorn the lawn. Typical are remarks attributed to the Chair of Bord Failte (the Irish Tourist Board) in a 1989 interview in *Newsweek:* "Visitors are looking for a land of shamrocks and leprechauns, and we should give it to them" (Sullivan 21).

This process of domesticating the strange, unknown, and inexpressible, of taming the fantastic, is admirably caught in Tom Stoppard's example of the sighting of "a unicorn": a fantastic mythical beast of no time or place which becomes reduced through familiarity and repetition to the known and easily described "horse with an arrow in its forehead [which must have] . . . been mistaken for a deer" (Stoppard 14-15).[4] Literary criticism is far from immune to the temptation to transform the unicorns of the fantastic into "the horses of instruction," as is apparent in the interpretation of much of Irish literature, including Samuel Beckett's plays or James Joyce's "Circe" chapter in *Ulysses.* Geoffrey Hartman might have been speaking about the reading or misreading of such texts, as well as "Leda and the Swan," when he warned:

> That writing is a calculus that jealously broods on strange figures, on imaginative otherness, has been made clear by poets and artists rather than by the critics. The latter are scared to do anything except convert as quickly as possible the imaginative into a mode of the ordinary—where the ordinary can be the historically unfamiliar familiarized. (27)

Yet despite such efforts, Beckett's work remains outside the pale of "the ordinary" as a meditation on impotence and failure. What many spectators find unacceptable in his early plays, for example, is the "imaginative otherness" encountered in his view of reality as reflected in that startling, unremitting picture of life lived in time as "moments for nothing" (*Endgame* 83; see "'Fidelity to Failure': Time and the Fantastic in Samuel Beckett's Early Plays"). What remains most valuable in Beckett is exactly what we also value in Yeats's extraordinary plays: this "imaginative otherness" which is so much a part of the fantastic and which both playwrights capture and present so well (see Csilla Bertha "Myth and the Fantastic: The Example of W. B. Yeats's Plays"). This imaginative otherness is also part of the fantastic's estranging effect which Rosemary Jackson describes and which may be perceived in the fantastic settings, characters, and actions of Yeats's and Beckett's plays:

> To introduce the fantastic is to replace familiarity, comfort . . . with estrangement, unease, the uncanny. It is to introduce dark areas, of something completely other and unseen, the spaces outside the limiting frame of the "human" and "real." (179)

Many of the writers discussed in this collection, such as Jonathan Swift (C. N. Manlove "Swift and Fantasy"), Tom Murphy (Csilla Bertha "Thomas Murphy's Psychological Explorations"), Stewart Parker (Anthony Roche "Ghosts in Irish Drama"), and James Joyce (Aladár Sarbu "The Fantastic in James Joyce's *Ulysses:* Representational Strategies in 'Circe' and 'Penelope'") aim at replacing "familiarity . . . with estrangement, unease." Because "Circe" is probably the most famous use of the fantastic in all of modern Irish literature, I will discuss Joyce's specific uses of the fantastic in some detail, showing how the fantastic may yield new insights into human beings, their behavior, feelings, and thoughts, as well as how it leads to innovations in art. (For an example from a different field, see Péter Egri's discussion of John Field's invention of the nocturne.)

Hume might well have been referring directly to "Circe" when she states: "Fantasy . . . aims for richness, and often achieves a plethora of meanings. This polysemousness of fantasy is its crucial difference from realism as a way of projecting meaning" (194). Drawing upon the conventions of the fantastic, Joyce presented not simply the strange, unfamiliar setting of what Richard Ellmann has called "the worst slum in Europe"—a reality unfamiliar to most readers of *Ulysses* then and now—but also the hallucinations of Stephen Dedalus and Leopold Bloom, a running commentary on events and characters in the chapter, and then the tour de force at the center of the chapter and the book itself: the kaleidoscopic presentation of the images from Bloom's unconscious. For the latter the fantastic appears an ideal choice, as Bellemin-Noël observes: "One could define fantastic literature as that in which the question of the unconscious emerges" (quoted in Jackson 62).

"Hovering between the marvelous and the mimetic modes . . . floats fantasy, a mode that confounds and confuses the marvelous and the mimetic. It plays one mode off the other, creating a dialectic which refuses synthesis," writes

Lance Olsen (Olsen 19; cf. Jackson 34-37). In "Circe" we encounter: the mimetic in Bloom's and Stephen's peregrinations through Nighttown complete with the Watch, dogs, whores, dialogue, music, and so on; the marvelous in the appearance of the dead changeling child, Rudy, and the ghost of Stephen's mother—truly incredible events, but ones which are carefully grounded by Joyce in each character's actions, emotions, and physical states; and the fantastic in the brief comments on the action—mostly on Stephen's, in figures such as Lynch's Cap and "Gummy Granny"—and in the deeply disturbing nighttime world of Bloom's unconscious which "confounds and confuses the marvelous and the mimetic" in the fantastic.

The "Circe" chapter opens with the unfamiliar but "real" setting of the Mabbot Street entrance to "Nighttown." In the mimetic mode grotesque figures shuttle in and out of shadows:

> *A pigmy woman swings on a rope slung between the railings, counting. A form sprawled against a dustbin and muffled by its arm and hat moves, groans, grinding growling teeth, and snores again. On a step a gnome totting among a rubbishtip crouches to shoulder a sack of rags and bones. A crone standing by with a smoky oil lamp rams the last bottle in the maw of his sack.* (U 429-430).[5]

Strange cries echo down the street:

> I gave it to Molly
> Because she was jolly.
> The leg of the duck
> The leg of the duck.
> (*U* 430)

Insidious invitations are whispered from doorways: "Sst! Come here till I tell you. Maidenhead inside. Sst!" (U 431).

Into this already strange cityscape of the night comes the fog, not with "little cat feet" but as "*snakes . . . creep[ing] slowly*" (U 433). And with the fog comes Bloom out of breath, "*flushed, panting,*" to encounter mysterious "*cyclists, with lighted paper lanterns aswing,* [who] *swim by him, grazing him, their bells rattling*" (U 435), and the sandstrewer, dragonlike, enormous, "*its huge red headlight winking, its trolley hissing on the wire. The motorman bangs his footgong,*" and narrowly misses running Bloom down (U 435). All very strange, but nothing—as yet—truly fantastic. This is what Sarbu calls this "thin . . . narrative plane" of events, but which he also notes "is firm enough to support the elaborate fantasies enacted on it."[6]

Contrast Joyce's use of mimesis in Bloom's frightening, but substantial encounter with the sandstrewer with his use of the marvelous in Bloom's encounter at the end of the chapter with Rudy, his long dead son "*a fairy boy of eleven, a changeling, kidnapped, dressed in an Eton suit with glass shoes and a little bronze helmet"* (U 609). Bloom is *"Wonderstruck,"* and his reaction is as immediate as it is deeply felt: he "(. . . *calls inaudibly.*) Rudy!" (*U* 609). Clearly in the marvelous rather than the mimetic mode, this vision is a projection of Bloom's own deepest feelings. (It is he who recalls his son as a changeling—at once his own and a fairy child taken away cruelly and abruptly—the mauve face indicating the cause of death.) Similarly we are in the mode of the marvelous when Stephen raises the ghost of his mother through drink and physical exertion, when: "(*He lifts his ashplant high with both hands and smashes the chandelier)*" (*U* 583), as he attempts to destroy his projection of her with all its horrifying details contributed by his guilt (cf. Sarbu). Hence his violent and immediate reaction: "(*Strangled with rage.*) Shite! (*His features grow drawn and grey and old)*" (*U* 582). There is no doubt about what Stephen sees or that he sees it. Nor is there any doubt that he alone of all the people present encounters this apparition, since no one else in the room witnesses his horrifying confrontation with the ghost of his mother. Joyce thus takes great pains to make clear to the reader that at two separate moments in the chapter for well-established physical and emotional reasons, first Stephen, then Bloom hallucinate.

During the remainder of the chapter, however, we are plunged into neither the mode of the mimetic nor that of the marvelous, but into that of the fantastic: ". . . a mode that confounds and confuses the marvelous and the mimetic . . . creating a dialectic which refuses synthesis" (Olsen 19). There is, for example, no evidence that either man hallucinates the strange phantasmagoric scenes, characters, and events which occur beginning with the appearance of Bloom's father. Rudolph Virag is not an apparition born out of excessive drink, physical exhaustion, or emotional imbalance—to say so is to "convert . . . the imaginative into a mode of the ordinary" (Hartman 27) and thus to do away with the strangeness of this chapter and its attendant insight into the character of Bloom. Given such a setting, in time and place and given Bloom's physical condition it might not surprise us if he did hallucinate, seeing his father *"Yellow poison streaks"* and all (*U* 437ff). But there is no evidence that Bloom notices or is aware of him. He gives him no greeting (something impossible to imagine for the son of a Hungarian father); evinces no surprise at his strange appearance, but behaves as if such encounters were perfectly normal; and returns readily to his role as the guilty son in attempting unsuccessfully to hide the forbidden pig's trotter. At the end of their meeting, Bloom continues where he left off before their meeting—indicating that nothing has happened, no time has elapsed, no event has occurred of which he is aware. Similarly with the fantastic set pieces in the chapter: Bloom as Lord Mayor or as Blazes Boylan's flunky, Bloom and the new Bloomusalem, or Bloom and Bella-Bello are each an image drawn from the unconscious without Bloom's awareness.[7]

As readers, we must accept the dialectic created by this use of the fantastic which "refuses synthesis" rather than attempting to make sense out of events as Bloom's hallucinations[8] or, worse, reducing the incredible to the "ordinary," as Wolfgang Iser does when he contends that such events are "potential revelations of character" (216). Iser attempts to account for the sequence of events as if they took place in "real time" by suggesting that "everything becomes real for Bloom that is omitted, concealed, or repressed in his daily life" (216), but surely the point of "Circe" is that none of the events which takes place in his unconscious is "real" for Bloom, because he remains unaware of them. Iser's comments are reminiscent of many early readers attempting to puzzle through the novel as if it were wholly mimetic.[9] For example, Paul Jordan Smith wrote in 1927: "Bloom in the red-light district imagines himself met by respectable folk. He imagines defenses, imagines the overthrow of the defenses, imagines himself persecuted for his conduct; has illusions of grandeur, followed immediately by a debased wallowing in the very pits of humility" (81). Yet Smith, one of the best of Joyce's early public readers, sensed what lay at the center of "Circe" when he remarked: "This entire chapter ["Circe"] is made up of noble nonsense, a tissue of remarkable day-dreams—of what Mr. D. H. Lawrence would call fantasia of the unconscious" (86). "Nonsense . . . daydreams . . . fantasia . . ." or what we today term the mode of the fantastic.

Thanks in large measure to Joyce's use of the fantastic, we know Bloom far better than he knows himself or we can ever know ourselves! While a similar statement might be made of, say, Oedipus, the difference between Sophocles and Joyce's hero lies in the nature of the reader's or audience's knowledge of him. *Oedipus Rex* remains rooted in dramatic irony, since we in the audience have knowledge of the king's past and know the outcome of events of which he remains ignorant. There is no such dramatic irony in "Circe."

Although we encounter images which reside in Bloom's unconscious, that does not enable us to predict future events; nor is any action described or new knowledge given of Bloom in future or past space/time. (For such possibilities, see "Ithaca.") Instead, our knowledge is of the dark mirror of the unconscious wherein we see refracted events, people, and emotions experienced during the daylight hours in the real space/time of turn-of-the-century Dublin on 16 June 1904. Compare, for example, the daytime Bloom we meet in the prosaic images of the nurturing man feeding and comforting people, animals, and birds with the nighttime androgynous Bloom we encounter in the fantastic images of the "new womanly man" fathering children and giving birth. Of the people we meet during the day in Dublin, Bloom alone feeds the gulls, the dog, the cat; he alone at the lying-in hospital identifies with poor Mrs. Purefoy during her long labor and goes and visits her; only he truly sympathizes with Mrs. Breen having to cope with her slightly mad, addled, husband Denis who "is off his chump." When challenged he stands up for his rights, but also defends love in the face of prejudice and hate. If the male cast of characters in *Ulysses* consists of alcoholic layabouts (Bob Doran), failures (Simon Dedalus), sentimentalists (Father Cowley), and myopic chauvinists (The Citizen), with a huge gathering of hangers-on, freeloaders, and generally ineffective men, Bloom stands out clearly as the exception: he is "the competent keyless citizen" who negotiates his way through a difficult day, earns a modest living, while performing acts of charity, and generally behaves as "the most Christian man" in Dublin. Much of his effectiveness arises from his acceptance of his anima, the feminine side of his character and personality which most of the other male characters reject.[10]

He is, in other words, a model of emotional health in the daytime, male-dominated world of Dublin. But in the images of his unconscious, the images of "Nighttown," his feminine traits and his passive behavior become transformed into the fantastic images of the "new womanly man" who gives birth to *"eight male yellow and white children . . . with valuable metallic faces"* (*U* 494), and who must undergo Bello's examination and humiliating treatment (*U* 530-544). Joyce thus uses the fantastic to establish the relationship of Bloom's conscious acts to his unconscious self. In doing so he illustrates Hume's contention that: "There is an elegant efficiency to fantasies" (191) which enables a writer to express ideas, emotions, and insights not available through mimesis:

> Mimesis still demonstrates its power when an author's [such as Joyce's] chief concerns are social interaction and human behavior. Mimesis excels at establishing the relationships between people and the likenesses between the fictive world and our own . . . Fantasy serves many other functions . . . It provides the novelty that circumvents automatic responses and cracks the crust of habitude. Fantasy also encourages intensity of engagement, whether through novelty or psychological manipulation . . . provides meaning-systems to which we can try relating our selves, our feelings, and our data . . . encourages the condensation of images which allows it to affect its readers at many levels and in so many different ways . . . [a]nd it helps us envision possibilities that transcend the purely material world which we accept as quotidian reality. (195-196)

Where daytime logic and mimesis see two opposing forces or statements as a contradiction and demand that such contradictions be resolved, nighttime unreason and the fantastic allow Joyce — or any author — to hold two opposing forces together as an oxymoron without moving toward resolution (Jackson 20-21). For example, during the day Bloom experiences deeply conflicting emotions which will return in "Circe": he dreads and abhors the approaching assignation of Boylan with Molly, but neither resists nor resents it, and even cooperates in it by not going home. (One of his biggest conscious worries is that Boylan might be diseased and so infect Molly!) Such conflict demands resolution: Is he a man or is he not? Why does he not go home and confront them? How can he do nothing? Why does he not divorce her? These are questions provoked in readers by this unresolved situation. Within "Circe," however, we encounter not Bloom's calm acceptance of the inevitability of events (that will happen in "Ithaca"), but the vivid turmoil produced in his unconscious by both his dread of the event and his failing to resist or effectively prevent it. Joyce offers a series of fantastic, unresolved images: first those which name Bloom as a well-known cuckold (*U* 469; and see 468-470); then those where he conspires in his own cuckolding by aiding Boylan. After Boylan *"hangs his hat smartly on a peg of Bloom's antlered head*," Bloom "*in a flunkey's plush coat and kneebreeches*" watches through a keyhole and cheers on Molly and Blazes as they copulate: "Show! Hide! Show! Plough her! More! Shoot!" (*U* 565, 567). There is no possibility of bringing such images into the daylight world of space/time or into Bloom's consciousness—that is, to domesticate them—without destroying the humanity and heroism of Bloom. During the day it is enough that he experience the humiliation caused by Molly's adultery and his conspiring in it. Although it involves deep suffering, he "turns the other cheek," accepts what happens with "equanimity" (*U* 732, 733), forgives, and goes on loving. "Circe" reveals, in the searing images of Bloom as Boylan's flunky and Bloom as exposed cuckold, what "the pain of love" actually entails for him, and it is that pain which lies at the very heart of *Ulysses*.

Besides employing "the dialectic which refuses synthesis," Joyce also makes good use of another characteristic of the fantastic in literature: its insistence on literalness; that is, the fantastic does not say one thing in terms of another (Jackson 84). Gregor Samsa is not *like* a cockroach, he *is* a cockroach. Leopold Bloom is not *like* the Lord Mayor of Dublin, in "Circe" he *becomes* the Lord Mayor of Dublin; it is not *as if* Leopold Bloom gives birth, he *does* give birth. Moreover, Bloom undergoes metamorphosis literally as he changes from male to female to male. Yet, as in many traditional fantasies (cf. the Alice books), no meaning resides in these changes. The sequence of Bloom's images "does not lend itself to assimilation into pleasurable or consoling schemes. It has," as Massey maintains of post-romantic metamorphosis, "something typically ugly, monstrous, unabsorbable about it" (Massey 17 quoted in Jackson 82). Like most modern fantasy, there is "little purposive transformation. Changes are without meaning. There is no overall teleological scheme to give the transformation a meaning" (Jackson 85). This lack of an overall scheme emphasizes the radical instability of the images themselves in the unconscious as they meld into one another. Such metamorphosis is congenial not to conscious, rational, articulate thought, but to the dark, inarticulate, and unarticulable side of humans.

The fantastic also proved congenial to Joyce, since at the time he wrote *Ulysses* it had, according to Jackson

> move[d] away from orthodox demonology towards psychology, to account for difference and strangeness. Literary fantasies from *The Castle of Otranto* to *Jekyll and Hyde* are determined by these transitions: from conventional diabolism in Beckford's *Vathek*, through the equivocations of *Frankenstein*, *Melmoth* and *The Confessions of a Justified Sinner*, to the internalized figures of Dorian Grey or . . . (158)

might we add to the internalized images in Leopold Bloom's unconscious. Thus Joyce's use of the fantastic emphasizes his insistence on a secular as opposed to a sacred interpretation of character in *Ulysses*.

But there is also something very Irish in Joyce's use of the fantastic in "Circe," since he followed "the Irish tendency to draw fantasy from what is real and experienced" (Pyle "'My Unshatterable Friend'"), as is also true of Swift, Synge, Murphy, and Jack Yeats. In 1901 Æ remarked to William Byrne: "I started from the stars and never succeeded in getting my feet firmly on the earth, but if you start from the earth you can go as far as you like" (quoted in Pyle "'My Unshatterable Friend'"). For Beckett, "starting from the earth," for example, meant using the fantastic to explore the reality of human impotence and ignorance which led him almost inevitably to such works as the "aesthetically terminal remnant" "Breath" (Olsen 49), whereas for Joyce it meant using the fantastic to explore the unconscious, which in turn led him to the richly human portrait of Dublin's most famous citizen, Leopold Bloom.

Each of the writers and artists discussed in this collection of essays drew upon the fantastic as the best, clearest way of expressing what he or she had to express. In our desire to chart critically the unknown "territory" of the fantastic, we must beware of domesticating their vision, but instead must ensure that the unicorn remains its fantastic self by refusing to reduce it to "a horse with an arrow in its forehead." If we will allow the imaginative to remain the imaginative and not "convert [it] as quickly as possible . . . into a mode of the ordinary," then we may discover that the fantastic allows each writer and artist, though in very different ways, to do what fantasy has always been best at; that is, to "assert the importance of things which cannot be measured, seen, or numbered" (Hume 98), which for many of us are those most worthwhile in human experience. A few decades ago C. S. Lewis summed up the power of the fantastic, a power which can be found in each of the Irish writers and artists discussed in this volume. Lewis said:

> At all ages, if it [the mode of the fantastic] is well used by the author and meets the right reader, it has the same power: to generalize while remaining concrete, to present in palpable form not concepts or even experiences, but whole classes of experience, and to throw off irrelevancies. But at its best it can do more; it can give us experiences we have never had and thus, instead of "commenting on life," can add to it. (38)

In other words, the fantastic can give us "things more real than reality" (Jack B. Yeats quoted in Pyle "'Unshatterable Friend of Clay'").

Notes

1. For example, after reviewing some of the important scholarship on the fantastic, Gary K. Wolfe concludes: "The criterion of the impossible . . . seems firmly in place in the academic study of fantasy literature; it may indeed be the first principle generally agreed upon for the study of fantasy" (1-2).

2. See: "'Fidelity to Failure': Time and the Fantastic in Samuel Beckett's Early Plays" for Landow's full remark on the relation between "our conception of what is fantastic [and] . . . our view of reality."

3. For a more detailed discussion of the relation of fantasy to belief, see Morse, "Monkeys, Changelings and Asses."

4. Stoppard makes his point brilliantly in *Rosencrantz and Guildenstern Are Dead:* "The more witnesses there are [to any given fantastic event] the thinner it gets and the more reasonable it becomes until it is as thin as reality, the name we give to the common experience" (Stoppard 21).

5. Because of the controversy surrounding the various texts of *Ulysses* and the non-controversial nature of the quotations in this article, I have felt free to use the Random House edition of 1961.

6. Professor Sarbu's and my readings of "Circe" differ: he emphasizes "the mind dramatized," whereas I emphasize the unconscious. I am indebted to Professor Sarbu for reminding me of Iser's argument.

7. Surely it would be impossible to take seriously Joyce's claims for the considerable significance of Bloom, or the views of those who see him as a true hero performing extraordinary deeds in his ordinary life, or as the modern representative man, if he were a conscious participant in the truly fantastic events in "Circe." Richard Ellmann eloquently claims for Bloom that "Joyce was the first to endow an urban man of no importance with heroic consequences. . . . Joyce's discovery, so humanistic that he would have been embarrassed to disclose it out of context, was that the ordinary is the extraordinary" (3).

8. Readers have often been misled by applying too rigidly or too generally Joyce's suggestion that the Art of "Circe" is Magic, while the Technique is Hallucination.

9. For a discussion of the changing readership of *Ulysses* see Morse, "Source Book of Book of Conduct? Changing Perspectives on Reading Joyce's *Ulysses.*"

10. "Anima" and "animus" are Carl Jung's terms for that part of the personality rooted in characteristics of the opposite sex without which no healthy relationship is possible. For example, Jung might be accurately describing Bloom's empathy for women when he observes that "an inherited collective image of woman exists in a man's unconscious, with the help of which he apprehends the nature of woman" ("Anima and Animus" (160).

Works Cited

Beckett, Samuel. *Endgame: A Play in One Act.* New York: Grove Press, 1958.

Cahill, Susan and Thomas. *A Literary Guide to Ireland.* New York: Charles Scribner's Sons, 1973.

Ellmann, Richard. *James Joyce.* New York: Oxford University Press, 1959.

Hartman, Geoffrey H. *Criticism in the Wilderness: The Study of Literature Today.* New Haven: Yale University Press, 1980.

Heaney, Seamus. *Death of a Naturalist.* London: Faber and Faber, 1966.

Hume, Kathryn. *Fantasy and Mimesis: Responses to Reality in Western Literature.* New York: Methuen, 1984.

Iser, Wolfgang. *The Implied Reader: Patterns of Communication in Prose Fiction from*

Bunyan to Beckett. Baltimore: The Johns Hopkins University Press, 1974.

Jackson, Rosemary. *Fantasy: The Literature of Subversion*. London: Methuen, 1981.

Joyce, James. *Ulysses*. New York: Random House, 1961.

Jung, Carl G. "Anima and Animus." *The Relations Between the Ego and the Unconscious*. In *The Portable Jung*, ed. Violet Staub de Laszlo, 158-182. New York: The Modern Library 1971.

Landow, George P. "And the World Became Strange: Realms of Literary Fantasy." In *The Aesthetics of Fantasy Literature and Art*, ed. Roger C. Schlobin, 105-142. Notre Dame: University of Notre Dame Press, 1982.

Lewis, C. S. *Of Other Worlds: Essays and Stories*. Ed. Walter Hooper. 1966 New York: Harcourt Brace Jovanovich, 1975.

Mac Manus, Dermot. *The Middle Kingdom: The Faerie World of Ireland*. Gerrards Cross, Bucks.: Colin Smythe, 1973.

Martin, Augustine. "Fable and Fantasy." In *The Genius of Irish Prose*, ed. Augustine Martin, 110-120. Dublin: The Mercier Press, 1985.

Martin, F. X. "The Image of the Irish—Medieval and Modern Continuity and Change." In *Medieval and Modern Ireland*, ed. Richard Wall, 1-18. Gerrards Cross, Bucks.: Colin Smythe, 1988.

Morse, Donald E. "Of Monkeys, Changelings and Asses." In *Aspects of the Fantastic*, ed. William Coyle, 197-202. Westport, CT: Greenwood Press, 1986.

—-. "Source Book or Book of Conduct? Changing Perspectives on Reading Joyce's *Ulysses*." *Hungarian Studies in English*. XXI (1990): 67-71.

Olsen, Lance. *Ellipse of Uncertainty: An Introduction to Postmodern Fantasy*. Westport, CT: Greenwood Press, 1987.

Smith, Paul Jordan. *A Key to the Ulysses of James Joyce*. 1927 San Francisco: City Lights, 1970.

Stoppard, Tom. *Rosencrantz and Guildenstern Are Dead*. New York: Grove Press, Inc., 1967.

Sullivan, Scott. "The Irish Miracle." *Newsweek*, 26 June 1989, 21.

Wolfe, Gary K. "The Encounter with Fantasy." In *The Aesthetics of Fantasy Literature and Art*, ed. Roger C. Schlobin, 1-15. Notre Dame: University of Notre Dame Press, 1982.

Part I

ANCIENT KNOWLEDGE AND THE FANTASTIC

Poetry and the poet have always occupied a special place in Irish life, one that reaches far back into Irish history. The scholar and poet Sean Lucy warns that:

> The English word "poet" gives very little idea of what was and to some extent is still meant by the Gaelic *file*. It is a commonplace that in pre-Christian Ireland *file* implied magical and religious powers and responsibilities which made their holders second only in real wealth and influence to the rulers, the kings. They were the memory of the people, the voice of its identity, and, finally, its spokesman to and link with all natural and supernatural powers. They could recall everything of interest and value, they could celebrate and give significance, they could curse and bless, blast and heal. (21)

The writers and artists discussed in this volume descend from such *file*, from enchanters and magicians, from the great makers of legend, fable, and story, or from the ancient scribes who fantastically illuminated the sacred texts and the anonymous artists who embellished the lives of saints and martyrs for the edification of the blest. But, as Csilla Bertha demonstrates in her essay, there is a great difference between the ancient synthetic power and universality of myth with its certainty of order, proportions, and values or a community's commonly shared belief in its extended reality, such as the *file* enjoyed, and the more individual and subjective endeavor of later writers and artists expressed in fantasy and the fantastic in the desire to go beyond or escape from visible reality. The two modes, the mythic and the fantastic, however, can and often do exist together, overlapping, enriching, and complementing each other's effects, as in the example of Yeats's plays. Maureen Murphy draws indirectly upon this distinction between the mythic and the fantastic when discussing the various Irish legends of the mermaid and seal women and their relationship to Irish life in ancient and contemporary times. All such legends have in common the entrance into the human world of beings from a supranatural realm which for the Irish, an island people, is — not surprisingly — often located in the sea. Although such beings may live among humans for a time, they will always return to their original element. These legends, Murphy concludes, reflect the human desire to connect with the supranatural world, as well as mirror many of the social situations in this one.

Anthony Roche also explores the human desire to connect with a world beyond this one through the phenomenon of otherworldly visitors on the Irish stage in "Ghosts in Irish Drama," where he discusses the spirits of the dead calling upon the living in plays by W. B. Yeats, J. M. Synge, and the contemporary Northern Irish dramatist, Stewart Parker. In these plays, he argues, the departed refuse "to remain either symbolic or conveniently off stage but . . . force . . . [their] way into full carnal presence and in so doing transform . . . the stage space into a site where the living and the dead interact on equal terms." He concludes that "the return of the dead to haunt the living, their refusal to stay dead, is the loophole by which the fantastic is admitted to the predominantly naturalistic Irish stage."

Bettina Knapp discusses Yeats's use of the fantastic, but from the viewpoint of his interest in the many forms of thought which we now label as "lost knowledge"; that is, forms of human knowledge now ignored or scorned which in the past were respected. Alchemy, for example, was once the foundation of all knowledge of the properties of physical things, and possessed "numerous links of absorbing interest with history, literature, mythology, astrology, folklore, mysticism, philosophy, religion, pictorial art, and even music" (Read xxi-xxii). It fell into disrepute, however, with the rise of modern science and the scientific method, beginning in 1661 with the publication in London of Robert Boyle's *Sceptical Chymist* (Read 31). In the twentieth century, the psychologist Carl Jung rediscovered the usefulness of alchemy, not to describe how the physical world works, but as a metaphor for the inner emotional and spiritual life of human beings. Jung's application of the laws of alchemy to describe the psychological processes gave new possibilities for modern writers to explore the invisible realms of human existence and to project them onto the page or onto the stage: in this way the fantastic transformations of the human soul can be made nearly tangible. Seen from the other side, characterization can be extended to include the fantastic as integrated into the whole of the human psyche.

Using Jung's cyclical concept of psychological evolution which closely parallels the alchemist's view of the perfection of metals, Knapp discusses W. B. Yeats's play, *The Only Jealousy of Emer*. To experience the unconscious during the seven alchemical/psychological operations enables an individual to transform chaos into cosmos, she contends. The previously unadapted attitude has now been transformed into a productive view in which the whole of the psyche operates as an integrated force.

It is no accident that three of the four essays in this section on "Ancient Knowledge and the Fantastic" focus in part or in whole upon the work of W. B. Yeats, and especially on his plays, for Yeats devoted much of his life to making visible what is usually considered the invisible, which places him within the ancient tradition of Irish poets who communicate "with the unhuman presences which . . . [make] up all of the worlds, including the everyday" (Lucy 21). As Richard Ellmann observes: "Yeats knew himself to be one for whom the invisible world existed" (87-88). To give this invisible world form and substance he drew upon both myth and the fantastic, making him an ideal subject to begin and conclude not only this opening section but also the complete collection of essays on the fantastic in Irish literature and the arts.

Works Cited

Ellmann, Richard. *Wilde, Yeats, Joyce, and Beckett: Four Dubliners*. Washington: Library of Congress, 1986.

Lucy, Sean. "Presences and Powers." Review of *Mount Eagle*, by John Montague. *The Irish Literary Supplement* 8,2 (Fall 1989) 21.

Read, John. *Prelude to Chemistry: An Outline of Alchemy, Its Literature and Relationships*. 1936 Cambridge, MA: MIT Press, 1966.

Csilla Bertha

Myth and the Fantastic: The Example of W. B. Yeats's Plays

The words "mythic" and "fantastic" are often interchanged as synonyms or mistaken for each other. Both myth and the fantastic are used in many senses in daily life as well as in literary criticism, but while myth has been thoroughly studied and has hundreds of different definitions, fantasy and the fantastic have only recently been given serious scholarly attention. Kathryn Hume's definition of fantasy is one of the most inclusive: *"Fantasy is any departure from consensus reality"* (21). Yet "consensus reality" differs from age to age, culture to culture. In modern times—mostly from the Renaissance on in Europe—consensus reality has been rather restricted, narrowed, confined only to the visible, material world, so everything that goes beyond what we see is considered fantastic. While it is true that the mythic and the fantastic modes can exist together, and sometimes it is difficult or arbitrary to divide them, seeing the major differences between them will help throw light on the nature of literary fantasy itself.

In prelogical thinking—which included all spheres of knowledge about the world in a synthesis—the distinction between reality and fantasy did not exist. As Levy-Bruhl asserts: "In primitive thinking the mystical feature was not added to things and phenomena but was identical with them; the supernatural was part of nature, so what we call miracles, were natural to them" (quoted Bak 65-66). Thus one of the most important features of myth is its synthetic view, which naturally and unquestionably holds the four-dimensional universe, the visible and invisible worlds together in a unity. In myth everything is conceived as real, the supernatural figures are personifications of the great, unknown forces of nature or the cosmos, while the heroes embody human forms of behavior in their struggle with these powers. That the two spheres meet comes as no surprise, for human beings are considered to be part of the universe, living among and participating in the interrelations of these forces. Fantasy differs from myth, as Colin Manlove points out, "in the wholly imagined character of its fictional worlds" ("Elusiveness" 50). The author of fantasy may introduce the supernatural but it will remain perforce on a different plane, with both the reader's belief and disbelief sustained at the same time: "something that we know at the outset to be impossible . . . may by virtue of the strength and skill with which it is created make us feel simultaneously that it does and does not have reality" (Manlove "Nature of Fantasy" 18). Thus fantasy does not extend our reality: "fantasy is not to do with inventing another non-human world: it is not transcendental. It has to do with inverting elements of this world, re-combining its constitutive features in new relations to produce something strange, unfamiliar and *apparently* 'new,' absolutely 'other' and different" (Jackson 8, her emphasis). In contrast, myth is the image of the extended reality, which, however, is felt to be extended not in the original synthetic view, but only by the modern analytical mind.

Mythic figures and events were believed to be real because they arose out of the collective experience of a community (whereas fantastic beings are a product of an individual imagination); hence myth, while being universal, is also closely related to the life of a community where it has the function of uniting its members. "Have not all races had their first unity from a mythology that married them to rock and hill?" — asks Yeats in his *Autobiographies* (194). Fighting against the inhuman powers, the heroes of myth usually symbolize mankind, and, more concretely, the heroes' tribes or their people. In such archaic communities, "life is communal and members achieve their fulfillment not by individuating themselves but by identifying with the traditions of their culture" (Hume 32). The heroes are heroes inasmuch as they are able to follow the mythic pattern of behavior and so embody the physical, moral, and spiritual ideals of the community. The modern emphasis on originality and individuality is the product of a nonmythic age and outlook, and it can be a feature of literary realism as well as of literary fantasy. Several of the fantastic heroes are such because they are different from the people around them. They are, however, more passive — even if not always Cinderella-like — than their mythic counterparts, more helpless in their power, and often "raised up and determined by the supernatural" (Manlove "Elusiveness" 13).

At the end of literary fantasy magic appears ephemeral and is often withdrawn which may be, again, the consequence of the individual human experience of life; whereas the collective, mythical vision produces a cyclic pattern familiar especially from vegetation and astrological myths. Consequently, instead of the circular plot — of at least one major type (if not all works) — of fantasy where everything returns to the starting point, and what is gained is lost again, myths often give the promise or hope of renewal and revival. This is just like nature on which the myths rely. The cyclic view of the world makes time reversible. Mythic time is timeless, annihilates natural time, and, like what Eliade calls "sacred" or "holy" time, dissolves past and future in a continuous, eternal present, which can be experienced again and again through rites (Eliade 62). While suggesting inevitable destiny, the cyclic view also dissolves its tragedy by eliminating the feeling of passing away in time into nonbeing. The synthesizing power of myth thus unites not only the natural and the supernatural, but also past, present, and future. In contrast, fantasy is "often acutely aware of time," which is "a condition of [the hero's] being, part of the air he breathes" (Manlove "Elusiveness" 49).

These differences are part of or consequences of the overall feeling behind myth and fantasy: myth offers the certainty and security of an order in the world in which everything has its place, and so proportions, relationships, and values are clear. Fantasy, on the other hand, acknowledges the elusiveness and un-knowability of truth in the modern world and tries to provide "a new method for turning chaos into something positive and useful" (Schwartz 28). Both myth and fantasy present the quest for wholeness and completion, but while in myth the quest is based on a commonly shared belief in certitudes about humans and the universe, in fantasy it is an individual endeavor to realize dreams and desires or to escape from the existing, frustratingly incomplete world.

The arts and literatures of peoples who preserved their ancient culture for long periods of time naturally incorporated myth and the fantastic. Due to various external and internal circumstances, the Irish retained their organic, mythic vision of the world well into the twentieth century. Their way of thinking, folk beliefs, customs, traditions, including even the law, present remarkable resemblances to the essentially mythic view in Eastern culture; indeed, among the modern Indo-European peoples in Europe, their outlook shows the closest similarity to that of the Indians and to the old Indo-European tolerance in matters of religion (Thornton 51-59; 64). In Eastern cultures people ex-perienced the world in its wholeness and respected not only what was visible but also what was invisible, hidden behind every part of nature, every tree, flower, or stone. So, too, the Irish peasants, in Patrick Kavanagh's poem "The Great Hunger," can see the unity of nature and spirit; can recognize God the Father "in a tree," where the Holy Spirit is identified with "the rising sap," and Christ with the leaves that come to life "at Easter from the sealed and guarded tomb" (38).

In Ireland pagan, pre-Christian beliefs survived alongside Christianity, often blending into it in a holistic view, because the church did not try to eliminate them; thus conversion to Christianity went on more peacefully there than elsewhere in Europe. This ability of the Irish to create synthesis is also manifested in their strong belief in the power of the *imagination* that can easily hold the totality of human experience in unity—including its real or apparent contradictions, such as subjectivity or objectivity, body, soul, and spirit (Thornton 51).

Whether the cause is ontological or historical, the Irish way of thinking differs from the western European way in being much less rationalistic. The western Europeans tried to take the world into their possession and rule over it. In order to rule they had to divide it and shape it into categories of logical thinking. The Irish mind, however, according to Richard Kearney,

from the earliest times ... remained free, in significant measure, of the linear, centralising logic of the Greaco-Roman culture which dominated most of western Europe. This prevailing culture was based on the Platonic-Aristotelian logic of non-contradiction which operated on the assumption that order and organisation result from the dualistic separation of opposite or contradictory terms. Hence the mainstream of western thought rested upon a series of fundamental oppositions—between being and non-being, reason and imagination, the soul and the body, the transcendentally divine and the immanently temporal and so on. . . . In contradistinction to the orthodox dualist logic of *either/or*, the Irish mind may be seen to favour a more dialectical logic of *both/and*: an intellectual ability to hold the traditional oppositions of classical reason together in creative confluence. (*The Irish Mind* 9; author's emphasis)

In the modern Western world the mythic view has been mostly lost and replaced by the dominance of reason, logic, and — in the mainstream of art — by realistic presentation of the visible world; by mimesis. The portrayal of the essential, of "what you know," gave way to that of the accidental, to "what you see" (Hume 32). Although the desire to go beyond realism toward the fantastic has always been there, attempts to do so have been denigrated. Lance Olsen observes that: "throughout history fantasy has been considered somehow inferior to the mimetic mode. . . . At least since Aristotle's declaration that the essence of art is imitation, fantasy has been marginalized and identified as a relatively minor genre" (14-15). The exceptions are those cultures in which the long-preserved mythic concept of the world could easily transmute into fantasy and into the fantastic mode of art, since fantasy, along with religion, philosophy, and art, is the descendent of myth, the all-inclusive knowledge of the world. So when the twentieth-century Irish writer works with myth and/or the fantastic, he or she does so not in pursuit of fashionable literary trends or as part of the general reaction to nineteenth-century naturalism or realism, but because it is the best approach to the expression of his/her own people's spirit.

The Example of Yeats

Nobody dedicated himself more passionately to reviving or keeping alive the archaic, mythic spirit of the Irish than W. B. Yeats. In his works he also introduced the products of his own creative fantasy, and so his plays offer interesting examples of how mythic and fantastic outlooks can exist side by side or may be mixed in literature. Having been naturally inclined toward everything beyond the visible world, and committing himself to creating a system of "heterogeneous mysticism" out of the various mystic, magic, irrational philosophies of the world, Yeats happily absorbed into his system the immanent mysticism of the Irish way of thinking. In his plays this mythic vision becomes an organizing force, uniting figures, events, and thoughts produced by reality and fantasy.

Yeats's plays dramatize both the mythical and the fantastic kinds of quest.

The majority of his plays are mythic in two ways: they reflect the mythic view of the world in general, and they also use figures, events, and situations of con-crete — usually Irish, sometimes other — myths. Although Yeats took most of his images and symbols from the Anima Mundi or Great Memory (which is similar to Jung's "collective unconscious"), he arranged them and transformed them to suit his own imagination. Thus some of his plays are mostly mythical while others mix elements of fantasy with those of myth.

Yeats was painfully aware of the tragedy of the modern world and human beings — of the split between the two substances of the same reality, the natural and the supernatural. The natural order, as he saw it, was tragically cut off from the divine and thus from original completeness. The metaphysical dualities manifest themselves within the human being too: through his purified, heroic passions, which elevate him to immortality, he is able to participate in the supernatural, while his physical nature binds him to the mortal world. Yeats dramatizes the human condition in many of his plays: humans, in their distance from the divine, are engaged in a constant fight to reattain the one-time mythical unity and so to achieve a spiritual identity. In his mythical plays the repre-sentatives of the two spheres are conceived of as beings of the same reality, participating in the cosmic mystery of struggling with each other, while in the plays closer to fantasy the supernatural creatures move farther away from the human order. The plays, most interesting from the point of view of the fantastic, can be divided into three groups according to the structure which the relation-ship between the natural and the supernatural brings about: (1) in a linear plot the human being quests for the spiritual; (2) in a circular plot the natural level opens up to let the supernatural intrude but soon closes, returning to the original; and (3) the figures and the plot are constantly oscillating between the two. Those of the first type seem to be either essentially mythic or dominantly fantastic, whereas those of the second and third types mingle elements of both.

Comparing two plays of the first type with a linear plot reveals the differen-ces between Yeats's mythic and fantastic plays. Both the fantasylike *The Shadowy Waters* and the mythic *At the Hawk's Well* dramatize efforts to transcend the human condition through the quest for immortality. But in the first, the two spheres of existence remain definitely apart, while in the latter everything is subordinated to a unified vision. The atmosphere in which the hero's symbolic journey toward the unknown takes place in the first is more mystical, whereas in the second there is a purely mythical encounter between the two worlds. The hero and heroine of *The Shadowy Waters* are more passive; indeed, their enchanted ship on the sea is in the power of supernatural forces, like that of Coleridge's Ancient Mariner, while Cuchulain in the second play is full of action and individual energy. The messengers of the spiritual world take the shape of birds, or rather half-human, half-bird forms in both, yet in *The Shadowy Waters* they are mysterious and elusive creatures whose messages are enigmatic. The Hawk-Woman in *At the Hawk's Well*, on the other hand, is a far more concrete image of the mediator between the two worlds, and her function is perfectly clear: although she also lures the hero, she can be, and actually is, confronted by him.

Forgael, the hero of *The Shadowy Waters*, follows the birds but even he cannot communicate with them, let alone those other, "normal" thinking people around him, who, with their practical, sober speeches create the ordinary human world. The supernatural intrudes into this world from outside, through magic and miraculous events and phenomena. Its effect is surprising: under the magic spell cast by Forgael's harp, even the most sober and rough sailors are enchanted. So, too, is queen Dectora, lured to forget her hatred and instead to love Forgael—much in the same way as the demonic power of Richard III changed Anne's spiteful hatred into love. A real Orphic miracle happens when at the end of the play the harp burns by itself "as if by fire." Yet the hero, Forgael, gains the power from forces greater than what he can account for, and although he appears as agent, he is in fact rather an object of the miracle, an instrument of the supernatural. He himself acknowledges his dependence on higher powers, which emphasizes the helplessness of human beings against fate. The recurring image of the net symbolizes the forces that neither he nor Dectora can escape. At the end the net will turn into Dectora's hair, thus the impersonal power descends to become her personal attribute and she, like Forgael, becomes both object and agent of the miraculous.

All these phenomena awaken wonder but the miracle is elusive; the sailors wake up from their spell and return to the ordinary world. The hero has received the gift of his life: the woman of his dreams, through a miracle, which is basically a fantastic feature. As Manlove remarks: "the element of receiving gifts could also be called central to fantasy" (Manlove "Elusiveness" 14). Now Dectora and Forgael together set out on their journey toward the unattainable. They embody the desire typical in fantasy: to escape from reality and to aim at the impossible. This voyage obviously leads to death. Like the heroes of fantasy in general, they, too, while trying to reach their spiritual aims, undergo the process of self-denial as far as the richness of natural life is concerned, and that "of reduction of being, right back to the apparent nothingness of death" (Manlove "Elusiveness" 14).

While Forgael's quest for mystic love in the realm of the "Everliving" is an entirely individual effort, Cuchulain, the central character in *At the Hawk's Well*, embodies archetypal heroic behavior. The very choice of Cuchulain as hero confirms this aspect: being one of the best-known and most respected, fearless, mythic Irish heroes, the evocation of his figure revitalizes the collective memory of the nation by setting an example of ancient heroism and courage that the people needed so badly at the time Yeats wrote the play (1916).

The Hawk-Woman cannot be found in the myth of Cuchulain, yet as conceived by the author she perfectly suits her mythical function. At one level she can be regarded as the representative of nature's power that would not let humans gain immortality no matter how bravely or persistently they fought for it. It is the law of nature that if someone attempts to violate its order, he or she will be punished and defeated. On the other hand, human heroism consists in struggling with or for what is known to be impossible. When Cuchulain is denied his primary aim, immortality, he seeks to establish at least a momentary contact with the supernatural, not to be dissolved in it but to gain a deeper and more intense understanding of life.

Miracles happen in *At the Hawk's Well*, too, but unlike *The Shadowy Waters*, they do not evoke wonder. The water of immortality that the hero is seeking does bubble up in the well from time to time, but it is taken rather as a natural phenomenon which follows its own supernatural laws, unknown to humans. For this reason no human being can control or possess it.

The play is set far from any human setting and so can easily be accepted as the meeting place of the two worlds. Nothing is ordinary here – even Cuchulain's human rival, the Old Man, although representing a more mediocre, cowardly behavior, is not shown in a natural human environment and is not engaged in any "normal" activity – the supernatural does not intrude into a naturalistic scene but instead the whole play goes on in a mythic time and space. It goes on in a timeless time which is present and past simultaneously, unique and eternal – as in the myths.

In some other plays Yeats mixes mythic and fantastic elements within the same work. In those of the second structural type the circular plot opens up allowing the supernatural to enter: it reveals itself to one or several characters – whether they were seeking it or not – and influences human lives and fates in some way. When the supernatural disappears the plot closes, returning to the original situation and bringing the characters back to where they were but with some new understanding or knowledge – even if it is only the realization of their deprived state. Thus, the basically mythical situation is combined with this fantasylike elusiveness.

Citing examples of this structural type from Yeats's early, middle, and late plays reveals how the mixing of the mythic and fantastic components helps him to express his perennial concerns but changing attitudes. The early play, *The Land of Heart's Desire*, the mature *The Only Jealousy of Emer*, and the late *Purgatory* all dramatize Yeats's central theme: the relationship between the two worlds, the visible and the invisible, and the basic mythic situation of the clash between them. The supernatural appears in a well-defined human world: in *The Land of Heart's Desire* in a realistically drawn peasant milieu where even the threads of a family conflict are outlined; in *Emer* in a domestic scene, although the characters themselves are mythic; and in *Purgatory* in a sordid scene with very earthbound human beings. In each the supernatural evoked by fantastic means differs, and so does the human attitude to it.

In *The Land of Heart's Desire*, due to Yeats's early romantic idealism, the fairyland is full of mystical attraction. The existence of the other world is taken for granted by all the humans; the magic objects and actions used by the fairies for taking possession of the human sphere are those of tradition – as the whole play itself is close to a fairytale or folktale. The antirealistic theatrical means, such as the mystical lights outside the door, the song, the magic words, and, especially, the enchanting dance of the Faery Child, all symbolize and give a glimpse of the superior beauty, the freedom, and eternal youth in the land of the spiritual. Such beauty and happiness appear in the young bride, Mary's indefinite longing for the unattainable (as opposed to the gray prospects of ordinary earthly life), which is then embodied in the images of fairyland. She, like the typical passive heroines of fantasies, makes her important decision in a trance, while under the spell of the supernatural. Magic is elusive: by the end of the play it recedes from the world of nature, leaving behind all the human beings except Mary. She can keep the magic and join the fairies, but only through her physical death.

Although the two worlds do exist side by side and communicate with each other, *The Only Jealousy of Emer* dramatizes the tragedy of human helplessness and distance from wholeness, from Unity of Being. The supernatural world still contains perfect beauty; Emer's vision of it would suit a work of pure fantasy. Fand the fairy has all the qualities of a supernatural creature in her shining, metallic dress, with her hair of "metallic suggestion," with her magic dance, and with all the details of her appearance, words, and movements. But the spiritual world is not wholly beautiful: the evil spirit, Bricriu, is also present in his distorted bodily form and with his offer of cruel alternatives. The attraction of the superior beauty is more dangerous than in the previous play; requires deeper suffering and sacrifice from humans who come in contact with it; and, like the golden bird of Byzantium, disdains "in glory of changeless metal" all that is transitory and imperfectly human (*Collected Poems* 281).

Yeats's treatment of the heroes is fantastic rather than mythic. Cuchulain, the fearless mythic hero of *At the Hawk's Well* and other plays, remains completely passive in *Emer*: seemingly dead but in fact totally in the hands of the other world. The split of the personality of both man and woman enacted on the stage further emphasizes human helplessness. Cuchulain actually appears in two shapes: his inferior, physical body and, separately, his pure, spiritual self; only his spirit meets the supernatural. His tragedy lies not in having to return to physical life but in not even being in the position to choose, since his fate depends on his wife Emer's decision, and on the fact that his momentary encounter with the spiritual world does not give him inspiration, or a deeper understanding of or intensity in life. When he returns to life, he only vaguely remembers his adventure as if in a bad dream, which, instead of being enriching, merely frightened him.

Emer, herself a combination of the mythic and fantastic heroine, plays the role of the mythic deliverer, yet hers is, above all, an ambiguous victory. She proves capable of a heroic self-sacrifice in order to save her husband's life, and she is the one who gains a deeper insight from the encounter with the messenger of the supernatural. However, her decision remains only partly her own, partly an acting out of the spirit's will. Moreover, what she gains for Cuchulain is only physical life, deprived of enlightenment or any other spiritual benefit. She understands that she cannot unite the two aspects of Cuchulain's love or rather, cannot unite the two aspects of Woman: ephemeral, physical attraction and spiritual beauty (embodied in the play in the two different figures of Fand the fairy and Eithne Inguba, Cuchulain's earthly mistress). The process of her self-denial, her heroic acceptance of having to give up possession, is ethically (while Cuchulain's "reduction of being" is ontologically) central to fantasy (Manlove "Elusiveness" 14).

Neither the plot nor the figures of *Purgatory* are directly rooted in any special myth. The playwright's own creative fantasy gives shape to the fundamental mythic situation: the confrontation of the visible and the invisible worlds. Having lost his youthful romanticism and idealism, having become more pessimistic in his views on history and the human condition, Yeats now evokes the supernatural in far less shining colors than earlier. The supernatural that manifests itself in the vision of human beings in *Purgatory* is no longer the "land of heart's desire"; neither is it of any great beauty. The spirits are only projections of a suffering human soul and, in their symbolic meaning, representative of an earlier generation's form of living and values. They do not, therefore, exist so unquestionably as the Faery Child or Fand, but behave rather like phenomena in fantasy: at one and the same time they do and do not have reality. The dramatic presentation has such great force that although the spirits first appear to be the products of the Old Man's raving mind, gradually even the Boy, who is entirely deprived of any faith and imaginative power, comes to share the vision and to see the light and figures in the window of the ruinous, floorless house.

The human being, in his attempt to contact the spiritual, first appears to succeed, but finally suffers defeat. Moreover, the supernatural proves never to have been really affected by human will, or to have communicated with the earthly sphere. In *Emer* human sacrifice, although intolerably painful, at least influenced life and fate, whereas here it turns out to be absolutely in vain. The unbridgeable distance from the physical human world to the spiritual, and thus to completeness and unity, is more bitterly enacted in *Purgatory* than in the earlier plays discussed.

The Herne's Egg embodies the third structural type of the mythic-fantastic in Yeats's plays, where plot and characters oscillate between the natural and the supernatural, while the hero and spectator alternate between belief and disbelief. Some basic mythic situations, such as those of Leda and the Swan or the Fall are enacted in a fantastic mode full of ambiguity. Thus the Leda and the Swan relationship in the play becomes more complicated than in the original: seven men consummate the God's love for an earthly woman instead of the godhead incarnated in the form of a bird. The Fall, breaking God's law by eating the forbidden fruit and so setting independent human will against the divine, is enacted in the farcical attempts of the hero Congal to steal the Herne's egg. The fantastic means (parts of the miraculous plot, events, figures, stylized and grotesque grotesque movements, symbolic stage design) enhance this feeling of ambiguity and ambivalence: as does the unusual shape (Great Herne) and strange, sometimes concrete, sometimes abstract, appearance of the godhead, the stylized fight and mock-heroic actions of the hero. Yeats intends these means to produce an alienating effect, as the supernatural activity, magic occurrences and miracles are experienced both as real and miraculous — alternately or both at the same time — with the result that they are to be and not to be believed in simultaneously.

One of the functions of fantasy, according to Rosemary Jackson, is to subvert the existing order and values. Yeats uses the fantastic in *The Herne's Egg* to subvert his own ideals: the hero, the heroic confrontation with the supernatural, and the union with the spiritual. But he does so in a way that at the same time maintains those ideals. Congal the hero is himself heroic *and* foolish, powerful *and* helpless, victor *and* defeated, all at once; the heroine, raped by seven men, still meets her divine husband untouched by humans. Such anomalies can be accepted as true, without conflict, only in fantasy, "where . . . logic and mimesis see two opposing forces or statements as a contradiction and demand that such contradictions be resolved, . . . unreason and the fantastic allow . . . any author to hold two opposing forces together as an oxymoron without moving toward resolution" (Morse, "Introduction," 8). According to our general definitions of myth as the product of the collective mind and fantasy as that of the individual creative imagination, it appears that those of Yeats's plays that are dominantly fantastic express individual desires, while those that are essentially mythic dramatize collective experiences. It also appears that the fantastic elements help to bring to the surface indefinite longings for the unknown, fears of the superior powers, or the tragedy of human helplessness in this fallen world. Myth, with its certainty gained from relying on tradition and collective views, makes the formation of more definite desires for union with the spiritual possible. It allows us to see even in modern literature man's defeat in the encounter with the greater powers as part of the cosmic mystery of the constant, infinite struggle between the antinomies of the world. Often in Yeats's plays the mythic and the fantastic work together, and those plays that mingle elements of both unite individual efforts with the collective needs, hopes, and fears of the tragic condition of the Irish people and of humankind.

Works Cited

Bak, Imre. "Mitosz, művészet, jel." *Kapcsolatok*. Budapest: Népművelési Intézet, 1980.

Eliade, Mircea. *A szent és a profán*. Trans. Gábor Berényí. Budapest: Európa, 1987.

Hume, Kathryn. *Fantasy and Mimesis: Responses to Reality in Western Literature*. New York: Methuen, 1984.

Jackson, Rosemary. *Fantasy: The Literature of Subversion*. London: Methuen, 1981.

Kavanagh, Patrick. "The Great Hunger." In *Collected Poems*. London: Martin Brian and O'Keeffe Ltd., 1972; New York: W. W. Norton & Co., Inc., 1973.

Kearney, Richard. *The Irish Mind: Exploring Intellectual Traditions*. Dublin: Wolfhound

Press, 1985.

Manlove, Colin N. "On the Nature of Fantasy." In *The Aesthetics of Fantasy Literature and Art*. ed. Roger C. Schlobin.16-36. Indiana: Notre DameUniversity Press, 1982.

—-. "The Elusiveness of Fantasy." *Fantasy Review*. V. 9,. No. 74. (April 1986) 13-14;49-50.

Olsen, Lance. *Ellipse of Uncertainty: An Introduction to Postmodern Fantasy*. Westport, CT:: Greenwood, 1987.

Schwartz, Richard Alan. "The Fantastic in Contemporary Fiction." In *The Scope of the Fantastic: Theory, Technique, Major Authors*. ed. Robert A. Collins, 27-32. Westport, CT: Greenwood, 1986.

Thornton, Weldon. *J. M. Synge and the Western Mind*. Gerrards Cross, Bucks.: Colin Smythe, 1979.

Yeats, William Butler. *Collected Poems*. London: Macmillan, 1950.

—-. *Autobiographies*. London: Macmillan, 1956.

—- . *Collected Plays*. London: Macmillan, 1960.

Maureen Murphy

Siren or Victim:
The Mermaid in Irish
Legend and Poetry

Irish supernatural tradition is rich in its associations with the sea. There are customs and superstitions about all aspects of fishing; there are stories of encounters with all kinds of sea creatures, and there are legends and beliefs that link certain Irish families with seals and seafolk continuing down to our own day. The nonchalance with which an Irish country woman remarks, "Tá na róna gaoilte leis na muintir Conghaile," (The seals are related to the Conneely people) is reflected in the offhand familiarity of the lines from Seamus Heaney's "The Singer's House":

> People here used to believe
> that drowned souls lived in the seals.
> At Spring tides they might change shape.
> They loved music and swam in for a singer
>
> who might stand at the end of summer
> in the mouth of a whitewashed turf-shed,
> his shoulder to the jamb, his song
> a rowboat far out in evening.
> (*Field Work* 27)

A "sea-woman unscaled" features in the list of wonders enumerated in Austin Clarke's "Paupers," a poem that imagines Lady Gregory collecting mermaid stories from the inmates of the Gort Workhouse, and Nuala ní Dhomhnaill's "Parthenogenesis" speaks to the widespread legend of mortal women and their lovers from the sea, concluding with lines suggestive of W. B. Yeats's "Leda and the Swan" that offer an image of the annunciation from Irish folklore to complement those from the Christian and the classical traditions:

> Instear an scéal seo, leis, i dtaobh thíos do chnoc
> Leitriúch na gCineál Alltraighe, cé gur ar bhean

de mhuintir Flaitheartaigh a leagtar ansan é.
Tá sé acu
chomh maith theas in Uibh Ráthach i dtaobh bhean de muin
     tir Shé
is in áiteanna eile cóstaí na hÉireann.
Ach is cuma cér dhíobh í, is chuige sea atáim
gurb ionann an t-uamhan a bhraith sí is an scáth
á leanúint síos is an buaireamh a líon
croí óg na Maighdine nuair a chuala sí
clog binn na n-aingeal is gur inchollaíodh
ina broinn istigh, de réir deal ramh, Mac Dé Bhí.

                                        (*ní Dhomhnaill* 134)

(The story is told at the foot of a hill in Connemara
although there it is put down to a woman of the O'Flahertys.
They have it as well south in Iveragh about one of the
     O'Sheas.
and it is heard in other places along the Irish coast.
But wherever she's from, my point is,
that when the shadow followed her below the sea
she felt the same fear as that which troubled the young
heart of the Virgin Mary when she heard the sweet bells
of the angels and conceived in her womb, so we're told,
the Son of God.)[1]

Among the various sea creatures, enchanted seals, swan maidens, mermen, mortal wives, and seafolk spouses, the mermaid—despite her reputation as bearer of bad luck—is one of the most attractive and, in some cases, most sympathetic figures in Irish supernatural tradition. She appears as a siren, a figure with whom she is often confused; she leaves the sea and her means of survival in search of love or a soul, or she becomes a wife to a mortal man who has captured her by stealing her magic cloak. She can be confused with other Irish supernatural beings insofar as she is known to take mortals to her own kingdom as the fairies do, and she is sometimes reckoned to be the harbinger of death in the manner of the banshee.[2] Modern and contemporary Irish writers have made her their own by turning tradition to irony or metaphor.

The variety of mermaid roles goes back to earliest Irish literature. Amid the chronicles of kings and clergy, battles and burnings, famine and fire in the *Annals of the Kingdom of Ireland* (1632-1636), popularly known as the *Annals of the Four Masters*, one finds accounts of a mermaid called Liban who was captured in the net of a fisherman named Beoan near Inbher-Ollarbha, the ancient name for Larne, County Antrim, in 558 A.D. and of a gigantic mermaid that washed up on the Scottish coast in 887 A.D.[3] A later text, *The Annals of Loch Cé: A Chronicle of Irish Affairs from A.D. 1014 to A.D. 1590* records another remark able instance of captured mermaids in 1118. "Another wonderful story also in Eirinn, viz.: – a mermaid was captured by the fishermen of Lis-Airglinn in Osraighe (Ossory) and another at Port-Láirge (Waterford)" (Hennessy 1:111). A story explaining the origin of the name Port-Láirge appearing in the "Rennes Dindsen chas" introduces the mermaid as a destructive force. It describes the voyage of Roth, son of Cithang, son of the Kings of Inis Aine, around the boundary of his territory at the time of the Fomorians. Roth hears the mermaids singing in Muir nIcht, the English Channel. They sing him to sleep only to savage and dismember him, sending his thigh to the place that was thereafter called Port-Láirge, the Port of the Thigh (Stokes 432-434).[4]

Seathrún Ceitinn's (Geoffrey Keating) *Forus Feasa an Éirinn* (1629-1634), a history of Ireland that is part mythology and legend, reflects a Homeric influence in its account of Milidh's meeting with mermaids near the mouth of the Caspian Sea:

> Thence they set out, having four leaders
> named Ealloit, Laimhfhionn,
> Cing and Caicher and mermaids came
> in the sea before them, and these used to
> discourse music to the sailors as they
> passed them, so they might lull them
> to sleep and then fall upon them and slay
> them and Caicher the Druid applied a remedy
> to this by melting wax in their ears so that
> they could not hear the music lest it might
> put them to sleep.
>
> (Ceitinn 2:35)

Both of these stories reflect the tendency of early writers to confuse the mermaid and the siren. Each is a sweet singer with a human head/upper body and a fish's tail; however, the siren has, in addition, bird's claws with which to tear her prey to pieces. The mermaid, on the other hand, seldom destroys her victim directly. Instead, she lures her sailors to certain death by attracting them with her beauty and her captivating song.

It was this image of a mermaid that was appropriated by Christian iconographers in order to suggest the danger to the unwary soul posed by sensual temptations. When the Continental religious orders were introduced to Ireland in the Middle Ages, they carved the figure in some of their churches. A mermaid holding a comb and a glass appears to lure two cheerful fish, a symbol for Christ, in a relief panel carved on the screen between the south transept and the sacristy in the Cistercians' Kilcooly Abbey, County Tipperary, that was built by Donal Mór O'Brien, King of Thomond, around 1182 (figure 1).

The lesser sin of vanity is represented by a figure of a black mermaid holding a comb in her right hand and a round glass in her left hand in the fifteenth-century restoration of the chancel arch of the Augustinian priory at Clonfert, County Galway (frontispiece). There are other mermaids in other Augustinian priories: one carved on one of the cloister piers in Inistioge, near Jerpoint, County Kilkenny, and another carved on the right side of the west doorway of Clontuskert, County Galway, a doorway that dates to 1471 (figure 2).

The mermaid who continues to appear in Irish folk forms down to our own time is kin to other supernatural figures who people Irish legends about those who meet untimely deaths. As Máire MacNeill observed in the introduction to her translation of a collection of fairy legends from Donegal, Irish country people appeared to distinguish between untimely accidental death and other kinds of death. The former, she suggests, may have been a reflection of "the anxieties of life and livelihood, the fear of calamities which, while not everyday occurrences, happen frequently enough in a fishing and subsistence-farming community to be ever present in the imagination" (Ó hEochaidh 22).

The well-known ballad "The Mermaid" (Child 289) which begins "Twas Friday morn when we set sail," expresses the belief that merely sighting a mermaid means disaster, and there are many legends like that of the Kerry storyteller Seán O'Connaill about a Dingle man's good sense in leaving a fishing ground after he catches a mermaid in his lines. He warns others away, but they believe he is only trying to protect a good fishing spot, so failing to heed his advice they stay on and lose a man to the sea (Ó Duilearga 277-278).

In modern Irish literature the bronze Miss Douce and the gold Miss Kennedy are the putative mermaid/sirens of James Joyce's *Ulysses*; however, in an ironic twist, as they crouch under the reef of the counter, it is Miss Kennedy who plugs her ears so that she will not have to hear Miss Douce's story about Bloom. The barmaids attract Simon Dedalus and his friends but as for Bloom, he is preoccupied with his own sirens—with Martha and especially with Molly. As he listens to the sirens' songs—not those of the bar maids but those of Dedalus and company—he, like Odysseus, holds his ground against the music, in this case the sentiments of songs like "The Croppy Boy," the 1798 ballad of betrayal that would tempt him to follow Blazes Boylan to his assignation with Molly and then to confront the lovers.

Later in the chapters mermaids add to Joyce's sexual imagery. Simon Dedalus ramps tobacco into the bowl of his pipe, "shreds of hair, her maiden-hair, her mermaid's" and the blind, youthful piano tuner taps his way past Daly's window, "where a mermaid, hair all streaming (but he couldn't see), blew whiffs of a mermaid (blind couldn't), mermaid coolest whiff of all" (Joyce 261, 289).

Along with the tradition of mermaids as agents of unprovoked disaster, there are legends of mermaids taking revenge on those who mistreat them by interfering with them physically or by failing to respond to their love. These legends are part of a wider body of cautionary tales having to do with the interaction between Irish country people and the supernatural. A fisherman who kills a mermaid despite her plea for mercy is not only pursued and drowned by an "avenging wave," but also his descendants' appearance in the same waters

Figure 1. Mermaid Carved on a Relief Panel in the Cistercian Abbey at Kilcooly, County Tipperary

Figure 2. Mermaid Carved on the Right Side of the West Doorway of Clontuskert Abbey, County Galway

raises the wave again (Benwell 158).

A well-known legend about a mermaid who is abused was told about the O'Briens who lived near Killone Lake, three miles from the town of Ennis in County Clare. John O'Donovan's version of the legend recorded in the second volume of his *Ordnance Survey Letters from Clare* (1839) describes how O'Brien captured a mermaid, brought her home, and imprisoned her in a crib, but ordered that she be cared for humanely. A fool who lived on O'Brien's charity decided to make her speak by throwing boiling water on her. She screamed, ran from the house, and cursed O'Brien saying:

> Filedhan bhradráin on sruith,
> File gan fuil gan feoil
> gur ba mar sin imtheochas siol mBriain
> Na ndeasacha fiadh as Chilleóin
> (O'Donovan 43-44)

> (As the return of the salmon from the stream,
> A return without blood or flesh
> May such be the departure of the O'Briens,
> Like ears of wild corn from Killone.)

The O'Brien's soon disappeared from Killone and no O'Brien has owned the property since that time.

More benign versions of the legend told today rationalize the human behavior, describing the mermaid as stealing wine from the cellar. Apprehended by the butler, she is thrown into boiling water whereupon she is reduced to jelly; however, she returns every seven years. In still another account, she is variously stabbed by an O'Brien butler or shot by a MacDonnell for her theft, but she manages to escape back into Killone Lake and every forty years the lake turns red as a result of her wounding (Spellissy 48).

There are other legends of a mermaid as a captive or as a victim—sometimes by her own choice. Christian syncretists were fond of stories that brought Irish pagan heroes like Oisín, and kings like the Middle Irish Suibhne to the Church before they died, or stories that turned pagan figures to saints. In his 1854 edition of the *Annals of the Four Masters*, the nineteenth-century antiquarian John O'Donovan identified Liban, the mermaid caught in the fisherman's net, with Liban the saint who appears in O'Clery's *Calendar of Irish Saints*. In the Leabhar-na-hUidhri she is the daughter of Eochaidh from whom Lough Neagh takes its name. When Lough Neagh erupts, Liban survives for a year under the sea. Then she asks to be transformed into a salmon and she remains in the sea until the time of Saint Comhgall of Bangor (d. 601). Comhgall sends a fisherman named Beoan on an errand to Pope Gregory. En route, Beoan's crew hears angels beneath their boat who herald Liban. Liban tells the crew that she has spent three hundred years in the sea and that she will meet

them in a year's time at Inbher-Ollarbha (Larne). Beoan goes to Inbher-Ollarbha at the appointed time, sets his nets, and captures Liban. Comhgall
baptizes her Muirgen (Born of the Sea) or Muirgeilt (Traverser of the Sea)
(O'Donovan 201-202).

The best-known story of a mermaid who seeks a soul is not Irish at all but
Danish. The heroine of "The Little Mermaid" falls in love with a prince, follows
him to land, and becomes a mortal in order to have a soul. When the prince
marries someone else, her heart breaks, but her soul offers her the chance for
immortality. The Irish counterpart to Hans Christian Andersen's story is
Thomas Moore's "The Origin of the Harp" from Moore's *Irish Melodies* (1845).
Moore's lines describe a sea-maiden whose unrequited love for a mortal youth
moves heaven to transform her into a harp whose music mingles the sounds of
love and sadness in recognition of her love. The Irish painter Daniel Maclise
based a painting on Moore's poem.[5]

Even when a mermaid's love is returned, all does not always go well. The
mermaid that appears on the O'Sullivan coat of arms at Dunkerron Castle, the
stronghold of the O'Sullivan More near Kenmare, County Kerry, is the subject
of T. Crofton Croker's "The Lord of Dunkerron" (1825). O'Sullivan More's
love for a mermaid brings him to an undersea palace. The mermaid leaves
O'Sullivan More to get permission from her chief to remain with him, promising
that only death would prevent her return. As he waits the sea turns violent, the
palace vanishes and a wave washes O'Sullivan More ashore where he is found
by his retainers (Croker 216- 221).

In his poem "The Mermaid," the third poem of the eleven-poem cycle "A
Man Young and Old" from *The Tower* (1928), W. B. Yeats's mermaid, in a spasm
of "cruel happiness," seizes her young man in a love grip that drowns both of
them. The oxymoron "cruel happiness" speaks also to Yeats's unrequited love
for Maude Gonne who, for the poet, combined the traits of beauty and heart-
lessness that traditionally characterize the mermaid. Imprisoned though Yeats
might have been by his love for Maude Gonne, in Irish tradition the mermaid
is far more likely to be captive than captor.

The most popular Irish mermaid legend is the type that the Norwegian
folklorist Reidar Th. Christiansen identified as "The Seal Woman" in *The
Migratory Legends* (ML 4080, 1958). In the legend, the seal woman or mermaid
comes ashore and puts aside a magic cloak or object while she suns herself or
combs her hair. A mortal man who is attracted to her steals the magic cloak
and hides it. The mermaid, who often begs unsuccessfully for its return, finally
follows the man, lives with him and bears his children. Years later, one of her
children discovers the cloak, reveals its location or gives it back to her. She dons
the cloak, abandons her human family and returns to her people in the sea.

There are variations to the basic legend. Sometimes the mermaid leaves
special gifts or good luck to her family; on the other hand, she can bring special
destruction on her own — turning children to stone or trying to upset the fishing
boat carrying her son.[6]

The seal woman legend is widely distributed over the west of Ireland with especially heavy concentrations in the Kerry peninsulas of Corca Dhuibhne and Iveragh. Patricia Lysaght, who is making a study of the legend, has noticed the similarities between it and a similar legend called "The Comb Legend" that is associated with the banshees (Lysaght 159-160). Seamus Heaney and Nuala ní Dhomhnaill have written poems about this legend, Heaney staking out his poetic territory in English and ní Dhomhnaill bringing a new passion and contemporary sensibility to poetry in modern Irish. Seamus Heaney's "Maighdean Mara" (Mermaid) is dedicated to Seán Ó h-Eochaidh, the Donegal folklore collector whose "Eoin Óg agus an Mhaighdean Mhara" (Young Eoin and the mermaid) supplied the metaphor for the poem.

"Maighdean Mara" appeared in *Wintering Out* (1972), a collection whose title alludes to the lines from Richard III, "Now is the winter of our discontent," and whose poems address the public suffering of Northern Ireland as well as the private distress of marriage and early family life. The poem is one of a series of six middle poems of the seventeen that make up Part Two and they concern women who reject their families in different ways: the mad young woman whose ghost returns in "A Winter's Tale," the "Shore Woman" who escapes her husband to walk on the strand, the woman who drowns her unwanted infant in "Limbo," the woman in "Bye-Child" who imprisons her son in a henhouse till he is discovered frail and speechless and even the woman in "Good-Night" who closes darkness behind her as she leaves the room.

Part One of "Maighdean Mara," describes the mermaid's homecoming, her first great sleep in her own place after her land years, and the suicide by drowning of a young mother:

> She sleeps now, her cold breasts
> Dandled by undertow,
> Her hair lifted and laid.
> Undulant slow seawracks
> Cast about shin and thigh,
> Bangles of wort, drifting
> Weeds catch, dislodge gently.
> (Heaney *Poems* 88)

The lines mimic the rhythm of the sea, the ebb and flow in the assonance of "dandled by undertow," the alliteration of "lifted and laid." Part Two retells the legend in fourteen spare lines: the theft of a cloak, the mermaid's pursuit of the man who took it, her captive years, children, the cloak recovered. Part Three describes the entry into the sea at night, leaving family behind.

Heaney's mermaid is a woman who chooses the darkness of the ocean over the warmth and light of family life. Nuala ní Dhomhnaill would no doubt consider her escape preferable to the fate of her mermaid in "An Mhaighdean Mhara" who is caught above the high water mark. Ní Dhomhnaill's mermaid is a metaphor for someone who is in the wrong place, trapped in a hostile environment redolent with fish faces, Nazi inquisitors, and a final terrifying image of a rat gnawing at the sun. With time running out and her natural defenses useless in such surroundings, the mermaid doesn't fight but withdraws — perhaps to extremes of anorexia or autism. One might be tempted to give the poem an autobiographical reading: ní Dhomhnaill the Irish language poet who fears time is running out for the language but who, left high and dry like the mermaid with water going down but no tide turning, will not capitulate to English.

Ní Dhomhnaill's sympathetic portrayal of the mermaid as a creature who has broken "the natural law" and who is a proverbial fish out of water stranded in a hostile environment offers an insight into the popularity of the mermaid marries man legend. If folklore is a projection of the yearning, fears, and anxieties of a people, one might read the legend as a metaphor for the woman in an arranged marriage, the match that was the practice in rural Ireland up almost to the second World War: a marriage based on a woman's property which was taken by her husband and that held her captive away from her own people and from which she only escaped by silence and distance or by madness or death.

Notes

1. All translations from the Irish are my own.

2. Patricia Lysaght cites an example from a Kerry School Manuscript (42) in the Archives of the department of Irish Folklore that describes a harbinger of death of the Walsh family who was believed to be a descendant of a mermaid (45-46).

3. The date of Liban's capture is variously recorded in the *Chronicum Scotorum* as 565 and in the *Annals of Ulster* as 571.

4. In the Book of Leinster version of the *Táin Bó Cuailnge*, Port Láirge gets its name from the final battle between Donn Cuailnge and Findbennach where the latter is dismembered and his thigh is sent to Port Láirge (O'Rahilly 272). The "Rennes Dindsenchas" also records another place name, Inber n-Ailbine or Oillbine, where the river Dilvin flows into the Bay of Mallahide, which marks the spot where a mermaid mother killed her son and hurled the child's head at his father (Stokes 295).

5. Jeanne Sheehy says that Moore got his inspiration for the poem from Edward Hudson who made a drawing of this fanciful origin of the harp on the wall of his cell in Kilmainham Gaol, where he was imprisoned for his part in the Rebellion of 1798 (48-49).

6. The Hennessys are given good luck by a mermaid in "The Three Laughs" (ÓDuilearga 123). Lysaght reports a gift of knowledge to the Walshes (41). Crofton Croker's "Children of the Mermaid" explains the origin of the large boulders in the townland of Scurmore, Co. Sligo, as the seven children of a mermaid that she turned to stone before she disappeared. The story of "Eoin Og agus an Mhaighean Mhara" ends with the mermaid trying to wreck her son's boat.

Works Cited

Benwell, Gwen and Arthur Waugh. *Sea Enchantress, The Tale of the Mermaid and Her Kin.* New York: The Citadel Press, 1965.

Bond, Francis. *Wood Carvings in English Churches.* London: Henry Fowde, 1910.

Ceitinn, Seathrún. *Forus Feasa ar Eirinn*, Vol. 2. Ed. Patrick Dinneen. London: Irish Texts Society 8, 1908.

Christiansen, R. Th. *The Migratory Legends: A Proposed List of Types with a Systematic Catalogue of the Norwegian Variants.* Helsinki: Folklore Fellows Communication 175, 1958.

Croker, T. Crofton. "The Lord of Dunkerron." In *Fairy Legends and Traditions of the South of Ireland*, 216-221. 1825. Reprint. London: Swan Gonnenschein, n.d.

Gregory, Augusta. *Visions and Beliefs in the West of Ireland.* 1920. Reprint. Gerrards Cross, Bucks.: Colin Smythe, 1970.

Hayes, Edwards. *The Ballads of Ireland.* 5th ed. Dublin: James Duffy, n.d.

Heaney, Seamus. "The Singer's House." In *Field Work.* New York: Farrar, Straus, Giroux, 1979.

—-. "Maighdean Mara." In *Selected Poems.* London: Faber and Faber, 1980.

Hennessy, William, ed. *The Annals of Loch Cé: A Chronicle of Irish Affairs from AD 1014 to AD 1590.* London: Longman and Trubner, 1871.

Joyce, James. *Ulysses.* New York: Randon House, 1961.

Lysaght, Patricia. *The Banshee: The Irish Supernatural Death-Messenger.* Dublin: Glendale Press, 1986.

Ní Dhomhnaill, Nuala. "An Mhaighdean Mhara," "Parthenogenesis." In *Selected Poems/Rogha Dánta.* Dublin: Raven Arts, 1988.

O'Donovan, John. *Ordnance Survey Letters, Clare II.* 1839. Typescript, 1928.

Ó'Duilearga, Séamus. *Sean Ó Conaill's Book.* Trans. Máire MacNeill. Baile Átha Cliath: Comhairle Bhéaloideas Éireann, 1981.

Ó hEochaidh, Séan, Máire Ní Néill, and Séamus Ó Catháin. *Síscéalta ó Thír Chonaill.* Baile Átha Cliath: Comhairle Bhéaloideas Éireann, 1977.

O'Rahilly, Cecile, ed. *Táin Bó Cuailnge.* Dublin: Institute for Advanced Studies, 1961.

Sheehy, Jeanne. *The Rediscovery of Ireland's Past: The Celtic Revival, 1830-1930.* London: Thames and Hudson, 1980.

Spellissy, Jean. *Clare: County of Contrast.* Galway: Connacht Tribune, 1987.

Stokes, Whitley. "Rennes Dindsenchas." *Revue Celtique* 15 (1883): 432-434

Wood-Martin, W. G. *Traces of the Elder Faiths of Ireland.* 1902. Reprint. Washington: Kennikat Press, 1970.

Anthony Roche

Ghosts in Irish Drama

This essay will consider a phenomenon associated with the fantastic or the supernatural, namely the return of the dead to haunt the living, and its particular provenance in Irish drama written in the English language. After briefly looking at James Joyce and Henrik Ibsen, it will concentrate on two classic and one contemporary dramatic treatment of ghosts in J. M. Synge's *Riders to the Sea*, W. B. Yeats's *The Only Jealousy of Emer*, and Stewart Parker's *Pentecost*.

What is true for modern European literature in general applies to Irish literature, that not only the lives of the characters represented but also the very space they occupy is haunted by the dead, who bring their dimension of being to bear interrogatively on those lives. A key modernist text is Joyce's aptly named "The Dead," where the exhumed ghost of the long-dead Michael Furey proves more real to Gretta Conroy than the living presence of her husband. The ending of the story not only transforms Gabriel's view of himself and his past existence but also through the hypnotic, repetitive, incantatory nature of its prose moves toward "that region where dwell the vast hosts of the dead" (241). In so doing, the ending provides an enlarged perspective which transforms everything that has occurred earlier in "The Dead" as well as all the preceding stories in the volume. Up to this point, the lives depicted in *Dubliners* have been viewed through the desolating gap of the author's pervasive irony. But Joyce is aiming for a different effect at the close in bringing on a dead protagonist and allowing Michael Furey's ghostly presence to dramatize the gap between aspiration and reality. Such a move strains the limits of his hitherto minimalist realism, the "scrupulous meanness" of Joyce's prose style, in giving access through language to another dimension.

Joyce was the Irish disciple of Ibsen and is clearly following him in "The Dead" by showing the extent to which the lives of people in the present can still be determined by, and outweighed by, the influence of dead figures from their past. That Joyce, with the exception of *Exiles*, chose to develop this and related themes through the medium of prose puts him outside the scope of this essay. But the figure of Ibsen is inescapable, because of his pre-eminence as an influence on the drama written at the time and because any consideration of the subject of ghosts in drama is inevitably haunted by his play of the same name. In *Ghosts*, the lives of Mrs. Alving and her son Oswald, for all of their insistence on acting as free agents, are overshadowed by the patriarchal ghost of the old man. Ibsen never brings Captain Alving on stage or directly back to life, since his ghost would cut a ludicrous figure in the realistic bourgeois setting of the play, but signifies his presence in other symbolic ways: the orphanage which is to be named after him; the bequeathed gestures, speech, and movement which both his son and his half-daughter inherit; and the legacy of syphilis which Oswald has contracted.

The Irish Dramatic Movement was singularly ambivalent on the score of Ibsen.[1] It would initially appear that, having shared the stage of a new Irish drama in 1899 with an avowed Ibsenite like Edward Martyn in plays such as *The Heather Field*, neither Yeats nor the movement he ran was prepared to encourage that school; accordingly, Martyn and his fellow Ibsenites were banished in favor of a drama not of social realism but of poetic surrealism. But Ibsen continued to exert a discernible influence on the plays of Yeats and Synge, for all of the rude noises they made about him. As Yeats admitted, "Neither I nor my generation could escape him" ("Tragic Generation" 279); and his talk of carrying Archer's translation of the collected works "to and fro upon my journeys to Ireland and Sligo" ("Tragic Generation" 280) suggests an Irishing of Ibsen rather than a repudiation of him. The Irish Dramatic Movement offers a translation of Ibsen in the sense that his narratives of strong characters wishing to assert their independence in an oppressive environment are transposed from the middle-class homes of Norway to the peasant cottages of Wicklow and the west of Ireland. In Synge's *In the Shadow of the Glen* another woman called Nora is forced to walk out and close the door on an unsatisfactory husband.

The most frequent criticism leveled by Synge and Yeats at Ibsen has to do with the nature of his dramatic speech. While sharing their aim in dealing "with the reality of life" he did so "in joyless and pallid words" (Synge "Preface" 53) and in writing "dialogue so close to modern educated speech that music and style were impossible" (Yeats "Tragic Generation" 279). They opposed the deliberate narrowing and restriction of the linguistic range, of the verbal expressivity available to Ibsen's trapped characters. But this derives from what I take to be the fundamental difference between them and the source of the objections—the restrictions placed upon Ibsen's representation of life by the bounds of a narrowly conceived stage realism. Yeats and Synge could not uncritically acclaim or emulate a form of drama which in their eyes kept some of the most important characters or issues off stage, or forced them there, a drama which prevented any direct representation of imaginative or supernatural energies. It is no surprise, therefore, to learn that the plays by Ibsen consistently exempted by Yeats from his strictures were those written outside the commercial theater, the phantasmagoric dramatic poetry of *Peer Gynt* especially; and Frank McGuinness's 1988 version of the play brings home just how much the young Peer anticipates Synge's Christy Mahon in making himself a mighty man through the power of a lie.[2] But in a play like *Rosmersholm* Yeats objected to the "symbolism and stale odour of spilt poetry" ("Tragic Generation" 280). Ibsen's most famous plays (unlike *Peer Gynt*) deny any direct exchange between the prosaic daytime world and the poetic regions of dream and nightmare, concentrating the action on the first and placing the other in quarantine. Ibsen is therefore forced in dramatic terms to bring the poetry onto the living-room stage in a specimen jar rather than allow for mutual, reciprocal leakage; and since he cannot admit the influence of the dead in incarnational terms, he must do so by displacing their ghostly energies onto objects which come to represent them at one remove — hence the importance of symbolic objects in Ibsen, especially those that, as in Hedda Gabler's portrait of her father, resemble the absent figure. But this to Yeats seemed a remarkably tendentious way of theatrically representing the dead; and much of his own dramatic endeavor was to search for a means of representing on stage contact and spoken communication between the living and the dead.

Yeats's other unusual objection to symbolism (unusual, because as a poet he himself relied so much upon symbolism) has again to do with drama, specifically his comment on the Irish public's reaction to *The Countess Cathleen*: "In using what I considered traditional symbols I forgot that in Ireland they are not symbols but realities" ("Dramatis Personae" 416). Yeats can hardly object to the practice per se. The striking point about the debate over *The Countess Cathleen* is that neither side in it objected to or found ridiculous the presence of demons or the mingling of realistic characters from a recent period of famine with avowedly supernatural creatures dressed in a cross between Ali Baba and medieval mystery plays. The Faustian pact that the play dramatizes did not seem in any way archaic, incredible, or irrelevant to the audience or those who argued the matter in the newspapers and pulpits; what they objected to was the dramatic fact that the peasant characters submitted to the supernatural powers. In this inaugurating event of the Irish Literary Theater, and Irish drama of the last hundred years in general, both sides were perfectly prepared to accept the coexistence on stage of two levels of theatrical reality, the actual and the symbolic, the living and the dead, and their intimate interchange as the very stuff of drama, as equally necessary to represent "reality." The argument arose over the difference of interpretation to be assigned these otherwordly figures, not over their phenomenological presence.

It is this ghostly factor which cuts across and complicates the apparent divide Yeats bemoans in his essay "A People's Theatre" between a socially and politically relevant theater in which the lives of people are held up for their inspection on the one hand, and a poetic drama which works obliquely to represent the regions of dream and myth on the other. The great majority of Irish drama would be seen as belonging to the first category. Yeats is almost alone in the second, although he has been bolstered by the late plays of Samuel Beckett, which abandon even a vestige of verisimilitude and are conspicuously set in a realm of ghosts. Indeed, virtually the only event in a play like *A Piece of*

Monologue is the speaker's witnessing of a burial as another of his tribe is laid to rest:

> So ghastly grinning on. From funeral to funeral. To now. . . . Rain pelting. Umbrellas round a grave. Seen from above. Streaming black canopies. Black ditch beneath. . . . That place beneath. Which . . . he all but said loved one?"
> (Beckett 428)

Here, he speaks as so many of the protagonists in Yeats's and Beckett's plays do, both as a man coming to the end of his individual life and as the end of a generational line. For the Anglo-Irish Protestant Ascendancy as the nineteenth turned into the twentieth century in Ireland, the writing was on the wall. As first their power waned and then their numbers diminished, they retreated into the ancestral region, the remains of a Big or Gothic House, occasionally venturing forth for solitary walks in an alien and inhospitable landscape but more habitually staying in, sitting in an armchair and attending to "all the dead voices" (*Godot*, Beckett 57). If the Catholics were in the political ascendant, then they were so out of a background marked by swift and bloody reprisals at any sign of attempted uprising and recurrent ravages caused by insufficient or blighted food. I believe it is because of the particular nature of Irish history that its drama insists on the presence of ghosts and on their corporeality, refusing a purely symbolic treatment as unreal and a form of betrayal of the dead through inadequate representation. By insisting on the materialization of its ghosts, Irish drama engages closely with the nature of the theatrical act in terms of its carnal immediacy. For the Catholic writer, there would be a clear debt to the ritual of the mass and the doctrine of transubstantiation, less a matter of symbolism than of metamorphosis (and Yeats's jibs at how traditional symbols are viewed in an increasingly Catholic Ireland may be read in this sense).

It was not only the leaders of the 1916 Rising who drew on the dramatic power of the Easter ritual to suggest an individual's continued active presence in the lives of an Irish audience after the moment of physical death. Irish playwrights, be they Catholic or Protestant, have continually drawn on Christ's death and resurrection as a motif, even in such outwardly naturalistic plays as Thomas Kilroy's *The Death and Resurrection of Mr. Roche* (1968). In Kilroy's play, if the sudden death of the title character comes as a surprise to the audience on and off the stage, then his even more unexpected return from the dead in Act two shatters the characters' and the play's facade of daytime normality.[3] Indeed, the return of the dead to haunt the living, their refusal to stay dead, is the loophole by which the fantastic is admitted to the predominantly naturalistic Irish stage, an influence which once admitted works to transform the nature of that space.

Synge and the Return of the Dead

The greatest instance of the death-and-resurrection motif in Irish drama is of course Synge's *The Playboy of the Western World*. Before proceeding to discuss his *Riders to the Sea* in some detail, where the ghostly presence is most extensive, I would like to consider *Playboy* and *In the Shadow of the Glen*, the two other Synge plays where the dead return to challenge the living and where the supernatural character of the event is apparently explained away.

Christy Mahon, as more than one critic has pointed out,[4] shares many similarities with his namesake Christ, and manages to stage his own resurrection after the Mayo villagers have turned on him. But it is the repeated capacity of his father to keep returning from the dead that is most remarkable. Old Mahon's first reappearance, while unexpected, can be accounted for in comic/realistic terms: Christy overestimated the lethal effects of "the tap of a loy" (Synge 4:161) and left before he had ascertained his father's death. Synge decided in his extensive revisions of *Playboy* not to leave it at that, as the farcical comeuppance of a young boaster by the return of an all-too-real authority figure, but to keep pushing the material in the latter stages of Act three in an increasingly unreal direction and into an area of increasingly explicit theatricalization. Specifically, there is the physical enactment of the second attempted murder and not only Christy's but also the entire community's certainty that he has effected it, with Old Mahon crawling in to be asked: "Are you coming to be killed a third time or what ails you?" (4:171). The line establishes that Christy is dealing with the ghost of his father, seeking to overcome and subdue the patriarchal tyranny under which he has suffered. The audience simultaneously registers the ghostliness along with the corporeality of a father figure who refuses to remain either symbolic or conveniently off-stage but, in the manner I have been arguing for Irish drama, forces his way into full carnal presence and in so doing transforms the stage into a space where the living and the dead interact on equal terms.

Playboy's full staging of the death-and-resurrection theme helps to establish Christy Mahon and his father as almost purely dramatic creations. As opposed to the "realism" of the shebeen and its inhabitants, they are not as fully bound by the laws of nature and probability. Where Pegeen Mike's existence is directly represented on the stage in credible and detailed terms, the two Mahons emerge out of nowhere and return to it in the end. Where Old Mahon is Synge's subtle deploying of the roistering, drunken figure of the Stage Irishman, calculating the effects of his larger-than-life storytelling in whiskey measures, Christy is much more open in terms of theatrical possibility and can be molded by the desires and needs of the onstage audience. His final struggle is for an identity independent of both the stereotyping of stage tradition and the coercive demands of an audience.

If Synge drew on the Bible for his own characteristic handling of the death-and-resurrection motif, his other great source of ghostly narratives was the oral folklore of the west of Ireland. As Mary King has pointed out, the stories in Synge's *The Aran Islands* are not detached from the living contexts which generated them but are interrelated with the activities of the people on the islands to form a complex weave of their mundane and imaginative lives, their waking and dream worlds.[5] Much of the folklore Synge recorded on Aran has to do with living people who are taken "away" by the fairies or, to put it another way, people who die but are imagined living an alternate existence elsewhere; they do so in opulent conditions the exact reverse of the deprivation they have left behind, enjoying an abundance of all good things. The belief in this otherworld manages to conflate and respond to two central factors in the Aran islanders' existence; death by drowning, and emigration. Unlike those who have departed for England or the United States, however, the dead retain the power to return and intervene in the lives of the island community. They do so under special conditions around which a body of practices has evolved.

In *In the Shadow of the Glen*, Synge drew on these folk materials to provide the play's plot, characters, and such details as the Tramp asking Nora Burke for a needle by saying, "there's great safety in a needle, lady of the house," and proceeding to stitch "one of the tags in his coat, saying the 'De Profundis' under his breath" (Synge 3:41). Since the Tramp is about to be left on his own with what he has every reason to believe is a recently deceased corpse, he is looking for safety and protection from any possibility of the dead man's return. While on Inishmaan, Synge had been drawn aside by the old story teller Pat Dirane and advised: "Take a sharp needle . . . and stick it in under the collar of your coat, and not one of them [the fairy forces] will be able to have power on you" (Synge 2:80). Later, in Part four, another old man tells of his encounter with the uncanny and the danger he was in, "remembered that I had heard them saying none of those creatures can stand before you and you saying the *De Profundis*, so I began saying it, and the thing ran off over the sand and I got home" (2:180). In joining the muttered words of the *De Profundis* to the talisman of the needle, the Tramp is making assurance doubly sure by drawing on and fusing Christian and pagan beliefs in a way Synge regarded as characteristic of the islanders.[6] As we and he learn very shortly after, Dan Burke is only feigning death in order to catch his wife in the act of adultery. But the audience has not been allowed in on this "trick" from the start and has, along with the Tramp and Nora Burke, believed the corpse to be a true one. In terms of the stage, as Falstaff demonstrates when he feigns death to avoid being killed, playing at and being dead are representationally one and the same. So Dan Burke's protestations do not entirely convince us to the contrary that he is fully alive; they allow for dramatic weight to be given to Nora's suggestion that her husband was "always cold" (3:35). In realizing that what she has shared with him in their marriage has been a kind of living death or entombment, Synge's Nora thus comes closely to resemble Ibsen's Nora in *A Doll's House*. But the method of staging her dilemma is very different, even allowing for the shift in setting from comfortable bourgeois household to a very basic peasant cottage. Synge has placed a corpse at center stage and gone on to enact a full-blown (albeit mock) death-and-resurrection scene, with many of the details appropriate to a wake ritual and the propitiation of the dead not to return.

In his dramatic treatment of Dan Burke as of Old Mahon, then, Synge breaks down the barriers normally separating the living from the dead and makes it increasingly difficult to say which they are. In *Riders to the Sea*, Synge does not go so far as to bring the dead son Michael on stage; but he does bring Michael's ghostly presence to bear on the women in the cottage and with it the increasing pressure of the accumulated folk beliefs surrounding the dead. The most graphic account of a burial in *The Aran Islands* is that of a young man drowned at sea. As he talks to the men working on the grave, Synge remarks that he "could not help feeling that I was talking with men who were under a judgment of death. I knew that every one of them would be drowned in the sea in a few years and battered naked on the rocks, or would die in his own cottage and be buried with another fearful scene in the graveyard I had come from" (2:162). The morbidity already apparent in an early work like *Etude Morbid*, and which long precedes his awareness that he was also dying from Hodgkins disease, finds dramatic outlet and objectification through the Aran Islands, where life is lived under the visible shadow of death—the men of their own deaths, and the women a living death, deprived of their menfolk. Rather than concentrating exclusively on the stark facts of disappearance or physical decay, what *The Aran Islands* increasingly records is an oscillation between the realm of the living, where the decaying mortal remains are laid to rest, and the realm of the dead, where paradoxically the remains enjoy an extended imaginative existence. It is primarily through storytelling that reality is extended to encompass two worlds, what Synge in his theory calls "real life" and "a land of the fancy" (2:347),[7] which these figures traverse and which he as a playwright similarly wants to traffic between.

Riders to the Sea presents an audience with two alternative views of what has happened to the missing Michael, one from his sisters, one from his mother. Maurya has broken her vigil for Michael to plead with Bartley, the sole remaining son, not to put to sea; and when he refuses, she has hastened after him with the bread and blessing she has neglected to bestow. Nora and Cathleen have contrived their mother's absence so that they can examine "a shirt and a plain stocking were got off a drowned man in Donegal" (3:5) to determine whether they are their brother's. As they scrutinize the few remnants, the play is unflinching in having its audience face up to the consequences of drowning at sea, especially the extent to which physical features are obliterated. The sisters finally identify Michael by counting the stitches in the cloth and equating him with his personal effects: "And isn't it a pitiful thing when there is nothing left of a man who was a great rower and fisher, but a bit of an old shirt and a plain stocking?" (3:17). Maurya re-enters and begins the slow, inarticulate wail of the keen, the cry of pagan desperation that Synge described in *The Aran Islands* as lurking beneath the islanders' quietude:

This grief of the keen is no personal complaint . . . but seems to contain the whole passionate rage that lurks some where in every native of the island. In this cry of pain the inner consciousness of the people seems to lay itself bare for an instant, and to reveal the mood of beings who feel their isola tion in the face of a universe that wars on them with wind and seas.

When her daughters ask if she saw Bartley, Maurya will only reply "I seen the fearfullest thing" (3:19) and goes on to invoke the whole realm of supernatural apparitions when she specifies what she has seen as a vision: "I've seen the fearfullest thing any person has seen, since the day Bride Dara seen the dead man with the child in his arms." When their mother insists that she has seen not only her living son Bartley but also her dead son Michael accompanying him on the grey pony, Nora and Cathleen immediately deny her claim by pointing to the empirical evidence that Michael was drowned in far-off Donegal. But their first instinctive reaction to hearing of Bride Dara's vision of the dead man has been a joint and inarticulate response, "Uah," which signifies not denial but anguished assent. There is, therefore, a dual recognition scene, one in response to the few tattered fragments of Michael's clothing after a week's immersion in the sea, the other Maurya's epiphanic vision of her dead son, fully clothed and also in a fashion well beyond their meager means: "I looked up then, and I crying, at the grey pony, and there was Michael upon it — with fine clothes on him, and new shoes on his feet." Maurya has been rewarded by the sight of her son who she has been entreating throughout the play; but that vision is a mockery, since it is insubstantial and fleeting. Michael has returned from the dead only to drag the final living son after him, to confirm a double loss for her.

Synge has prepared the dramatic ground for the audience to give at least provisional credence to Maurya's supernatural vision by carefully and consistently doubling the living Bartley with the dead Michael through the early stages of *Riders to the Sea*. When he enters belatedly, Bartley steps into a zone already charged with the three women's collective act of attention on the absent figure of Michael. Bartley takes the rope which is to be used for his brother's coffin as a halter, and steps not into the dead man's shoes but into his shirt, as the sisters later realize when they search for the identifying flannel of Michael's shirt "I'm thinking Bartley put it on him in the morning, for his own shirt was heavy with the salt in it" (3:15). The rope serves to bind together the figures and fates of the two brothers, blurring the absolute distinction between their two identities and their separate status, one living and the other dead. Nothing is as inevitable as that Bartley will be drowned, and soon, as the pressure from the other side of the grave intensifies.

With her last son gone, Maurya lists the family line of her dead. The brothers Michael and Bartley serve as the first in a ritual naming of the eight "fine men" of the family and their separate fates. The number of dead begins to outweigh the living, as a succession of off-stage presences comes to surround the three women: "There were Stephen, and Shawn, were lost in the great wind. . . . There was Sheamus and his father, and his own father again, were lost in a dark night, and not a stick or sign was seen of them when the sun went up. There was Patch after was drowned out of a curagh that turned over" (3:21). A story Synge recorded in *The Aran Islands* tells of the gathered hosts of the dead and numbers them in the hundreds, providing a numerically stark and poignant contrast with the bare handful of survivors eking out a living on these barren, windswept islands. The returned ghost of a dead woman "told them they [the dead] would all be leaving that part of the country on the Oidhche Shamhna [the night of the Celtic feast Samhain, November 1], and that there would be four or five hundred of them riding on horses, and herself would be on a grey horse, riding behind a young man" (2:159). These are the riders to the sea evoked in the play's title and, while there may be passing reference to the Four Horsemen of the Apocalypse, those four biblical riders are subsumed by the hundreds of horseback riders who make up the pagan hosts of the dead.[8] Bartley may assert that he is riding to the Galway fair and that he will not be drowned; but other forces in the play assert that he will and that his ultimate destination is the sea which wields the presiding influence on the islanders' lives. As the play puts it in its most lethally ambivalent pun: "It's the life of a young man to be going on the sea" (3:11).

The doubling of living and dead brothers not only breaks down the notion of individual identity but also undercuts the sense of chronological time. Both events (the drowning of Michael and the feared drowning of Bartley) seem to be occurring simultaneously during the play's brief duration, since they are repeatedly referred to and interrelated as the dominating object of the characters' verbal energies. But in strictly temporal terms one drowning is being reconstructed from the immediate past, the other projected into the immediate future. The stage effect of timelessness and cyclic recurrence is increased when, as Maurya recalls the death by drowning of a previous son Patch, what she evokes verbally is enacted before her and the audience as the door opens, the men enter bearing a body, and the old women follow keening.

This acting out on stage of Maurya's description of the past is akin to the single most uncanny moment in Ibsen's *Ghosts* when Mrs. Alving's account to the pastor of the flirtation between her husband and the maid is simultaneously enacted, in the play's present, by her son and the maid's daughter. At that point, she responds hoarsely with the play's title: "Ghosts!" (Ibsen 54). But Synge pushes such a ghostly incident further into a full-fledged re-enactment of all eight men dying in one simultaneous moment, abolishing chronological succession and presenting one archetypal scene which can be repeated an endless number of times. We are in the region of ghosts, as Mrs. Alving correctly intuited, where the invocations, incantations, and repetitions of Maurya's heightened speech have replaced realistic dialogue: "It isn't that I haven't prayed for you, Bartley, to the Almighty God. It isn't that I haven't said prayers in the dark night till you wouldn't know what I'd be saying; but it's a great rest

I'll have now, and it's time surely. It's a great rest I'll have now, and great sleeping in the long nights after Samhain" (3:25). The drama has moved into a place where the measured, hieratic movements of this ritual of worship for the dead, audaciously combining the Christian and the pagan by referring in the same breath to holy water and the feast of Samhain, have taken over from the more mundane activities of island life and the forward propulsion of plot.

This description is not quite true to the ending of *Riders to the Sea*. Maurya, for all of her undoubted authority, is not given the absolute final say, nor does her vision of things prevail. Nora and Cathleen are equally allowed to give voice to their skepticism, to the feeling that the strain of loss has been too much for their mother: "It's getting old she is, and broken." But I have emphasized the nonrealistic elements of the close of *Riders* as a gloss on Synge's assertion that on "the stage one must have reality, and one must have joy" (4:53-4), and to pave the way for a consideration of W. B. Yeats's *The Only Jealousy of Emer*.

Yeats and Ghosts

Where Synge always preserves a realistic base in his drama, Yeats in *The Only Jealousy of Emer* works through an avowedly poetic theater and conventions derived from the Japanese Noh drama to go one crucial transformative step further. He stages directly the encounter between the living and the dead which Synge had kept (just) off-stage and had conveyed primarily through oral storytelling. The line, "We're but two women struggling with the sea" (Yeats *Plays* 541), establishes the extent to which Yeats's play has Synge's *Riders* as one of its frames of reference, as mediated by the dramatic techniques of the Noh. The play similarly focuses on a drowning, and the setting evoked by the chorus is detailed, naturalistic, and in all respects closer to the fishermen's humble cottages described by Synge in *The Aran Islands* than any dwelling out of elaborate legend:

> *First Musician* [speaking]. I call before the eyes a roof
> With cross-beams darkened by smoke;
> A fisher's net hangs from a beam,
> A long oar lies against the wall.
> I call up a poor fisher's house;
> A man lies dead or swooning . . .
>   (532-33)

The corpse is male and has perished by drowning; those who watch over it are women, though their roles are sexual (wife and mistress) rather than familial (mother and sisters). Yeats's Emer and Synge's Maurya are the still, suffering centers of their respective plays and emerge as tragic figures through the loss of the same thing: hope of a future reunion with the man or men they have lost. Both are mocked by an image of wish fulfillment without any corporeal substance. Maurya sees her son Michael restored and refurbished, but only as an image she cannot contact or release. Emer only wins her husband Cuchulain's return from the dead by bartering away "the hope that some day somewhere/ We'll sit together at the hearth again" (537). But Emer differs from Maurya in being a less passive figure, and this difference has implications for the kind of ghost drama Yeats is writing. Where Maurya is struck dumb by the supernatural manifestation and rendered powerless to intervene, Emer stands her ground in the grotesque face of the changeling Bricriu, resolute in her determination to press through to the other side, to make contact and negotiate with it. This was no less true of Yeats in his life long efforts to win wisdom from the dead, to appropriate a measure of the knowledge he believed lay beyond the grave. This aim binds together his early interest in Irish folklore, his occult research, and the later automatic writing of Mrs. Yeats. Posited in terms of the drama, it helps to explain Yeats's frustration with conventional realistic dramaturgy, his sense that it represented only one half of reality, and that the less essential.

The Only Jealousy of Emer deals almost diagrammatically with Yeats's desire to bring the natural and the supernatural within the same frame of the stage by dividing the space in half: "*The folding of the cloth shows on one side of the stage the curtained bed or litter on which lies a man in his grave-clothes. . . . Emer is sitting beside the bed*" (531). The bed on which Cuchulain lies is the only property on an otherwise empty stage. It is not placed in a dominant central position but pointedly confined to the "one side" while the other so far remains unoccupied, empty, open, charged with possibility.

The drama that is centered on the bed, with the younger mistress Eithne Inguba insisting that Cuchulain is dead while the older wife Emer replies repeatedly that despite all appearances he "is not dead" (535), has its textual antecedents in Synge's *Riders to the Sea*. But Yeats's expanding from the familial to the sexual, from the ideologically endorsed bond (in Irish nationalism) between mother and sons to the institution of marriage and explicitly adulterous liaisons, moves closer to the dramatic terrain of Ibsen. The exchange between Emer and Eithne Inguba that takes place around Cuchulain's bed brings to the surface a clearly psychological drama as the wife urges the mistress to confess her intimacies with Cuchulain. At the realistic level, on that "side" of the stage, we witness the triangular relationship of wife, husband, and "other" woman. But that side is only one half of the story in Yeatsian dramatic terms; it is what occupies the other zone, and the final synthesis he manages between the two, that take Yeats beyond Synge or Ibsen.

This dramatic development was made possible by Yeats's discovery via Ezra Pound of the materials of the Japanese Noh drama, and then, the form Yeats fashioned from them. Most of the scenarios hinged on an encounter between a travelling priest and the ghost or god haunting some local site; and what the Noh therefore offered was an elaborate and interlocking series of dramatic conventions explicitly designed to stage an interaction between the worlds of the living and the dead. Of the many ways in which it did so, space will only permit a focus on one of the most relevant, the use of the mask and its central role in *The Only Jealousy of Emer*.

Yeats's first direct experience of the mask as a theatrical device had come through Gordon Craig. Craig had designed a mask for the Fool in Yeats's *The Hour-Glass* (though the design was never executed)[9] and, in a note accompanying the design, listed the four qualities he intended it to convey: "hint of clown / a hint of Death / and of sphinx / and of boy."[10] Yeats took the hints from Craig but was unable to develop them until through the Noh he found a dramatic form into which the mask could be integrated.[11]

The first "hint" of clown is not only appropriate to the character but also increases the degree to which the Fool is both an individualized creation and a readily recognizable role with a lengthy popular tradition. Whatever the role, the mask will enhance this suggestion, suppressing the individual player by highlighting the archetypal nature of what is being represented. Yeats's writing in the Noh technique openly acknowledges the properties of drama as a medium: we are shown, not "people," but players wearing and changing masks; not an actual but an imagined setting called "to the eye of the mind" (399); not casual circumstances but a fundamental life-and-death struggle of the entire being. The "hint of Death" reminds us of death masks, the living person's features permanently embodied in clay but at the expense of animation. Yeats could admit the possibility that "being is only possessed completely by the dead" ("Certain Noble Plays" 226). The death mask captures the paradox embodied by Keats's urn, that the figures represented on it purchase immortality at the expense of breathing, just as *The Only Jealousy of Emer* makes it clear that Cuchulain will only acquire immortality at the cost of his humanity.

But the figures on the Grecian urn remain eternally youthful, like the Woman of the Sidhe; and Craig's fourth hint, of boyhood, suggests how the mask can represent an inhabitant of the Land of the Ever-Young (*Tír na nÓg*) by eliminating the process of aging. The Sphinx is another stone embodiment, a traditional symbol and sign of the wisdom which Yeats believed the dead to possess. The mask in his drama gives concrete expression to the meeting of the natural and the supernatural on which so many of his plays are centered. More precisely, since the mask is an imposition of one material upon another, it images the constraining of the natural by the forms of the permanent and increases Yeats's awareness that the relation between the two worlds is not an easy one. For the mask externalizes the idea of contending personalities within a single human frame and signifies that one of them is supernatural or dead. So, at a key moment in the play, the heroic mask of Cuchulain is switched in favor of its antithesis, the grotesque distorted mask of the "god" Bricriu. The mask indicates that the area on stage is located between the borders of the living and the dead, and that all the major figures inhabit more than one dimension.

Yeats had for many years brooded over the possibility of writing a stage version of *The Only Jealousy of Emer*[12] But what had effectively stalled him until his discovery of the Japanese Noh was the central problem posed by the episode out of Irish legend: how to dramatize the condition of Cuchulain "away"? What were the means by which Cuchulain's dual existence, lingering on a sickbed watched over by his wife while simultaneously encountering the Woman of the Sidhe in an otherworldly setting, could be represented on stage? Any approximately naturalistic staging would tip the balance in favor of the deathbed scenario and reduce the other ghostly dimension to a purely verbal, after-the-fact account by a reawakened Cuchulain of what he had experienced there. A more simultaneous trancelike communication would risk the kind of incoherence, through a failure to keep the two realms sufficiently distinct, that finally sabotaged Yeats's earlier play *The Shadowy Waters*. There is also something perilously undramatic in a scenario which threatens its audience with the prospect of a completely immobilized protagonist for most of its duration. Of all the various elements of the Noh, the mask most enabled Yeats to overcome this disabling fixity and to maintain a consistently dual dramatic perspective in *The Only Jealousy of Emer*.

The opening stage directions show not only a man in a heroic mask on his deathbed but also another "*man with exactly similar clothes and mask [who] crouches near the front*" (531). As this opening makes clear, the mask has freed the playwright from the strict realistic necessity of confining the multiple aspects of his hero's personality to a single incarnation. By duplicating Cuchulain's image, the superimposition of the mask makes possible a more exact doubling than even the traditional disguise of costume. There is no reason why this need be restricted to two. Yeats's rewriting of the play in prose eleven years later as *Fighting the Waves* adds another Cuchulain to the sum, and the number is potentially as endless as the supply of masks and the number of phases into which the single personality can be divided. The two Cuchulains are differentiated in the cast list as "The Ghost of Cuchulain" and "The Figure of Cuchulain," broadly speaking the departing spirit and the physical shell or husk it has vacated. The doubling clarifies one essential point: neither of these images represents the whole man but rather different aspects of the self. The doubling also makes it possible to view the entirety of what is happening on the stage as a psychic drama emanating from the prone Cuchulain.

With the arrival of Bricriu, signified by the changing of masks, the possibilities for a dramatic interchange between the two zones are enlarged. This exchange is posited in the familiar Yeatsian terms of a bargain: Emer is asked to renounce the hope of ever being loved by Cuchulain again in order to secure his return from the dead. And she demands, quite understandably, that she be given a greater degree of insight into the place and situation that currently claim her man before she can decide. To so demonstrate, Bricriu gives Emer (and by extension the audience) access to the inner drama unfolding in the otherworld between the Ghost of Cuchulain and the Woman of the Sidhe: "Come closer to the bed / That I may touch your eyes and give them sight" (547). What Emer now sees for the first time is what we have seen all along, the continuing presence on stage of the Ghost of Cuchulain as evidence that the play admits of spiritual life after apparent physical death, and as confirmation of Emer's negative to the repeated question: "And is he dead?" But until her eyes are opened to his presence, the Ghost of Cuchulain has been prone, crouching, awaiting release.

Emer is now called upon to perform the role of witness-audience-spectator by Bricriu in his role as playwright/director/stage manager. His urging her to come "closer to the bed" stresses the sexual intimacy of this particular play and the more general wish Yeats had to abolish distance and establish intimacy as the foundation of his new drama (*Certain Noble Plays* 224). Emer has been mounting a watch and, as a result of her concentrated scrutiny, is granted a vision, specifically the ability to view other areas of the stage which have so far been screened from her sight: "My husband is there."

But the mirror is only one-way so far as Emer is concerned, since it soon becomes clear that Cuchulain can neither see her image in return nor hear her entreaties. The most the Ghost of Cuchulain has been able to discern is the fact that there is an audience urging his presence: "The longing and the cries have drawn him hither" (549), as Bricriu reveals, and kept him literally in suspense until Emer is explicitly informed of and set up in her role as active spectator. Her darkness is lightened by Bricriu's touch and her gaze is directed toward the so-far vacant other side of the stage, which now reveals a figure ready to be reanimated.

When the Woman of the Sidhe enters and is identified, Emer reacts by drawing a knife and attempting to strike at the image of the "other woman." Apart from making the point that such an action is futile under the supernatural circumstances, Bricriu also makes the larger point that violent actions have no place or efficacy in this kind of drama. Emer's effort to express her jealousy by drawing a knife is forestalled by the admonition that her passion can achieve greater and more effective expression by being channeled into the role of a privileged spectator:

> *Figure of Cuchulain*:   No knife
> Can wound that body of air. Be silent; listen;
> I have not given you eyes and ears for nothing.
>   (551)

What has already become clear is that the absolute separation between the two areas or sides of the stage, the distinction between the "real" world of Emer's bedside vigil and the avowedly theatrical realm of Cuchulain's ghostly sojourn, is more apparent than real. For one thing, the crouching Ghost is identified by Emer with and as her "husband" whereas the physical creature by her side with the withered arm is a ghostly impostor. And what is about to ensue between Cuchulain and the Woman of the Sidhe now takes precedence over any other onstage situation and will have permanent consequences back in the waking world. The effect increasingly is to break down any clear-cut distinction between the two worlds and to produce the dramatically uncanny effect that

Yeats recorded with pleasure from his first staging of *At the Hawk's Well*: "Nobody seemed to know who was masked and who was not on Tuesday. Those who were not masked were made up to look as if they were. It was all very strange" (Letters 610-611). Initially, to judge from the dramatis personae, it would appear that masks are worn by those who are of exclusively supernatural provenance, the Woman of the Sidhe or Bricriu, or those of semihuman, semidivine origin, like Cuchulain; whereas the women, Emer and Eithne Inguba, are made up to appear as if they were wearing masks, the physical stress and coloration falling on their human character. But as Yeats notes, this distinction breaks down in practice. Similarly, Bricriu's injunction is as much to each member of the audience as it is to Emer, urging them to be silent, listen, and so help to create the drama about to be witnessed which, if successful, will finally bring together the two sides of the stage and the third side, the audience, into a comprehensive unity of atmosphere.

What follows is an inner drama in the sense of a psychological exploration of the self and of a play within the play, something implicit since the opening with its double-masked incarnations of the hero. The two Cuchulains have also resembled each other in their paralysis. The freeing of the physical, Cuchulain's return to life, is going to depend upon the prior feeling of the soul and a necessary working out of his situation in a consciously dramatic form.

The form chosen by Yeats for this psychic drama is what he called in *A Vision* the "dreaming back" to describe one of four stages he believed the soul passes through in its progress toward reincarnation. "Dreaming back" is his variation on the familiar conceit of the events of a drowning man's life passing rapidly before his eyes. Here, the review of Cuchulain's life follows immediately after rather than preceding the drowning. Instead of reliving the events of his life in their original chronological order, the dead man reverses the sequence and takes his end as his beginning, dreaming "the events of his life backward through time."[13] Cuchulain is dreaming throughout *The Only Jealousy of Emer* in his truncated sleep of death, but it is a waking dream, one that has "place and weight and measure" (Yeats "Swedenborg" 63). This dramatized dream or phantasmagoria brings before him a succession of figures — his wife, his mistress, his otherworldly muse/daimon — and articulates their various relationships with him. It has been argued that Cuchulain appears to have little to do with, or indeed in, the play.[14] But everything we see on stage proceeds from him and returns to him as the center of the drama, literally and symbolically.

The following exchange with the Woman of the Sidhe confirms that the Ghost of Cuchulain is undergoing the "dreaming back":

> *Woman of the Sidhe*: . . .
> What pulled your hands about your feet,
> Pulled down your head upon your knees,
> And hid your face?

Ghost of Cuchulain: Old memories:
A woman in her happy youth
Before her man had broken troth,
Dead men and women. Memories
Have pulled my head upon my knees.
(551-553)

Of the troop of figures in his life that pass before Cuchulain's inner eye
Emer is foremost, especially in the moments of greatest shared intensity: "O
Emer, Emer, there we stand; / Side by side and hand in hand / Tread the
threshold of the house / As when our parents married us" (556-557). This is a
complex dramatic moment. Cuchulain is addressing a figure that we see
standing before him on stage. But he cannot see her and his remarks are
directed, not to Emer as she is in the play's present, but to an image of her as
they were in the past, at the moment of their greatest happiness. And this past
union serves only to heighten by contrast their estrangement and isolation in the
present, since "as each but dreams again without change what happened when
they were alive, each dreamer is alone" (*A Vision* 226- 227).

The "dreaming back" is no simple reverse screening of the dominant
experiences of a lifetime. For, as the above exchange makes clear, the
protagonist of the dream scenario can no longer retain or plead the innocence
that may have accompanied such events; rather, he is forced to relive them with
full knowledge of their consequences: "The man must dream the event to its
consequence as far as his intensity permit; not that consequence only which
occurred while he lived, and was known to him, but those that were unknown,
or have occurred after his death" (A Vision 227). The events are a working
through in both a psychological and dramatic sense, a full exploration of the
consequences of an event. Thus it is that Cuchulain in his "dreaming back"
concentrates on Emer, the woman he married but repeatedly passed over in his
drive for new amorous conquests. The consequences of his actions for Emer
are what Cuchulain now takes on in his own person, directly experiencing the
painful emotions caused by his heedlessness. This is the closest Yeats comes to
a concept of hell. It is closer indeed to the state termed purgatory (compare
his play of the same name), which also promises an end to suffering when the
dead person has worked out his or her guilt in an act of expiation. For Yeats,
"there is no punishment [in the afterlife] but the prolongation of the *Dreaming
back*" (*A Vision* 228). In place of a predetermined and irrevocable Christian
guilt and virtue, a hell or heaven, in imagining what happens after death, he opts
for a process much closer to the Freudian working-through, a more conscious
and consciously dramatic re-enactment of all the events, impulses, thoughts,
and emotions of a single life.

The Ghost of Cuchulain cries for a way out of the self-created labyrinth of
that life at the moment of greatest suffering. He is offered oblivion by the
Woman of the Sidhe, whose kiss promises to remove him from the burden of his

past to the freedom and ease of the otherworld. She in her turn, who lacks completion by only an "hour or so" (553), can find it only through direct physical contact with Cuchulain. For "the dead," Yeats writes, "cannot originate except through the living," for all of their perfection, just as the Sidhe must replenish themselves by drawing "away" children and newlyweds. In the play, it becomes apparent that Cuchulain has not attained the expiation of his human life with Emer that the otherworldly seductress has urged him to do. Where union with Cuchulain will bring the Woman of the Sidhe to Unity of Being, Phase fifteen at which no human life is possible, there is a disturbing disjunction in his own case, a sense of emotional division. His cries alternate between "Your mouth," as they are about to kiss, and "O Emer, Emer," as he turns away (555-557). And if we bear in mind the staging, what is taking place between the Ghost of Cuchulain and the Woman of the Sidhe cannot be viewed as the whole emotional or dramatic truth. For Yeats has placed this ghostly drama in the framing context of Emer as impassioned witness, and in so doing has matched Cuchulain's continuing memory of her with Emer's embodiment of their lives in a complementary dream which the very shape of the play mirrors. The grit of memory which continues to trouble Cuchulain's vision is referred to disparagingly by the Woman of the Sidhe as the "Wind-blown dirt of their memories" (557), but is polished by the friction of the play into the pearl of great price which neither can relinguish. The cost to Cuchulain is the promise of immortality. For Emer, it is to continue as knowing, conscious witness to a drama from which she is excluded as her act of renunciation delivers her husband from a deathlike trance into the arms of his living mistress. The final and abiding image is of Emer's isolation on stage, the marginalized other woman, as Cuchulain passes directly from one mistress to another.

In *The Only Jealousy of Emer* Yeats undertook his fullest dramatic exploration of the interaction between the living and the dead. But the subject continued to preoccupy his drama through such late works as *The Words Upon the Window- Pane* (1934), where a seance in contemporary Dublin is invaded by the ghostly triangle of Dean Swift, Stella, and Vanessa; and *Purgatory* (1939), where the Old Man sees the ghosts of his parents and tries to abort the "dead night" (1049) of his conception. As the members of his Anglo-Irish Ascendency class followed a loss of political power with a decline in living numbers, Yeats drew increasingly on the spirits of the departed, both for company and as the chosen ones of his pantheon; the threat of the extinction of his caste was at least one motive behind a late play like *Purgatory*.

Synge's own morbidity, aggravated by this inherited condition, was to seek an objective correlative in the fates of the Aran islanders. The contemporary equivalent of such social and cultural pressures on an individual playwright is the situation in the North of Ireland. There, the threat of imminent extinction afflicts both sides not only on an individual basis but also in a larger context of implicit genocide; so it is Northern drama which has witnessed a return to the subject of ghosts, and with no less an emphasis on their direct onstage manifestation.

I had already decided upon Stewart Parker's *Pentecost*, presented by Derry's Field Day Company in 1987,[15] as my chosen contemporary text when news arrived on 8 November 1988, of Parker's untimely death at the age of forty-seven; and so I have ended up in this chapter not with two dead and one living dramatist but with a trio of ghosts. The reading which follows is haunted, then, by that unexpected ghost of its author and an even greater insistence on pressuring the text(ure) of a script from which he is absent to summon up his whimsical, humane presence.

Stewart Parker and the Haunting by the Dead

The dead figure in Stewart Parker's *Pentecost* who returns to haunt the living is not the victim of sectarian assassination, as one might reasonably imagine from the play's setting of Belfast in 1974. Rather, Lily Matthews, respectable widow of Alfred George Matthews, has died of natural causes at the re spectable age of seventy-four, making her as old as the century and in many ways a representative of the history of the Northern Protestant community over that period. It is the lives of the living characters in the play which are under threat at one of the numerous crisis points in the ongoing turbulence of Northern Ireland's last twenty years. Or as Lenny the trombone player ruefully remarks: "Sure, every bloody day in the week's historic, in this place" (Parker 171).

But even so a particularly historic turning point was the Ulster Workers' Strike of 1974 – the period during which *Pentecost* takes place – given its determination to force the hand of the British government in bringing down the recently established power-sharing Executive, Northern Ireland's first (and so far only) concerted effort at something resembling democratic government. With the army and police standing idly by and the streets full of gun-toting civilians, nobody out there is safe, as we discover when Lenny's estranged wife Marian returns from searching out her car: she is revealed *"in the light of the torch, mud-spattered with her coat ripped, and scratch marks on her face"* (189). Given the life-threatening reality of what is just on the other side of a/the door, the onstage space functions as it does in so many Northern Irish plays as a kind of stay or refuge, an asylum or temporary holding ground, one step removed from the (war) zone of historical circumstance. Marian identifies the house in which she has chosen to live and which provides the play's setting in just these terms – as a refuge – when she complains to Lenny: "You've been living with me again, here in this house, the very place I chose as a refuge" (192). But the larger point Marian misses is that her estranged husband, and the two friends of theirs who follow in his wake to make up the ill-assorted quartet of the cast, are all equally in need of a refuge, a site for healing in which their psychological, more than their actual, wounds can be tended.

Lenny's relationship with Marian – cannot live together, cannot live apart – has certain features in common with Northern Ireland itself; but both

Catholic husband and Protestant wife are reluctant to declare their "marriage" a failed entity. Ruth, a friend of Marian's from ten years earlier, is on the run from her truncheon-wielding policeman husband not for any crime she has committed beyond that of marriage. And the fourth stray who finds his way to the house Marian has chosen for splendid isolation is not (as we might expect and as someone prophesies) Ruth's pursuing husband but a new, belated character, Peter. An ex- college friend of Lenny's, he has returned to Belfast from years in Birmingham and so brings the perspective of the outside world to bear on the local situation.

But *Pentecost* is more crowded than the cast of four would suggest. For the house into which Marian moves at the beginning of the play, *"a respectable working-class 'parlour' house, built in the early years of this century"* (141), is a haunted site and not as empty as it strikes the pragmatic Lenny. He has come to inherit it by way of a great-aunt, and when Marian declares a wish to take it over in return for finally granting him a divorce, he protests: "Marian, you can't possibly live in this gaff, it's the last house on the road left inhabited! – the very road itself is scheduled to vanish off the map" (154). Here, Marian's concern is to preserve the house as an example of the lived culture of a Belfast working-class Protestant community from the early years of the century. But this fossilization of the past, or Ulsterization, is finally resisted by Marian in a change of heart by which she decides that what the house needs is air and light, in order to be lived in.

The agent of this change of heart is the ghost of Lily Matthews, the house's last tenant, who refuses to be evicted even by death. Marian conjures up the ghost of Lily at least partly out of her own loneliness and need; her motives for so doing, like those for moving into the house in the first place, remain initially unclear, even to herself. When she and Lenny first enter the house, it is within hours of Lily vacating it, and the space is still very much suffused with the presence of the dead person. Entering the area where a woman has just died, they are both paradoxically made aware of her presence, evidenced by a half-finished cup of tea, and Marian begins the process of identification which is central to the play by trying to imagine the moment of Lily's death. Since they never knew her and so do not remember her, Marian is consciously working to reconstruct a past, a memory where none had previously existed. Marian cannot do it all by herself; the process is going to require the active presence and participation of the ghost of Lily Matthews.

The process by which the dead person is evoked in Irish drama usually depends on a theatrical, symbolic, and personal prop, like the half-drunk cup of tea, a physical synecdoche by which a more complete reality is summoned onto the stage. In the second scene, in ways reminiscent of the discovery scene in Synge's *Riders to the Sea*, Marian lifts a piece of unfinished knitting out of a basket. In both plays the knitting signifies a severed lifeline and the distinctive fabric of one person's existence which the play is going to draw out. But in Marian's suggestion that "I might just finish it off for you" (155), there is also the larger point of the overall pattern which is beginning to emerge, the dramatic weave of the ensemble. Here, the two reactions which Synge kept dramatically separate, the skeptical and visionary, are fused in Marian's response. Her superficially ironic yet emotionally engaged dialogue with the absent figure now calls Lily forth, bringing her on stage dressed as she exited two months earlier:[16]

> (*Lily Matthews, in Sunday coat and hat and best handbag, appears in the shadowy doorway leading from the pantry*).
> LILY: I don't want you in my house.
> (*Marian keeps her eyes on the knitting pattern: on guard but not entirely frightened, aware that her mind is playing tricks on her*).
> MARIAN: You needn't try to scare me, Lily.
> LILY: Don't you "Lily" me. I don't want you in here, breathing strong drink and profanity. (155)

As in Hugh Leonard's *Da* (1973), where Charlie returns from his father's funeral to find the old man sitting in an armchair, the person is dead but refuses to lie down (or to stop talking). Parker's *Pentecost* is in a strong Irish dramatic tradition which realizes that, far from keeping to narrowly realistic boundaries, theater is a means of bringing the dead back to life. And in the objective and ineluctable materialization which is theater, those ghosts cannot be read entirely in psychological or Ibsenite terms once the playwright has decided to show them on stage. Clearly, as even Marian herself is aware, her own isolation, the strong drink, and her confession that she does not much like herself are all psychologically sufficient to project an imagined alter ego as a way of dramatizing her own divided self. Brian Friel did no less with his youthful protagonist Gar O'Donnell in *Philadelphia, Here I Come!*, requiring two actors to represent:

> *two views of the one man. Public Gar is the Gar that people see, talk to, talk about. Private Gar is the unseen man, the man within, the conscience, the alter ego, the secret thoughts, the id. Private Gar, the spirit, is always invisible to everybody. Nobody except Public Gar hears him talk.* (Friel 11-12)

The same is true of Lily Matthews in relation to the other characters in *Pentecost*; to them she is invisible, nonexistent, a sign merely of Marian's cracking up: "You've been talking to yourself, you've been counting spoons, you've been babbling in tongues in the middle of the night!" (192). But in theatrical terms once you have assigned an actor to embody an alter ego, a doppelganger, or a dead person, there is nothing to choose between the real and the ghostly. Yeats makes this clear from the opening of *The Only Jealousy of Emer*, with its precise, masked doubling of the Figure of Cuchulain and the Ghost of Cuchulain. Nor is the "real" figure given precedence or consistently placed in the foreground; both Yeats and Friel preserve a fine equilibrium between their split persona(e) in a dramatic double act as balanced as that of

Vladimir and Estragon in Beckett's *Waiting for Godot*. This doubling not only erodes any distance between the real and the uncanny but redefines the nature of the surrounding drama. For the inhabitants of Ballybeg in Friel's *Philadelphia, Here I Come!*, there is only one Public Gar to see and commune with; but for the audience there are the two Gars who become more real to us than the two-dimensional characters of the fictional rather than the theatrical space.

The same holds true for Lily Matthews's manifestation in Parker's *Pentecost*. Her ghost not only challenges Marian's reality and her grip on it, but also that of the reality the play is representing. The irony is that Lily appears to urge strict segregation into Catholic and Protestant and (we might add) living and dead, while her presence on stage succeeds in crossing all kinds of boundaries and established lines of demarcation. When the ghost invokes her dead husband's absence by saying: "You'd be singing on the other side of your face if my Alfie was here" (156), Marian, closing her eyes, insists: "There's nobody here. Nobody." The audience at this point must register a double take by applying Marian's words reflexively to herself no less than to the ghost of Lily, since who, in theater, on the stage, is *really* there? Parker has fun with this phenomenon of theater all the way through the play. He has Lily insist on her greater materiality by way of having more of a right to be in the house, reversing the situation by treating Marian as the interloping ghost who needs to be exorcised; her appearance is usually accompanied by a bout of hymn singing to keep the Antichrist at bay. But Marian plays along with the inverted terms of the identification by stressing the interdependence between living and dead:

> I need you, we have got to make this work, you and me. . . . You think you're haunting me, don't you. But you see it's me that's actually haunting you. I'm not going to go away. There's no curse or hymn that can exorcise me. So you might just as well give me your blessing and make your peace with me. (179-80)

What Lily's active questioning presence does with the drama, in ways similar to both the Yeats and Friel plays, is to double it. The urgency with which Marian examines this *revenant* on the details of her life history, of the intimate hidden life which lies behind the imperturbable respectability of Lily's facade, is the psychic secret which this updated Gothic drama seeks to discover in its haunted house. As she does so, Marian becomes increasingly drawn into the process, in effect taking over and subsuming the role of Lily as she comes to understand and identify with it.

As is usually the case in a ghostly scenario, which Yeats would liken to a phantasmagoria or psychic procession, the appearance of one ghost soon draws others in its train. For example there is Lily's dead husband, Alfie, a ghost in a double sense. He may have died and left her widowed only fifteen years earlier, in 1959, but it turns out that Lily was wed as an eighteen-year-old virgin to this man who, having endured the trenches of World War I and been one of only two on his street to survive, was already a living corpse: "Alfie had come back, that's why. Back from Passchendaele. Hellfire Corner. Back from the dead.... All in the one week, married and moved in, he couldn't wait ... not after what he'd seen ... this house was his life, same as mine" (156).

Marian confronts Lily, however, with incriminating objects, strands of evidence that weave a very different story from the one her house embodies: a rent book signifies the ghost of a third party, Alan Ferris, an English airman; and in a photograph of the three, husband, wife, and lodger, the outlines of a triangular relationship may be discerned. In regard to her and Alfie's childlessness and the sterility the house ultimately represents, Lily is confronted by Marian with a 1930s child's christening gown, which gives the lie to their married relationship. Lily's husband had also been sexually maimed, and her one brief experience of passion had been with the airman. In her most crucial exchange with Marian, Lily evokes a visionary landscape of water and air redolent of her sexual need: "All we did was stand and look, across the water" (194). This scene, which develops in ways reminiscent of Beckett's *Rockaby*, has Marian sit in the rocking chair and begin speaking Lily's thoughts for her, based on reading her diary: "That was the moment when it hit you, though ... the moment you realised that you were going to give yourself." The fruit of Lily's relation ship with her airman was the baby she could not bring herself to acknowledge and so abandoned, the sign of her betrayal as she saw it.

There is more than one buried child being exhumed in this interchange. Lenny has let fall to Peter that he and Marian had a baby, which comes as a revelation in the play's second half, a child which is never acknowledged whenever they are together on stage discussing their marriage. The irony is that they only married because Marian was pregnant and then, in having the baby, she and Lenny learned to love each other. Ruth, too, has had more than one miscarriage, not least because her policeman husband repeatedly beats her, and she has been told she can have no more pregnancies. At the close of the first half, the three women are linked across the generations, across the sectarian divide, and across life and death as the revelation of the dead Lily's dead child leads the two living women to acknowledge their own. When Lily completes her suppressed story of the affair with Alan that lay behind the fact of her child, Marian responds with an eloquent gesture, reaching out the hand of the living to that of the dead and holding it against her heart as an act of restoration:

> (*Marian takes Lily's hand and holds it against her own heart*).
> MARIAN: Forgive me, Lily.
> (*Lights fade to blackout*). (197)

For Lily's husband Alfie was impotent, neither "the first nor the last to come back from the dead in that condition" (196), and the house was the sole witness to Lily's labor, birth, and what she suffered in giving up her child. This denial of life and her sense of abandonment are the emotional truths which Lily's

Unionist cry of "no surrender" tries to deny and silence.

Lily does not appear again after this. When Marian speaks in the play's closing scene, there is no longer any need to present them as two separate or distinct selves on the stage. This final scene has generally been criticized, in the context of the overall praise *Pentecost* has attracted, as Parker's imposing an overtly religious and didactic conclusion on his play through wholesale quotation from the Bible. There is dramatic overkill with four epiphanies *and* four pentecostal speeches; the biblical speaking in tongues is not sufficiently refashioned in terms of the individual speech of each of the characters. Finally, only Marian's speeches are dramatically convincing. The other three, in offering their solution to how a vision of Christ can be wedded to the reality of street life in contemporary Belfast, speak too exclusively for themselves and in overly rhetorical terms. Marian is the only one who follows the Pentecostal injunction to "speak with other tongues, as the Spirit gave them utterance" (204). She does so, first, by speaking for and as Lily Matthews in the culmination of a dramatic process we have witnessed throughout the play. She does so by imagining a scene during a Second World War bombing raid on the Belfast house, with Lily alone on the parlor sofa on which she and Alan had made love. In a direct evocation of Ibsen's *Ghosts*, Peter and Ruth had earlier entered that same parlor and made love there, the past repeating itself in the present, and the hidden sexual history of these interconnected lives being brought to the surface. But with Marian's subsequent storytelling the past is not allowed to dominate and determine the present as in Ibsen. Rather, it is reshaped in the light of present possibilities. Marian as actress/playwright takes on and speaks out of her own understanding of Lily Matthew's twilight existence, imagining a unique moment of sexual and spiritual ecstasy in which Lily wishes to die as the bombs rain down from her demon lover. Instead, Lily is suffered to survive, "condemned to life. A life sentence" (202). Marian realizes that her own making present of that life, her articulation of what lay hidden in Lily's journal, has released the petrified ghost from the bonds of hypocrisy.

Marian goes on to speak for and in the tongue of yet another denied ghost, her dead son Christopher. In so doing Marian speaks up effectively for the Christ in each of them that is the tenor of the play's closing: "I denied . . . the ghost of him that I do still carry, as I carried his little body" (207). There is a ghost trio at this point, since Marian's talk of Christopher is also Lily speaking for the love-child whose exist ence she has denied. As *Pentecost* ends Lenny touches Marian's hand, as she had earlier touched Lily's, in a reciprocal gesture of support and restoration.

Ghosts are a strong and recurrent feature of Irish drama. It is less a case of Ireland being in thrall to its past (though that specter is raised and confronted in all of the plays discussed) as one in which the past is always living as a potential to be resurrected in the endless present of theater. The lives of those who have died are keenly felt and registered in Irish drama's insistence on treating ghosts as nothing more (or less) than full corporeal presences and the stage itself, as a necessary meeting ground to mediate between the claims of the living and the dead.

Notes

1. I am grateful to Professor Katharine Worth for providing me with a copy of her to-be-published essay, "Ibsen and the Irish Theatre." A further stimulus was Thomas Kilroy's 1989 version of Ibsen's *Ghosts*, which updates the play, transposes it to Ireland, and replaces syphilis with AIDS.

2. See "Yeats's 1904 review of Ibsen's *Brand*, "The Stone and the Elixir," in *Uncollected Prose of W. B. Yeats*, 346, where Yeats regrets that "the later and less imaginative though profoundly interesting plays [of Ibsen] have been acted and expounded to the neglect of the works of his prime, and until two or three years ago neither *Brand* nor *Peer Gynt* had been translated." See also Diderik Roll-Hansen, 155-160. Synge's reading of Ibsen's plays (in German) is recorded in his diary of 1893 (Trinity College, Dublin Synge Manuscripts, 4415). Frank McGuinness's version of *Peer Gynt* was directed by Patrick Mason at Dublin's Gate Theatre in October 1988 and published by Faber and Faber in 1990.

3. See Anthony Roche, "The Fortunate Fall: Two Plays by Thomas Kilroy," 159-168.

4. See Howard D. Pearce.

5. See Mary C. King: "The religious, political and aesthetic themes in *The Aran Islands* are carefully contextualised in time and place." Further, Synge highlights "the transformation into art of the day-to-day lives, activities and preoccupations of a community" (20).

6. See Anthony Roche, "Christianity Versus Paganism in J. M. Synge."

7. "For a long time I have felt that Poetry roughly is of two kinds, the poetry of real life . . . and the poetry of a land of fancy. . . . In all the poets the greatest have both these elements" (Synge 2:347).

8. See Nicholas Grene.

9. See Katharine Worth, 52; and see also "The Syntax Achieved," for what Yeats learned from Craig, 48-71.

10. See Liam Miller, 163. Miller's book reproduces the projected Craig designs for *The Hour-Glass*, 163ff.

11. Cf. Yeats's letter to Lady Gregory of 26 March 1916: "I believe I have at last found a dramatic form that suits me" (Letters 610).

12. See Lady Gregory for Yeats's source, her English rendering of the Irish original as "The Only Jealousy of Emer," 210-224.

13. See *A Critical Edition of Yeats's 'A Vision'* (1925), 225. The 1925 edition is chosen over the 1937 edition because it is closer in time and intertextual dependency to *The Only Jealousy of Emer*. The editors note that "this play, finished on 14 January 1918, receives far more attention than any other of Yeats's creative works in the AS (Automatic Script)" (xxxi). Future references are to this edition and will be noted in the text as *AV*, while references to the *Variorum Plays* will be by page number alone.

14. See, for example, Richard Taylor. Taylor holds that the play's "action" only

indirectly focuses upon Cuchulain, that he is "a mere occasion for the action that takes place around [him]," 140.

15. Stewart Parker's *Pentecost*, directed by Patrick Mason, was premiered in Derry's Guild Hall in September 1987. My thanks to the late Stewart Parker for providing me with a script. The play has been published (1989) as part of a trilogy, with *Northern Star* and *Heavenly Bodies*.

16. As a ghost Lily initially assumes the form in which she died. In subsequent appearances, which reflect different stages of her life, her dress and appearance are altered accordingly.

Works Cited

Beckett, Samuel. *The Complete Dramatic Works*. London: Faber and Faber, 1986.

Friel, Brian. *Philadelphia, Here I Come!* London: Faber and Faber, 1965.

Gregory, Lady [Augusta]. *Cuchulain of Muirhemne*. Gerrards Cross, Bucks.: Colin Smythe, 1970.

Grene, Nicholas. *Synge: A Critical Study of the Plays*. London: Macmillan, 1975.

Ibsen, Henrik. *Ghosts and Other Plays*. Trans. Peter Watts. London: Penguin Books, 1964.

—. *Peer Gynt*. A new version by Frank McGuinness, from a literal translation by Anne Bamborough. London: Faber and Faber, 1990.

Joyce, James. "The Dead." In *The Portable James Joyce*, ed. Harry Levin. Harmondsworth: Penguin Books, 1966.

King, Mary C. *The Drama of J. M. Synge*. Syracuse: Syracuse University Press, 1985.

Leonard, Hugh. *Da/A Life/Time Was*. Harmondsworth: Penguin Books, 1981

Miller, Liam. *The Noble Drama of W. B. Yeats*. Dublin: The Dolmen Press, 1977.

Parker, Stewart. *Three Plays for Ireland: Northern Star, Heavenly Bodies, Pentecost*. Birmingham: Oberon Books, 1989.

Pearce, Howard D. "Synge's Playboy as Mock-Christ," *Modern Drama* 8, no.3 (1965): 303-310; reprinted in *The Playboy of the Western World: A Collection of Critical Essays*, ed. Thomas R. Whitaker, 88-97. Englewood Cliffs: Prentice-Hall, 1969.

Roche, Anthony. "Christianity Versus Paganism in J. M. Synge." In *A J. M. Synge Literary Companion*, ed. Edward A. Kopper, Jr., 107-134. Westport, CT: Greenwood Press, 1988.

—. "The Fortunate Fall: Two Plays by Thomas Kilroy." In *The Writer and the City*, ed. Maurice Harmon, 159-168. Gerrard's Cross, Bucks.: Colin Smythe, 1984.

Roll-Hansen, Diderik. "The Playboy of the Western World: An Irish Peer Gynt." In *Studies in Anglo-Irish Literature* ed. Heinz Kosok. Bonn: Bouvier, 1982.

Synge, J. M. *Collected Works, Vol. 2; Prose*. Ed. Alan Price. London: Oxford University Press, 1966.

—. *Collected Works, Vols. 3 and 4; Plays*. Ed. Ann Saddlemyer. London: Oxford University Press, 1968.

—. "Preface to *The Playboy of the Western World*." In *Collected Works. Vol. 4; Plays*. Ed. Ann Saddlemyer. London: Oxford University Press, 1968.

Taylor, Richard. *The Drama of W. B. Yeats: Irish Myth and the Japanese No*. New Haven: Yale University Press, 1976.

Worth, Katharine. *The Irish Drama of Europe from Yeats to Beckett*. London: The Athlone Press, 1978.

Yeats, W. B. "Certain Noble Plays of Japan." In *Essays and Introductions*. London: Macmillan, 1961.

—. *A Critical Edition of Yeats's 'A Vision'*. 1925. Eds. George Mills Harper and Walter Kelly Hood. London: Macmillan, 1978.

—. "Dramatis Personae." In *Autobiographies*. London: Macmillan, 1955.

—. *The Letters of W. B. Yeats*. Ed. Allan Wade. London: Rupert Hart-Davis, 1954.

—. "The Stone and the Elixir." In *Uncollected Prose of W. B. Yeats*. Vol. 1. Ed. John P. Frayne. London: Macmillan, 1970.

—. "Swedenborg, Mediums, Desolate Places." In *Explorations*, ed. Mrs. W. B. Yeats. New York: Macmillan, 1962.

—. "The Tragic Generation." In *Autobiographies*. London: Macmillan, 1955.

—. *The Variorum Edition of the Plays of W. B. Yeats*. Eds. Russell K. Alspach and Catherine C. Alspach. London: Macmillan, 1969.

Bettina Knapp

"The Only Jealousy of Emer": Recycling the Elements

The alchemist's belief in monism, or cosmic unity, appealed strongly to W. B. Yeats, the man haunted throughout his life by conflict and duality. Yeats sought to heal the breach corroding his existence by transcending the workaday world or the state of human consciousness, which he believed was composed of "a series of antinomies" (Berryman 117). The *prima materia* is devoid of conflict. Only in the phenomenological world does it take on many forms, combining and recombining in a state of perpetual becoming. Nothing ends; nothing is destroyed; all is transformed in an eternal death-birth mystery. The goals of the Yeatsian hero and of the alchemist are similar. Each seeks to transcend the human condition – the differentiated, phenomenological world – by shattering the existing outlook or arrangement of chemicals. Each then examines and evaluates entities from which new blendings emerge, bringing fresh behavior patterns or alloys into existence and, with them, a *renovatio*.

In *The Only Jealousy of Emer* the characters are put through two alchemical operations. They begin as *prima materia*, in the preformal state of oneness, and move to *separatio* and *coagulatio*. The "subtle separation" which takes place within their beings is experienced via the water and fire rituals. During these transformative procedures, matter (personalities or events) is liquefied or made malleable through the alchemist's heating process. Old attitudes are thus separated, objectified, and explicated, finally to surface in a new manner. With their expanded understanding, new insights and potentials develop in the characters and then, in alchemical par lance, fixate.

The Goidelic mythical hero Cuchulain was eternalized in *The Tain* (*Táin Bó Cuailnge*), the Irish epic dating from the seventh or eighth century AD. After numerous battles and as many loves, Cuchulain loses a powerful struggle with the waves. His wife, Emer, brings his lifeless body to a fisherman's cabin. Yeats's play opens as Emer is caring for her husband. She calls for Eithne Inguba, Cuchulain's mistress, who is standing at the door of the cabin, and asks her for help. Although Yeats's hero is sophisticated – a highly personal and poetic individual – he bears many of the ancient Goidelic hero's characteristics.

The mythical figure, Yeats's Cuchulain is a man of instinct and prone to blind rages. He feels his way into events and situations. He acts and does not think. Unlike the original Cuchulain, however, Yeats's protagonist does not possess an anthropoid psyche. He is a sensitive and suffering hero whose ways and words are marked with finesse. He is a man who, while needing to be loved for his personal well-being, also uses his passion for creative purposes: to transform feeling into poetry.

According to Goidelic heliolatry, the original Cuchulain's name was Sétanta. His birth was quasi miraculous. He was said to have been born three times. His mother Dechtirde, an Irish princess, swallowed the god Lugh in the form of a winged insect (Graves 75). (This fly remains in its nymphal state for two years, only emerging in its adult state for one day in order to mate and die.) Cuchulain seems to mirror the primitive and adolescent condition of the winged creature. It has also been said that Cuchulain could swim like a trout and was endowed with the strength of a bull as soon as he was born. Cuchulain's foster parents, Sencha, Fergus, and Cathbad, taught him wisdom, warfare, and magic. His exploits were many and included the killing of the smith Culann's watchdog, a heroic feat, after which he was called the "Hound of Culann." He was then given the honor of guarding the kingdom of Ulster.

Hero figures throughout history have been marked with certain unusual physical traits and Cuchulain is no exception. In *The Tain*, he is described as having seven pupils in each eye, seven toes, and seven fingers—comparable, perhaps, to the seven alchemical operations. His cheeks were colored yellow, blue, green, and red; each of these colors has an emotional and alchemical value. Three colors were visible in his hair: a dark color close to the roots, red in the middle, and a lighter red at the tip of each strand. In battle a "spot of blood or spark of fire" was visible on each hair. From his mouth "spurted fire," and from the top of his head "a jet of black blood" (*Celtic Mythology* 232).

The sensitive, suffering, and disenchanted Cuchulain of *The Only Jealousy of Emer*, patterned after Yeats's own personality, experiences his battle in "The labyrinth of the mind," in those lunar spheres where spirit and matter blend, where the ancient druid and creative artist communicate, and not in the environs of Ulster (Yeats 185). Alchemically, the original Cuchulain may be associated with the element air, since his mother was inseminated by a winged insect. Because this fly appears in Ireland during the month of March, one may assume that a relationship exists between Cuchulain's birth date and the planet Mars and its corresponding metal, iron. Cuchulain's struggle with the waves (an alchemical recycling of the elements), compels him to experience a *regressus ad uterum*, thus paving the way for the *separatio and coagulatio* processes.

Cuchulain's association with air indicates that he possessed sublimating characteristics which usually accompany "air born" or winged creatures. Basilius Valentinus expressed the alchemist's understanding of air:

It is the Principle to work Metals . . . being made a spiritual Essence, which is a meer Air, and flyeth to and fro without Wings, and is a moving Wind, which after its expulsion out of its habitation by *Vulcan* [fire], is driven into its *Chaos*, into which it entereth again. ... By this Spirit of Mercury all Metals may be, if need requireth, dissolved, opened, and without any corrosive reduced or resolved into their first Matter. This Spirit reneweth both Men and Beast, like the Eagle; consumeth whatsoever is bad, and produceth a great Age to a long life. (quoted in Read 186-187)

According to other alchemists, air represents breath and is an intermediary between heaven and earth; it combines spirituality and fertility. Claude de Saint-Martin believed it to be a sensible manifestation of the invisible world, a vibrating and communicating principle.

Air may also be looked upon as an eternal present, a space/time continuum, or as a transpersonal force in the shape of a mythical hero. Because it is a mysterious force, air represents a world *in potentia* – that Other World or *Anima Mundi* – as does Yeats's Cuchulain. Since the Celts considered air creatures to be messengers of the gods and thus representatives of superior types of beings, so Cuchulain, the Goidelic hero, was endowed with great strength and energy. Yeats's creature was imbued also with poetic insight.

The mythical Cuchulain's association with the fiery red planet Mars is another indication of his energetic, violent, and ardent temperament. Always tense and dissatisfied, he became disruptive and unpredictable as time passed. Cuchulain's desires and wants were always potent. Mars's redness found an emotional equivalent in Cuchulain's flammable traits: his petulant, fickle, childlike, choleric nature. As god of war, Mars was known for his irascible, cruel, and inflexible nature. The Yeatsian hero possesses these qualities in a mitigated form, reflecting the psychological and aesthetic outlook of a man at odds with himself and with the creative process.

The variety of red in the mythical Cuchulain's hair was an accurate measure of his emotional state. In this *rubedo* condition, according to the alchemists' color chart, Cuchulain would be capable of liquefying solids and melting iron. He thus becomes a mediating principle between forms as well as a symbol of regeneration and action. Fire purifies, spiritualizes, and illuminates. It also destroys, consumes, engulfs, and overpowers. In *The Tain*, Cuchulain is described as being powerful, violent, and passionate during a battle: he is inflamed. After he was knighted he became a threat to the community; once his fury was so great that a way to cool him had to be found. A vat of cold water was thrown on him at the height of one of his rages. "In the second vat the water escaped [by boiling over]; in the third, the water was still hotter." By this time his fury died down. The fire was subdued by the water. In the third magical vat of water he was restored "to his natural form and feature" (Moore 35).

Since Cuchulain's flame for conquest and domination had turned into blind violence, thereby creating an unbalanced situation within his psyche, the cold water was transformed into steam. In this form, the solid liquid became gaseous; the combustible energy was sublimated. Alchemically, it could be said that Cuchulain had transcended the norm, that he had opted for a superhuman rather than a human state. The spirit of fire contains gold, and when Cuchulain was in harmony with himself and acted in consort with his people and community, his gold scintilla came to the fore. That was his condition when he became the protector of Ulster, but not when Yeats eternalized him in *The Only Jealousy of Emer*. The elements of earth, water, air, and fire were not in harmony; his kinetic energy did not work positively; he was no hero, but rather was victimized by his own sensuality and frenetic drive. He had lost the freshness of inspiration and the joy of love.

A moon appeared on Cuchulain's forehead, indicating the duality of his nature. As a masculine solar hero, he symbolized strength, courage, bravery, and spirituality. His lunar female side was the powerful and unconscious force within him. This dual personality likened him to Achilles, who was also given to erratic and highly volatile behavior.

Yeats tells us in the beginning of *The Only Jealousy of Emer* that Cuchulain struggled with the "waves" and that "he fought the deathless sea" which then "washed his senseless image up" (186) and placed it at the door of the fisherman's cabin in a state "beyond hearing or seeing" (184). Throughout the play, reference is made to water in a variety of forms: stormy, troubled, dark, foamy, white. In accordance with Archimedes' principle, which Yeats mentions in the opening lines of his drama, Cuchulain was raised above the waters and brought back to land.

Water, an indifferent mass representing infinite possibilities and the un-formed germ of all matter, is that force in nature which paves the way for Cuchulain's rebirth. According to Plato, water is the most powerful solvent: it can liquefy stone (49). Like Plato, Paracelsus considered water to be a universal solvent which enabled liquefaction or a reshuffling of views to take place. Only through dissolution or a fusion of elements could the later processes of filtration, distillation, and decantation occur (Read 137). Solids—whether metals or elements—can be dissolved by water. In psychological terms, personal and limited views may be fused into impersonal and larger frames of reference. When Cuchulain's masculine ways are immersed in the maternal waters of the unconscious (or the feminine components of the psyche), he acquires new perspectives with their reemergence. A blending of antithetical ways prepares him for a *coniunctio*. Jagged edges are rounded out; harsh corners are smoothed.

Before his immersion in the waves, Yeats's Cuchulain was one-dimensional. His attitudes and ways had become arid and ossified. He had to be dissolved in order to regenerate. Such a transformation is dangerous because loss of identity and drowning could result, yet Cuchulain had to expose himself to the water ritual. He had to allow himself to be absorbed by this solvent, inviting danger in order to return to nearly embryonic state. As Arnold of Villanova wrote: "The oftener the Medicine is dissolved, sublimed and coagulated, the more potent it becomes. . . . In each sublimation its protective virtue is multiplied by ten" (quoted in Read 141). Only after the dissolution of the original material has taken place can the stagnant ruling authority or idea be altered. Cuchulain had reached a state in his development where his strength, candor, and creative force had ceased to be fruitful. His negative characteristics, cruelty and immorality, predominated. An inner and outer revaluation of his being had to be undertaken if he were to evolve. His ego had hypertrophied; his arrogance and aggressive ways had become repetitive and unproductive and had to be washed away or cleansed. The *regressus ad uterum* motif into the undifferentiated primal state of oneness could pave the way for the creation of new poetic insights.

After Emer brought Cuchulain's body into the cabin, she placed it in a curtained bed. Yeats refers to the inert Cuchulain as the "Figure of Cuchulain," and he wears a heroic mask. Another Cuchulain is crouching in the corner, unseen by the protagonists. He is referred to as the "Ghost of Cuchulain." He remains in the shadow because he represents the unconscious self, the darkened and blackened being, the alchemist's *umbra solis* (sun's shadow). As the representative of the unregenerate aspects of the psyche, the Ghost of Cuchulain must pass through "the valley of the shadow," altering that which is defective and illuminating that which remains shrouded in darkness.

The fisherman's cabin sets the stage for the powerful transformation ritual. Fish live in the interior and subterranean realms of deep waters. They stand for the inner riches and potential forces within the psyche; they are representative of both the formal and the physical universe. They allow mankind to be nourished by them; as psychic beings, they symbolize spiritual fecundity. Christ was called "the fisher of men" since wisdom was extracted from him. Parsifal meets the Grail King as a fisherman.

Emer's fisherman's cabin is a closed and protective area which calls for introspection. In just such an inner sanctum Apuleius was initiated into the rites of Isis and Faust experienced the Realm of the Mothers. Emer will be forced to sound out her depths, to come to terms with her needs and motivations. It is in this halfway station between life and death, earth and water, that Emer's consciousness will expand.

Emer's conviction that Cuchulain is not dead, but that some cosmic force possesses his body, enables the alchemical process to pursue its course. In very powerful and moving language she tells of Cuchulain's past. She describes his feelings of guilt after having killed his son in a rage.

> And being mad with sorrow, he ran out;
> And after, to his middle in the foam,
> With shield before him and with sword in hand,
> He fought the deathless sea.
> [No one dared disarm Cuchulain or call him back.]
> . . . . all stood wondering

. . . .
Until at last, as though he had fixed his eyes
On a new enemy, he waded out
Until the water had swept over him;
But the waves washed his senseless image up
And laid it at this door.

(186)

In alchemical terms, the Figure of Cuchulain lies in a grave. In this regressive, unconscious state, he experiences the waters of forgetfulness. The undifferentiated ego has become a *massa confusa*. Yeats delineates the chaotic emotions involved in terms of antithetical eidetic images, rhythms, and tonalities. The frail seabird is opposed to the bold and aggressive eagle, and the wind which brings storms is opposed to the gentle breath of air. Verticality adds to the scope and breadth of the emotions involved; the vision of the bird spells ascension or elevation, while the mole represents a descent into abysmal depths. A separation of earth and heaven, higher and lower spheres, coarse and fine, light and heavy particles or feelings, prepares for the ensuing objectification of feelings and situations, the *separatio*. Nuances of color also activate the dichotomy implicit in the personalities: the white seabird and the dark furrows, the white color of shell, foam, and wing are set against the blackness of the storm. Black usually accompanies sensations of fear and tremulous excitement and earthiness, caves, and closed, magical domains where the ancient initiate relived his death/birth mysteries. The color white, or the alchemist's *albedo* condition, indicates a cold, feminine world.

When Yeats refers to the white "foam of the waves," he indicates abrupt changes in the emotional reactions of his protagonists. Waves may be looked upon as the realization of sudden disruptive qualities emerging from the unconscious, inner forces or drives ready to assault the spirit and overwhelm the rational function. The "white shell" (115) is reminiscent of an inner, subterranean world where creativity occurs, as in the case of Aphrodite who was born from the foam surrounding a shell. "White wing" suggests a creature inhabiting the higher realms, the sky. Driven by wind or spirit, he is seemingly disoriented. When a Yeatsian storm arises, agitation, instability, and inconstancy permeate the atmosphere:

At daybreak after stormy night
Between two furrows upon the ploughed land:
A sudden storm, and it was thrown
Between dark furrows upon the ploughed land.

(184)

A titanic principle is at work—blinding, passionate, and instinctual. *Pneuma*, or spirit, begins to predominate. It is God's spirit which moves about the primordial waters as it had when endowing Adam with a soul or in sending the Great Flood. For the druids, wind was an arcane power, a vehicle for magic, an energetic principle, a manifestation of a hermetic light.

Emer calls to Eithne Inguba. Her position close to the door indicates the role she plays in the drama. The door represents a passageway between two states and two worlds: the known and the unknown, sea and land, heat and cold, wind and calm, life and death. It was Emer, as the earthly and conventional wife, who helped Cuchulain through the early part of his ordeal. It is Eithne Inguba, symbolizing the hetaera type, the sensual and ever-alluring inspirational woman, who will take him through the *separatio*, the next step of the initiation process.

The stage is set. A fire must be lit to dry out the watery masses in the form of the two Cuchulains. Emer lights the hearth, comparable to the alchemist's athanor. Now the secret fire will burn; subterranean forces will start their work. The coals glow. The operation starts. The alchemical waters recede, and the "dreaming foam" dries out. The *massa confusa* stills as the components separate. Analysis can now begin as anguish, pain, and guilt are expelled in dialogue form, bringing about a *purgatio/purificatio*.

Emer, the earth wife, tells Eithne Inguba to come close to Cuchulain's bed and summon his soul. Only when the feeling principle is activated can blood again begin to circulate in Cuchulain's heart and life's energy be restored. "We're but two women struggling with the sea," Emer states (188). To battle death means to transform inert into kinetic energy, to counter *stagnatio* with *circulatio*. Only by means of emotions can the double movement of life, systole and diastole, pave the way for transformation. These feelings affect will and intelligence and become activated in Yeats's drama at the very moment the fire is lit in the hearth. While Emer stirs the living coals, Eithne Inguba kindles the emotional flame. Cuchulain moves. Love has changed the rigid metal into molten mixtures. The transubstantiation begins. Eithne Inguba kisses him. The elements activate the immortal brew—the blood of life, the *aqua permanens*.

Eithne Inguba, however, starts back after her kiss, saying: "I felt some evil thing that dried my heart / When my lips touched it" (188). Something has altered. She hardly recognizes her lover. The heat of passion has dried him out and he has grown remote. She comments on his withered right arm. That it is no longer able to function indicates that Cuchulain's relationship with reality is defective and that his unconscious is in full sway. The right arm usually symbolizes a rapport with the workaday world. It is also aggressive: it grabs things; it holds weapons. Cuchulain is now incapable of such activity. He has become a passive entity.

Eithne Inguba's kiss brought Cuchulain back to life, but not as the great hero previously known to his wife and mistress. He returns as Bricriu, the god of discord, to inhabit the Figure of Cuchulain. As Bricriu, the Figure of Cuchulain sits up. He is no longer wearing the heroic mask, but a "distorted" one. Yeats uses the mask as a metaphor, a theatrical convention further to suggest the divergence between conscious and unconscious attitudes. Eithne Inguba leaves, and Bricriu becomes the catalyst. He is in charge of continuing the alchemical operation. He will arouse conflict and objectify the emotional situation. As Yeats wrote: "We can only become conscious of a thing by comparing it with its opposite. The two real things we have are our natures and the circumstances that surround us. We have in both a violent antithesis" (quoted in Berryman 32).

As the *separatio* process begins, the personalities are reshaped. What had been fluid is dry; what had been dark is enlightened. Bricriu, the messenger of self-knowledge, will be the separating agent and bring the light. The distorted mask he wears represents the pain involved in bringing lucidity and the split engendering illumination. He is a composite of Nietzsche's Superman and the Ugliest Man (Jung 14:520). A "bridleless horse" brought Bricriu to the fisherman's cabin. As the agent which carries him from the watery depths of the unconscious to the rational sphere of the articulate being, the horse symbolizes the intense energy needed to pave the way for illumination and lucidity. Endowed with the strength to surge forth from the primal depths to the drier spheres of solid matter, Bricriu is the one who will force Emer to choose and thus mold her destiny.

Emer has a dilemma. She must either renounce Cuchulain's love forever or pursue her fruitless attempts to possess him. Another possibility is that she will lose Cuchulain to the death-dealing Fand, a new figure whom Yeats introduces. Emer refuses to sacrifice her earthly love. She claims to live for two things: the memory of her life with Cuchulain and the hope of being his once again. To warn her of the possible outcome of her indecisiveness, Bricriu touches Emer's eyes "to give them sight." That his left hand is the healthy one is significant. The left side is usually equated with the unconscious, the liquid realm; this is no longer the daylight or rational sphere, but the darkened realm of subliminal life. Both worlds will be experienced simultaneously during the play.

The Ghost of Cuchulain, as the unconscious personality, lives in a world inaccessible to mortal beings. As a shadow figure, he symbolizes the primitive factors in the personality which until this point are in their embryonic state. Untouched by human reason, they live in darkness and operate according to their own logic. The Figure of Cuchulain, with Bricriu as its spokesman, represents the conscious outlook that is needed in the differentiated, mundane world. That Bricriu, as the Figure of Cuchulain, confronts his opposite, the Ghost of Cuchulain, indicates that a *separatio* has been accomplished. An objectification of feelings and needs is coming into being. Previously Emer had never understood Cuchulain's shadowy nature. It had either remained invisible to her or she had repressed any knowledge of it. Now that Bricriu is concretizing it before her, she begins to understand the situation and may learn to cope with it.

Yeats's drama takes on a new dimension as the *separatio* process continues to divide, cut open, and disconnect. Fand enters. She tells the Ghost of Cuchulain, who seems to be suffering from guilt and remorse, that she has come from "the Country-under-Wave" (190). She promises him beatitude and forgetfulness, the obliteration of everything, including the memory of his wrongdoings.

Fand, referred to in Celtic mythology as *"a Woman of the Sidhe"* (190), represents Ideal Beauty. She is cold and remote, *"more an idol than a human being"* (191). An archetypal figure, she emerges from the deepest areas of the unconscious. Her function is to mesmerize and overpower man in her embrace. Her desire is to re-enter the realm of the absolute. As Yeats presents her in her still partly mortal state, she longs for Cuchulain's embrace. Only after his acquiescence can she know "Unity of Being" or experience a complete separation from the existential domain. If Cuchulain gives her the kiss she seeks, he will know oblivion — which means death to individuality, activity, frustration, and, ultimately, death to life.

Emer, Fand's antagonist, represents the weariness of the workaday world with its struggle for survival and its frustration of activity. Emer would use any means to destroy her rival and even attempts to slay her with a knife. Bricriu warns Emer that no weapon "can wound that body of air" (190); no earthly force can destroy man's dream or fantasy figure — the Eternal Feminine, the ideal which the poet nourishes in his heart and mind — and bind the ethereal to the physical universe.

Fand begins her seductive gyrations, dancing around the crouching Ghost of Cuchulain. Ever-alluring, she attempts to captivate her victim and enclose him in her embrace. Her undulations grow quicker, like those of Salome. She circles about her prey, leans over him, and enshrouds him with her lustrous hair. The Three Musicians whose songs opened the play now accompany Fand's arabesques with flute, drum, and stringed instrument. The Ghost of Cuchulain moves. He begins to question Fand as she pursues her wave-like patterns in space.

> Who is it stands before me there
> Shedding such light from limb and hair
> As when the moon, complete at last
> With every labouring crescent past,
> And lonely with extreme delight,
> Flings out upon the fifteenth night?
> (191)

He sees her as a "labouring crescent," a moon figure ready to enclose him in her world and bring his world of conflict to an end. Fand, in turn, taunts him, and grows more aggressive, fighting to conquer her host and bring him to her realm "beyond the human" sphere, to possess him totally and eternally. No longer is he to be loved by many earthly women, but only by the Eternal Feminine.

The Ghost of Cuchulain must choose between the atemporal realm of bliss and the temporal realm of suffering. He is no longer the youthful dreamer, the idealist, the poet. His memories "Weigh down my hands, abash my eyes" (191). Once he had been an "amorous" and "violent" man (185); ruthless, cutting, destructive. Resembling the eagle, with whom Yeats associates him, he represents power and ability; like the mole, to which he is also compared, he burrows beneath the ground, refusing to take stock of his immoral deeds. Endowed with equine energy, Cuchulain has galloped through existence, surging forth in Dionysian frenzy from one amorous adventure to another, from one battle to the next. Fand's goal was to force him to give up his power, which had instilled in him feelings of guilt and suffering, as well as lusty joy and the satisfaction of conquest. Should he succumb to Fand, Cuchulain would never know want or thirst, for his heart would be forever stilled.

The Ghost of Cuchulain turns away. He clings too desperately to life with all of its difficulties and traumas. He calls for Emer. Fand grows angry and insists upon kissing him. Tension heightens. The alchemical brew boils. Bricriu cries out to Emer, "Renounce his love," just before Cuchulain succumbs to Fand's wiles. "And cry that you renounce his love forever," he repeats (192). Still Emer refuses. She has not yet understood the forces at stake. Her all-too-human ways indicate the limitations of her perception. Bricriu speaks:

> Fool, fool!
> I am Fand's enemy come to thwart her will,
> And you stand gaping there. There is still time.
> . . . .
> There is still a moment left; cry out, cry out!
> Renounce him, and her power is at an end.
> Cuchulain's foot is on the chariot-step.
> Cry—-.
>
> (192-193)

Emer yields. She stabilizes her emotions, coagulates her spirit. The alchemist's flame of anguish, which had brought an upsurge of emotion, subsides. The emotions involved in the relationships have been disconnected, dried out, and aired. Lucidity has cut through feelings and aided her in facing her ordeal. "I renounce Cuchulain's love for ever," she cries out (193).

No sooner is her decision made than the Figure of Cuchulain "sinks back upon the bed" (193). He has donned the heroic mask once again. Eithne Inguba kneels in front of him. Vitality now predominates. Joy, lust, heroism, and suffering will invade his existence. He beckons Eithne Inguba to come closer. "Your arms, your arms! O Eithne Inguba, / I have been in some strange place and am afraid" (193). With life's return the Other World, Fand, and the

Ghost of Cuchulain vanish.

The battle of the elements has subsided for the moment. The solution has been found. Matter has coagulated into a new mixture, though it is perhaps no better than the first if a hierarchy of values has to be established. Emer's decision, though painful for her, allows Cuchulain to pursue his flighty loves, to suffer from guilt and remorse again, and to re-enter the Wheel of Life.

For Yeats, the true hero-poet, exemplified by Cuchulain, must endure suffering and guilt in order to experience life's dichotomies viscerally; he must also learn to evaluate the actions and feelings which he encounters in the phenomenological world. Only then can he begin to create from his own substance, mold from his flesh and blood, and drive through the core of conventional material to reach the domain of the ideal — the created work of art.

Anima Figures

Emer, Eithne Inguba, and Fand are anima figures. Psychologically, the anima is defined as "an autonomous psychic content in the male personality which can be described as an inner woman" (Edinger 10). Anima figures have been depicted since time immemorial in all forms, from virgin to harlot. They stand for Eros, love, and relatedness: they personify the feminine principle within man. As an Eros image, the anima figure establishes feeling relationships between protagonists which may be described in terms of taste (bitter or sweet) or of color (white, red, black, golden). When man falls in love, he projects his anima onto another person. If his ego, the center of his conscious personality, identifies with the anima figure, danger arises; he is victimized by this unconscious force and is rendered psychologically impotent. A psychologically developed man who experiences the anima figure consciously, on the other hand, may be provided with the deepest type of human relationship.

Emer, Eithne Inguba, and Fand may be viewed as projections of Cuchulain's psyche. Once they begin functioning in the phenomenological world, each struggles in her own way to assert herself. The artist in whom these forces exist attempts to embody them in his work. Yeats described the battle to articulate feelings and visions as taking place

> in the depths of the soul and one of the antagonists does not wear a shape known to the world or speak a mortal tongue. It is the struggle of the dream with the world—it is only possible when we transcend circumstances and ourself, and the greater the contest, the greater the art. (quoted in Nathan 160)

Fand is the most alluring and most dangerous of the three. In Ireland, the Sidhe were associated with the moon goddess and thus with tides, water, the "magic of poetry," and the mysteries of the creative spirit in man. When mesmerized by the Sidhe, the individual yields to absolute passion, the ideal; the dream world becomes his realm and not the workaday domain. Since Fand comes from that "Country-under-Wave," she represents infinite riches, the alpha and omega of existence: a world *in potentia* (Graves 10). She becomes an active force in the drama. Rather than withdrawn into some remote area of the room (or psyche), she comes forth and demands her prey; "for the Sidhe / Are dexterous fishers and they fish for men / With dreams upon the hook" (190). Fand corrupts the imagination. She tries to entice Cuchulain with her sweet song and rapturous sensuality. She wants him to experience her as complete woman and no longer as a "bird of prey."

In alchemical terms, what Fand seeks is a "spagyric marriage" with Cuchulain — that is, an inner psychic union with a blending of conscious and unconscious factors. If this union is accomplished, hostility and differentiation come to an end. No opposition exists, no polarities, no differentiation, no coagulation. The preformal state returns. Fand types are present in all societies and in all epochs. Though it has various names (Lorelei, Mélusine, Siren, Bird-Woman, Fish-Woman), this kind of female force captures the unsuspecting male and then devours him in an embrace.

Fand is also a lunar force, and therefore silver is her color. This noble metal represents the glimmering, shining, and mysterious tones she casts on those who fall within her sphere. When associated with the moon, silver expresses the occult side of nature, the unconscious as opposed to the sun principle which relates to clarity and cerebrality. It represents volatility, multiplicity, and fragmentation. For the poet, it stands for a world of fantasy and creativity. The alchemist likens moon figures to quicksilver, to the "fluid body of Man," or to the "non-formal" dynamic aspects of the personality, because they both dissolve and coagulate (Jung 14:520). Fand lives in the powerful waters of the unconscious, the collective sphere where the poet draws his inspiration and the alchemist projects his struggle upon matter.

The moon is cold and moist and shines only with reflected light, so it both receives and pours out. It is both passive and active — a kind of vampire who feeds on men in order to pursue and finally complete her monthly course. In its more positive aspects, the moon, equated with the unconscious, is dependent upon the sun, or consciousness. Without the unconscious, consciousness would not exist, nor could the poet create. Without consciousness — with the disappearance of the sun and the domination of the moon — an unlimited void would arise. The alchemist's silvery stage must then be watched and tended so that the illumination which radiates from the metal may bring about the *albedo* phase and operate the transformative process. Once the anima is freed from the *prima materia* and can navigate autonomously in the spheres above, she may spread her poison, ensnare, and then suffocate her victim in her embrace. It is this elemental force which becomes personified in *The Only Jealousy of Emer*.

Since Fand has been incarnated, she is not absolute. Her image-making power is still a potent force. She lives as form and idea and thus as a reality, and can express herself in a variety of phenomena inhabiting the physical universe. She acts as a powerful anima figure for the Ghost of Cuchulain because she is still alive. She wills; she wants. To increase her statuesque and godly nature, Yeats associated her with gold, bronze, brass, and silver. She "seems more an idol" (191) than a flesh-and-blood woman. Everything about her is metallic, including her hair. Like Salome, she surpasses the human sphere; like metal, she is unfeeling. As a moon figure, she represents the unconscious. Her blatant sensuality inspires Cuchulain and entices him, as does the hetaera woman who seeks to rid man of his responsibilities and lure him into the nondifferentiated realm of serenity.

After Fand begins her dance, she comes to life in the various tones of shining metals, as though the moon itself were revealing its subdued and glimmering hues. Like other moon figures—Ishtar, Isis, Hathor, Artemis—so Fand dominates the cycles of life. Death and rebirth practices were powerful in matriarchal societies. To underscore the collective nature of Fand's dance, Yeats links her to the Three Musicians whose songs open and close the play. Yeats, like the alchemists, saw the connection between sound, metal, and quantity. Numbers could be heard in a type of music of the spheres. Indeed, it was said that alchemists used to dance and play musical instruments during their experiments, thus according them entry into various levels of the unconscious (Jung 14:272, 240, 130-132).

The lascivious spatial forms of Fand's dance produce new relationships in the created world. Each gesture and sign is an abandonment to cosmic force, a linking of time and energy in visual designs. The sounds emerging from Fand's lips as she dances in spirals and circles suggest numerical relationships in the musical scale. Nature itself, as Plato suggested, was based upon a mathematical plan. Matter was an expression of mysterious cosmic harmonies (Yeats *A Vision* 135, 90-100). Fand's kinetic and spatial forms become relationships between sound, harmony, and rhythms, each communicating with the other in a "Unity of Being." Like the ancient Celts who played their harps in three different modes—sleep, smile, lamentation—so Fand undulated about in spellbinding configurations.

Since Fand represents perfection and ideal beauty, she is out of man's reach, always eluding him and arousing his desire. Her collective and impersonal nature can never be possessed. Man can be overwhelmed by her if he succumbs to her wiles and promises of ecstasy, but then he rejects his individuality, his human memory. Although he is released from pain, he is denied his heroism and nobility. It is the earthly aspect of Cuchulain's personality, his attachment to the lustiness of life, that saves him from Fand's grasp. He chooses life, not death; struggle, not oblivion.

Terrestrial love, incarnated in Emer, is subject to change. It stands for the soul of man, the incomplete, accessible, differentiated feelings. Yeats suggested: "All power is from the terrestrial condition, for there opposites meet and there only is the extreme of choice possible, full freedom. And there the heterogeneous is, and evil, for evil is the strain one upon another of opposites" (quoted in Nathan 161).

Emer is the brutal light of reality. It is she who feels the bitterness of consciousness, the tears of sorrow, the disappointment of loss, the dread alternative belonging to the human condition. It is she, as a projection of Cuchulain's psyche, who struggles to choose the best course to follow and is made lucid by the dichotomy Bricriu makes visible to her. Emer is a transient figure. She is Cuchulain's first love, but she dries up as an anima figure and becomes routine. She no longer offers the poet the excitement he needs to create. Cuchulain will succumb to his fickle nature and seek another woman. Emer is the stable force in his life. She waits patiently and in vain for her husband's return, offering him understanding, tenderness, and comfort. She is nourished by memories and hope. Alchemically, it is she who must sip the "bitter water of reason and judgment." As is stated in *The Hermetic Museum*: "O water of bitter taste, that preservest the elements! O nature of propinquity, that dissolvest nature! O best of natures, which overcomest nature herself! . . . Thou art crowned with light and art born . . . and the quintessence arises from thee" (Jung 14:252). This secret substance, with its moral and psychological ramifications, is the water "that springs from the *lumen naturae*" (light of nature); "the *aqua permanens* or . . . primal water which contains the four elements" (Jung 14:252-253).

In contrast to Emer is Eithne Inguba, the passing love. She is youthful, beautiful, passionate, and joyful. Cuchulain experiences her as an escapade. On the contrary, she understands Cuchulain's need of her because he is poet in search of inspiration. It is she who excites his creative faculties until the next lover appears. Emer sees Fand as the real and only danger. Once his dream-world or unconscious takes over and Fand has complete sway, the poet grows impotent; memories cease and, without these archaic feelings and sensations, creativity vanishes. When Emer observes Fand's power increasing, her fear mounts. Fand is the catalyst at this juncture, just as Bricriu had been the light-bringer. Emer is compelled to act. Her sacrifice is fruitless, however, since it requires Cuchulain to return to Eithne Inguba and to re-enter the world of time. With his re-entry, he is doomed to rebirth and differentiation.

Yeats's tragedy, *The Only Jealousy of Emer*, dramatizes the alchemical operations which take his protagonists from a state of primal oneness to *separatio* and *coagulation*. The alchemical dictum reads: "Take the old black spirit, and destroy therewith the bodies until they are changed" (quoted in Read 138). The *separatio* experienced during the play broke up undifferentiated attitudes and allowed heretofore buried unconscious contents to emerge into the light of consciousness. A variety of possibilities thus came into being, and with them the power of discrimination began to develop. The alchemical experience as dramatized in *The Only Jealousy of Emer* was assimilated by the protagonists with all of its psychological and poetic ramifications. The journey once accomplished, however, did not lead to *sublimatio* or evolution into a higher sphere of existence, but rather to another *separatio*, another war and another rebirth. So continues Yeats's Wheel of Life.

Works Cited

Berryman, Charles. *W. B. Yeats: Design of Opposites, a Critical Study*. New York: Exposition Press, 1987.

"Celtic Mythology." In *New Larousse Encyclopedia of Mythology*, ed. Felix Guirand, trans. Richard Aldington and Delano Ames 222-244. London and New York: Prometheus Press, 1974.

Edinger, Edward. "An Outline of Analytical Psychology." Unpublished article.

Graves, Robert. *The White Goddess: A Historical Grammar of Poetic Myth*. New York: Vintage Books, 1958.

Jung, Carl G. *Mysterium Coniunctionis: An Inquiry into the Separation and Synthesis of Psychic Opposites in Alchemy. Collected Works*. Vol. 14. New York: The Bollingen Foundation and Random House, 1963.

Moore, John Rees. *Masks of Love and Death: Yeats as Dramatist*. Ithaca: Cornell University Press, 1971.

Nathan, Leonard E. *The Tragic Drama of William Butler Yeats: Figures in a Dance*. New York and London: Columbia University Press, 1965.

Plato. *Timaeus*. In *Plato's Cosmology: The Timaeus of Plato*, trans. Francis MacDonald Cornford. Indianapolis: Bobbs Merrill Co., Inc., n.d.

Read, John. *Prelude to Chemistry: An Outline of Alchemy, Its Literature and Its Relationships*. 1936 Cambridge, MA: The MIT Press, 1966.

Yeats, William Butler. *The Only Jealousy of Emer*. In *The Collected Plays of W. B. Yeats*, 183-194. New York: Macmillan, 1953.

—-. *A Vision*. 1937 New York: Macmillan, 1966.

Part II

THE FANTASTIC AND THE IRISH ARTS: THEATER, MUSIC, AND PAINTING

Ireland's most famous export for the past three centuries has been its writers. In the twentieth century, for instance, it would be impossible to consider literature written in English without beginning with the Irish writers: W. B. Yeats in poetry, James Joyce in prose, and Samuel Beckett in drama. Each in his own way significantly changed the very form in which he wrote. Moreover, if Yeats's and Joyce's work helped define "modern literature," then Beckett's work is surely part of what we mean by the postmodern in literature. Less well known outside Ireland, however, are its composers, represented in this section by John Field; painters, here represented by Jack B. Yeats; and the many other dramatists (several of whom are discussed here by Christopher Murray), besides the most famous, John Millington Synge, Sean O'Casey, and Beckett (the latter three will be discussed individually in the next section, "Uses of the Fantastic by Irish Playwrights.")

Christopher Murray, in discussing "the role of fantasy in modern drama," suggests that: "generally speaking, [it] is radically to overthrow the easy assumptions regarding the nature of perception and experience." After presenting a survey of the uses of the fantastic in the Irish theater, he concludes by asserting that the fantasist's unique role on the contemporary Irish stage is as "a subversive who offers audiences a dream of an alternative, more tolerable, life magically but humanly transformed."

Perhaps no modern painter is more unjustly a victim of the neglect which comes from being virtually unknown beyond the seas surrounding Ireland than Jack B. Yeats. On the occasion of the centenary of his birth, Roger McHugh wrote: "He was our first great painter and found his real subject in the current Irish scene and in its association [sic], including those of its fragmented culture" (15). A truly remarkable painter—Sir Kenneth Clark once exclaimed about Yeats's paintings: "Colour is Yeats's element in which he dives and splashes with the shameless abandon of a porpoise" (quoted in Rosenthal 3). Excellent water colorist, as well as an interesting writer of plays, prose, and poetry, Yeats captured exquisitely life in the town of Sligo in the west of Ireland, which his brother, William Butler Yeats, memorialized in poetry. Hilary Pyle contends that "no one brought the ability to observe life to such a high level of imagination as Jack B. Yeats." There is great energy in his paintings along with genuine human sympathy for his subjects; yet, as Pyle also demonstrates, for him to give expression to both it was necessary to draw not upon the mythic, which had preoccupied his brother for much of his career (see Bertha, "Myth and the Fantastic"), but upon the fantastic — and always the fantastic rooted in life. This relation of fantasy to reality, of the stars to the earth, is also important for Yeats's early contemporary John Millington Synge, as Toni O'Brien Johnson points out in "Interrogating Boundaries: Fantasy in Synge's Plays," as well as for Joyce and other Irish writers.

One of the genuine innovations in nineteenth century music occurred when the Irish composer John Field invented the nocturne. Made famous by Chopin, who much admired Field, the nocturne is now well-ensconced within the canon of accepted forms of musical composition. Péter Egri, in his essay, places Field and his work within its axiological context and within the larger confluences of the nineteenth century, discussing his compositions in relation to the poetry of Shelley, the painting of Turner, and the music of Chopin. In doing so he demonstrates Field's importance for the development of music and the arts contending that he "initiated a new way of telling, a new kind of sensibility, a new course of imagination" (Egri).

Each of these essays approaches its subject from the fresh vantage point obtained by considering the importance of the fantastic in the artists' work, thereby throwing new light on Irish drama, Yeats's painting, and Field's music, while at the same time linking each to other creative Irish artists discussed in this volume.

Works Cited

McHugh, Roger. "Introduction." In *Jack B. Yeats: A Centenary Gathering*, ed. Roger McHugh. Dublin: The Dolmen Press, 1971.

Rosenthal, T. G. "Jack Yeats 1871-1957." In *The Masters: Yeats*, 2-6. Paulton, UK: Knowledge Publications, 1966.

Christopher Murray

Irish Drama and the Fantastic

In a well-known passage in Shakespeare's *A Mid summer Night's Dream* Duke Theseus makes a comparison between the lunatic, the lover, and the poet to the effect that whereas each sees what does not exist, each is capable of providing a new reality for "airy nothing" because each has

> Such shaping fantasies, that apprehend
> More than cool reason ever comprehends.
> (5.1.5-6)

This is quite a claim when taken thus out of its context, for Theseus is actually on the other side, the side of the rationalists. The play in which he appears demonstrates that he speaks truer than he could know. For Shakespeare, fantasy provided an alternative mode of knowledge, if not of being, and in *The Tempest* he ends up claiming that *we* are such stuff as dreams are made on (4.1.156-157). The audience – everybody – is incorporated in the notion that life is but a dream.

Fantasy was, one may say, important to Shakespeare, and yet he did not use it without irony or without leaving his audience the option of discarding what they were given as unimportant:

> If we shadows have offended,
> Think but this and all is mended,
> That you have but slumbered here
> While these visions did appear.
> (*A Midsummer Night's Dream* 5.1.430-434)

The history of English drama after Shakespeare moves well away from fantasy to endorse empiricism, scientific objectivity, and naturalism. To find fantasy on the stage in the eighteenth or nineteenth centuries one must seek out the popular forms, pantomime, extravaganza, or afterpieces as they were termed: afterthoughts we may just as well call them, for they had no serious role to play in the continuing dialogue between stage and auditorium.

Nowadays, however, we recognize rather more fully the need for fantasy, its place in the whole realm of play, and its significance as imagery, psychological and cultural alike. Before looking at Irish drama at all, then, one must inspect for a moment or two the nature and role of fantasy in modern drama in general. First, perhaps, we need to get clear our notion of the term itself.

Kathryn Hume's study, *Fantasy and Mimesis: Responses to Reality in Western Literature*, provides a simple definition of fantasy: "*Any departure from consensus reality*" (21, her emphasis), together with a well-argued account of its functions, which all relate to "ways of giving a sense of meaning" (44), especially in modern literature. Although her study is based entirely on narrative literature, that is, prose fiction, her approach to fantasy may be applied to drama well enough since in her diagram of the relationship between author, work, and world she constantly uses the term "audience." The audience receives and is affected by the "work," and in turn the audience may or may not, depending on the aim of the work, experience a sense of "engagement" with or "disengagement" from the world (57). As I interpret this model, the "world" of the author is not necessarily the "world" of the audience; there may or may not be persuasion that the author's world, as transformed in the work, should open doors into the audience's world (outside the theater). Thus one can have a play like George Bernard Shaw's *John Bull's Other Island* (1904) or Brian Friel's *Freedom of the City* (1973) on the one hand, putting pressure on an audience to apply the contrived or fanciful events to the real world, or on the other hand one can have plays such as Hugh Leonard's *Madigan's Lock* (1958), *Time Was* (1976), or *Pizzazz* (1983) in which the world outside is sealed off and the audience is confined to the experience of the work itself, as a play.

Scholars in the field of drama studies, such as John Gassner, see little value in dramatic fantasy as such. Gassner clearly regards formalism (or a mixture of realism and nonrealism) as both more challenging and more effective on stage:

> Conventional fantasy has been deliberately written and staged as though it were "true," the purpose being to provide the same illusion of reality that common realism affords. At the same time we tend to believe . . . that fantasy will call attention to itself more strongly when unnatural events occur in an everyday manner and in an environment in which only humdrum occurrences are to be expected. (174)

Formalism, in Gassner's view, is preferable to fantasy in drama because formalism exploits the theater itself in its assumptions: "The premise that theatre is art and that art is a tissue of conventions is inherent in the formalistic approach. The aim of theatricality is to create a new reality — a reality of art — on the stage" (174-175). Gassner here distinguishes between realism or representationalism, which he calls a mode of actuality, and presentationalism or theatricalization, which he calls a mode of theater. The two may and frequently are combined. Theatricalism, he further comments, ruled the stage in classical times, subsequently in the age of Shakespeare and in the age of Molière, but was forcibly sidelined in the twentieth century into the music hall, vaudeville, and musical comedies. Nevertheless, *some* degree of theatricalism has been an element of all efforts since 1890 to depart from realistic drama and staging (148), since "A theatre freed from all pretense of reproducing reality has been the modern theatricalist ideal" (145). Thus the various experimental forms used in the theater since the 1890s, symbolism, expressionism, surrealism, and so on, may all be regarded as various attempts to bring fantasy into an active relationship with realism. In effect, this means that the role of fantasy in modern drama, generally speaking, is radically to overthrow easy assumptions regarding the nature of perception and experience. Its function is twofold, indeed: to subvert such assumptions and to open up by various means and with varying effects an audience's understanding of the world.

We may accept, then, that in modern drama in general fantasy fulfills a quite specific role, that of revising, in a theatrical context, an audience's concepts of experience and reality. It is the context that arouses and activates the audience's collaboration in the process of imaginatively transforming perceived events into "play" and hence into vision.

Modern Irish drama was born – in part – out of an impulse to counteract the stage Irishman. As W. B. Yeats and Lady Gregory put it in their manifesto for the Irish Literary Theater: "We will show that Ireland is not the home of buffoonery and of easy sentiment, as it has been represented, but the home of an ancient idealism" (Gregory 20). It follows that the Irish Literary Theater hoped to tell the truth about the Irish character. The first and one of the most effective achievements in this area was Carden Tyrrell, in Edward Martyn's *The Heather Field*, the play that alongside Yeats's *The Countess Cathleen* launched the Irish Dramatic Movement in Dublin in May 1899. *The Heather Field* is not fantasy in Gassner's sense: the form remains realistic, with no incursion of dream states or the like. But because the central character is a dreamer, a romantic with a particular obsession which drives him into opposition with those around him who preach common sense, *The Heather Field* can be said to qualify as fantasy by Hume's definition. Indeed it marks the first in a particular category of Irish fantasy in drama: fantasy and character.

There are, broadly speaking, two subdivisions in this category: the fantasist as madman and the fantasist as escapist. Both categories use realism as the basic dramatic form but make the central point that realism both as a mode of seeing and of living is restrictive and destructive. What this type of play establishes is the validity of the unrealistic, unseen world over against the denying power of the empiric vision.

Carden Tyrrell, in *The Heather Field*, a landowner who has cleared a field of native heather, plans to drain it and turn it into fertile land. He has mortgaged himself to the hilt in order to pursue this pet project, much to the dismay of his nagging wife Grace. But for Carden the field is no mere agricultural experiment; it is a special environment, a place apart where he hears voices from the past and feels yearnings toward "that immortal beauty – so far away – always so far away" (Martyn 68). The effect on him of his obsession with the field is a sense that "persons and objects are receding from me and becoming more unreal," so that, as he tells his sympathetic brother Miles, "I often think that my life of pain and unrest here is only a dream after all" (19). Carden's voices call him back to his "real" life before he "wandered into this dream" (50). To Grace, Carden is simply going mad, and she enlists the help of two doctors to have him so certified. In the end Carden does go mad when the heather field reasserts its natural wildness and makes vain all his efforts at cultivation.

Martyn's play is a complex presentation of the conflict between subjective vision and objective reason, art versus reality, imagination versus common sense. The case is not a simple one: Carden's relationship with Grace, for example, is an unexplored factor in his whole estrangement. Moreover, he is something of a sentimentalist, literally wishing to return to and recapture the past. So to some extent we see his folly as folly, and his destruction as inevitable. It is doubtful whether Martyn fully understood the implications of his own play, which at once dismisses Grace and the doctors as predatory and indicts Carden as hubristic in the face of nature's untameable power. Because the sexual relationship with his wife is shown as emasculating, Carden's defeat is really a comment on his failure to come to terms with Grace. Thus his heather field really is an illusion, a fantasy into which he escapes in order to civilize nature and create a garden of Adonis. In today's jargon, the heather field is Carden's "text," which he reads in one way, his wife in another, and which we read in a totally different way.

It could be said that Martyn's play presented fantasy in a vacuum. Yet he sounded a note in *The Heather Field* which many Irish dramatists were subsequently to echo, with suitable variations, down to the present time. Martyn himself, however, soon rooted his theme in a way which better indicates how this category of fantasy most fruitfully operates. In *Maeve* (1900), he offered a clearer and simpler basis for alienation. Maeve O'Hynes, descendant of an ancient Gaelic family now fallen into poverty and decay, is about to marry an Englishman, Hugh Fitzwalter. She is full of unease at the prospect, however, because the alliance will remove her from her native soil and all it means to her. Like Carden Tyrrell she is a visionary, but her visions are clearly focused on Ireland's ancient past, in particular on Queen Maeve and her heroic times, "such beautiful dead people!" (Martyn 88). She feels she is dying "because I am exiled from such beauty" (89). An old peasant woman, Peg Inerny, encourages Maeve to choose "the grandeur of that other life" (106) in preference to the meanness of this life. She begins to see Hugh as a destroyer of this alternative life, "like his English predecessors who ruined every beautiful thing we ever had" (113). Thus a political element enters the fantasy. Maeve's estrangement and ultimate death may be understood as her coming to political consciousness and her self-sacrifice to assert and enter "the empire of the Gael" in Tír-na-nÓg (121). The fact that Maeve actually identifies with Queen Maeve highlights the question of identity; her vision of Queen Maeve and of ideal beauty provide a focus lacking in *The Heather Field*. Something is gained by this strengthening of focus, undoubtedly, but something is lost also, because in anchoring the dreamer's vision in patriotism Martyn narrows his range. The specific location of Maeve's fantasy makes it less disturbing than Carden Tyrrell's vague, unanswerable hunger for eternity.

Edward Martyn depicts Irish society as oppressive to the imaginative spirit. The function of his fantasy, as embodied in Carden Tyrrell and Maeve O'Hynes, is to open the eyes of the audience to specific alternatives to mundanity. George Fitzmaurice was another playwright who showed up this dichotomy. Fitzmaurice, however, was always a more embattled writer than Martyn, the distinguished landowner and landlord. Fitzmaurice was one of the new dispossessed, a poor Protestant descendant of a once-powerful Kerry family, eking out a living as a junior civil servant in Dublin. He could ill afford the grand gestures of Martyn. His work is closer to Synge's but on a smaller scale. In several of Fitzmaurice's plays, *The Pie Dish*, *The Magic Glasses*, and *The Dandy Dolls*, to mention only his early work, there is a preoccupation with the eccentric in society who is obsessed with some activity that is an analogue for the artist's vocation. The fantasy resides in this relentless preoc cupation with a private and irrational dream: it is a dangerous obsession, so far as the "ordinary" people are concerned who surround this central figure. In *The Pie Dish* Leum O'Donoghue is frantically trying to complete even one pie dish before death claims him, yet every one he makes somehow breaks or is destroyed whether by accident or supernatural design. As his death hour approaches and his family urge him to leave aside his "folly" and turn to the more important task of saving his soul, Leum panics, his concentration on his dream intensifies and he ignores even the priest who — like doctors with Carden Tyrrell — tries to return him to "normality." To the last, however, Leum refuses to be bound by the constraints of society, and preferring his pie dish he dies vainly pursuing his own notions of wholeness and joy. The priest's verdict is ominous: "He is dead, and 'tis likely he is damned! . . . What folly and vanity there do be in this short world! But what was in this at all? (*Takes up piece of pie-dish.*) What was in this at all?" (*Plays* 2.56).[1] The implication is that Leum's obsession was demonic.

In *The Magic Glasses* Jaymony Shanahan lives as a recluse, upstairs and away from his family, spending all his time gazing into three brown glasses, three red glasses, and three blue glasses, containing between them visions of all the wonders and pleasures of the world. His parents regard him as sick, but it is clear that they also regard him as sinful: "Two months now since he was at church or chapel, and 'tis years since he [has] seen a priest" (*Plays* 1.12). When asked why he lives thus, anti- social and self-indulgent, Jaymony replies:

> Wisha, 'tis better than being in the slush—same old thing every day—this an
> ugly spot, and the people ignorant, grumpy, and savage. (11)

Like Martin Doul in John Millington Synge's *The Well of the Saints*, then, this visionary retreats deliberately into fantasy in condemnation of the terms for living meekly accepted by others. Just as in Synge's play, the visionary in *The Magic Glasses* is not allowed the freedom at once to remain in the society he despises and to exercise or express his anticlerical celebration of beauty. After the doctor figure (actually a quack of awesome presence) fails to cure Jaymony of his dependence on the glasses the family comes to the conclusion that "The devil himself [is] above in the top loft!" (15). They come to the bottom of the rickety stairs and, victims of fantasy themselves, see the horns and hooves of the devil upstairs, smell the brimstone, and see hell's flames. In their hysteria they pull down the stair ladder, killing Jaymony: "Glory be, if it isn't kilt entirely he is, and his jogular cut by the Magic Glasses!" (16). Fitzmaurice finds here an image for the fate of the Irish fantasist. The real enemy, he asserts, is religious fear which insists on absolute conformity. Sean O'Casey was later to take on this same analysis of Irish culture, particularly in *Cock-a-Doodle Dandy* (1959), but Fitzmaurice is less satirical than O'Casey and his priest figures are far less powerful. In Fitzmaurice, the real danger lies in the fierce conservatism of the people themselves. Fitzmaurice was able to imagine such a society as not only violently repressive of the fantastic impulse when that impulse is turned actively into a way of life, but also as absurdly, cravenly in awe of the supernatural and its manifestations. The ending of *The Dandy Dolls*, too long to quote here, bears out this point. There, the people witness what they regard as one more punishment of a wayward fantasist (Roger Carmody), but the form it takes is a triumph for the pagan forces of mischief and elemental energy.

The history of Irish drama after Martyn and Fitzmaurice, each of whom wrote a great deal more than fantasy, shows that where fantasy depends on a central character it also establishes a specific theme and a particular plot structure. The theme, as will be clear from what has been said already, concerns opposition to a community view or culture, a war on the order of the ordinary, whereby the claims of a visionary world are established. As suggested, this theme can be social or political. Where it is political, as in *Maeve*, it veers toward propaganda—or in Yeats's *Cathleen Ni Houlihan* (1902) it more than veers. There the "world elsewhere" which is asserted as primary is a field of experience altogether allegorical; what is gestured toward is a choice, that is, of involvement in history by way of a fight for national independence. That particular theme was later to be mocked by Denis Johnston in *The Old Lady Says 'No!'* (1929) and (less famously) in Maurice Meldon's *Aisling* (1953). Each of these later fantasies is satiric of the Yeatsian ideal. Fantasy thereupon becomes a matter of dramatizing history as nightmare, Ireland as decayed to the point where patriotism is only a front for self-promotion and profiteering. In Johnston's version (discussed below) Yeats's embodiment of Ireland becomes a grotesque hag; in Meldon's version Ireland is still beautiful but up for auction to the highest bidder.

The plot structure of the fantasy plays discussed earlier derive from this theme of a world elsewhere in rivalry with the safety and mundanity of the here and now. One could also instance Yeats's early plays, from *The Land of Heart's Desire* (1894) to *The Shadowy Waters* (1904). There is always this binary structure, even if the other world is far less detailed than the realistic world in which the play is set. It is a world of illusion, a world liberated from the constraints of peasant realism. The title of a later play, Paul Vincent Carroll's *Shadow and Substance* (1937), encapsulates this plot feature. In Carroll's play the visionary simplicity of the young girl Brigid is set against the "substance" of a peasant community terrified of change. It is not Brigid of whom the "ordinary" people are terrified but O'Flingsley, a rebel schoolteacher who has written an inflammatory book under the title *I Am Sir Oracle*. Carroll subtly relates the simple mysticism of Brigid to the idealism of O'Flingsley, and, rather like Fitzmaurice in *The Magic Glasses*, shows how the forces of conservatism combine to destroy the visionary. Carroll resolves the plot by an accident (a stone meant for O'Flingsley kills Brigid), but this is necessary to reinforce the theme. Thus it may be said that the plot of fantasy, in this restricted sense of fantasy, is either didactic or satiric.

A sense of place or setting is also a feature of Irish fantasy. Indeed, it follows quite plainly that if an invisible world is being championed or explored, its contrasting setting must have a local habitation and a name. The lack of just this clearly stated or realizable ordinary world seriously damaged Yeats's early plays. For example, as Frank Fay (among others) protested: "The Theater is a very practical thing; Mr. Yeats is too much a theorist. ... Before he will be even on the road to achiev ing greatness as a dramatic poet, Mr. Yeats must tackle some theme of a great, lasting, and living interest. In Ireland we are at present only too anxious to shun reality" (Fay 51, 52, 53).[2] Thus Edward Martyn's early plays provide a far better model for the development of Irish drama: they have a firm basis in realism, with a setting clearly indicated as the west of Ireland, details of locale being added in *The Heather Field* and *Maeve*.

The much-noted reliance in Irish drama on the trappings of realism some-times blinds readers to the role of fantasy within the setting. In Synge's plays, for example, the flights into creative dream, memory, or future bliss take their force from the contrast with the sordid circumstances and setting from which they emanate: Martin Doul's bleak background at Timmy the Smith's forge offers a striking example; but so, too, do Christy Mahon's lofty transformations of Pegeen Mike and her environment, for as the Widow Quin notes ironically, "There's poetry talk for a girl you'd see itching and scratching, and she with a stale stink of poteen on her from selling in the shop" (Synge, *Playboy* 4, 2.127). The ideal is constructed from a rejection of the real.

The setting and place, however, are usually rejected through the exile or expulsion of the fantasist. We have seen that exit into death or madness is the form taken in the plays of Martyn and Fitzmaurice, as also in Yeats's and in Synge's tragedies; in comedies the exit is to another locale, looked forward to as infinitely preferable and more sustaining. The "come away" motif of the tramp at the end of *In the Shadow of the Glen* (1903) conjures up a way of life straight out of the pastoral world. Nora's wry reply indicates that she is not blind to the harshness and severity that must also be implied:

> I'm thinking it's myself will be wheezing that time with lying down under the Heavens when the night is cold, but you've a fine bit of talk, stranger, and it's with yourself I'll go. (Synge 3.57)

So, too, at the end of *The Well of the Saints* (1905) Martin Doul exits with Mary to freedom and a new life, but realistically:

> There's a power of deep rivers with floods in them where you do have to be lepping the stones and you going to the south, so I'm thinking the two of them will be drowned together in a short while, surely. (3.151)

As Synge envisages Irish society, however, it is better to drown like this than suffer the slower suffocation of unimaginative "settled" living. The gesture by which Martin Doul dashes the saint's can of holy water to the ground describes an energetic repudiation not only of orthodoxy but also of its healing agents. Such subversiveness inevitably implies exile.

O'Casey uses the same kind of exile motif in his fantasies, especially in *Cock-a-Doodle Dandy* and *Behind the Green Curtain* (1961). In O'Casey, however, Ireland as a whole is repudiated; nature alone does not provide a viable alternative to Ireland's social repressiveness. The rebel, whom O'Casey champions, must seek fulfillment and freedom in another country. The problem with this use of place, so far as dramatists of the 1950s and after were concerned, is that exile implies no problems.

The later playwrights are more sociologically aware. In the plays of M. J. Molloy—such as *The Old Road* (1943) and *The Wood of the Whispering* (1953)—emigration is a painful and distressing alternative to domestic deprivation. This, too, is the attitude of John B. Keane in *Many Young Men of Twenty* (1961) and *Hut 42* (1962). Brian Friel probably puts this point strongest of all from *The Enemy Within* (1962) onwards: exile is a heartrendering experience, the cost of which elevates the homeland in spite of its deficiencies. Indeed, the pain of enforced exile, in the plays of Keane and Friel (up to and including *The Gentle Island* (1971), registers the failure of Irish society to *be a patria*, a fostering, paternal force. "Place" becomes dislocation, which in turn becomes an accusation of mismanagement.

The role of language must also be taken into account. Here a distinction may be made between realism and formalism. For the most part, the drama before national independence never used formalism, and fantasy operated either within the parameters of naturalism or else as an element in poetic drama, such as that of W. B. Yeats. O'Casey was the first Irish playwright to allow fantasy to modify the form itself, as in his one-act play *Kathleen Listens In* (1923).

In *The Plough and the Stars* (1926), moreover, he wrote in the expressionistic mode as much as in the realistic, a point Denis Johnston acutely observed in his contemporary review (*O'Casey* 82-85).[3] Yet it is to Johnston himself one must turn to find the first comprehensive formalist play in which fantasy and satire blend and fuse totally. The language of *The Old Lady Says 'No!'* is parodic. The first few pages of the text comprise a virtual anthology of nineteenth-century romantic Irish verse (Canfield 479-81), which in the mouths of Robert Emmet and Sarah Curran serves to mock romanticism in history as in love. The language parodies an established literary tradition. Whether or not Johnston's title also makes fun of Lady Gregory as the "old Lady" of the Irish theater, the play undisguisedly mocks Yeats and his *Cathleen ni Houlihan*. The Flower Woman, an aged street seller, goes about calling for her four "bewtyful gre-in fields . . . . Penny a bunch th' gre-in fields" (32-33), in clear parody of Yeats's lines:

> *Old Woman*: I have had trouble indeed.
> *Bridget*: What was it put the trouble on you?
> *Old Woman*: My land that was taken from me.
> *Peter*: Was it much land they took from you?
> *Old Woman*: My four beautiful green fields.
>
> (*Plays* 81)

The "four beautiful green fields," of course, represent Ireland. Johnston mocks Yeats's romantic conception of sacrifice and heroism by transforming the line into the shrieking of a latter-day harridan. The language of Synge and O'Casey is also mocked as part of Johnston's exposure of contemporary Ireland's preoccupation with rhetoric. *The Old Lady Says 'No!'* is a tour de force of mockery and fantasy, since the form of the play borrows from Pirandello, whereas the commentary it offers on Ireland after the Civil War takes seriously Yeats's own rueful admission in "Meditations in Time of Civil War" about the heart "fed . . . on fantasies" from which it has "grown brutal" (*Poems* 230). The language of fantasy had never before in Irish drama operated in so devastating a style as in Johnston's precocious antimelodrama.

The distance from Martyn's *The Heather Field* (1899) to John B. Keane's *The Field* (1965) — a tale of a sordid rural murder to gain possession of a field — measures the extent of Irish drama's journey away from romanticism. By the mid-1960s, when *The Field* was first staged, Ireland had become industrialized and was beginning to shed most if not all of Martyn's kind of idealism. True, after the death of Yeats there were still occasional fantasies in the theater, such as Michael MacLiammoir's *Where Stars Walk* (1940), Donagh McDonagh's *Happy as Larry* (1946), or Jack B. Yeats's *In Sand* (1949). But such plays, together with the poetic fantasies of Austin Clarke and the brilliant satire of Maurice Meldon's *Aisling*, made no impact on the dominant taste for realism-as-mirror. Fantasy in Denis Johnston's terms (*The Old Lady Says 'No!'*) had no future, as the fate of even his own *A Bride for the Unicorn* (1933) too plainly shows: it failed miserably at the Gate Theater and Johnston gave up mythic fantasy for good.

Most recent playwrights, however, especially Brian Friel, Thomas Murphy, Thomas Kilroy, Stewart Parker, and Tom Mac Intyre, have returned to fantasy as part of their much less tolerant attitude toward audience comfort and mass opinion. Apart from Mac Intyre, easily the most experimental of contemporary Irish playwrights, all of those named integrate fantasy into a firmly realistic mode. The general purpose is at least twofold: to dramatize a consciousness at odds with authority or dominant social ideas; and to criticize or attack that same authority or those same dominant social ideas. For example, in Friel's plays from *Philadelphia, Here I Come!* (1964) on, the self is presented as divided into public and private forms. The private self lives on memories, recreated as fantasies; the public self tries in vain to accommodate to an unsympathetic environment. As in the earlier form of Irish drama, in Martyn's *The Heather Field*, the imaginative misfit serves to suggest the narrowness and repressiveness of the values against which he rebels. The difference is that now the rebellion, being hopeless, is secret; it is also thereby psychologically damaging in a general sense. Friel shows in several of his plays the cost of authoritarianism. More than once, also he awards the blame to the Catholic clergy, whose job it is, as he puts it in *Philadelphia*, to "translate all this loneliness, this groping, this dreadful bloody buffoonery into Christian terms that will make life bearable for us all" (96). (The charge against the clergy is more strongly put in *Living Quarters*, 1977, where the priest is a drunkard.) Unlike the characters in Fitzmaurice's plays the hero in Friel's and his successors' plays is not driven mad or broken by society: he is usually young, intelligent, happy-go-lucky, and determined to beat the system. In short, he is an anti-hero of our time. Thomas Murphy's John Joe Moran is a typical example, in *A Crucial Week in the Life of a Grocer's Assistant* (1969).

Although John Joe resembles Friel's Gar O'Donnell to a considerable extent, the real link is with Tennessee Williams's Tom Wingfield in *The Glass Menagerie* (1945). John Joe is in conflict with his nagging mother rather than (as in Friel) with his authoritarian father. He does not so much take refuge in dreams (like Gar O'Donnell) as experience certain dreams in bed that characterize the nature of his oppression. (The dream scenes in this play are more Freudian than anything to be found in Friel.) Murphy notes that on stage these scenes must be registered as dream states: *"Unusual lighting suggests the unreality of the dream scenes: movement and speech become stylized and the characters become caricatures"* (*Grocer* 10). One scene in particular (8) is a surrealistic one, in which all the characters who torment John Joe – including the priest, his former employer, his associates, and his girlfriend – participate in an expressionistic series of assaults, verbal as well as physical. In the course of the scene Mr. Brown, the employer who gave him the sack, repeats his dismissive cry, "You're only . . . a dreamer!" (44), which is exactly the accusation

Amanda Wingfield flung at Tom when he quit his job and walked out at the end of *The Glass Menagerie*.

The difference between the two plays, however, is not only (obviously) that Murphy has no Laura but also that John Joe Moran stays rather than runs away. Here is Murphy's most original dramatic statement in this play. He presents a hero who neither goes mad nor emigrates but who stands his ground, cries out in the public street all the home truths which shame his family, and thereby liberates himself. Murphy finds a way of cutting through the Joycean "nets" of religion and social tyranny which keep Irish youth imprisoned. The gesture may recall Martin Doul's, but the context is entirely new and the result is strikingly different, as existentialist revolt finds a new voice in the Irish theater. Fantasy plays its part in this "finding" process inasmuch as fantasy registers the pressure under which imaginative man is placed; to ease that pressure the hero must abolish fantasy, even if he was energized by it, and take his place among his oppressors as a free man.

A similar liberation process, worked out in diverse and more complex forms, can be seen at work in Murphy's *The Morning After Optimism* (1971) and *The Gigli Concert* (1983). Suffice it to say that in these plays, as in Thomas Kilroy's *Tea and Sex and Shakespeare* (1976) or in Stewart Parker's *Nightshade* (1980), the modern Irish hero is no longer overcome because he is a fantasist. On the contrary, the richness and sensitivity of his personality are vindicated through a form of fantasy which, far from being a symptom of weakness or derangement, allows him the stature of a visionary who *has* a gesture to make which is positive and life-enhancing.

The fantasist in Irish drama today, operating within the framework of realism, is a subversive who offers audiences a dream of an alternative, more tolerable life, magically but humanly transformed. In that regard, it can be said that contemporary Irish drama favors "engagement" over "disengagement," to use the terms Kathryn Hume employs about the effects of fantasy (57). Hugh Leonard is the exception here: his plays luxuriate in a fantasy that folds back upon itself, as in *Madigan's Lock* or *The Mask of Moriarty* (1985). In general, however, Irish playwrights now use fantasy to alert audiences to images of a world elsewhere within reach of the striving spirit.

Notes

1. Howard K. Slaughter, who edited and wrote the introduction for volume 2, *Folk Plays*, includes *The Pie Dish* with the folk plays rather than with the fantasies, but the categorization of Fitzmaurice's plays is notoriously difficult. See McGuinness (27-29), and Achilles.

2. The date of the review is 4 May 1901.

3. Johnston concluded: "As a realist he is an impostor. . . . His dialogue is becoming

a series of word-poems in dialect; his plots are disappearing and giving place to a form of undisguised expressionism" (85).

Works Cited

Achilles, Jochen. "George Fitzmaurice's Dramatic Fantasies: Wicked Old Children in a Disenchanting Land." *Irish University Review* 15 (1985): 148-163.

Canfield, Curtis. "Titles and Authors of Poems Used in the Prologue of 'The Old Lady Says "No!".'" In *Plays of Changing Ireland*, Appendix B: 479-481. New York: Macmillan, 1936.

Coyle, William. "Introduction: The Nature of Fantasy." In *Aspects of Fantasy: Selected Essays from the Second International Conference on the Fantastic in Literature and Film*. Westport, CT: Greenwood Press, 1982.

Fay, Frank J. *Towards a National Theatre*. ed. Robert Hogan. Dublin: Dolmen Press, 1970.

Fitzmaurice, George. *The Plays of George Fitzmaurice*. 2 vols. Dublin: Dolmen Press, 1967-1969.

Friel, Brian. *Philadelphia, Here I Come!* London: Faber and Faber, 1965.

Gassner, John. *New Directions in Modern Theatre and Drama*. New York: Holt, Rinehart and Winston, 1966.

Gregory, Lady [Augusta]. *Our Irish Theatre*. Gerrards Cross, Bucks.: Colin Smythe, 1972.

Hume, Kathryn. *Fantasy and Mimesis: Representations of Reality in Western Literature*. New York: Methuen, 1984.

Johnston, Denis. *"The Old Lady Says 'No!'"* Vol. 1. *The Dramatic Works of Denis Johnston*. Gerrards Cross, Bucks.: Colin Smythe, 1977.

—-. "Sean O'Casey: An Appreciation (1926)." In *Sean O'Casey: Modern Judgements*, ed. Ronald Ayling. London: Macmillan, 1969; Nashville: Aurora, 1970.

Martyn, Edward. *The Heather Field and Maeve*. London: Duckworth, 1899.

McGuinness, Arthur E. *George Fitzmaurice*. Lewisburg: Bucknell University Press, 1975.

Murphy, Thomas, *A Crucial Week in the Life of a Grocer's Assistant*. Dublin: Gallery Books, 1978.

Synge, J. M. *Collected Works*. Vols. 3 and 4. Gen. ed. Robin Skelton. London: 1962-1968.

Tremayne, Peter, ed. *Irish Masters of Fantasy*. Dublin: Wolfhound Press, 1974.

Yeats, W. B. *The Collected Plays of W. B. Yeats*. London: Macmillan, 1952.

—-. *The Collected Poems of W. B. Yeats*. London: Macmillan, 1963.

"My Unshatterable Friend of Clay": Fantasy in the Paintings of Jack B. Yeats

The original meaning of the term fantasy comes from the Greek "phantasia," meaning "a making apparent," a movement of the imagination which is capable of containing truth without limit. In modern English the term has been watered down to suggest something considerably less substantial — a whimsy or hallucination without foundation in solid fact.[1] The poet and painter Æ (George Russell) must have had this in mind when he admitted to William Byrne in 1901: "I started from the stars and never succeeded in getting my feet firmly on the earth, but if you start from the earth you can go as far as you like" (Letter). He had observed the new mood among the young Irish writers then emerging. They were bypassing the impersonal world of myth — that had preoccupied him and W. B. Yeats — to come down to earth in search of genuine people and actual happenings (Yeats 52-53). John M. Synge, for one, in his preface to *The Playboy of the Western World* (1907) was sure that a writer could be free and inventive in his use of words, "and at the same time . . . give reality, which is at the root of all poetry, in a comprehensive and natural form" (184). For him, poetry — like timber — has its roots in clay and words,[2] and the poet could be brutal to be authentic.

The term fantasy is not generally applied to the work of Irish artists around the turn of the century. They tended to be conservative, even in their illustration of legend. But a spirit of imaginative reality was developing among Irish artists of the generation of Synge, who were tired of the world of myth and saw possibilities for subject matter in the genuine understanding of their own country. No one brought the ability to observe life to such a high level of imagination as Jack B. Yeats, who was Synge's exact contemporary, although he outlived him by half a century, dying in 1957. Yeats, at all stages of his career, sought to "make apparent" what was beyond the naked eye: but, like Synge, he was only too aware of the brutality which is as much a part of life as beauty is.

In his early years as a black-and-white artist, he was infected by the fairy-tale world of Dick Doyle, contributing elvish borders and caricatures to *The Vegetarian* at the age of seventeen. These gave way to similarly comic but tough cartoons of sporting events in the nineties. Such impish reportage was counter-balanced by the humorous fantasy of his pirate illustrations and watercolors, which, with the help of the English writer, John Masefield, grew into a verbal and visual legend (Pyle "Letter" 43-47).

But the main body of Jack B. Yeats's work was developing in a new direction for Irish art: for, while he lived in Devon and made studies of farming life there, from 1898 he determined to make Irish life, as it was lived by the people in the west of Ireland, his concern. About the same time as Synge, who was coming from Wicklow and Paris to live for periods among Aran farmers and fishermen, Yeats came from Devon, via Liverpool and Dublin, to view the townspeople of Sligo – among whom he had grown up as a boy – with a new eye.

His drawings and watercolors of races and fairs, of local personalities such as the squireen and the cow doctor, or of various hardened or fallen characters, image in an uncanny fashion the idealism and the reality of western Ireland before the 1916 Easter Rising. This phase of his work came to a climax in his book of illustrations, *Life in the West of Ireland* (1912), and the oil paintings carried out for George Birmingham's *Irishman All*.

However, along with a genuine sympathy for the pleasures and hardships and humanity of the people Yeats portrayed, the seeds of a growing dream can be seen, which in the end he could only express in a fantastical way. Yeats himself felt the imaginative stimulation of melodrama and music-hall theater from the time of his first arrival in London as a schoolboy to live with his family in Bedford Park. Before that, romance had touched his life in Sligo, where he lived for long stretches with his grandparents and heard tales of tropical places from the sailors on the quays, or learned of the colorful doings of returned Americans during their emigrant years. The eyes of the traveler silhouetted against his native peninsula in *Memory Harbour* are filled with a vision beyond the immediate happenings on the shore behind him.[3] The vision is not one of myth, but derives from an experience private to himself, inspired by a real world, where imagination has as much place as common sense.

Perhaps the best way of understanding Jack Yeats's blend of reality and imagination or fantasy is to compare one of his watercolors of a musician with some illustrations of musicians worked by his father a few years before. J. B. Yeats (1839-1922), who spent his life in the shadow of his more famous sons, W. B. and Jack, abandoned portraiture for illustration during the 1890s, and contributed full-page wash drawings to *The Leisure Hour* from time to time. *Music's Golden Tongue* (1894) shows a girl wearing a kerchief, listening to a boy with sailor's cap playing a concertina (43. 546). The following year, *Music Hath Charms* (1895) has a similar girl, though this time probably modeled on his daughter Lily, who posed for most of his drawings, sitting on a grassy bank, herself playing a concertina, watched by three cows and a hare (44. 49). The third drawing – and they are so close as to seem to form a series – is of a peasant girl sitting on a bog, playing a concertina, watched by cows. It is called *Never Less Alone Than When Alone* (1897) (46. 682). The drawings are very much in the Victorian mode, as evidenced in Anglo-Irish illustrations, being romantic but slightly heroic as well. They all call up twilight, a grassy bank, water, and youth to create the mood of wistful melancholy. In these, J. B. Yeats starts "from the stars," as Æ did in his poetry; though he was quick to replace his feet on the ground when he returned to portrait painting shortly afterwards.

Jack B. Yeats's musicians, worked in water-color at the end of the same decade and the beginning of the next, have, by contrast, a rough reality, treated in his individualistic manner, which was then developing and readjusting itself all the time. *The Melodeon Player* (1903) (figure 3) sits on a wooden bench placed against the whitewashed wall of a room in a cottage, tapping his foot, glancing at some unseen dancers or company with half his attention, but engrossed in his wheezy music. He is perhaps a sailor, the member of the crew who was known and revered in those times as "the music." His comrade looking through the door at him, hand stuffed in pocket, has the same rough reality observed by the artist during his tours of the west. But between their heads a note of romance or fantasy is suggested. "The Belle of the Pacific" is drawn almost humorously, seeming indignant at her placement between two such ruffians. Her position is obviously crucial, since the artist had originally put her to the right of the musician, and on second thoughts centered her. (The pentimento is still visible to the right of the melodeon player's head.) So through the spirit of the music, the dreams of the two seafaring men are encapsulated in a romantic, unrealistic image of a far-off beauty with a flower in her hair.

Arthur Symons pinpointed Jack B. Yeats's way of linking reality and fantasy when he reviewed his London exhibition in 1905. He likened the display of forty water-color sketches, hanging "in happy confusion," to "a child's paradise." He was not altogether complimentary. "There is next to no drawing, and the colour, though it has often a queer kind of emotion, is often mere fun." But he was very aware of the vitality which pictured what he called "the drunk and disorderly side of existence." "In his way," Symons commented, "he is as much a visionary as his brother; but while Mr. W. B. Yeats sees heroic and fairy things with delicate precision, Mr. Jack Yeats sees all the real and unreal world of a boy's romance, and he renders them like the maker of penny toys" (225). The critic liked best the village scenes and characters; and approved of the artist's uncontrived manner. "He means something," was his conclusion, "and we catch his meaning. Mr. Yeats is like a dumb man who can only explain himself by signs; but he does it so gaily and so well that he tells you at least all he wants to, and amuses you mightily into the bargain" (225).

"He means something" seems to be one explanation of this Irish tendency to draw fantasy from what is real and experienced. That Yeats meant something is obvious from the vantage point of hindsight. He, with youthful energy, attempted to capture in his watercolors all the aspects of work and recreation, of idealism and imperfection that he found in his part of the west. It was a pictorial realization of the Ireland which had every expectation of at last becoming independent — if political developments were anything to go by. He

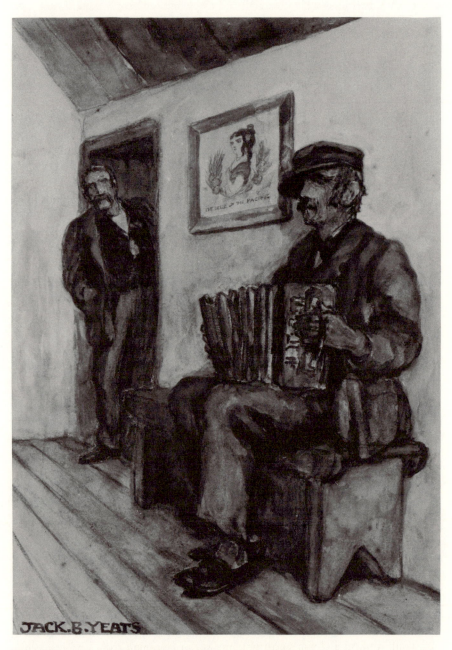

Figure 3. Jack B. Yeats, *The Melodeon Player*, 1903

was probably not yet aware of what he meant: but he was working out a theme, and he was making signs that were interpretable by his contemporaries.

Later in life Yeats invited the spectator to interpret what—in his mature work—were vastly less orthodox signs. Marilyn Gaddis Rose has commented that "his paintings bewitch us and his writings dumbfound us. The qualities which in his painting lead from complexity to beauty and, hence, to pleasurable satisfaction in the viewer," she says, "in his writing lead from complexity to confusion and, hence, to amused exasperation in the reader and spectator. With paint Yeats achieves harmony and completeness; with words, disharmony and incompleteness" (93). If this is true, is it because, if painted, we can accept an image or a sign instantly, whereas in prose we await an explanation? *Death for Only One* (1937) is a haunting scene of a man standing over his fallen companion on a moor. We are shown no more than that. We can interpret it as an incident in war, as the result of violence or an accident, or as natural death: but the purport rather than the explanation of the visual image is projected in the highly charged title.

In Jack Yeats's play *La La Noo* (1943), on the other hand, death seems trivial and a useless waste because it is particularized in the narrative. The Stranger, in order to give a lift to some woman stranded in the rain, takes out a truck which—because he has never driven before—crashes into a tree, and he is killed. There is no high point to death here. His chivalrous action appears negative and baffling. And yet, as Robin Skelton points out, the theme of the play, which the author hints at here and there, is not the actual event which dumbfounds us, but the frailty of life and the inevitability of death. The play, he indicates, "uses realism in the interests of symbolism, and does not attempt esotericism or prophecy" (263).

This reasoning can be applied to both the paintings and writings of Jack Yeats. Realism, which is always at the root of his imagery, is used in the interests of symbolism and very often at the level of fantasy in his late work. He found this first in his circus paintings. Circuses as he knew them in boyhood in Sligo widened a knowledge of the world beyond the immediate locality. They brought life and excitement into an enclosed society. Even the entry of the circus into the country town was staged in a ritual fashion. His early pictures of circus processions project a sense of wonder at this parade of "Challengers of the World," as he referred to the circus performers in his book *Sligo* (1930) (124).

Circus imagery could be a means of expressing joy in late paintings like *They Come, They Come*, or the carefree *Clown of Ocean* (1945). In this last, a grotesque bare-legged buffoon, rather like a joking skeleton in harlequin dress, punts his way across the waves toward the horizon. The image derives tenuously—inflated to an extreme of fantasy—from the ship's entertainment he describes in his novel, *The Careless Flower* (1947). The second steward, he tells us, would put on a clown's costume and give a one-man show on board ship, with various homemade musical instruments, imitating an old gaffer with a red-spotted handkerchief and clay pipe, or his wife with no teeth—"an old world touch of old-world clown of ocean" (60).

Circus imagery also matured into something tragic in his middle period clown paintings, such as *The Singing Clown* and *The Clown Among the People;* and in the symbolic late work, *The Great Tent Has Collapsed* (1947). The idea of the tent in this last had been teasing his mind for years, as we see from a passage in *Sligo* of 1930: "Let the Beginning be in a circular confined place," he wrote, "a circus tent. There is nothing like a circus tent, I mean a single pole tent, the double pole tent has its dark corners, and its mystery. But it's not so complete as the old single pole whirl-a-gig round and round, over the garters and through the balloons" (34). In *The Careless Flower* he went even farther. Not content with seeing the tent as the birthplace of creation, he invested it with a celestial significance in the phrase: "circus tent above the great round dish of grey-blue sea" (130).

Such a symbol intimated in the title swells the power of *The Great Tent Has Collapsed*, painted in the same year that *The Careless Flower* was published. The artist himself may be equated with the ringmaster, that remote and majestic figure of his early drawings, in the oil painting bereft of all his dignity as the great tent is swept away from over his head by a gale. The spectators flee to safety. In his flapping, shabby, tailed coat, he strides forward into an empty field, watched only by a curious bystander — who again may be taken to be the artist. (Yeats had a habit in his late period paintings of including himself as a detached observer.) Here the suggestion and the setting he knows, and of the artist who looks on, have an appropriate irony. The picture was painted shortly after the death of the artist's wife in April 1947.

Yeats also found fantasy in melodrama and in the music-hall, which he attended in search of themes. He enjoyed the absurdities of booth performances, reveling in one he saw in New York, where the hero leapt into a real water tank in order to save the heroine; he depicted it in his drawing, *In a Booth Theatre* in *Life in the West of Ireland* . He wrote his own melodramas for his model theater, and published three of them. "We reel away from a Theatre, where we have been watching a crook- drama, with more grateful hearts than from a Thinking Drama, where the Author had to think hard to write it, and the Actors and Actresses, had to think very hard indeed to thrill things into it," he wrote in *Sligo* (42). Late in life, he painted *The Student of Drama* as a melancholy Hamlet, brooding over his lines outside a booth theater. Anticipation of fantasy to come could give mystery to the dim interior of *The Ticket Office* of 1949.

In the title of another painting, *He Will Not Sign*, the artist transfers melodrama to a scene of real life, which portrays the mental anguish of a man reaching the limits of his endurance. The drama is heightened by contrasting the macabre figures who threaten him with the serene landscape stretching beyond them through the window.

His painting of a Christy Minstrel music-hall act, in *Singing "Way Down Upon the Swanee River"* (1912), similarly underlines how narrow the gap is between fantasy and reality. The Negro minstrel of the Great American Circus is as tragicomic a symbol as the more familiar clown of these islands. Yeats had already used the act as the theme of a pastel in 1900: and in *Sligo* he introduced the simile, "sitting, like a half hoop of Christy Minstrels on a Music Hall stage" (41), the image he adopted for the painting of twelve years later, where the chorus is grouped in a semicircle about the singer of the song. The picture has yet a further dimension when we recall his words elsewhere, describing the Minstrels' faces as "not Masks, they are the faces of our brothers, our own faces made all awry" (132).

About to Write a Letter (1935) (figure 4), like *Death for Only One* mentioned earlier, through the force of the title decides the direction of emphasis for a fairly straightforward image. The picture is melodramatic in its use of a rich ruby color in the foreground, the emerald green heightened with chrome yellow on the back wall, and the obviously theatrical pose of the man portrayed. It has all the artificial traits that excited Yeats when he attended music halls in his youth. The painting takes its theme from a small book produced by Masefield and Yeats in 1906. *The Fancy* — the name derives from the word "fantasy," and was used in the early nineteenth century to denote those who "fancy" a particular sport, especially pugilism — was a collection of poems originally published by John Hamilton Reynolds, a close friend of Keats. Reynolds was wild and dissolute as a young man, a member of "The Fancy," and found himself in a predicament when he wanted to marry and had to abandon the carefree existence that appealed to him. Under the guise of "Peter Corcoran" he bade farewell to the wild days, as well as to his career as a creative writer. It was probably Yeats who divined that Reynolds was the author of Peter Corcoran's *The Fancy*, since he had been taking an interest in his work (Pyle "Letter" 46), but it was Masefield who edited the volume and wrote the introduction, while Jack Yeats provided the illustrations. The young man with the ghastly complexion in *About to Write a Letter* — painted thirty years after the book was published — bears a striking resemblance to the dying Corcoran of *The Fancy* illustrations. He averts his eyes from the swan-like portrait of a young woman on the wall, dominating the shadowy sketches of racehorses and sportsmen, and looks down at the paper and pen lying on his table.

Yeats does not seek to explain the painting, and might well dismiss the reference to his Corcoran illustrations as irrelevant. The emotional struggle which he so brilliantly portrays in a single melodramatic moment — a moment of fantasy — should more aptly be paralleled with Vermeer's *The Letter*, where through the simple image of a girl writing and the subtlety of the few details of the room where she sits, a baroque allegory of love is created. But Yeats's title is important, as it is in all his late paintings. It suggests the moment of hesitation, the doubt, and emotional anguish that may be experienced in many another situation of choice: and so carries the picture beyond the actual image to something broader and infinitely more subtle than the visual narrative proposes. Fantasy, as we see, does not exclude the suffering imposed by separation, or by

Figure 4. Jack B. Yeats, *About to Write a Letter*, 1935

104

Figure 5.   Jack B. Yeats, *A Race in Hy Brazil*, 1937

Figure 6. Jack B. Yeats, *On the Move*, 1950

death or old age – because it is grounded in real existence for Jack B. Yeats. All his paintings of the later period rely on memory for inspiration, aided by his numerous sketchbooks, and of course the constant habit of observation which kept his art fresh and exploratory. "The distortions," notes Robin Skelton, "are less the product of a fallible memory than of an intention to transform, dignify, dramatize, and elucidate the actual, and cast over it 'a colouring of the imagination'" (256). Thus the strand races of Sligo in the 1880s were lifted by Yeats in 1937 into the magical setting of the island of old Irish lore, *Hy Brazil* (1937; figure 5). Hy Brazil was another *Tír na nÓg*, or Land of Eternal Youth. The artist transforms and casts "a colouring of the imagination" over what he remembers in his book, *Ah Well* (1942), when he is musing on childhood, and with his imagination conjures up his "oldest friend" – "my unshatterable friend of clay," "he is the small man come away from his setting" – who sits on his table, casually dangling a leg while they chat (5).

But in the same book Yeats makes it clear that fantasy, or as he also calls it, romance, is not to be sought hiding under stones, nor is it smeared on the surface like facial makeup. It is hot and flows in the air. It is composed of sweat and sin. "Where there is Romance," he states in *Ah Well* (1942), "there is the grain, the seed of the charlock bui the wild gold weed of a free sovereign people growing. It was in Mother Eve's Garden and when the snake came sliding he circled it" (7). In this, he echoes his brother's musings on the fantasies in "Meditations in Time of Civil War" (1923), which W. B. Yeats warned wryly had led to the subsequent brutalities.

Jack Yeats does not represent sin or violence so harshly or crudely as some of the present-day Irish expressionists do, in their rather different forms of fantasy. He provides powerful visual metaphors for war in *The Tinkers' Encampment: The Blood of Abel* (1941), for violence in *Humanity's Alibi*, for guilt in *The Face in Shadow:* yet in all he is conscious of the "great arc of indigo" he refers to in *Ah Well* (5) and elsewhere that stands behind them, everlasting, never fading and which vividly related his art to his spiritual thinking.

So fantasy in his late paintings is fantasy with a definite message. *Rise Up Willy Reilly* (1945) shows a ballad singer singing to a boy, with much the same elements of composition as might be found in an early broadsheet illustration by the artist, and certainly recalling the shawled ballad singers who thronged fairs and race meetings in his early days. But the girl's shawl has become a mantilla which she holds out like a veil about her head. She stands in a mountain landscape that sings with color, her eyes alight at some invisible marvel, while the boy sinks to his feet, his hands clasped to his breast. The invitation to Willy Reilly to come away is now transformed into something far deeper and more far-reaching.

Men of Destiny (1946), of the following year, shows some fishermen mooring their boat on a western peninsula and walking up the point in the evening light, their bodies illuminated with color. Even without the telling title, the radiance of the figures and the sunset landscape speak for themselves of vision. These

Figure 7. Jack B. Yeats, *For the Road,* 1951

are followed by a series of celebratory paintings such as *Fag a Bhothar*, *Follow My Leader*, *Music of the Morning*, and *Shouting* (Pyle "There is no night" 37), which, through the medium of music used more realistically in his early water-colors, create a fantasy of joy, itself a metaphor for some invisible spiritual reality. A child appears repeatedly in Yeats's late visionary landscapes. An image suggesting hope from the time of his first oil paintings, the child or youth is seen in *On the Move* (1950) (figure 6) as a symbol of life to come. A stranger passing in shadow on the fantasy moor takes his hat off to the small boy who waves in the sunlight as he passes. The boy dances on his way, and yet his eyes and expression are serious and wise.

On occasion the metaphor can be more specific. *For the Road* (1951) (figure 7), through the horse responding to the call of its master at the end of an avenue of trees, imagines the spiritual bond between the real and the unseen worlds — in much the same way as Stephen Spender envisaged it in his poem, "I Think Continually of Those." The truly great, from the womb, "remembered the soul's history through corridors of light."

While Yeats's very individual approach can be seen to have influenced the artists who came after him in different ways, the greatest effect his paintings had was to open Irish art to forms of fantasy, which had their origin in personal experience. Artists like Nano Reid, or Patrick Collins, or Alicia Boyle could feel free to paint landscape or imaginative subjects outside traditional perspective and idiom. Mary Swanzy, after a period with Post-impressionism, evolved a personal style of fantasy as erratic in its references as that of Yeats. His influence was felt, even after his long career came to an end in 1957, until the first *Rosc* exhibition in Dublin ten years later turned Irish art to international trends and post-painterly abstraction.

A new generation of artists, though, is now beginning to look at reality again, as a starting point for imaginative expression. There has been a revived emphasis on figure drawing, which has led to vigorous representational canvases and sculptures, imbued with an element of fantasy, underlined with irony. Interestingly, the inspiration of Padraic O Flaihearta, exhibiting only for the past two years, derives directly from his background on Aran Mor in the Aran Islands, where he grew up. Curraghs and crayfish are the principal sources for imagery in his fantasy drawings and sculptures. Their distinctive shapes are still faintly recognizable. But they are always conceived in huge, partial forms whose completeness depends on a movement of the imagination to make them apparent. Perhaps he would agree with what Yeats had to say to Shotaro Oshima when he visited him in Dublin in 1938. Yeats told Oshima, "Even in mere phantasy there often are things inseparable from truth, or things more real than reality itself. It is the very world a true artist lives in" (55).

Notes

1. This definition is based upon that given in the *Oxford English Dictionary*.

2. Compare Paul Klee's simile of the tree/artist in his treatise, *On Modern Art* (13ff).

3. J. White and H. Pyle, *Jack B. Yeats: A Centenary Exhibition*, no. 18, repro. (34), 1971. Many of the paintings referred to in this article are reproduced in this catalogue.

Works Cited

Klee, Paul. *On Modern Art*. 1924 London: Faber and Faber, 1966.

Pyle, Hilary. "About to Write a Letter," *Irish Arts Review* 2, no. 1 (Spring 1985): 43-47.

—-. "There Is No Night," *Irish Arts Review* 3, no. 2 (Summer 1986): .

——, and J. Rose, Marilyn Gaddis. "Mixed Metaphors: Jack B. Yeats's Writings," in *Jack B. Yeats: A Centenary Gathering*, ed. Roger McHugh, 92-106. Dublin: The Dolmen Press, 1971.

Russell, George W. [Æ]. Letter to William Byrne. Letters from G. W. Russell transcribed by Alan Denson. MS. 9967- 9969. Dublin: National Library of Ireland.

Skelton, Robin. "Unarrangeable Reality: The Paintings and Writings of Jack B. Yeats," in *The World of W. B. Yeats*, eds. Robin Skelton and Ann Saddlemyer. Dublin: The Dolmen Press, 1965.

Symons, Arthur. Review. *Outlook*, 18 February 1905.

Synge, John Millington. *Dramatic Works of J. M. Synge*. Dublin: Maunsel, 1921.

White, J. and Hylary Pyle. *Jack B. Yeats: A Centenary Exhibition*. Dublin, New York: Martin Secker & Warburg, 1971.

Yeats, J. B. "Music's Golden Tongue," *Leisure Hour* 43 (1894):546.

—-. "Music Hath Charms," *Leisure Hour*. 44 (1895):49

—-. "Never Less Alone Than When Alone," *Leisure Hour*. 46 (1897):682

Yeats, Jack B. *Ah Well: a Romance in Perpetuity*. London: George Routledge & Sons, 1942.

—-. *The Careless Flower*. London: The Pilot Press, 1947.

—-. *La La Noo*. Dublin: The Cuala Press, 1943.

—-. *Life in the West of Ireland*. Dublin: Maunsel and Company, Ltd., 1912.

—-. *Sligo*. London: Wishart & Co., 1930.

—-. "Interview with Jack Butler Yeats." By Shotaro Oshima. *Jack B. Yeats: A Centenary Gathering*, ed. Roger McHugh. Dublin: The Dolmen Press, 1971.

Yeats, W. B. *Imaginations and Reveries*. Dublin: Maunsel and Company, Ltd., 1921.

Péter Egri

John Field's Imaginative Achievement: Parallels with Chopin, Shelley, and Turner

In 1836, a year before the death of the talented Irish composer John Field, Robert Schumann wrote an enthusiastic assessment of Field's *Piano Concerto No. 7*:

> I am full of it, and can think of hardly anything sensible to say about it except unending praise. Away with your forms and your thorough-bass conventions! Your schoolroom desks were carved from the cedar of genius, and not just once! Do your duty, i.e. have talent, be Fields, write as you wish, be poets and persons, I beg you! (Schumann 2:106)

Expounding the principles of his romantic aesthetics, Schumann hails here the Irish composer as an authentic talent. This is high praise from a high place, extended with a mixture of emotional *Aufschwung* and witty irony, not unlike the disposition of the scherzo movements of Schumann's *First* and *Fourth Symphonies*, and lavished by the romantic composer-critic of *Fantasiestücke* on a fellow-"fantasist" (Schumann 1:45).

Schumann's praise of Field is all the more significant since it is in sharp contrast with the typical nineteenth-century appraisal of English music by German critics, who usually looked upon England as "the land without music" (Raynor 137). While this evaluation is somewhat rash and harsh, it is undeniably true that throughout the eighteenth and nineteenth centuries native imaginative music in England (Arne, Boyce, Stanley, Crotch, Hook, Bennett, and even the work of such a distinguished initiator of a musical revival in the second half of the nineteenth century as Parry) was far less important than realistic fiction based on rational, critical, utilitarian, and ameliorative norms (Defoe, Richardson, Fielding, Smollett, the Brontë sisters, Dickens, Thackeray, or George Eliot).

The tentative tendency of a reciprocal relationship between the relative importance of music and fiction can be observed in other periods of British culture as well. The golden age of British music (Dunstable, Tallis, Byrd,

Morley, Dowland, Weelkes, Wilbye, and Purcell) marks but the embryonic stage of the history of British fiction (Sidney, Lyly, and Nashe). At the time of the second efflorescence of British music in the twentieth century (Warlock, Elgar, Delius, Holst, Vaughan Williams, Walton, Tippett, Britten, Searle, and Fricker), the traditional realistic novel, even if it did not disappear (Galsworthy, Bennett, Wells, Amis, Braine, and Wain), lost the central significance it had enjoyed earlier; and as traditional values came to be replaced by experimental ones, an important branch of the novel became subjectivized (Woolf) and even adopted poetic techniques and musical structures (Huxley and Joyce). Viewed in this axiological context, John Field's music—with no comparable British achievement in the Irish composer's lifetime (1782-1837)—should be considered as an Irish exception to a British "rule," or at least a tangible trend.

The development of German and Austrian culture would seem to corroborate the validity of this axiological pattern from the other side of a comparable constellation. The tendency of reciprocity in the achievement of great music and (traditional) fiction can be equally observed in Germany and Austria in the eighteenth and nineteenth centuries, but there it was music which reached an unprecedented and unsurpassed level (Bach, Handel, Haydn, Mozart, Beethoven, Schubert, Schumann, Mendelssohn, Brahms, and Wagner), to which the performance of the novel (even in Goethe's *Werther* and *Wilhelm Meister*) was unable to rise.

Other national developments also testify to a similar dichotomy. In the United States even the music of a Barber, Copland, Ives, Gershwin, or Cage cannot compete with the longer and more prominent range of novelists such as Cooper, Hawthorne, Melville, Mark Twain, London, Crane, James, Dreiser, Hemingway, Fitzgerald, Steinbeck, Faulkner, or Styron.

In France in the first half of the nineteenth century with his *Symphonie fantastique* Berlioz emerged as a lonely giant, while the realistic novel was a strong and broad stream (Balzac, Stendhal, and Flaubert). In the second half of the century, when this type of novel was replaced by naturalistic fiction (Zola) and the lyrically refined and musically balanced artistic novel of introverted Impressionism and psychological analysis (Proust), the importance of music increased (partly Bizet and Gounod, but mainly Debussy and Ravel).

In Italy at the beginning of the nineteenth century the novelist Manzoni was an isolated phenomenon, and until the last decades of the century the Italian novel could not live up to the standard of the Italian opera (Rossini, Bellini, Donizetti, Verdi, and Puccini).

The imaginative achievement of John Field's music may be an Irish exception to a British rule, but it is very much a part of the more comprehensive, more universal tendency just delineated. Those Irish-born novelists who *approximated* the realistic pattern (Swift and Sterne) combined English social raw material with distance-keeping, imaginative Irish wit, and had considerably predated Field. The representative nineteenth-century Irish novelist, Sheridan Le Fanu, had romantic, "Gothic" leanings.

The development of nineteenth- and twentieth-century Hungarian culture was also characterized by the outstanding role of music (Erkel, Liszt, Bartók, and Kodály) which the Hungarian novel rarely approached.

These examples are too numerous to be dismissed as merely accidental. They suggest, if not a rule without exception, a tendency which consists in a reciprocal historical relationship between the heyday of realistic fiction and great music. The uneven development of culture relies on a correlation between values outside and inside art. From an axiological point of view a work of art is a specific model of value (cf. Lukács 2:193-226), a sensuous value judgment, rather than a mere illustration of ethical tenets.

Such a historical connection is supported by aesthetic considerations as well. The historical polarity of traditional fiction and significant music corresponds to their aesthetic polarity. Whereas the novel satisfies the Hegelian claim of objective totality and provides a vast, moving, and changing panorama of a three-dimensional social crosssection represented as an objective network of social types, music expresses an emotionally and imaginatively focused and minutely graded interior universe, weaving a sensitive network of inner relationships without any immediate reference to a visible or tangible world of external objects. While this opposition does not deny the ability of music to suggest the objective essence of a historically determined human predicament, the visual wealth and auditory poverty of fiction and the auditory richness and visual poverty of music do constitute two opposed poles as far as the artistic molding of human reality is concerned.

The parallelism between the historic and aesthetic reciprocity of fiction and music might throw some light on why golden ages of fiction and music are often dichotomous. Homogeneous, objective, widespread and far-reaching social changes, such as the consolidation of bourgeois society with a definite direction, evaluation, and a discernible trend favor the unfolding of the traditional realistic novel, which represents a completed phase of social development in a vast tableau. A composer's imagination, however, can soar high under different sociopolitical conditions as well. Marx observed that the achievement of classical German philosophy relied on the fact that the Germans were tracing in intellectual terms what the French were doing in political terms (137). *Mutatis mutandis*, if classical German philosophy was an intellectual contemporary of the period of the French Revolution, classical German music was an emotional and imaginative contemporary of these events. Such reflections may explain why the musical imagination is sometimes able to compose an organic and coherent whole even from contradictory and fragmented material, in periods when a realistic narrative attempt at a synthesis of a comparable magnitude would be doomed to failure or would result in empty utopianism. The tardiness of bourgeois development and the historical necessity to lead a national life in the axiologically emphatic medium of culture created the conditions of an imaginative self-expression of national identity in Ireland. This axiological constellation is responsible for the importance of folktales, folklore in general, poetry, and poetic drama in Irish culture, and it may also throw an explanatory beam of light on the imaginative achievement of John Field's music.

The Originality of John Field

Field was not only a talented composer, he was also an original one. W. S. Bennett may have been "an English Mendelssohn" (Blom 185; E. Walker 313-314), but nobody has ever thought of referring to Mendelssohn as an English Bennett. Even much of good music in England in the nineteenth century was historically imitative. Field, by contrast, was no imitator; he was an initiator, an inventor. A case in point is Field's creation of the genre of the nocturne, which earned him the admiration of Franz Liszt. In his introductory essay to Field's *Nocturnes* published in 1859 Liszt extols

> the poignant charm of these tender poems, [their] balmy freshness . . . vague Aeolian tones . . . half-sighs . . . plaintive wailings, ecstatic moanings . . . [and] delicate originali ty, which excluded neither extreme simplicity of sentiment, nor variety of form and embellishment. . . . For him, invention and facility were one, diversity of form a necessity. . . . His tranquility was well-nigh somnolent. . . . Field was the first to introduce a style in no way derived from the established categories, and in which feeling and melody, freed from the trammels of coercive form, reign supreme. . . . The title *Nocturne* aptly applies to the pieces so named by Field, for it bears out thoughts at the outset toward those hours where in the soul, released from all the cares of the day, is lost in self-contemplation, and soars toward the regions of a starlit heaven. (1, 2)

Written with romantic passion and pathos, this is an evaluation worthy of Field and characteristic of Liszt.

In the era of sentimentalism and romanticism, to attribute value to nocturnal moods was, of course, very much in the air. Schiller's typological discrimination between the "naive" and "sentimental" (413-503) was developed into the "classical" and "romantic" by the Schlegel brothers, as Goethe remarked (Ecker mann 350), and modern critics maintain (Lovejoy 1-10, 136-146; Wellek 133). Schiller's metaphors of the "naive" poet being at one with nature and the "sentimental" poet only seeking it can be axiologically conceptualized: while the "naive" poet or artist can easily and naturally express his values in a plastic manner in terms of existing conditions, often even of external reality, the "sentimental" writer or artist cannot: his value system is basically divorced from that immediately found in philistine reality, so he must develop special means to give a sensuous form to his values. Although a composer does not, as a rule, work with representational images, he may embrace (Haydn, Mozart, and Beethoven) or discard plastic ways and forms of molding his emotional material. Schiller's generic categories characterizing the sentimental attitude and method can be amply exemplified by Field's *Nocturnes*. Those in the minor key are invariably elegiac, *No. 2 in C minor, No. 10 in E minor*, and *No. 13 in D minor*, those in the major key are usually idyllic, *No. 1 in E flat, No. 3 in A flat, No. 4 in A, No. 5 in B flat, No. 6 in F, No. 7 in C, No. 8 in A, No. 9 in E flat, No. 11 in E flat, No. 12 in G, No. 14 in C, No. 15 in C, No. 16 in F*, and *No. 19 in C*, have a vivacious, dancelike character and — as Patrick Piggott has convincingly pointed out (143-144) — are not really nocturnes at all, and despite their usual inclusion in most collected editions of Field's *Nocturnes*, should not be considered as such.

The imaginatively idyllic nature of some of the *Nocturnes* is also underlined by their alternative titles and sometimes by their origins: a variant of *Nocturne No. 5* is named *Serenade*; *Nocturne No. 8* was also published as one of *Three Romances* (1814) and had earlier appeared as the *Pastorale* movement of *Divertissement No. 2* (1811); *Nocturne No. 12* had previously figured as a lyric interlude in the first movement of Field's *Piano Concerto No. 7*; *Nocturne No. 16* contains a phrase which Field took over from his *Fantaisie sur une Polonaise favorite*; and *Nocturne 17* is the solo version of Field's *Grand pastorale*, an elaborate piece for piano and string quartet.

The musical pattern of the nocturne develops and crystallizes the sentimental attitude in a generic form. Hence its novelty even in comparison with such delightfully vigorous and plastically articulated lyric pieces as Mozart's *Serenata nottuma* (K. 239) or *Eine kleine Nachtmusik* (K. 525). The same applies to poems ranging from Young's *The Complaint; or Night Thoughts on Life, Death and Immortality* which predates Schiller's essay to Shelley's "To the Moonbeam," "A Summer Evening Churchyard," "The Waning Moon," or "To Night"; as well as to paintings like Turner's *Fishermen at Sea, Moonlight, a Study at Millbank*, and *Shield Lighthouse* or Friedrich's *Two Men Watching the Moon* and *Moonrise at the Sea*.

In his fine analysis of Field's *Nocturnes* Liszt extends the nocturnal period to include dawn. With his unique ability to associate tone with color, he writes:

> The third and sixth Nocturnes bear a pastoral character: their melodies seem as woven of the balmiest breezes, sighing warmly and moistly; they appear to reflect the changing shades that dye the vapors of dawn, rose tints giving way to bluish, and these in turn to lilac. In the latter, however, the forms stand out more clearly, with sharper outlines, as if oppressive heat had already dissipated the mists of morning. One meets therein with sinuosities like those of a great wave bearing sparkling wavelets resembling diamond chips, rolling its serpentine swells across a landscape radiant with light and freshness. (3)

Such a free treatment of the nocturnal duration is, in the case of *Nocturnes* in the *major* key, not surprising; Field's *Nocturnes* are, after all, "half-waking dreams. ... They live and move only in the dreamy imagination of the poet, and not in waking reality" (Liszt 3). (Seeing any kind of images while listening to the *Nocturnes* is, of course, not necessary.) What is surprising, even intriguing and exhilarating, is the fact that Liszt describes Field's *Nocturnes* in terms of Turner's landscapes and seascapes. The serpentine swell of sparkling waves, drifting diamond-shaped reflections is often encountered in Turner's "sinuous" paintings, from the more traditional early *Egremont Sea Piece* to the Impressionistic late *Yacht Approaching the Coast*. The "vapors of dawn," "rose tints," "bluish" and "lilac" colors mark the color scheme of paintings like Turner's *Venice, Looking East from the Guidecca: Sunrise* with conspicuous accuracy. The subdued and delicate quality of "changing *shades*," "rose" tints, and "bluish" hues are also the properties of Turner's watercolor of *Venice* painted with spots of semitransparent pastel layers. Liszt's reference to *"changing shades,"* "rose tints *giving way to* bluish, *and these in turn to* lilac" correlate with Turner's comparable interest in emphasizing—even in his spatial medium—modifications of views and impressions, evoking and expressing changing moods, "modulations of . . . sentiment" (Liszt 1), the transformation of one state into another. Liszt's association of aural manifestations, "melodies," with visual impressions, "tints," and tactile as well as heat sensations, "balmiest breezes, sighing warmly and moistly," is also parallel to Turner's fusion of impressions in his watercolor of *Venice*.

The phenomenon can hardly be explained away by claiming that this was after all the way Venice appeared. In Canaletto's classical Venetian *vedutas* Venice looks very different. His views are sharp, clear, brilliant, factual, and topographically accurate, apparently painted by an artist who was able to represent his internal values through depicting external reality. Turner, however, was not; he belonged to the romantic trend which developed from Schiller's sentimental attitude. The painter of the Venetian *Sunrise*, as well as of *Sunrise, with a Boat between Headlands, Sunrise with Sea Monsters, Norham Castle, Sunrise*, and *The Blue Rigi: Lake of Lucern—Sunrise* has transformed external reality to give an impression of his own internal system of values, and in some respects foreshadowed the Impressionism of Monet (Ritchie 14; Gatt 26), just as some of Field's *Nocturnes* and several of Chopin's *Nocturnes*—for example his *Nocturnes in E flat major*, Op. 55, No. 2; *B major*, Op. 62, No. 1; or *E minor*, Op. posth.—give a foretaste of Debussy's music. There are parallel passages even between an *ostinato* section for violins in the first movement of Field's *Piano Concerto No. 6* and Debussy's *Petite Suite* (Piggott 173-174). This is why Liszt—himself anticipating in his own later musical developments—was justified to express, with the instinctive insight of involuntary intuition, his impression of Field's *Nocturnes* in terms of Turner's paintings.

The anticipation of quasi-Impressionistic procedures within a romantic idiom can also be observed in Field's *Nocturne No. 7* where the simple melody in continuous, *moderato* motion and in three-four time is played by the left hand, over which a broken octave of a dominant pedal is heard. After ten occurrences this motif is ornamentally transformed and persistently returns. This effectively simple arrangement "finds an interesting parallel in the work of certain Impressionist painters who rendered special effects of light with the use of a palette limited to only two or three colours" (Piggott 128). In this connection Piggott aptly mentions the example of Whistler, who, touched by some Impressionistic procedures, entitled his fine decorative canvases as *Arrangement in Grey and Black*, and even as *Nocturne in Blue and Green* or *Nocturne in Blue and Gold* and *Nocturne in Black and Gold*. The latter type of painting did not leave Debussy's *Three Nocturnes* unaffected (Piper 284; Rawley 76). Turner had achieved a comparable color scheme in his paintings *Moonlight* or *The Evening Star*.

Field's Impressionistic foresight also has its harmonic aspects. In the final version of his *Nocturne No. 2* he finishes the piece with "a wistful, almost Impressionistic coda, containing one of his favorite pedal effects — a haze of shifting harmonies above a sustained tonic" (Piggott 119). *Nocturne No. 11* reveals "imaginative asides in harmonic ambiguity" (Young 465). In *Nocturne No. 14 in C major*, after the final cadence of an episode in G major, its "left-hand arpeggio continues with slight shifts of harmony, until it settles on a repeated G, whereupon the music of the introduction returns in the key of A flat, the connecting link being the note G, which is absorbed in the dominant seventh of the new key" (Piggott 138). The emphasis is not on energetic advancement and aim-propelled progress, but on sensitive transition and sensuous transference; on an "endless modulation of the ... chord of the sentiment" (Liszt 1), the gentle modification and shifting readjustment of an emotional state, the gradual reevaluation of a fragile mood and a tonal shade from the aspect of another mood and shade.

The phenomenon may be called a musical metaphor. That a metaphor can be transplanted from one artistic medium to another is graphically proved by the literary description of a pictorial metaphor in Proust's *Remembrance of Things Past*. Proust applies the term in the extended sense of sensuous transference to describe the Impressionistic seascapes of the painter Elstir, who, in depicting the harbor of Carquethuit on the Balbec coast, used "one of his metaphors ... employing, for the little town, only marine terms, and urban terms for the sea" (Proust 2:629). The resulting "poetic" suppression of the line of demarcation between land and sea is also typical of Turner; see, for example, *Dort, or Dordrecht, Storm-clouds: Sunset, The Chain Pier, Brighton, Archway with Trees by the Sea, The Evening Star, Sunrise, with a Boat between Headlands*, or *Yacht Approaching the Coast*). The saturation of Shelley's poetry with metaphors (and tropes derived from metaphors) based on the linguistic transference of a name to another phenomenon is equally conspicuous in "Ode to the West Wind," "The Sensitive Plant," "The Cloud," "To a Skylark," and so on. Such an extended sense of metaphor may invoke impressionistically rich blended sensations, but the notion itself is not metaphorically ambiguous: whether it refers to a literary, pictorial, or musical phenomenon, it invariably involves a sensuous — linguistic, visual, or auditory — transference of qualities. Cutting across various areas and branches of art, it also focuses a formal procedure of selecting, condensing, generalizing, and evaluating phenomena conceived and captured differently in the naive and sentimental groups. Hence its axiological importance: if value is considered to be the human significance of phenomena, then the function of form is to highlight value by patterning quality.

Liszt's analysis of Field not only suggests specific romantic traits paving the way for Impressionistic effects; it also points out the pioneering significance of Field's *Nocturnes* for romantic music at large: Field "opened the way for all the productions which have since appeared under the various titles of Songs without Words, Impromtus, Ballades, etc., and to him we may trace the origin of pieces designed to portray subjective and profound emotion" (2-3). Liszt's mentioning "Songs without Words" immediately calls to mind the music of Mendelssohn; the "Impromtus" evoke Schubert; the "Ballades" in this context suggest Chopin; the mood of the *Nocturnes* summons up Liszt's *Consolations*; and the very name and character of Field's *Nocturnes* conjure up the most important field of generic irradiation, Chopin's *Nocturnes*.

By the time Chopin composed his posthumously published early *Nocturne in E minor* (1827), Field had already been widely known both as a perfect pianist and as an accomplished composer. The grandson of an organist and the son of a violinist in Dublin, the boy betrayed talent in music at an early age. In 1792, not yet ten years old, he played a concerto by his teacher, Giordani, with success in Dublin. In 1792 and 1793 he also started writing music, arranging for the piano an Irish air, *Go to the Devil and Shake Yourself*, and two rondos on Giordani's songs. In London in 1794, he performed a sonata by Clementi, who gave him lessons and employed him as a salesman in his piano shop. Field's talent was acknowledged by Haydn, Dussek, and Cramer (Branson 3; Piggott 12). In 1799, at the age of 17, Field already performed his own first *Piano Concerto* which was very well received. In 1802 Clementi took him to France, Germany, and Russia, where he gave concerts and earned acclaim. Settling in St. Petersburg, Field led the actual life of "the fictional Irishman" (Gorer 33), and soon became a bohemian, a teacher — one of his students being Glinka — a pianist, and a composer of fame. He did his best to keep his personal independence and artistic autonomy. When Count Orlov offered him the title of "Court Pianist," he refused the honor with a characteristic *bon mot*: "*La cour n'est pas fait pour moi, et je ne sais pas lui faire la cour*" (Nikolayev 26). Field was certainly right: the court was not made for him, and he was not made to court it.

The year 1811 saw the publication of Field's *Divertissement avec Quatour No. 2 in A — Pastorale et Rondeau*, whose *Pastorale* movement, somewhat shortened and reshaped, came to be resurrected as *Nocturne No. 8*. In 1814 Field's first three *Nocturnes* were published; in 1815 his *Piano Concerto No. 1 in E flat* with classical tones and overtones and his *Piano Concerto No. 2 in A flat* with a romantic fabric were printed. In 1816 his *Piano Concerto No. 3 in E flat*, *Piano Concerto No. 4 in E flat*, and *Romance in E flat* (the later *Nocturne No. 9*) appeared. In 1817 *Nocturnes No. 4, 5*, and *6* as well as *Piano Concerto No. 5 in C* were published and soon became popular (Flood 12-13).[1] By 1822 *Nocturnes No. 7* and *No. 8* had been brought out; and in 1823 Field's *Piano Concerto No. 6 in C*.

Thus Chopin had a chance of knowing much of Field's work before 1827; and he, in fact, taught his pupils Field's *Nocturnes* and *Concertos*, and himself often played Field's *Nocturnes* and *Concerto No. 2* (Branson 19-20, 25-26). In 1833 Chopin heard Field perform his *Piano Concerto No. 7* in Paris.

The stylistic affinity between Field's and Chopin's *Nocturnes* — as David Branson has pointed out in summary fashion and with polemic passion (31-56) — is conspicuous. It is not merely a matter of mood, sensibility, tone, or the appearance of a *cantilena* melody over an *arpeggio* accompaniment (as in Field's *Nocturnes Nos. 5, 13,* or *15* and Chopin's *Nocturnes Op. 9, No. 1, No. 3, Op. 15, No. 2,* and *Op. 27, No. 1, No. 2,* and so on): the pianistic equivalent of an operatic *bel canto*. The stylistic convergence also appears in the cumulative and increasingly imaginative effect of particular details.

The falling and rising melodic phrases of Field's *Nocturnes No. 1, No. 10, No. 11,* and *No. 13* are paralleled by a comparable undulation in the opening theme of Chopin's *Nocturne Op. 27, No. 2*. Like Field in his E flat *Nocturne No. 1*, Chopin in his E flat *Nocturne Op. 9, No. 2* also couples a descending passage with a chiming close. Both Field's *Nocturne No. 1* and Chopin's *Nocturne Op. 15, No. 1* are characterized by a yearningly open, romantically conceived and songlike *bel canto* (Szabolcsi 2:208-209).

Placing the melodic line under a repeated over-note appears in Field's *Nocturne No. 2* and reappears in Chopin's *Nocturne Op. 32, No. 1*. The rhythmic figure in Field's *Second Nocturne*, of a triplet with a lengthened — or rest-complemented — second note and a shortened third note followed by the same note, also occurs in several of Chopin's *Nocturnes* (*Op. 9, No. 3, Op. 32, No. 2, Op. 55, No. 2,* and *Op. 62, No. 1*).

A decorative pattern repeated an octave higher, as in Field's *Nocturne No. 5*, is also heard in Chopin's *Nocturne Op. 32, No. 1*. The throbbing chord passage in Field's *Fifth Nocturne* has a parallel in the middle section of Chopin's *Nocturne Op. 32, No. 2*. A phrase in the ninth bar of Field's *Nocturne No. 6* has its equivalent in the fourth bar of Chopin's *Nocturne Op. 9, No. 2*. The descending phrase ending of three chromatic notes cropping up in bar six of Field's *Nocturne No. 8* is also present in bar twenty-six of Chopin's *Nocturne Op. 55, No. 2*.

Field's *Nocturne No. 9* and Chopin's *Nocturne Op. 9, No. 2* appear to be especially closely linked by the fall-rise of the opening theme, the key of E flat major, the melody starting on the note G (not counting the upbeat in Chopin), the rising triplets of the accompaniment, the time signature six-eight in the Field and twelve-eight in the Chopin, the *dolce* character of both pieces, and by the fact that even the decorative turn embellishing the melody appears at the same place (between the fifth and sixth triplets of the bass). Field's *Nocturne No. 14* (in Liszt's order *No. 16*) and Chopin's *Nocturne Op. 27, No. 1* share a chromatic bias (Szabolcsi 2:215-216).

Further examples could, of course, be quoted, but this much may suffice to suggest that Field did not simply hit upon the name of the nocturne; he also initiated a new way of feeling, a new kind of sensibility, and a new course of imagination: indeed, a new norm and form of evaluation which Chopin developed, elaborated, and brought to exquisite, elegiac perfection.

Field's Treatment of the Storm

Field's imaginative originality also asserts itself in the treatment of the storm. To show the way in which his innovative romantic fantasy worked, it is necessary to take a look at the classical solution of the problem. In Haydn's oratorio, *The Seasons* (1801), the storm is a formidable threat. Already Simon's, Lukas's and Hanne's recitatives (No. 16) in "Summer" express ill forebodings: Simon sings of "unusual darkness" and "wrathful vapors," Lukas of the "threat'ning storm" and "disaster," and Hanne of "fear" and "a deathlike silence." In No. 17 the full chorus and the full orchestra combine to render the fearful rage of the tempest. In the words of Gottfried van Swieten's libretto, based on James Thomson's poem:

> Hark! the storm's tremendous voice,
> Heaven protect us!
> The mighty thunder rolls!
> The rushing tempest rages!
> Where shall we fly! away!
> Sheets of livid flame wrapping ether in a blaze!
> The fierce ragged lightning bursting the clouds,
> Now the flood in torrent descends.

The C minor key of the storm scene also performs its tonal function in conveying tempestuous tension. Between the G minor of the opening and the C major of the closing of the oratorio, the C minor key in the progressive tonality of the work "serves a function similar to that in *The Creation*; for Haydn it was the key that symbolized the world before light. Therefore it is used at the beginning of 'Summer' to describe the pre-dawn and later the storm during which the heavens are darkened. The lightless beginning of 'Winter,' and the symbol of old age, is also expressed by C minor" (Landon 128-129). The chromatic notes in the fugue of Haydn, inspired by Handel, in the concluding phase of the storm also contribute to contrapuntal suspense.

Although unsupported by the evidence of words and expressed with the continuous personal presence of a tempestuous temperament, the storm in the fourth movement of Beethoven's *Symphony No. 6* (1807-1808) unquestionably transmits the sense of an even more fundamental threat. In Beethoven's work the storm appears in unsurpassed symphonic pomp in F minor with thundering drums, lightning flutes, running violins, and the raging of the whole orchestra. Chromatic dissonance plays its part as it steps up the horrifying intensity of the tempest. When the storm is gone, the shepherds have a very good reason to rejoice and sing a hymn of gratitude in the last movement of the symphony.

In a branch of romantic music—Schubert's *Stormy Morning* in the song cycle *The Winter Journey* (1827), Berlioz's *Fantastic Symphony* (1830), Mendelssohn's *Scottish Symphony* (1831-1842), Bellini's *The Puritans of Scotland* (1835), Wagner's *The Flying Dutchman* (1841), Liszt's *Les Préludes* (1848-1850), Berlioz's *The Trojans* (1855-1858), or Verdi's *Otello* (1887)—the ominous character of the storm is maintained and in some respects even sharpened. The usual attraction of the romantic imagination to the extreme found a natural medium in the storm: the extreme state of nature.

Field, however, was not content with this much. In his *Piano Concerto No. 5* in C major, which he subtitled *L'Incendie par l'orage* (1815-1817), he seems to have started in a different direction. The difference does not lie in Field's effort to reach a powerful effect: all composers depicting a storm have endeavored to do so, and romantic composers were especially keen on enlarging their resources to outdo their predecessors. Field became acquainted with Daniel Steibelt's *Piano Concerto No. 3* (*L'Orage*) as early as 1798, when it enthralled London audiences with its evocation of the storm in the middle of its final rondo movement. Steibelt's program concerto also scored a great success in St. Petersburg even in the 1810s, and it was Field's ambition to outdistance Steibelt in a friendly rivalry. Accordingly, Field fortified his orchestra, added a bass trombone, used some extra percussion, employed a bell, and in the storm section even prescribed a second piano to obtain extra sonority and to reinforce the solo instrument without hammering inordinately the soft-toned and square-shaped piano of his day. As against Steibelt's *L'Orage*, Field evoked the impression of *L'Incendie par l'orage* suggesting "not merely a storm but some kind of catastrophe resulting from it; though whether this was merely a fire caused by lightning or a symbol of some larger event (the burning of Moscow?) one can only guess" (Piggott 167).

But Field's originality does not simply lie in the onomatopoeic depiction of lightning, thunder, wind, and fire. His innovative spirit is chiefly revealed in his imaginative reinterpretation and revaluation of the storm. Changing the key to C minor lends the storm scene a passionate quality. Placing the tempest into the development section of the first movement of the concerto creates the conditions for a modification of meaning: the phase of development is the most unstable part of any piece in the sonata form. Field increases the impression of instability by large-scale modulation, intensive and inventive passage work, roaring tremolos in the bass range and sparkling ornaments in the high register, dynamic runs, chromatic effects, and ragged (dotted and syncopated) rhythms. The romantic outcome of this climate of transformation is a veritable change of musical content: from an awful force the storm becomes an awesome power, an awe-inspiring, even sublime agent, the fantastic proof of creative fantasy. The peak of the process is the enormous *fortissimo* outburst of the orchestra and the piano shrieking in ecstatic semitone friction and submerging metric stress in phrase accent in bars 379 to 382: an eruption of flames not unlike the bursting "black rain and fire" of Shelley's "Ode to the West Wind" or Turner's image in *The Burning of the Houses of Lords and Commons, October 16, 1834*. It is a flashing fireband shooting up, curving down, sparkling up, dying down, and giving way to a *scherzando* passage in A minor.

This passage shows some melodic, metric, and rhythmic similarity, though, of course, no identity, with the main theme of the last movement in Chopin's *Piano Concerto in F minor* (1829-1830), while the prolonged phrase at the peak of Field's storm with its circular movement rising above, sinking below, and returning to the initial note foreshadows the shape of the central phrase – appearing, as it were, in diminution – in Chopin's *"Winter Wind" Study, Etude No. 11* in the *Op. 25* set (1832-1836). What Field had begun, Chopin brought to full fruition. He did not do so in conscious imitation, but in creating a form which carried further Field's achievement in reinterpreting and revaluating the meaning and human significance of the tempest. The form used by Chopin developed the norm established by Field. Essentially this is the axiological basis of the stylistic affinity between their music.

Chopin's *"Winter Wind" Study* opens with a four-bar introduction. It was, in fact, a friend of Chopin's, Charles A. Hoffmann, who suggested to the composer that such a preparatory section might enhance the overall effect (Collet 136). So the introduction was an afterthought; but what a thought! Chopin took the hint and composed his musical preface with perfect autonomy and ingenuity.

When the haunting and singing phrase is first presented in the right-hand part, it is immediately present in the alert consciousness of the listener; yet since it is played *lento* and *piano*, it is also distant and elegiac. The double curve of its gentle and fragile melodic line is entirely unaccompanied, so its key is mysteriously undecided: it can be both C major and A minor (bars 1-2). A *fermata* renders its musical gesture increasingly tentative.

When the phrase is repeated in bars three and four, the riddle seems to be solved; the notes C, G, and C under the melodic E set the tune in C major. Yet the initial duality persists on another plane: if the melody is now filled in and rounded off by chords which lend it a measure of corporeality and solemnity, it is also made more remote and enigmatic by the *pianissimo* mark. Its groping character is further emphasized by another *fermata*. The presence and absence of the phrase are simultaneously enhanced. Beauty is the object of romantic yearning.

The third cell in the introduction is the last chord of bar four. The D in the treble register and the B in the deep bass might – *in insolation*, and after the repeated alternation of tonic chords in C major and subdominant chords in F major – point to G major, which, as dominant, could prepare a return to C major. This, however, would be a platitudinous solution.

Under the note D the right hand also plays a G sharp rather than G. Thus considered, the chord would suggest not the fifth degree of C major but the seventh degree of A minor; it would constitute a compound diminished fifth chord consisting of two minor thirds. It would be the closest relative of the diminished seventh chord consisting of three minor thirds which, as James Anderson Winn wittily remarks, was to romantic music "what the adverbial clause beginning 'where' or 'when' was to romantic poetry: a smoothly plausible way of continuing motion, a means to juxtapose and associate images or key-areas without committing oneself to one unequivocal grammatical relation between those elements" (279- 280).

This, however, is not the full truth about the imaginative nature of this chord. The previous chord has a *fermata* over it and contains an E. Because of the *fermata*, the E is *held* long; since however, it is a minim, it also *sounds* long and, if ever so gently, losing even a part of its *pianissimo* volume, it affects the last chord of the introduction, making it tactfully and gracefully the dominant seventh chord of A minor. It also has a *fermata*, the third one in four bars, indicating that the phrase is feeling its way in an ambiguous course.

In bar five the storm breaks out vigorously *allegro con brio* in A minor, which proves to be the basic key of the study. The left hand plays the opening phrase of the introduction energetically, *forte* and *risoluto*. The dramatic shift in dynamics is not only a quantitative but also a qualitative change: the phrase has now lost its elegiac nature and has assumed a passionate quality, which is increased by the rapid chromatic action and counteraction of the right hand, indicating the fact that the contradictory principle in the introductory section is not lost but reproduced on a higher level as an energizing factor and explosive agent. "This study must be treated throughout as a polyphonic duet between the two hands with attention to the melodic writing implicit in most of the semiquaver figuration," states Collet (136-137). The piece is also made "virile, energetic and boisterous" (Hedley 145) by the sectional return and dynamic increase of the basic theme; by a fantasy-driven range of large-scale modulations; as well as by the practice of joining "two entirely foreign harmonies by chromatic progressions in all parts. Thus . . . an E major and a C minor triad can be joined together . . . (bars 49 and 50)" (Badura-Skoda 274). Such an imaginative joining of distant harmonic poles in romantic music corresponds to the equally imaginative linking of distant linguistic poles in romantic poetry — Shelley's similes and metaphors in "Ode to the West Wind" — as well as to the atmospheric fusion of diverse masses of whirling color in romantic painting (Turner's *Snow Storm*).

The enormous increase of tempestuous energy is also expressed by the changing range and shape of the basic phrase. The left hand starts playing it in the deep bass, but soon (already in bar eleven) a treble clef notation crops up on the bass staff, and is repeated in bar twenty-one; while in bars forty-one to forty-four the phrase rises to the treble range, is played by the right hand, and is counterpointed by the figurations on the left hand, which now also plays in the treble clef. The identical dotted notes of the first motif of the first phrase are either reinforced by repetition or are replaced by triplets (bar 10, and so forth), which may be widely placed (bars 17, 18, 35, 36, 81, and 82) and often point upward, swordlike (bars 11, 21, 29, 38, 39, and so forth). If we also take into account the dynamic surge of the *Etude* from *piano* and *pianissimo* to *forte*, *fortissimo*, and *forte-fortissimo* (fff); if we consider the summarizing last blasts of the crucial phrase with its second motif appearing heavily accented and in augmentation; and if we listen to the passionate and parallel run, ascending rush and upward thrust of both hands at the very end of the *Study*, then we have so many good reasons to regard it as a tour de force of romantic imagination: a fantastic and cathartic reassessment of the tempest. The emphasis is not on onomatopoeic effects or tone painting, but on the rendition of a tempestuous mood and an imaginative revaluation of that mood. Field's pioneering achievement is brought here to organic perfection.

The clue to understanding this miraculous transfiguration lies in Chopin's *"Revolutionary" Study*, *Etude Op. 10, No. 12* in C minor, dedicated to Liszt. Composed in Stuttgart in September 1931, when Chopin was on his way to Paris and received news that the czar's troops had crushed the Polish revolutionary uprising and struggle for independence (Nádor 67-68, 74, 77, 79), *The "Revolutionary" Study* expresses not only the composer's tragic shock, but also his "terrific defiance" (Melville 24), his cathartic transformation of an acutely painful experience. "The defeated Polish revolution was bound to be victorious in Chopin's music" (Szabolcsi 1:333). Such a thoroughgoing change could only be effected by the power of creative imagination. Chopin's *Etudes* are a far cry from the didactic exercises of Clementi, Cramer, Czerny, and Bertini, and even from those of Dussek, Hummel, Moscheles, or Kalkbrenner.

Chopin's *"Winter Wind"* and *"Revolutionary" Etudes* are related not only in mood, passion, their minor key, *allegro* tempo, dynamic contrasts, sharp accents, the flash and flicker of high treble notes against a deep, dark bass, a final augmentation (Abraham 41), the parallel motion of both hands in the closing run, the enormously widespread interaction between chromatically colored, modulating, murmuring, roaring and rushing semiquaver figurations, and an eloquent, energetic, restated, reinforced, and reshaped two-motif phrase, but also to a certain extent in some traits of the pattern of the seminal phrase itself: in the dotted rhythm of the first motif and the semitone step up and back in the second motif (which in *The "Revolutionary" Study* is also dotted). The motifs in *The "Revolutionary" Study* may be sharper, more pointed, dotted differently, thrusting upward and immediately swordlike, but the parallels between *The "Winter Wind" Etude* and *The "Revolutionary" Etude* are strong enough to transfer, "transpose," and warrant the claim of István Kecskenéti (made in a different context and comparing different études): "Chopin has written two Etudes in C minor: both are cycle-closing pieces, and, regarding their content and expressive form, both could be called either 'Storm' or 'Revolutionary' Etudes" (22-23). The tempestuous or revolutionary character is also the property of the *B minor Study (Op. 25, No. 10) and of Nos. 3, 8, 22*, and *24* of the *Préludes* (1838-1839) in the *Op. 28* series (cf. Jemnitz 169, 199; Hedley 146-147). The link, however, is the closest between *The "Winter Wind" Etude* and *The "Revolutionary" Study*. In *The "Winter Wind" Etude*

> the left hand has a march-like theme and . . . the right hand "accompaniment" combines harmonic and melodic functions in a uniquely formulated and strongly characterised pattern, sweeping across the registers to create a dramatic and powerful counter point to the principal theme. It is the most impassioned of the later set, recalling "revolutionary" study in its heroic tone and its structural breadth. (Samson 72)

This is why in Chopin's creative imagination the storm has changed its charge, sign, and value: from a negative force it has become a positive power.

Such an axiological change, initiated by Field and completed by Chopin, can also be observed in the poetry of Shelley and the painting of Turner. Shelley was bound to know the threat of storm both in his life and death. He knew it and expressed it in his poetry as well ("A Vision of the Sea," 1820). Yet when his imagination has given an impalpably sensuous form to his utopis tically radical ideals, the tempestuous wind has become a value- bearing force of transformation and inspiration ("Ode to the West Wind," 1819). The change from Autumn to Winter and from Winter to Spring (Sections 1 and 5), from calm to thun derstorm (2) and seastorm (3), from passivity to activity (4), and from nature to society (5); the change of allegiances from things driven (a leaf, a cloud, a wave) to the phenomenon driving them: "Be thou, *Spirit fierce,* / My spirit! *Be thou me,* impetuous one!"; the change from long to short sentences; the change of subjunctive verb forms ("If I were a dead leaf") into imperatives ("Make me thy lyre," "Drive my dead thoughts," "Scatter . . . / Ashes and sparks, my words among mankind!"); the unexpected, uncustomary, and at this time unusual change of the rhyme scheme in the last structural section from *abc*, *bcb*, *cdc*, *ded*, *ee* into *aba*, *bc₁b*, *c₂c₃c₂*, *c₃dc₃*, *dd*, using — in the pronunciation of "hearth" and "wind" contemporary vowel and diphthong variants as rhymes (Cf. J. Walker, 225, 536), paralleling the augmented culminations of Field's and Chopin's storm scenes, and suggest ing, with the "mighty harmonies" of a powerful closure, the musical magic of "the incantation of this verse" and "The trumpet of a prophecy," the cumulative change of the overwhelming *crescendo* of sequential *terza rimas,* forceful alliterations, enormous enjambments, and the leitmotif like sectional recurrence of addressing the wind; and the general change of tone from the yearning elegiac to the triumphantly tempestuous: all these imaginative changes of value and evaluation correspond to the process and progress of the storm in Field's *Concerto No. 5* and Chopin's *"Winter Wind" Study*.

Comparable revaluation of the storm took place in Turner's *oeuvre*. Of his numerous stormy seascapes, the *Calais Pier* canvas, first exhibited in London at the Royal Academy in 1803, undoubtedly represents the tempestuous sea as the ominous medium of serious danger. "Nearly swampt" (Wilton 82), Turner noted tersely in his sketchbook, recording the perilous experience of his risky arrival in 1802 at Calais, the first stage of his first tour abroad.

The painting is composed in dramatic contrasts. The walls of waves threaten the fragile sailing boats, and rush against the stiff structural line of the wooden pier, which protrudes into the raging sea and constitutes a slanting axis. The lurching set of struggling boats tossed by the stormy sea draws another slanting axis pointing precariously and ambiguously both forward, to the middle of the sea, and backward, to the pier. The dual use of the axis heightens the dramatic effect: the fishermen make an effort to move away from the pier, but the waves force them back, and may easily knock them against the pier. Human endeavor and natural force fatefully clash. The partly lit up and slightly sinuous line of the horizon, where the sea and the sky meet, creates a third axis against which the diagonals of the composition are measured. A fourth axis is formed by the nervous line of variously tilted masts pointing upward, ending at different-ly placed, accented points, and reinforcing each other's position by what might be termed the visual equivalent of the syncopated *staccato* effect. The tempes-tuous drama is expanded from plane to space.

The spatial quality is further enhanced by the fifth axis embodied by the edge of the billowing clouds slanting from upper left to lower right, working against the direction of the masts, continuing, as it were, in the bending line and upright back of the pier, and supported by further diagonals of parallel beams of light. All these variously placed but invariably dynamic axes unite in a vertiginous vortex and universalize, as formative principles, the movement of the voracious whirlpool circling around a cone of wave in the foreground, where a diamond-shaped ravine is carved out of the surface of the sea, ready to collapse and crumble into the circular swirl it holds.

The color scheme of the painting is equally dynamic. It also suggests a circular pattern, each stage of which represents a contrast. The wall of waves more or less parallel to the position of the viewer is white and bright with spuming froth, but it is also counterpointed by the dark brown pier and the dark green sea. The shaking and shivering sail of the boat in the middle is a bit darker than the white of the wave, but it is still light, even sunlit against the heavy mass of a dark rain cloud. The sail to the left is russet brown and is contrasted by the light blue opening in the sky where the mast points. The extreme left of the picture is occupied by a deep, dark mass of clouds and by whirling waves which lead the eye back to the white foam indicating that the color scheme has come full circle.

The dramatic quality of the tempestuous scene is also increased by related opposites: the convex cone of waves in the foreground and the concave opening in the sky; the lit-up sail in the middle and its luminous and vaporous mirror image copied upon darker clouds. The sharp white of a waving flag and a flying gull, set against the huge dark surface of stormclouds, strikes the eye as a shrill shriek would the ear.

If in the early *Calais Pier* the tempest is definitely formidable, in the late *Snow Storm* (1842) it is positively sublime. The element of deep danger is a part of the sublime, a tense field of drama, the medium of cathartic triumph. In his crossing to Calais Turner was *surprised* by the storm. In the experience depicted in the *Snow Storm* he *exposed* himself to the storm. He is reported as having said, "I wished to show what such a scene was like; I got the sailors to lash me to the mast to observe it; I was lashed for four hours and I did not expect to escape but I felt bound to record it if I did" (Ruskin 445). Some scholars query the authenticity of this claim (Gaunt 45; Lindsay 146), but there can be no doubt about the fact that Turner made such a claim, subtitled his painting as "steam-boat off a harbour's mouth making signals in shallow water, and going by the lead. The author was in this storm on the night the Ariel left Harwich" (Wilton 286); and the composition of the painting is such that he must have been lashed to the mast. It is an extraordinary evocation of a deeply personal experience.

If in the *Calais Pier* the movement of the tempest tends to be circular, in the *Snow Storm* it is circular. While in the *Calais Pier* canvas the pier, the boats, the sea, and the sky are separate entities, people and objects are clearly recognizable, circularity is emphasized on the thematic level (the swirling sea and the shape of ropes in the foreground) and generalized in form by the cumulative effect of the various axes, the *Snow Storm* presents a cosmic whirlwind, deletes dividing lines, and suppresses most details. This is why for the average contemporary eye it looked like a "mass of soap-suds and whitewash" (quoted and refuted by Ruskin 161); and this is the reason why for the modern viewer it is the internalized evocation of a crucial experience, an eternalized impression of a seething swirl captured with the anticipation of a modern sensibility which had a liberating effect on Monet and Pissarro twenty years after Turner's death (Lindsay 160-161).

In his original, witty, and erudite book, *The Englishness of English Art*, Nikolaus Pevsner supposes that "Turner's world of fantasmagoria," his "atmospheric view," "unplastic, cloudy or steamy treatment" were basically consequences of the English climate which brought about "the incorporeal tradition of English art" (24, 173-174). While there can be no doubt about the fact that English moisture and mist and the frequent changes of atmosphere have left their mark on Turner's art, it is also true that the English climate did not change from Hogarth's to Turner's time, but that English art did; climatic conditions were the same in Turner's youth and old age, but his manner of representation became thoroughly modified; and Turner's influence on Monet was not the effect of the British climate on French weather. The Impressionistic incorporeality of the late Turner's art can be explained on an axiological, rather than meteorological, basis: as soon as the industrial revolution made it impossible for the romantic artist to express his values through the immediate forms of external reality, the imaginative transformation of that reality became a matter of paramount importance. In France a similar process took place later. This is the basis of the conspicuous modernity of the British romantic movement in poetry (Shelley), music (Field), and painting (Turner) alike.

In the *Calais Pier*, influenced by the seascapes of Willem van de Velde, even water is characterized by the solidity of glass. In the *Snow Storm*, even solid objects possess the fluidity of water. In the early seascape people are actual and, to a certain extent, even anecdotal figures. In the late picture no clear-cut figure is visible; however, configurations of vapor, light, and cloud suggest the possibility of an impalpable spiritual presence on either side of the mast. Are these shapes like the symbolic angel in the middle of the equally circular painting, *The Angel Standing in the Sun* (1846)? They are less definite, but they certainly have symbolic overtones. Or are they the mythical figure of Moses in the upper middle part of the experimental circular painting having the long title of *Light and Colour (Goethe's Theory) — the Morning after the Deluge — Moses Writing the Book of Genesis* (1843)? They are more impalpable, but they may have some mythical implications. Are they there at all? They may well be. The ambiguity of their presence is the ontology of the fantastic (cf. Landow 122, 126).

In the *Calais Pier* the center of the maelstrom is external to the sailing boats; it is placed at the bottom left corner of the composition. In the *Snow Storm* the center of the cosmic turmoil is the mast of the ship, the real or fictional position of the painter "at the center of the landscape" (Paulson 82). His body may be the target of the storm, but his fantasy is the power center of the tempest. The movement of the sweeping whirlpool is centrifugal (Roskill 39). "Turner's painting is a work not of self-effacement but of survival and triumphant self-assertion" (Heffernan 104). Its energy is the positive power of creative imagination. Its source is the Shelleyan wish of "Make me thy lyre" and "Be thou me" ("Ode to the West Wind"), the imaginary and imaginative paradox of pantheistic identification — without, of course, Shelley's explicitly verbalized social message. Its gesture is the sensuous form of a positive value judgment. Its achievement — like those of Field, Chopin, and Shelley — is the imaginative praise of human creativity.

Coda

At this point, a more quiet coda is in order. Even if Field's stature was admittedly smaller than Chopin's, Shelley's, or Turner's, and his sense of structure and grasp of pattern was less sure than theirs, "in a rich age of English poetry" and painting, "Field was the only musician capable of uncovering a complementary vein of lyrical music" (Young 465), whether elegiac or passionate. The fact that he can be compared to them at all is a measure of his significance. But his importance is not simply historical. He was not only the inventor of the nocturne, the initiator of the romantic revaluation of the storm, and not even merely one of the pioneers of romantic music. He was more than that: an imaginative composer worth listening to, in his own right, even today.

Note

1. I wish to express my gratitude to Dr. Wolfgang Zach, President of the Graz Centre for the International Study of Literatures in English, for his generous help in making it possible for me to study a handwritten copy of the orchestral score of John Field's *Piano Concerto No. 5* in the possession of the New Irish Chamber Orchestra.

Works Cited

Abraham, Gerald. *Chopin's Musical Style*. London: Oxford University Press, 1973.

Badura-Skoda, Paul. "Chopin's Influence." In *The Chopin Companion*, ed. Alan Walker. New York: W. W. Norton and Co., Inc., 1973.

Blom, Eric. *Music in England*. West Drayton: Penguin/Pelican Books, 1947.

Branson, David. *John Field and Chopin*. London: Barrie and Jenkins, 1972.

Collet, Robert. "Studies, Preludes and Impromptus." In *The Chopin Companion*, ed. Alan Walker. New York: W. W. Norton and Co., Inc., 1973.

Eckermann, Johann Peter. *Gespräche mit Goethe in den letzten Jahren seines Lebens*. Berlin und Weimar: Aufbau Verlag, 1982.

Flood, W. H. Grattan. *John Field of Dublin: Inventor of the Nocturne*. Dublin: Martin Lester, Ltd., 1920.

Gatt, Giuseppe. *Turner*. London: Thames and Hudson, 1968.

Gaunt, William. *Turner*. Oxford: Phaidon Press, 1981.

Gorer, Richard. "John Field and His Storm Concerto." *The Listener* 55.5 January, 1956.

Hedley, Arthur. *Chopin*. Revised by Maurice J. E. Brown. London: J. M. Dent and Sons, Ltd., 1974.

Heffernan, James A. W. *The Re-creation of Landscape: A Study of Wordsworth, Coleridge, Constable and Turner*. Hanover and London: University Press of New England, 1984.

Jemnitz, Sándor. *Fryderyk Chopin*. Budapest: Gondolat, 1960.

Kecskeméti, István. "Fryderyk Chopin: Tizenkét etüd" (Twelve Studies), Op. 10. In *A hét zeneműve* (The composition of the week), ed. György Kroó. Budapest: Zeneműkiadó, 1979.

Landon, H. C. Robbins. *Haydn: Chronicle and Works*. 5 vols. London: Thames and Hudson, 1977.

Landow, George P. "And the World Became Strange: Realms of Literary Fantasy." In *The Aesthetics of Fantasy Literature and Art*, ed. Roger C. Schlobin, 105-142. Notre Dame: University of Notre Dame Press, 1982.

Lindsay, Jack. *Turner: The Man and His Art* New York: Franklin Watts, 1985.

Liszt, Franz. "On John Field's Nocturnes." 1859. Translated by Theodore Baker. In *Eighteen Nocturnes for the Piano*. John Field, 1-3. Revised by Franz Liszt, with an essay by Franz Liszt and a biographical sketch of the author by Theodore Baker. *Schirmer's Library of Musical Classics* 42. New York: G. Schirmer, Inc., 1902.

Lovejoy, A. O. "Schiller and the Genesis of German Romanticism." *MLN* 35 (1920):1-10, 136-146.

Lukács, Georg. *Die Eigenart des Ästhetischen*. Vols. 1-2. Neuwied und Berlin: Luchterhand Verlag, 1963.

Marx, Karl. *A Contribution to the Critique of Hegel's "Philosophy of Right." Introduction.* Translated from the German by A. Jolin and J. O'Malley. Cambridge: Cambridge University Press, 1970.

Melville, Derek. *Chopin.* London: Clive Bingley, Ltd., 1977.

Nádor, Tamás. *Fryderyk Chopin Életének krónikaja* (The chronicle of Fryderyk Chopin's life). Budapest: Zenemükiadó, 1982.

Nikolayev, A. A. *John Field.* Translated by Harold M. Cardello. New York: Musical Scope Publish ers, 1973.

Paulson, Ronald. *Literary Landscape: Turner and Constable.* New Haven and London: Yale University Press, 1982.

Pevsner, Nikolaus. *The Englishness of English Art.* Harmondsworth: Penguin Books, 1978.

Piggott, Patrick. *The Life and Music of John Field 1782-1837: Creator of the Nocturne.* Berkeley and Los Angeles: University of California Press, 1973.

Piper, David, ed. *The Genius of British Painting.* London: Weidenfeld and Nicholson, 1975.

Proust, Marcel. *Remembrance of Things Past.* Vols. 1-2. Translated by C. K. Scott Moncrieff. New York: Random House, 1934.

Rawley, Thomas. *British Painting.* Oxford: Phaidon Press, 1976.

Raynor, Henry. *Music in England.* London: Robert Hale, 1980.

Ritchie, Andrew Carnduff. *Masters of British Painting 1800-1950.* New York: The Museum of Modern Art, 1956.

Roskill, Mark. *English Painting from 1500 to 1865.* London: Thames and Hudson, 1962.

Ruskin, John. *Works.* 7 vols. Eds. E. T. Cook and A. Wedderburn. London: Library Edition, 1903-1912.

Samson, Jim. *The Music of Chopin.* London, Boston, and Henley: Routledge and Kegan Paul, 1985.

Schiller, Friedrich. "Über naive und sentimentalische Dichtung." In *Schillers Werke* 20, Benno von Wiese, ed., 413-503. Weimar: Herman Böhlaus Nachfolger, 1962.

Schumann, Robert. "Two Sonatas by Carl Loewe." 1835. In *The Musical World of Robert Schumann: A Selection from his Own Writings,* ed. Henry Pleasants, 45. New York: St. Martin's Press, 1965. Referred to in the essay as Schumann 1.

—-. "John Field, Piano Concerto No, 7, 1835. In *The Musical World of Robert Schumann: A Selection from his Own Writings,* ed. Henry Pleasants, 106. New York: St. Martin's Press, 1965. Referred to in the essay as Schumann 2.

Szabolcsi, Bence. *A zene története* (The history of music). Budapest: Rózsa-völgyi/Athenaeum, 1940. Referred to in the essay as Szabolcsi 1.

—-. *A melódia története* (The history of melody). Budapest: Zenemükiadó, 1957. Referred to in the essay as Szabolcsi 2.

Walker, Ernest. *A History of Music in England.* Revised and enlarged by J. A. Westrup. Oxford: Clarendon Press, 1952.

Walker, John. *A Critical Pronouncing Dictionary and Expositor of the English Language.* London and Leipsic: Ernest Fleicher, 1826.

Wellek, René. *Concepts of Criticism*. New Haven and London: Yale University Press, 1963.

Wilton, Andrew. *J. M. W. Turner: His Art and Life*. Secaucus, N.J.: Popular Books, Inc., 1979.

Winn, James Anderson. *Unsuspected Eloquence: A History of the Relation between Poetry and Music*. New Haven and London: Yale University Press, 1981.

Young, Percy M. *A History of British Music*. London: Ernest Benn, Ltd., 1967.

Part III

USES OF THE FANTASTIC
BY IRISH PLAYWRIGHTS

Although many critics — as Christopher Murray observed in his essay "Irish Drama and the Fantastic" — refuse to believe that the fantastic belongs on the stage at all, since the birth of modern Irish national drama Irish playwrights have relied on their rich legacy of experiencing the world as a harmony of reality and fantasy. And although Irish drama is usually characterized as basically naturalistic and nonexperimental, it was in Ireland that the renewal of drama in the English language started around the turn of this century with Yeats's reintroduction of myth and nonimitative, nonrepresentational stage technique, Synge's grotesque realism enriched with poetry and fantasy, O'Casey's expressionism and surrealism — all contributing to the formation of western European modern drama.

The four Irish playwrights discussed here — John Millington Synge, Sean O'Casey, Samuel Beckett, and Tom Murphy — together illustrate the many different creative ways in which the fantastic has been used in Irish drama.

Toni O'Brien Johnson, in discussing Synge, maintains that grotesque realism "is the principal form he [Synge] gives to fantasy," which he then employs in order to "open the work and prevent it from becoming monological" by forcing the reader to become actively engaged with the text. By focusing on Synge's language, which she claims "interrogates the boundaries" between desire and reality, as well as between the fantastic and the ordinary, Johnson presents an illuminating discussion of three of Synge's best-known plays: *The Playboy of the Western World*, *Riders to the Sea*, and *In the Shadow of the Glen*.

Although a majority of the contemporary theater audience will be familiar with Sean O'Casey's earliest, most famous plays, only a small minority may know the later, less often produced ones. Jürgen Kamm considers the body of O'Casey's plays, then focuses on O'Casey's use of the fantastic in the late ones, in relation to their content and production, as well as to his earliest work. Kamm concludes that "the fantastical elements [in the late plays], in addition to their symbolic value, serve two major functions by being employed for structural and satiric purposes." As often in O'Casey, the butt of the satire is the "philistinism of the secular and clerical dignitaries as well as the . . . backwardness of the values they stand for." On the other hand, those characters in his plays who welcome the fantastic stand out as healthy, loving, and blessed with a good sense of humor. This positive group of characters points "the way toward the liberation from [the kind of] . . . stifling experiences" which O'Casey felt characterized many Irish people and all of those with political or social power. In contrast to Synge, O'Casey in his later years employed the fantastic for didactic rather than psychological ends.

All of the plays of Samuel Beckett, along with some of those of O'Casey and Synge, reflect Rosemary Jackson's contention that: "fantasy . . . is a literature of desire which seeks that which is experienced as absence and loss" (3). Yet Beckett, of all twentieth-century dramatists — and perhaps of all twentieth-century writers — most profoundly wrestles with these issues using the mode of the fantastic. Lance Olsen describes his work as "the journey toward minimalism through the window of entropy and exhaustion" (43). Through a long and distinguished career Beckett "gave voice to the third of every existence likely to be spent in decay" (Ellmann 104) — not an especially happy thought, but one which clearly preoccupied him in his writing.

In his essay, "'Fidelity to Failure': Time and the Fantastic in Samuel Beckett's Early Plays," Donald Morse traces the progression in Beckett's plays from the various "options for action or inaction in *Waiting for Godot* . . . to the other plays where the characters are driven to immobility" through their impotence and ignorance. Choice is meaningless; action is futile. Maddy Rooney, Beckett's brilliant comic creation in *All That Fall*, wittily sums up the choices life presents: "It is suicide to be abroad. But what is it to be at home? A lingering dissolution" (in *Krapp* 39). Pointing to this and many other speeches and actions, Morse contends that what many people find fantastic in Beckett's plays "is actually his view of life lived in time as 'moments for nothing.'"

If Beckett uses the fantastic to explore human ignorance and impotence, Tom Murphy uses it, Csilla Bertha suggests, to reveal psychological reality and enable that which "is invisible inside human beings to appear in the theater." In some plays this revelation takes the form of Freudian dreams "of unconscious fears and distorted desires, projected on stage"; in others it takes the form of the "struggle between the conscious and the unconscious," often confronted with the difficulty in integrating the "shadow figure," "the double . . . into the self." Murphy's use of the fantastic varies from play to play, but usually involves a miracle of some kind — most often one that leads to the restoration of wholeness to a character, and usually demonstrates the power of "creative confluence" rather than logical succession or cause and effect. As such his work illustrates the Irish mind's penchant for dialectical unity that holds "the traditional oppositions of reason together" and which finds the fantastic so congenial.

Theoreticians of the fantastic often argue that the fantastic is not suitable on the stage or that it is too difficult to use in drama, yet Irish drama by its very nature indicates the opposite, partly because the Irish theatrical tradition relies nearly entirely on words, "on talk, on language left to itself" (Deane 12), words which have the power to create whole worlds in the imagination. Dreams, desires, illusions — so central to the Irish way of thinking and to Irish life as well as to fantasy literature — exist in words and images; words are thus an ideal means of conveying them. Also, drama cannot help being fantastic when presenting reality as people experience it either in the many mythical-fantastic plays or in the so-called "realistic" and surrealistic peasant plays which already contain otherwordly figures or phenomena. In contemporary Irish drama where supernatural occurrences are rare, the fantastic is still present: in less traditional, sometimes more subtle, while in other times more shocking theatrical devices which serve to create a medium and atmosphere where "the invisible can appear" (Brook quoted in Murray 9).

Works Cited

Beckett, Samuel. *Krapp's Last Tape and Other Dramatic Pieces*. New York: Grove Press, Inc., 1960.

Deane, Seamus. "Introduction." *Selected Plays of Brian Friel*. London: Faber and Faber, 1984.

Ellmann, Richard. *Wilde, Yeats, Joyce, and Beckett: Four Dubliners*. Washington: Library of Congress, 1986.

Jackson, Rosemary. *Fantasy: The Literature of Subversion*. London: Methuen, 1981.

Murray, Christopher. "Introduction: The Rough and Holy Theatre of Thomas Murphy." *Irish University Review* 17 (Spring 1987): 9-17.

Olsen, Lance. *Ellipse of Uncertainty*. Westport, CT: Greenwood Press, 1987.

Toni O'Brien Johnson

Interrogating Boundaries:
Fantasy in the Plays
of J. M. Synge

The realist side of the plays of John Millington Synge operates as a contrasting base for the fantasy in the characters' language. This realism, with its heavy mimetic burden for those concerned with staging, inspired the minute attention to details of properties and costume for which Synge is noted. When *Riders to the Sea* and *In the Shadow of the Glen* were staged under his direction, authentic pampooties, flannel and a spinning wheel were conscientiously procured to maintain this illusion of "reality," and even the gestures of the actors were based on those observed among the people whom they were supposed to "represent."[1] However, such staging problems simply do not arise for the fantastic element in the plays, for whereas the difficulties of physically staging the fantastic generally preclude it from stage plays, Synge managed to include it by largely confining it to language, thus avoiding those mimetic responsibilities that he had otherwise so fully undertaken.[2]

Seamus Deane regards each of Synge's plays as presenting the story of a fantasy, an illusion which begins in an eloquence that survives the destruction of that illusion (Deane 57f). "Illusion" implies a deception in relation to some identifiable "consensus reality" that might be objectively defined (see Hume 21), and as Deane suggests, the eloquence of the characters survives the elimination of the deceptions. The capacity of their language to create a space for fantasy is not curtailed by the destruction of any particular fantasy, so that the fantastic dimension continues to interrogate the finite boundaries of the "reality" against which they live out their existence.

W. B. Yeats in his well-known account of Synge's language in the preface to *The Well of the Saints* was less concerned with any objective consensus reality that language might be measured against than with its origins and impulses in the subject. In support of his claim for the appropriateness of the strange rhythm of Synge's language, for the "measureless desire" for which he was seeking a dramatic form (Synge 3:64), Yeats states of Nora in *In the Shadow of the Glen*:

> She is driven by desires that need for their expression . . . words full of
> suggestion, rhythms of voice, movements that escape analysis. . . . She is
> intoxicated by a dream which is hardly understood by herself, but possesses her
> like some thing half remembered on a sudden wakening. (Quoted in Synge
> 3:68)

Yeats's location of the origins of desire in dream and sleep here links it
clearly with the unconscious; and his idea of possession by "something half
remembered" suggests the uncanny, or Freud's *Das Unheimliche*. Language,
as Yeats perceives it here, allows desire to slip through, between the lines as it
were. I propose to examine the fantasy of the plays in terms of its breaking into
language from desire, understood as a movement of the subject toward some
Other, and from fear, understood as a movement of the subject away from some
Other.

The uncanny involves knowledge that we would prefer not to recognize, or
that would ordinarily be kept repressed or held back in the unconscious
(Jackson 63-72). If desire as a movement towards some Other cannot be
fulfilled, knowledge of it will in time be repressed so as to avoid the pain of
hopeless recognition. The same applies to fear when it cannot be assuaged. But
when desire and fear are repressed, they do not actually go away or disappear:
instead, they well up unexpectedly, and at an inappropriate moment from the
unconscious where they have been repressed. Sometimes, they nag and possess
their subject, who consequently expresses them obliquely: Synge's Nora in *In
the Shadow of the Glen* is a case in point, for she is prevented from expressing
her desire directly, therefore it breaks through her language from the unconscious.

Desire *de facto* arises from within a subject's unconscious, but in Synge's
plays its surfacing coincides with an arrival from outside the community. In
Riders to the Sea, for example, the boat arrives to take Bartley to Connemara,
evoking Maurya's desire to keep her last son at home and save him from the sea.
The tramp arrives at Nora's cottage in *In the Shadow of the Glen* to evoke from
her an account of the desire that arises from the isolated confinement in which
her marriage has kept her. The saint arrives in *The Well of the Saints* to activate
in the blind couple the desire to see their respective "beauty." Christy arrives
at the Flaherty cottage in *The Playboy of the Western World* to set up Pegeen's
desire for a hero, which in turn inspires him. And in *Deirdre of the Sorrows* Naisi
and his brothers arrive to hunt in the remote woods where Conchubor has
sequestered Deirdre, to make concrete her desire for "a man with his hair like
the raven maybe and his skin like the snow and his lips like blood spilt on it"
(Synge 4:191). *The Tinker's Wedding* inverts this pattern in that the desire
originates with one of the tinkers, themselves outsiders in relation to the settled
community, so that Sarah's dream of a regular marriage occurs through contact
with that settled community, in particular with the priest. This overall pattern
of encounter between external factors and internal desires suggests that in-

dividual fantasy, though conceived in the unconscious, is engendered in an encounter with the limitations of the protagonists' environments. Accordingly, the fantasy in these plays arises from interaction between the conscious and the unconscious, and operates on the dynamic between individual desire and the restrictions of the society against which the protagonists function.

Individual fear or desire cannot ultimately be known by anyone other than its subject and is therefore a solitary experience, but those fears and desires that instigate the fantasy of these plays are connected with death and sex, and can therefore be known in an uncanny way. The uncanniness arises from the fact that although death and sex are universal, knowledge of them is repressed because of fear of a threat to the boundaries of individual identity to which they give rise. Besides, knowledge of sex is repressed for reasons of social "order" — because free-floating desire would threaten the patriarchal institution of marriage. Although the nature of Nora's desire may be "measureless" and "half remembered" — Yeats's words — for Nora herself because of its repression, it can nevertheless be clearly identified as sexual in origin by an audience prepared to read beyond Nora's conscious statements — to read between the lines. The dissatisfaction of the younger woman in the January/May combination has a long literary history, as well as a social history in Ireland, which underlies Synge's rendering of it in Dan and Nora. The textual evidence for this view is Nora's speech after the tramp has refused to lay his hand on Dan to verify whether he is cold:

> Maybe cold would be no sign of death with the like of him, for he was always cold, every day since I knew him,—and every night, stranger—[she covers up his face and comes away from the bed]; but I'm thinking it's dead he is surely. (3:35)

Her almost unconscious addition of "and every night" here is eloquent testimony of her unsatisfied sexual desire: in re-covering her husband's face, she recovers her own desire. The deliberation with which Synge calculated this effect is borne out by his alteration of an earlier typescript so as to mark this slippage with a pause. It had originally read:

> NORA [covering the face again].—Well he was always cold, every day since I knew him, and every night, stranger, and maybe cold would be no sign of death with the like of him. [She comes away from the bed.] I'm thinking it's dead he is surely. (3:34)

Here the phrase "and every night" is buried in the rest of the speech, so that there is no sense that it has slipped out almost unawares. In the final ver sion, Nora's stage business recovers her sexual desire. In a less subtle play, the phrase "and every night" might have been played with a knowing wink to the tramp, but such easy comedy is alien to Synge's work where so much occurs between the lines. Indeed, sexual desire in *The Shadow* is entirely subsumed into language: Nora leaves with the tramp because he has "a fine bit of talk" (3:57).

Although Synge deliberately reinstated the sex he found wanting on the Irish stage, he was strongly opposed to what he saw as drama that was bad because sex-obsessed, as he noted in a letter to Stephen MacKenna in January 1904:

> Heaven forbid that we should have a morbid sex-obsessed drama in Ireland, not because we have any peculiarly blessed sanctity which I utterly deny—see percentage of lunatics in Ireland and causes thereof—but because it is bad drama and is played out. On the French stage the sex-element of life is given without the other balancing [sic] elements; on the Irish stage the people you agree with want the other elements without the sex. I restored the sex-element to its natural place, and the people were so surprised they saw the sex only. (Saddlemyer 1:74)

Insofar as we can take Synge's own plays as a practical application of this theory, the "natural place" for sex in them turns out to be in language, where it slips through from the unconscious. The violent objections *The Shadow* and *The Playboy* gave rise to when they were first performed occurred because the audience would have preferred not to recognize this subtle presence of sexual desire: the uncanny was at work.

The notorious riot that broke out at the word "shift" in *The Playboy* did so only when this word occurred in the third act. "Shift" had already been used in the second act without any objection, but also without any sexual connection, when Pegeen tartly replies to the Widow Quin's pretense of wanting starch, "And you without a white shift or shirt in your whole family since the drying of the flood" (Synge 4:105). The second time this word is used is in Christy's response to the Widow Quin's offer (after Pegeen's withdrawal from him) to find him "finer sweethearts at each waning moon" (Synge 4:165), when he proclaims:

> It's Pegeen I'm seeking only, and what'd I care if you brought me a drift of chosen females, standing in their shifts itself maybe, from this place to the Eastern world. (Synge 4:167)

The main thrust of Christy's ill-received speech, given the unavailability of Pegeen to him, is disdain for the implied sexual availability of a "drift" (a term used in relation to cattle, meaning a "herd") of fine women clothed only in their undergarments. Ironically, Christy's disposition here is chaste, despite the breaking of the taboo on sexual matters in his speech that gave rise to the riot. The fantasy instigated in Christy's language by his desire for Pegeen transgressed the boundaries of social propriety as it was conceived at that time in Dublin. That the boundaries of propriety were regarded as coextensive to the play and "real life" was a reflex of the realism of the staging.

Whereas sexual desire emerges only obliquely from the unconscious through fantastic images in Synge's plays, there is a direct confrontation with possible death in each play, which produces another form of the uncanny related to the common fear of death. This fear arises from the notion of the individual identity being bounded by the body, which in death disintegrates or dissolves. When the dead body of Bartley is brought on stage in *Riders to the Sea*, it could feasibly be the body of Michael for both Maurya and the audience: the identity of one son can be confounded with that of another in death. In *The Shadow* the supposedly dead body of Dan is there on the stage, only to prove not to be dead. Thus the "clear" distinction between what is alive and what is dead is challenged, so that the boundaries between life and death are destabilized. Furthermore, the dead Patch Darcy reappears in the speech of the other characters, also mingling death with life. At the end of *The Well of the Saints*, death by drowning is the fate envisaged by Timmy for the expelled Martin and Mary, though the blind couple entertain a contrasting expectation of life as they leave for a destination unknown and unknowable to the discomfited audience. Michael, at the end of *The Tinker's Wedding*, threatens to drown the trussed priest in a bog-hole and is in a strong enough position to do so (4:47), thus introducing death as a possibility. The supposedly murdered Old Mahon appears literally "fighting fit" — apart from a rent in his crown — in the second act of *The Playboy*, and is reported as truly dead in the third act when Philly claims to have felt "the last gasps quitting his heart" (4:167). Yet he turns up alive a third time to evoke a questioning of the borders between death and life. *Deirdre of the Sorrows* ends with a grave on stage replete with newly dead bodies. The recurrent pattern in the plays is one of death in the midst of life, and the speech of the characters contains many references to death, the whole giving rise to the unease typical of the uncanny.

The important place of sex and death, and the accompanying prominence of the body in Synge's language, arises in part from the folk element in the plays and the consequent adoption and adaptation of a folk aesthetic. Mikhail Bakhtin, in perhaps the most influential work of this century on the functioning of such an aesthetic, has categorized it as *grotesque realism*. This aesthetic makes use of the bodily principle in its cosmic, social, and individual aspects for contrastive purposes with whatever is lofty or ideal, resisting attempts at severance from the material and bodily roots of the world. Typically, *grotesque realism* insists on facing death as a merging of the individual with the earth or cosmos, so that the identity held within the individual body is lost. It also acknowledges that in the sexual act, the boundaries of the individual body are transgressed, as well as in the primary dyad of mother and child that we see in the icon of the infant being suckled. It refuses to ignore the process of ingestion and discharge of food which also involves a continual transgression of the boundaries of the biological individual, and it questions such "easy" distinctions as those between animal, human and divine. Furthermore, it firmly situates the individual within the human mass, confirming the social body as continually decaying but continually being renewed (see Bakhtin, especially 18-23).

The fantasy of Synge's plays primarily takes form in their *grotesque realism*. In this process of transgressing boundaries, whether those of individual biological, social, or conceptual "bodies," *grotesque realism* often expresses anxiety concerning identity and incorporation, seen for instance in the possible confusion between the dead bodies of Michael and Bartley, already mentioned. This had been anticipated in Maurya's uncanny experience of seeing the live Bartley on the red mare with the dead Michael behind on the grey pony. Then, in reply to her daughter's reasonable protest that she could not possibly have seen the dead Michael, meaning that it was an illusion, she says defiantly:

> I'm after seeing him this day, and he riding and galloping. Bartley came first on the red mare, and I tried to say "God speed you," but something choked the words in my throat. He went by quickly; and "the blessing of God on you," says he, and I could say nothing. I looked up then, and I crying, at the grey pony, and there was Michael upon it—with fine clothes on him, and new shoes on his feet. (3:19)

Such a precise material record of what she saw, with details like fine clothes and new shoes, encourages confidence in Maurya's account, so that her evidence of the boundaries between life and death being blurred can be given some credence. Yet the repression of her fear clearly shows in the "something [that] choked the words in [her] throat."

Maurya earlier relates this experience to another occurrence of the same kind, this time to Bride Darra who saw "the dead man with the child in his arms" (3:19). No indefinite articles here: it was *the* dead man and *the* child, so that identity seems not to be in question. However, anxiety of identity surfaces again when Maurya realizes that Michael's body has been in the sea for nine days:

> There does be a power of young men floating round in the sea, and what way would they know if it was Michael they had, or another man like him, for when a man is nine days in the sea, and the wind blowing, it's hard set his own mother would be to say what man was in it. (3:23)

In death, the identity of a young man can be in doubt even for his mother, so that in that sea-ridden community, the women have evolved a way of identifying the disintegrating corpses of their drowned men: they count the stitches in the garments they knit in oiled wool for them. Since it survives the sea, Nora can say with confidence of the stocking found on Michael's body: "It's the second one of the third pair I knitted, and I put up three score stitches, and I dropped four of them" (3:15). The play shows death repeatedly confounding attempts to fix identity, so that Maurya, whose identity is restricted to that of mother, has only a story to tell of six sons, a husband, and a husband's father all of whose identities are ultimately submerged by death in the sea.

In *In the Shadow of the Glen*, the tramp is immediately identified as a stranger by Nora, which categorically places him outside the social body to which she belongs. However, their shared appreciation of fine talk not only allows them to identify with each other, but becomes the means for her to break out of the constraints of her marriage. They also share a fear of death, which causes the tramp to ask for the protection of a needle despite his assertion that "A man that's dead can do no hurt" (3:39). This categorical claim is ironically called into question when Dan sits up in bed and quotes this very phrase back to the tramp (3:41). Nora's fear is also shared by Michael: she observes Dan's orders not to touch his body under threat of a curse (3:35), and Michael refuses to pull down the sheet off Dan's face to check whether he is dead, explaining: "I do be afeard of the dead" (3:45). In these instances, fantasy instigated by fear is translated into action, not merely words.

Nora transgresses the conceptual distinction between human and animal when she identifies Dan's death with that of a sheep, saying he "stiffened himself out the like of a dead sheep" (3:35); and this stings him sufficiently to make him repeat it, with the additional threat of isolation when he envisages *her* death:

> It's lonesome roads she'll be going, and hiding herself away till the end will come, and they find her stretched like a dead sheep with the frost on her, or the big spiders, maybe, and they putting their webs on her, in the butt of a ditch. (3:55)

Dan's fantasy carries the dehumanizing transgression even further by evoking the dying animal's custom of withdrawing to die alone in contrast with most human societies where dying alone is viewed as anathema, and the moment of death is marked by presence and ritual so as to repress the fear of the actual isolation of the dying individual.

Nora's fantasy of the blurring of human and animal distinctions is activated not only by death, but also by the prospect of age and decay:

> Why would I marry you, Mike Dara? You'll be getting old, and I'll be getting old, and in a little while, I'm telling you, you'll be sitting up in your bed—the way himself was sitting—with a shake in your face, and your teeth falling, and the white hair sticking out round you like an old bush where sheep do be leaping a gap. (3:51)

The fantasy here is of the aging settled man as a fixed object — a bush — and only the tramp, who is a mobile outsider to the values of the settled community, can offer Nora the alternative of incorporation within the natural world where nothing is fixed and individual identity is lost (3:57). These repeated references to sheep are a reminder of that animal's renowned herd instinct, which operates against isolation. Although Nora is sufficiently engaged with "reality" to recognize that "it's myself will be wheezing that time lying down under the Heavens when the night is cold", she nevertheless settles for an *isolation à deux* wherein she is at least recognized as a subject of desire.

Likewise in *The Well of the Saints*, the blind couple at the end of the play opt for the possibility of death "on the road" together, rather than accepting the denial of their desire to remain blind on the edge of the settled community. Their continued blindness is necessary for maintaining their shared fantasy of physical beauty. Their opting for a fantasy world instead of consensus reality causes them to be regarded as mad by a community that cannot tolerate the kind of difference that favors blindness over sight, for not only does this choice defy social conformity, but it also opens up possibilities for thinking outside the established structures. For Western discourse has equated seeing with understanding (see Irigaray, especially 133- 227; also Jackson 45f), so that the kind of knowledge that comes from being prepared to forego seeing cannot be comprehended. The community in the play retains the right to create knowingly a collective "counterfantasy" in the lies it tells about the beauty of the blind couple in the first act, but it expels as strangers those who voluntarily maintain that illusion by remaining blind. It allows the kind of verbal structure that creates false connections between signifier, signified, and referent, but only within limits set by itself. Arbitrariness is all very well, but total disregard for established signifying practice on the part of an individual cannot be tolerated by a linguistic community; therefore those who choose to live out a fantasy are necessarily made outsiders.

In *The Playboy of the Western World*, Christy is likewise cast out by the Mayo community for trying to live out a fantasy, and he leaves with Old Mahon. However, the fantasy of parricide has taken him through a range of new identities, and he leaves with a new fantasy of himself as a "gallant captain with his heathen slave" (4:173). Pegeen's desire for him, and his for her, instigate the most fantasy-laden speeches of the play, as well as his confrontation with himself as Other in the scene where he takes down the mirror:

> Didn't I know rightly I was handsome, though it was the divil's own mirror we had beyond, would twist a squint across an angel's brow, and I'll be growing fine from this day, the way I'll have a soft lovely skin on me and won't be like the clumsy young fellows do be ploughing all times in the earth and dung. (4:95)

Liberated from earth and dung here, Christy differentiates himself from such fellows as he used to be, not without disgust, and projects a finer future identity for himself (his "soft lovely skin" is reminiscent of Mary Doul). However, this identity is too fragile to be tested by the gaze of the "Stranger girls" who then arrive, so that he says, "Where'll I hide myself away and my long neck naked to the world. [He looks out.] I'd best go to the room maybe till I'm dressed again." Here we see the privacy of his fantasy isolating him.

In contrast with Christy's "stranger" status, Pegeen is well within the boundaries of her own community at the opening of the play, as she inscribes herself within its patriarchal structures in writing to order supplies including material for her wedding dress. There is no fantasy in her conception of the marriage which, in the words of Shawn Keogh, is "a good bargain" between himself and her father (4:59). Pegeen herself seems mainly concerned to ensure that she is not left alone and frightened in her isolated home. Thus one could say that there is a space for fantasy in her life, a space which Christy readily fills as a fascinating stranger to the community.

Lonesomeness is a recurrent theme in the play, occurring notably in the speech of Pegeen, Christy, and the Widow Quin. The term "lonesome" has survived in everyday usage in rural Ireland in preference to "lonely" for signifying "solitary" or "companionless." Applied to women, it can mean "single" or "widowed," which implies that the solution to it is a union of two. Michael James endorses such unions after Pegeen has left him no choice but to accept Christy as his son-in-law:

> It's the will of God that all should rear up lengthy families for the nurture of the earth. What's a single man, I ask you, eating a bit in one house and drinking a sup in another, and he with no place of his own, like an old braying jackass strayed upon the rocks? (4:157)

The only way for the stranger to avoid lonesomeness is to marry into the community, yet the play ends without a marriage, for this particular outsider leaves with a new fantasy, also in an *isolation à deux*.

By the time we see Christy in his love scene with Pegeen in the third act (4:147-151), fantasy pervades his speech. The future he envisages for himself and Pegeen is in no way constrained by a cottage and the community in which it exists, and even extends to pity for God in *his* lonesomeness:

> CHRISTY: It's then yourself and me should be pacing Neifin in the dews of night, the times sweet smells do be rising, and you'd see a little shiny new moon maybe sinking on the hills.
>
> PEGEEN (*looking at him playfully*): And it's that kind of a poacher's love you'd make, Christy Mahon, on the sides of Neifin, when the night is down?
>
> CHRISTY: It's little you'll think if my love's a poacher's or an earl's itself when you'll feel my two hands stretched around you, and I squeezing kisses on your puckered lips till I'd feel a kind of pity for the Lord God is all ages sitting lonesome in his golden chair.
>
> PEGEEN: That'll be right fun, Christy Mahon, and any girl would walk her heart out before she'd meet a young man was your like for eloquence or talk at all.

Christy's eloquence identifies Pegeen and himself in extravagant terms, and in his following speeches fantasy recognizes no boundaries between what is mythological, human, and divine. But Pegeen's realistic disposition intervenes in these flights with, "But we're only talking maybe, for this would be a poor thatched place to hold a fine lad is the like of you" (4:159). As Rosemary Jackson points out about arbitrary, capricious combinations of the kind that occur in Christy's talk:

> Fantasy re-combines and inverts the real, but it does not escape it: it exists in a parasitical or symbiotic relation to the real. The fantastic cannot exist independently of that "real" world which it seems to find so frustratingly finite. (20)

Here in *The Playboy* and elsewhere in Synge's plays, fantasy is presented against such a background of the "real." The primary mode of the plays is mimetic, but the fantastic is incorporated to "open" the work and prevent it from becoming monological.

Lonesomeness is also a recurrent theme in *Deirdre of the Sorrows*, centering on Deirdre. First, the action is located at varying distances from the center of society at Emain Macha. There is a sense in which the social body is dismembered when Deirdre, Naisi, and his brothers leave for Alban; and the strange fighters that Conchubor has brought in to kill Naisi and his brothers (4:249) can also be seen as an invasion of that body. Fergus uses homesickness as an argument for persuading the runaways to return, adding, "Let you come this day for there's no place but Ireland where the Gael can have peace always" (4:225). Separation from the tribe and homeland is presented as something to be feared or regretted. Based on a heroic tale that promotes the notion of a unified social body, this play shows the disruption that individual desire causes to such a body.

The background desire is that of Conchubor for Deirdre as the young woman who will relieve the loneliness of his old age. But the desire that moves the action is that of Deirdre for Naisi. There is also Owen's desire for Deirdre, which instigates some of the most grotesque of the bodily images in the play, for instance:

> Well go take your choice. Stay here and rot with Naisi, or go to Conchubor in Emain. Conchubor's a swelling belly, and eyes falling down from his shining crown, Naisi should be stale and weary; yet there are many roads, Deirdre [he goes towards her], and I tell you I'd liefer be bleaching in a bog-hole than living on without a touch of kindness from your eyes and voice. It's a poor thing to be so lonesome you'd squeeze kisses on a cur dog's nose. (4:223)

These imagined kisses to a dog, resulting from loneliness, again transgress the animal/human boundary: unsatisfied desire leads to a collapse of the boundaries of species. But Deirdre recognizes how desire itself collapses in the presence of death: "by a new made grave there's no man will keep brooding on a woman's lips" (4:253). Desire, shared or not, is upstaged by death. In Deirdre's words: "We've had a dream, but this night has waked us surely" (4:255). Despite this awakening, her most eloquent speeches follow in her fantasy from the edge of her grave, where she incorporates her individual identity with that of her lover and his brothers: she too "leaves" with her chosen company, this time for an *isolation à quatre*.

Loneliness and incorporation are also preoccupations in *The Tinker's Wedding*, where the ring intended to symbolize the incorporation of Sarah Casey's identity in that of her partner Michael Byrne plays an important structural role. On the realist level, it causes Michael considerable pain to make the ring (4:7), and it is tight for Sarah's finger (4:9). For Mary, the wise old woman of the play, it is no protection against the woman's labor pains:

> Is it putting that ring on your finger will keep you from getting an aged woman and losing the fine face you have, or be easing your pains, when it's the grand ladies do be married in silk dresses, with rings of gold, that do pass any woman with their share of torment at the hour of birth, and do be paying the doctors in the city of Dublin a great price at that time, the like of what you'd pay for a good ass and a cart? (4:37)

Mary here undermines the symbolic function of the ring by bringing the consequences of physical union for the woman to the fore. By the same process of foregrounding physical consequences, she conveys the inappropriateness of rings for tinkers, denying any need for "drawing rings on our fingers, would be cutting our skins maybe when we'd be taking the ass from the shafts, and pulling the straps the time they'd be slippy with going around beneath the heavens in the rains falling" (4:47). The inseparability of the human body from the surrounding body of nature underlies Mary's view, and the inappropriateness of the social forms of the settled community for the tinkers is accordingly maintained.

The final use of the ring in the play occurs when Sarah puts it on the priest's finger before she leaves, to remind him of his oath not to denounce them to the police. Thus the usual function of this symbol for the settled community is altered: instead of binding the identity of the woman to that of the man, it binds the priest to a silence that will leave the tinkers their freedom. Yet their freedom has to be lived outside, off-stage, for the priest is pointedly left "master of the situation" at the end of the play, suggesting the social power that confronts fantasy.

Sarah's fantasy of adopting the settled community's formal mode of sexual union arises from her desire to stave off infidelity with Jaunting Jim (4:9, 11, 35). But once again Mary is skeptical, asking Michael: "And you're thinking it's paying gold to his reverence would make a woman stop when she's a mind to go?" (4:35). The priest, as regulator of desire in his role of marriage legalizer within his own settled community, is its only representative to appear on stage. But the respective views that these two social bodies have of each other are such that the priest's regulation cannot be transferred except in fantasy. For instance, the priest's distaste for what he perceives as the tinkers' invasion of the body of his church is evident when he says: "I wouldn't have you coming in on me and soiling my church" 4:(43). Few things are as sure to exclude one from the social body as objections to physical uncleanliness, which is what the priest is indicating here, as well as when he dismisses the tinkers: "Let you walk off now and take every stinking rag you have there from the ditch" (4:41). But the tinkers operate with other standards for the body; being notoriously thin and wiry, they can accuse this very priest of being "a big boast of a man" (4:13) and "near burst with fat" (4:43), conveying their distance from him. Furthermore, Mary accuses Sarah of waking her up with the unaccustomed sound of her washing her face, for "washing is a rare thing" (4:29), giving us another instance of the disruption that Sarah's fantasy is causing to their way of life as tinkers.

Only two things are in fact exchanged between the tinkers and the priest: the ring that Sarah puts on the priest's finger and the porter Mary gives him to drink (4:17). Porter can operate as a suppresser of desire, taken in sufficient quantities, or as a liberator of fantasy, depending on the individual, and while the priest has a reputation for consuming plenty of it (4:13, 19), he appears to have little fantasy. Mary, however, uses porter for another purpose, to combat loneliness by opening up social boundaries in the pub, where she will find an audience for her stories since she currently has none within the tinker community. She offers to tell a story to Sarah who is not interested and leaves. Left alone Mary thinks:

> What good am I this night, God help me? What good are the grand stories I have when it's few would listen to an old woman, few but a girl maybe would be in great fear the time her hour was come, or a little child wouldn't be sleeping with the hunger on a cold night? (4:27)

Here she sees the power of her fantasy as confined to the helpless. Thinking of the consequences of selling the can that Sarah has put aside to pay for her marriage, she muses: "What's a little stroke on your head beside sitting lonesome on a fine night" (4:27). Mary's need for an audience is acute, and she is clearly practiced at finding one in pubs (4:37). Thus, while on the realistic level boundaries cannot be crossed, it seems that fantasy structured into narrative can be taken from the tinkers by the settled community, and in addition to Mary's *telling* stories in pubs, she also *listens* to the "great talk" of the settled community (4:37). Language appears to be the only means of incorporation into a community.

This consideration of fantasy suggests that in Synge's plays individual fantasy, after having in some way attempted to incorporate the individual identity with some Other, tends to turn ultimately its subjects back upon themselves. Only social or communitarian answers acceptable within the social body can lead to any satisfaction of human desire which does not rely on transgression. Thus fantasy heightens but sublimates desire, and in so doing becomes a substitute for the satisfaction of desire in social life. The richest fantasy appears to be one that can be shared in talk and stories, for this implies a linguistic movement toward the Other and a refusal of notions of separateness and isolation.

None of the individuals who have a fantasy in Synge's plays succeed in substituting their dreams for consensus reality, or in finally subverting established society; and where death as the ultimate isolation is undone, it transpires that it was not, after all, true death. Yet fantasy does disrupt the status quo, and through the disillusionment but continuing eloquence of the central characters, the sympathy of the audience is enlisted for the fantasy which their desire has instigated. The desire for difference drives certain characters beyond the boundaries of their initial perceived identity, which sometimes involves incorporation with or separation from another. Desire and fear either instigate invasion or recoil from invasion by another. And the language of fantasy in the plays constantly has recourse to images of the body where its boundaries are never intact because such language is always in process, always unfinished. The continual transgression of boundaries, together with the lack of true resolution at the end of the plays, prevents them from being closed texts and creates a space for the audience or reader to enter a shared fantasy with the author: to be incorporated in the text.

Notes

1. See Ann Saddlemyer, in her "Introduction" to volume 3 J. M. Synge, *Collected Works*, for details of these early productions.

2. See Kathryn Hume for a brief discussion of the difficulties of staging fantasy (163).

Works Cited

Bakhtin, Mikhail. *Rabelais and his World*. Trans. Helen Iswolski. Boston: MIT Press, 1968.

Deane, Seamus. *Celtic Revivals: Essays in Modern Irish Literature*. London: Faber & Faber, 1985.

Freud, Sigmund. "The Uncanny." In *The Standard Edition of the Complete Psychological Works of Sigmund Freud*, 24 vols, trans. James Strachey, 17:217-252. London: Hogarth Press, 1964.

Hume, Kathryn. *Fantasy and Mimesis: Responses to Reality in Western Literature*. London: Methuen, 1984.

Irigaray, Luce. *Speculum of the Other Woman*. Trans. Gillian Gill. Ithaca: Cornell

University Press, 1985.

Jackson, Rosemary. *Fantasy: The Literature of Subversion*. London: Methuen, 1981.

Johnson, Toni O'Brien. *Synge: The Medieval and the Grotesque*. Gerrards Cross, Bucks.: Colin Smythe; Totowa: Barnes & Noble, 1982.

Saddlemyer, Ann, ed. *The Collected Letters of John Millington Synge*. 2 vols. Oxford: Clarendon Press, 1983.

Stallybrass, Peter, and Allon White. *The Politics and Poetics of Transgression*. London: Methuen, 1986.

Synge, John Millington. *Collected Works*. General ed. Robin Skelton. Vols. 3 and 4, *Plays*, ed. Ann Saddlemyer. London: Oxford University Press, 1962-1968.

Jürgen Kamm

The Uses of the Fantastic
in the Later Plays
of Sean O'Casey

On 10 April 1922 a Dublin playwright by the name of Sean O Cathasaigh submitted a copy of a short play under the title of *The Seamless Coat of Kathleen* to Lennox Robinson, already a distinguished dramatist and one of the Abbey Theater's directors, inquiring if the Abbey were interested in producing this "allegorical play in one act dealing with the present situation in Ireland — from my point of view" (*Letters* 1:100f). Robinson informed "Dear Mr. O Cathasaigh [sic]" (*Letters* 1:101) on 15 April that his request could unfortunately not be complied with, the play being "too definite a piece of propaganda for us to do it" (*Letters* 1:101), but he nevertheless encouraged the author of *The Seamless Coat of Kathleen* in his literary pursuits by stating: "The Directors and I have read your play and like a great deal of it — its humour and the element of phantasy in it" (*Letters* 1:101).

O Cathasaigh felt no doubt emboldened by this reply and on 12 April 1923 — he had meanwhile changed his name to Sean O'Casey — his first play, *The Shadow of a Gunman*, had its premier at the Abbey Theatre. The success of this production enticed the board of directors to stage a further play by O'Casey, who had by then revised *The Seamless Coat of Kathleen* and had retitled it *Kathleen Listens In*. The play opened at the Abbey on 1 October 1923 and failed disastrously, the audience receiving the playwright's view of "the present situation in Ireland" in stony silence.

The consequences of the play's reception on O'Casey's subsequent development as a dramatist are difficult to overrate. At least for a while he strenuously avoided nonrealistic, "phantastic" modes of presentation and instead continued in the realistic vein which he had so successfully pursued in *The Shadow of a Gunman*. While on a visit to London in 1926 the celebrated author of the Dublin plays remarked about his recent career:

> When *The Shadow of a Gunman* was produced at last by Abbey in 1923, I was elated, and began to write phantasies on politics. One of these, *Kathleen Listens In*, was done at the Abbey, but it was so badly received that I went home

brokenhearted, without going behind even to thank the artists. And that same night in my attic I sat down to write *Juno and the Paycock*. *("Sean O'Casey Sees London"* 4)

The disappointment at the failure of his early dramatic "phantasy" was so thoroughgoing that O'Casey did not venture to publish the text until 1961 when a first version appeared in *The Tulane Drama Review.*[1] In his prefatory note to the play, now under the title of *Kathleen Listens In*, he formulates an interesting distinction between "phantasies" and "realistic plays"

The one interest *Kathleen Listens In* has for me is that it is a "phantasy," done after my first play at the Abbey, showing this form was active in my mind before the "major" realistic plays were written, 'tho most critics maintain that phantasy began after I left Dublin. This, of course, is what they want to believe, and so, God be with them. ("Kathleen Listens In" 36)

The textual evidence as offered by *Kathleen Listens In* does indeed contradict the still widespread notion that O'Casey's early writings were exclusively realistic. Moreover, O'Casey himself acknowledged that in his later plays he returned to what in a letter to the critic Saros Cowasjee he called: his "first principle of phantasy" (Cowasjee 205). O'Casey never bothered to define precisely what the term phantasy was meant to signify, nor did he care to elaborate on the principles appertaining to it, yet what emerges clearly is that he employed the term as synonymous with "nonrealistic."

Meticulous research during the past decades on the peculiar qualities of fantastic literature has attempted to define fantasy more precisely by setting it off against mimetic literature and by describing it as an isolated phenomenon. As a result definitions of the term have become legion (see Hume 5-28) and the very existence of the fantastic as a genre still remains a matter of scholarly controversy. Tzvetan Todorov's theory that the fantastic relies on the ambiguity of phenomenal experience, luring the reader into irresolution as to the credibility of the narrated events, has largely been rejected, since a story's final resolution of such ambiguity altogether demolishes a generic concept of the fantastic and at best grants it a fleeting and escapist nature. Rosemary Jackson presses the point even further by flatly discarding the idea of the fantastic as an abstract entity. She acknowledges the existence of different literary works sharing similar structural characteristics, but these she views as being generated by similar unconscious desires (7-8). If, however, works with similar structural characteristics may be identified, the demand for a definition of this body of works through a poetological analysis of the ingrained similarities between them appears warranted.

Despite such controversies, a common denominator can be found by viewing fantasy as the literature of the impossible (Irwin 4), operating, as Kathryn Hume puts it, through *"any departure from consensus reality"* (Hume

21). The most salient feature of fantasy literature, therefore, is the violation of rules set up by empirical experience. Florian F. Marzin in his study *Die phantastische Literatur* concludes that the fantastic comes into being whenever the world of the empirically possible is brought into contact and, indeed, into conflict with the world of the empirically impossible. Hume broadens the issue yet further by embracing allegories, utopias, and science fiction since these forms of literature too depart from consensus reality and hence qualify as fantastic (22). Hume, however, does not seek to describe and define the fantastic as a literary genre but argues that the fantastic, along with the mimetic, represents a tool by which a writer may efficiently shape his visions of the universe, of "reality" (103, 113-114, 121-123).

Applying such a broad, "inclusive" notion of fantasy to O'Casey's dramatic writings, an allegorical one-act play such as *Kathleen Listens In* would qualify as being fantastic. Likewise, a number of O'Casey's experiments with nonrealistic predominantly expressionist modes of presentation could be subsumed under the heading of "fantasy." Thus, the famous second act of *The Silver Tassie* (1928) does not portray a world belonging to the empirically impossible but through his "fantastic" treatment of the all too frightfully "real" trench warfare of 1914 to 1918 O'Casey undoubtedly departs from consensus reality. Similarly, plays such as *Within the Gates* (1933), *Oak Leaves and Lavender* (1946) and *Red Roses for Me* (1948), represent important experiments with nonrealistic techniques. These plays mark important stages in the dramatist's artistic development which may well be characterized by O'Casey's gradual departure from a purely mimetic mode (see Achilles). Ultimately, this led the aging playwright to a (re-)discovery of the artistic potential which the fantastic holds in store. Looking back on his progress as a dramatist O'Casey himself remarked:

> To me what is called naturalism, or even realism, isn't enough. They usually show life at its meanest and commonest, as if life never had time for a dance, a laugh, or a song. I always thought that life had a lot of time for these things, for each was a part of life itself; and so I broke away from realism into the chant of the second act of *The Silver Tassie*. But one scene in a play as a chant or a work of musical action and dialogue was not enough, so I set about trying to do this in an entire play, and brought forth *Cock-a-Doodle Dandy*. It is my favourite play; I think it is my best play—a personal opinion. ("Cockadoodle Doo" 143)

Although critics may disagree with O'Casey's "personal opinion" there can be no doubt that *Cock-a-Doodle Dandy* (1949) is a masterly achievement. It is also the first of his later plays which include *Time to Go* (1951), *The Bishop's Bonfire* (1955), *The Drums of Father Ned* (1958), and *Figuro in the Night* (1961) which form a surprisingly homogeneous body of works as regards their subject matter and dramatic form.[2] All these plays are set in Ireland and — with the exception of *Figuro in the Night* — the stage actions manifest themselves in small rural communities far removed from the centers of culture and civilization. Each of the actions is restricted to a single day in a not precisely defined contemporary present, and each employs similar sets of dramatis personae. These comprise representatives of the politically and socially powerful group of profit-seeking local dignitaries who are in league with the representatives of the Catholic clergy. The village priest in these plays is the most powerful opponent of progress and change as O'Casey's priest figures reveal themselves as enemies to everything which the members of the younger generation and the representatives of the workers strive for.

The struggle between these groups of characters is at the root of the central dramatic conflicts and, while it serves to delineate the universal conflicts of good and evil, it also facilitates investigations into specific Irish problems during the forties and fifties as O'Casey saw them. Hence, these plays are thematically concerned with the problems of mass emigration and lives in exile, with the repression of sexual love and the resulting late marriage, with cultural ignorance, fierce anticommunism and literary censorship, with ruthless materialism and single-minded profiteering, and, finally, with the hegemonial power and influence of the Catholic clergy whose rigid dogmatism O'Casey held responsible for most of Ireland's predicament.

In the dramatic form of these plays O'Casey achieves an astonishing degree of originality by fusing into a new and coherent form diverse techniques of scenic presentation, which he had partly experimented with in earlier plays. Elements of realism are blended with symbolic stylization, farcical events are combined with allegorical components and, in addition, O'Casey employs features of expressionist drama, melodrama, satire, music, dance, and song. What is genuinely new with regard to O'Casey's oeuvre, however, is the introduction of fantastical components although the amount, range, and scope of such elements vary greatly between the in dividual plays, with fantasy being central to *Cock-A-Doodle Dandy* and only peripheral to *The Drums of Father Ned.*

The fantastic in these plays is embodied in the shape of empirically impossible figures or objects which are endowed with supernatural powers and which, when brought into contact with "realistic," that is to say empirically possible characters and settings, create confusion and occasionally havoc. The most impressive and artistically most accomplished of these figures is that of the human sized Cock in *Cock-a-Doodle Dandy* who makes Michael Marthraun's house shake to its foundations, who has thunder and lightning at his command, who magically transforms himself into a "silken glossified tall hat" (368), and who casts a spell on Michael's whiskey bottle turning it red hot. The fierce beating of his wings causes violent winds which whip off the trousers of those who oppose him, and all attempts to shoot the rebellious bird are doomed to fail because bullets pass right through this magic creature.

If the enchanted Cock is responsible for upsetting the lives of the people in Nyadnanave, the same can be said of Widda Machree and Kelly of the Isle of Mananaun in the short play *Time to Go.* Under their influence barren trees "suddenly flush with blossom, foliage, and illuminated fruit" (291); they use their supernatural powers to freeze other characters in their movements and they, too, resist arrest by simply sliding out of their handcuffs and they finally disappear in an act of inexplicable mystery.

Among such fantastical figures, that of Father Ned occupies a somewhat unusual position in that he never appears on stage. All that is ever heard of him is his incessant drumming, by which he summons the young and trusting to take part in the revelry of life. Although he exists solely in the sound of his drums and by oblique reference, the fact that he is reported to have been spied in several places at the same time bestows a fantastical quality on him, and the magical atmosphere of the play coheres around this invisible figure.

Poised similarly on the brink between realism and the fantastic is the figure of the Birdlike Lad in *Figuro in the Night*, who bears a striking resemblance to the Cock in outward appearance, being clad in "black narrow trousers, close-fitting black jersey . . . bright yellow socks, and yellow sandals or shoes" (361). This strange creature – partly human, partly animal – emerges mysteriously from the shadows and "while he speaks his words are accompanied by, not loud but clear, hoots of owls, caws from rooks, and rattles from corncrakes" (363). With "a gay cawing laugh" (361), not unlike a crow's, the Birdlike Lad proclaims to the astounded and confused Dubliners the news of "an abounding joy everywhere at last" (361).

The reason for such abounding joy is the Figuro of the title, a statue resembling that of *Manneken piss* in Brussels which, by some weird magic, has appeared in O'Connell Street and which, as the Birdlike Lad announces, has meanwhile surfaced everywhere in Ireland. The statue of the Figuro, "weavin' a fountain outa him in a way that was a menace to morality" (351), is the cause for numerous transformations, especially among the Dublin womanhood. Thousands of women crowd around the statue to get a closer look at its anatomical properties, and the men are in danger of having their clothes torn to shreds and of losing their "decent dangling accessory" (351). The fire brigade is just as powerless to restrain the tumultuous masses of women as are the Civic Guards and the Legion of Mary, and, worst of all, the Irish bishops "are seated at a Round Table in the Senate Room, Maynooth" (361), singing with full voices love songs such as "Come and Kiss Me, Sweet and Plenty."

Mysteries of quite a different nature emanate from yet another statue with supernatural powers, that of Saint Tremolo in *The Bishop's Bonfire*. While Councillor Reiligan and Canon Burren are feverishly preparing for the expected visit of Bishop Mullarkey to his native town of Ballyoonagh, the Bishop has sent on in advance the statue of his private saint, Saint Tremolo: "The statue is a big one, about three feet high, and its form takes the shape of a modern sculpture and somewhat fantastic" (69). Dressed in the uniform of a Roman legionary, the statue – irreverently referred to by one character as the "buckineeno boyo" – wears a buccina coiled around his body on which he is capable of emitting sharp blasts. Rumor has it that all Bishop Mullarkey's thoughts and actions are directed by Saint Tremolo's Roman wind instrument: "If his thinkin' right, the buckineeno blows a steady note; if his thinkin's goin' wrong, the buckineeno quavers" (57). Moreover, Saint Tremolo proves to be highly sensitive to his surroundings, and whenever improper thoughts are pondered or "indecent" actions are performed in his presence by any of the characters, he is quick at responding to such "unholinesses" with forbidding, wailing blasts from his buccina.

O'Casey employs these fantastic characters, fantastic objects, and the frequently fantastic actions which they trigger off, to fulfill diverse thematical and formal functions. The artistic success of his later plays, therefore, depends largely on the degree to which O'Casey achieves a satisfying incorporation of the fantastic elements into the overall structure of an individual play.

This brief survey of the fantastic components suggests that the playwright created them as symbolic representations of abstract concepts. Thus, the Cock embodies what O'Casey himself calls "the joyful, active spirit of life" ("Cock-adoodle Doo" 144), and this spirit becomes immediately evident in the Cock's outward appearance: the "black plumage" symbolizes his demonic and magical powers, the "bright green flaps" are an unmistakable reference to Ireland and the "big crimson crest" (122) asserts both the Cock's proverbial virility and his rebellious spirit.

In *Time to Go* the two fantastic characters are appalled at having committed "an ugly, mortal sin, an' a mean one, too" (269) since Widda Machree has asked too much for a cow and Kelly who has bought the animal is similarly conscience-stricken because he, for his part, believes that she has asked too little. In their attitudes toward business they reveal a boundless altruism which O'Casey employs to reevaluate in symbolic terms the humanistic spirit as it is codified in legends as well as in Christianity (see Pauli 183). The "otherworldliness" of these characters is realized dramati cally by their supernatural powers, and these they employ, among other purposes, to resist attempts at their arrest. The very fact that they cannot possibly be shot or put into chains underlines the nature of the spiritual concepts they symbolize.

In *The Drums of Father Ned* the background to the action is the Tostal which is being prepared and which O'Casey describes as "a yearly festival of promise in my country, Ireland; a festival of drama, music, dancing, folk-art, national games, and films, lasting a fortnight within the month of May" ("O'Casey's Drama Bonfire" 138-139). Father Ned takes over the role of presiding God at the festivities (see Templeton 61), beating his drum to awaken the youthful characters and to encourage them to set out for a future where the spirit of the Tostal is not restricted to a fortnight but prevalent throughout the year. The very spirit of the Tostal, the spirit of joy and celebration is embodied in the indefatigable figure of Father Ned, but the fact that he does not appear on stage "constitutes an admission that he cannot as yet be defined in visual terms" (Knight 180).

In contrast to the figure of Father Ned, the statues of the Figuro and of Saint

Tremolo function as visual symbols of opposing spirits. While the Figuro communicates in symbolic terms the concepts of love and sexual fulfillment, Saint Tremolo's piercing blasts are audible portents of the forces which suppress O'Casey's cherished values of joy, love, and sexuality. The fact that the bishop's statue is discovered to be "all holla underneath" (69) satirizes the Catholic clergy in an amusing way as well as being a delightful finishing touch to Saint Tremolo's symbolic quality.

It is precisely this opposition of values that concerns O'Casey. The introduction of the fantastical elements, in addition to their symbolic value, serves two further major functions by being employed for structural and satiric purposes. Since O'Casey attempts to investigate competing values, he is primarily interested in experimenting with basic situations which can be used as suitable testing grounds for such values. For this reason, plot in the sense of a logical sequence of events is replaced by numerous individual scenes (cf. Kosok *O'Casey the Dramatist* 238). Whereas such an approach does not pose too severe problems in the short plays, the danger of jeopardizing the unity of a full-length play through a lack of plot is counterbalanced with varying degrees of success by including the fantastic elements. In *Cock-a-Doodle Dandy* dramatic unity is safeguarded by the character of the enchanted Cock, who is either acting on stage and sparking off the events or who asserts his magical presence even when invisible. Similar structural qualities, however, cannot be ascribed to Saint Tremolo, who is clearly anything but the structural center of *The Bishop's Bonfire*, nor to Father Ned whose drum beating while supporting other characters in their beliefs and convictions is insufficient for sustaining dramatic unity.

Still, the fantastic in these plays is assigned a minor structural function in that Saint Tremolo's blasts in *The Bishop's Bonfire* and the mysterious Echo in *The Drums of Father Ned* (which repeats parts of the dialogue and is even listed under the dramatis personae), deliver ironic comments on the action. The effect of these devices is, however, marred by the lack of consistency with which they are employed. Thus, Saint Tremolo on some occasions remains silent while irreverent speeches are made in his presence, and the Echo, too, rests taciturn when an audience would expect it to come to life. Since they cannot be construed by the evidence of the text, such inconsistencies in the use of the fantastic are detrimental to the literary merits of these dramas. They suggest that O'Casey paid little attention to the possibilities of exploiting these devices for the sake of a densely wrought dramatic texture, and that he preferred to use them either as amusing gimmicks which enhance the farcical humor of individual scenes or as a means of alienating realistic stage settings in order to create a fantastic atmosphere.

Structurally, the fantastic serves a further function which is best designated by the term "catalytic." Whenever the fantastic clashes with the realistic, the dramatic action is significantly propelled forward and the dramatic conflicts are precipitated, since the fantastic is used to put into sharp relief the contradictions existing on the realistic level. It is this catalytic force of the fantastic which allows each action to be confined to a single day and which, in turn, contributes toward the dramatic unity.

If the clash between the fantastic and the realistic serves a catalytic function on the structural level, O'Casey further exploits this confrontation to expose and to scourge, often in a comic form, the philistinism of the secular and clerical dignitaries as well as the morbidity and backwardness of the values they stand for. That the fantastic characters are fashioned as sharp blades of satire is already hinted at in the stage directions: the Cock *"has the look of a cynical jester"* (122), Widda Machree *"has a semi-plaintive air, though this is occasionally changed into a humorous, half-cynical manner"* (269), Kelly's face is *"pale and grave-looking, though occasionally showing a satirical line in it"* (278), and the Birdlike Lad speaks *"with a cawing laugh of derision" (363).*

As soon as the world of the fantastic encroaches upon that of the realistic, the established order of the latter is challenged and its representatives are forced to put to the test every possible strategy at their disposal so as to defend the continuity of the old order. By doing so they fall back on well-tried devices such as intimidation, armed force, denunciation, and expulsion, thus exposing the means by which they have managed to maintain power. Since such ruthless contrivances prove to be utterly unsuited to fight the fantastic, the representatives of the old order reveal themselves as chicken-hearted, foolish, ignorant brutes. Their defeats nearly always provoke laughter, and they are often metaphorically and symbolically significant.

In *Cock-a-Doodle Dandy* Michael Marthraun, the prosperous bog owner, and Sailor Mahan, the equally well-to do haulage contractor, are constantly quarreling over prices and continuously contriving new schemes to exploit their workers: "My turf-workers an' your lorry-drivers are screwin' all they can get out of us so that they'll have more to spend on pictures an' in th' dance halls" (164-165). It is hardly surprising, therefore, that they are selected as victims of the Cock's magic: they are flung to the ground as their chairs collapse mysteriously under them, and Michael must watch helplessly as the infuriated bird picks his precious tall-hat, the symbol of Michael's bourgeois respectability, to pieces.

Similarly, the philistinism of the two characters is satirically exposed. While they pay lip service to virtue and chastity, they are only too eager to make passes at the women. But when Marion jovially responds to the men's flirtations, the ornament which the young girl wears on her head suddenly separates into two parts, *"forming two branching horns, apparently sprouting from her forehead"* (150). Fearfully, Michael and Mahan flinch back from what they believe to be the devil in a woman's guise but Marion's amusing remark, "Was th' excitement too much for yous, or what? . . . The way you slumped so sudden down, you'd think I'd horns on me, or somethin'!" (151), clearly shows that the fantastic device operates on a symbolic level. It satirically exposes the misled sexual imagination of the men who recognize in every woman nothing but the temptations of the devil. Partly, this is the result of superstitious tall tales about strange apparitions and wondrous specters as they are told by old Shanaar who points out to Michael and Mahan: "You might meet a bee that wasn't a bee; a bird that wasn't a bird; or a beautiful woman who wasn't a woman at all" (135). Shanaar's mysticism, however, is equally exposed to ridicule since his mumbo jumbo of bog Latin simply does not affect the Cock, and the old blatherer, supposedly "full of wisdom an' th' knowledge of deeper things" (135), quickly takes to his heels when the giant bird confronts him.

The most potent representative of the old order and hence the Cock's immediate antagonist is the village priest, Father Domineer, whose name amply suggests the paramount power of the Catholic clergy which "dominates" the thoughts and actions of the villagers. Father Domineer is, of course, a stylized figure, a devil incarnate who not only orders the burning of "blasphemous" books including one by Voltaire and another entitled "Ullisississies, or somethin'" (201) but who also prides himself quite openly on his misogynism. Having worked himself into a fury, Father Domineer even strikes dead Sailor Mahan's best worker for the simple reason that the man is "livin' in sin with a lost an' wretched woman" (186). To portray a priest on stage as a murderer who, moreover, uses the power of his office to cover up the deed ("Sure, we know that, Father — it was a pure accident" 189), came little short of inviting hostility, and O'Casey was reproached with exaggerating the criticism of the clergy (Cowasjee 92). And yet, in dramatic terms the playwright needed a character such as Father Domineer to create an equally potent opponent to the Cock. After the disciples of Father Domineer's repressive maxims have suffered further amusing defeats in the shape of black eyes and sore legs, after they have lost parts of their clothing and have finally been punished with immobility, the Cock plays his pranks on Father Domineer who, as the scene grows and a resonant clash of thunder is heard, is carried away on the bird's back.

To slightly lesser degrees, similar satiric uses of the fantastic can be identified in the other plays under consideration. *The Drums of Father Ned*, for example, closes with a scene which is as fantastic as it is satiric. As Mayor Binnington and Councillor Reiligan, the representatives of the old order, hurriedly prepare to put on their official garments, they suddenly find that *"the robes seem to have become too big for them, the chains dangle down too far, and the cocked hats fall down to their eyes"* (235). The scene abounds with farcical humor as the two men unsuccessfully try to disentangle themselves from the timeworn symbols of their offices, but it also criticizes in comic form their lack of intellectual mobility which, quite literally, causes their downfall.

Time to Go directs the thrust of the satire against ruthless materialism as practiced by Flagonson who owns the tavern, by Farrell who runs the general store, and by the rich farmer Conroy, whose minds are: "all bent down over the thought of gain" (278). When their attitudes to business are challenged and exposed by Kelly and Widda Machree the powers of repression resort yet again to intimidation: "You must be th' boyo who th' Sergeant told me was spreadin' ideas about incitin' to discontentation everywhere. I can tell you, th' polis'll soon be on your tail!" (279). Again, the mechanisms which are used to stabilize power are laid bare and again the fantastic characters remain unimpressed and unaffected by them. What is more, it even seems as if the fantastic could transform the realistic when the tune of "Jingle Coins," which Kelly had been singing to ridicule the realistic characters' outrageous greed, is heard in the background and the scene is suddenly and fantastically metamorphosed: "*The two barren trees in the background suddenly flush with blossom, foliage, and illuminated fruit" (291).* But what one character acknowledges as "Jayayus, a miracle!" (291) turns out to be only transient.

As soon as Mrs. Flagonson appears and urges her husband to help her tot up the day's takings, the miracle vanishes at once, the glowing trees "becoming dead and barren again" (292). The promise of a more gratifying existence which the fantastic proffered is utterly destroyed by the return of the materialistic spirit and the vision is finally down graded to "only a halleelucination" (292).

These examples illustrate that the forces of repression, the forces of the old order as they are represented by the priests, the influential land owners, the shopkeepers, and the politicians are on the receiving end of O'Casey's harsh, if often hilarious satire. The fierce wind of repression which even makes God heave "a long, sad sigh" (85) at the end of *The Bishop's Bonfire*, blows through all the later plays, albeit with different velocities. If the representatives of the old order are made the butt of O'Casey's criticism, the playwright's sympathies clearly reside with the victims of such repression. They are predominantly found among the younger generation, and in these characters O'Casey stakes his hope for a better future when life will again be filled with joy, love, dance, and song. While the councilors, mayors, rich farm owners, businessmen, and village priests are scared out of their wits by the "joyful, active spirit of life," the youthful characters, for their part, develop a much more friendly relationship with the world of the fantastic. Since they recognize the spirit for what it truly represents, the fantastic loses all its terrors and, moreover, becomes a most powerful ally in their revolt against an environment which is as drab as it is repressive (cf. Worth 185).

This liberating function of the fantastic is prominent in all the later plays (see Metscher 141; Pauli 165). In *Cock-a-Doodle Dandy* the Messenger, whose fanciful dress immediately singles him out as a potential supporter of the Cock, is the only one who, unencumbered by superstitious fears, volunteers to rescue the infuriated bird, eventually leading the peaceful animal out of Michael's house by a green ribbon. The Messenger has discovered the Cock's joyful spirit as he explains to Michael's wife Lorna:

> Looka, lovely lady, there's no danger, an' there never was. He was lonely, an' was only goin' about in quest o' company. Instead of shyin' cups an' saucers at him, if only you'd given him your lily-white hand, he'd have led you through a wistful an' wondherful dance. But you frightened the poor thing! (143)

If the "joyful, active spirit of life" has been "in quest o' company" in Ireland, he now gathers his followers, notably from among the women. First Lorna who, "looking at the Cock with admiration" (144) finds that "he's harmless when you know him" (144); and the Messenger affirms that the Cock is: "Just a gay bird, that's all. A bit unruly at times, but conthrollable be th' right persons" (144). In fact, the Cock is gentle, meek, and mild to "th' right persons"; that is, to those who sympathize with the spirit he represents. On stage this polarization of the dramatis personae is effectively realized when the fierce beating of the Cock's wings causes winds so violent that the followers of Father Domineer have their trousers torn off their legs while the supporters of the Cock remain visibly unaffected by the same gales. And yet, despite their repeated defeats, the forces of the old order finally reassert themselves once again. The beautiful and tempting Loreleen, who is clearly the Cock's alter ego since she embodies the same spirit and the two never appear on stage together, is driven out of the country by Father Domineer. If the dangerous spirit cannot be annihilated it can at least be expelled. But the alleged victory is as hollow as the statue of Saint Tremolo: Loreleen and the Cock are accompanied into exile by the poetical Messenger and by all the women. Having been liberated by the world of the fantastic, these characters turn their backs on Nyadnanave — a typical O'Casey tongue-in-cheek expression, the term meaning both "Nest of Saints" and "Nest of Knaves" — and, in allegorical terms, shut the door on the whole of Ireland as the flagpole with the Irish tricolor in Michael's garden suggests. Led by the fantastic Cock these realistic characters set out "To a place where life resembles life more than it does here" (221), leaving the barren, womanless country to its doom.

In *Time to Go* O'Casey advances a step further. The barrenness of the country is aptly symbolized in *"the remains of two trees. . . . Their branches are withered, and they look as if they had been blasted by lightning"* (261). If the world of the fantastic is being exiled at the end of *Cock-a-Doodle Dandy*, it returns to Ireland in *Time to Go*. The transformation of the barren trees into blossoming, fruitful plants must be read in symbolic terms as the promise of liberation from a sterile, joyless, and sordid existence. But the promise of redemption which the fantastic proffers is ultimately rejected and the "real" world returns to its former shape.

In *The Drums of Father Ned* O'Casey progresses yet further by dramatizing the moment when the old order is about to succumb to the liberating force of the fantastic as it manifests itself in Father Ned's drum beats and the joyful activities of the Tostal. In *Figuro in the Night*, finally, the forces of repression are defeated and the liberation is completed by the appearance of the fantastic Figuro. In these two plays O'Casey presents his vision of an Ireland liberated from religious dogmatism, selfish materialism, and cultural ignorance, and it is in this visionary trait that the fantastic mingles with the utopian. O'Casey himself regarded the thrust of his argument as not being restricted to Ireland

and he drew attention to the universality of *Cock-a-Doodle Dandy* in stating:

> The action manifests itself in Ireland, the mouths that speak are Irish mouths; but the spirit is to be found in action everywhere: the fight made by many to drive the joy of life from the hearts of men; the fight against this fight to vindicate the right of the joy of life to live courageously in the hearts of men. ("Cockadoodle Doo" 144)

In *Cock-a-Doodle Dandy* O'Casey employs the fantastic most skillfully and, as his wife Eileen discloses, he enjoyed himself tremendously while using it as a tool:

> Besides his other work [i.e. especially *Autobiographies*] Sean was excited about the creation of a new play, *Cock-a-Doodle Dandy*—as excited as when he had got the idea for *The Silver Tassie*. Once more, as so often when beginning a play, he sang a good deal; it was as if rhythm, mostly of Irish folk-songs, helped his thoughts. I am sure he was excited because of his resolve to break away from realism—not just in a single act, as in the war scene of the *Tassie*, but through the entire piece. (E. O'Casey 200)

O'Casey was, of course, perfectly aware of the fact that his use of the fantastic placed him firmly inside time-honored literary traditions (cf. Metscher 139; Pauli 151, 207). It has been claimed that fantasy frequently betrays a tendency of looking back to and draw ing on the great literature of the past (Manlove 31), and reverberating through *Cock-a-Doodle Dandy* and the later plays are unmistakable echoes of *The Tempest* and *A Midsummer Night's Dream*. Similarly, the contention that fantasy is often pastoral in setting (Manlove 30; Hume 60-64) is corroborated by the findings of Robert Hogan who argues convincingly that O'Casey exploited literary strategies prefigured in pastoral literature ("In Sean O'Casey's Golden Days"). The two most salient features are marked by the contrast between the real and an idealized, "golden" world, and the use of fantastical elements especially in the transformation scenes which are characteristic of pastoral writing (cf. Toliver). As a result there is a delight in being at the core of the pastoral mode, and it is precisely this joy of life that O'Casey is concerned about in his later plays.

While it remains difficult to pinpoint an immediate influence as far as the use of the fantastic is concerned by O'Casey's contemporaries such as Shaw (Metscher 139) or the Irish fantasist James Stephens (Kosok 239),[3] O'Casey's later plays are evidently indebted to ancient myths and legends. The cycle of ballads on Robin Hood (cf. Child 3:39-233) undoubtedly inspired the creation of the characters of Robin Adair and Marion in *Cock-a-Doodle Dandy*. Loreleen's name is suggestive of Lorelei, the redoubtable temptress of German mythology, but Loreleen would tempt men and women not to destruction but to lives full of dance, song, and joy. It is therefore interesting to note that

Loreleen in all her beauty is repeatedly compared to Deirdre of Irish mythology who, like Loreleen, returned to her native land only to find disillusionment and grief.

O'Casey himself acknowledged his indebtedness to Irish mythology and folk literature which he occasionally employed as models for his own dramatic ventures ("Bonfire Under A Black Sun" 141-142; *Sunset and Evening Star* 294). It would be the task of a separate study to investigate the parallels between O'Casey's later plays and the early Gaelic writings which abound with fantastical characters and fantastical incidents, especially such otherworld tales about the *Tír na nÓg* ("The Land of the Young") and the anonymous masterpiece of Irish comic genius, *The Vision of MacConglinne*, which O'Casey greatly admired (cf. *Letters* 2:592; *Sunset and Evening Star* 268). In his seminal study, *The Irish Comic Tradition*, Vivian Mercier investigates the relationship between the fantastic and the comic as it is established in the early Gaelic writings. If it is true, as Mercier asserts, that a peculiar mixture of the comic, the satiric, and the fantastic represents one of the hallmarks of Irish writing throughout the ages (23), then O'Casey's later plays must be regarded as an integral part of this tradition. By using the fantastic to expose and criticize the social, political, and clerical powers which dominated Ireland, at least in O'Casey's opinion, during the forties and fifties, and by employing it simultaneously to show the way toward the liberation from such stifling existences, O'Casey in his later plays teaches the gospel of the joyful, happy, and fulfilled life.

It is this didactic use of the fantastic which no doubt appealed to the aging dramatist, this peculiar quality of the fantastic in all its mysterious otherness which, in the words of the fantasist Ray Bradbury, "attempts to disrupt the physical world in order to bring change to the heart and the mind" (Bradbury vii). This is most probably what O'Casey was thinking of when he rejected "naturalism or even realism" because they "usually show life at its meanest or commonest, as if life never had time for a dance, a laugh, or a song" ("Cock-adoodle Doo" 143). The fantastic through all its various functional uses as outlined in this survey presents the writer with an efficient tool which can penetrate deeper into the mysteries of human existence and may approach universal truths about life more accurately than a mimetic code (see Hume 102-123). O'Casey's blending of the fantastic with the comic will appeal to audiences and readers alike, and it obviously delighted Lennox Robinson and the other Abbey directors who, it may be remembered, admired the "humour and the element of phantasy."

Notes

1. A slightly different version appears in *Feathers from the Green Crow: Sean O'Casey, 1905-1925*, ed. Robert Hogan (London: Macmillan, 1963), 277-299. O'Casey had previously revised the text for a revival of the play in 1925. See letter to Lady Gregory of 22 February 1925. (*Letters* 1. 132 3; "Kathleen Listens In" 36)

2. The following remarks are indebted to Kosok, 233-241.

3. O'Casey dedicated *Cock-a-Doodle Dandy* to "James Stephens the jesting poet with a radiant star in's coxcomb" (118) primarily to encourage Stephens in his literary work. See: *Letters* 2:1056-1061; 1069f.

Works Cited

Achilles, Jochen. *Drama als problematische Form: Der Wandel zu nichtrealis tischer Gestaltungsweise im Werk Sean O'Caseys.* Frankfurt: Verlag Peter Lang, 1979.

Bradbury, Ray. "Introduction." In *The Circus of Dr. Lao and Other Impossible Stories*, ed. Ray Bradbury. New York: Bantam Books, 1956.

Child, Francis James, ed. *The English and Scottish Popular Ballads.* 5 vols. New York: Dover Publications, 1965.

Cowasjee, Saros. *Sean O'Casey: The Man Behind the Plays.* Edinburgh and London: Oliver and Boyd, 1963.

Hogan, Robert. "In Sean O'Casey's Golden Days." In *Sean O'Casey: A Collection of Critical Essays*, ed. Thomas Kilroy, 119-37. Englewood Cliffs, NJ: Prentice Hall, 1975.

Hume, Kathryn. *Fantasy and Mimesis.* New York and London: Methuen, 1984.

Irwin, William R. *The Game of the Impossible: A Rhetoric of Fantasy.* Urbana: University of Illinois Press, 1976.

Jackson, Rosemary. *Fantasy: The Literature of Subversion.* London: Methuen, 1981.

Knight, Wilson G. "Ever a Fighter: *The Drums of Father Ned.*" In *Sean O'Casey: Modern Judgements*, ed. Ronald Ayling, 177-182. London: Macmillan and Co. Ltd., 1969.

Kosok, Heinz. *O'Casey the Dramatist.* Gerrards Cross, Bucks.: Colin Smythe, 1985.

Manlove, C. N. "On the Nature of Fantasy." In *The Aesthetics of Fantasy Literature and Art*, ed. Roger C. Schlobin, 16-35. Notre Dame: Notre Dame University Press, 1982.

Marzin, Florian F. *Die Phantastische Literatur: Eine Gattungsstudie.* Frankfurt: Verlag Peter Lang, 1982.

Mercier, Vivian. *The Irish Comic Tradition.* Oxford: Oxford University Press, 1962.

Metscher, Thomas. *Sean O'Caseys dramatischer Stil.* Braunschweig: Georg Wester-mann Verlag, 1968.

O'Casey, Eileen. *Sean.* Ed. J. C. Trewin. London: Macmillan, 1971.

O'Casey, Sean. *Blasts and Benedictions: Articles and Stories.* Ed. Ronald Ayling. London: Macmillan; New York: St. Martin's Press, 1967.

—. "Bonfire Under a Black Sun." In *The Green Crow*, 130-159.

—. "Cockadoodle Doo." In *Blasts and Benedictions*, 142-145.

—. *The Complete Plays of Sean O'Casey.* 5 vols. London: Macmillan, 1951- 1984.

—. *The Green Crow.* New York: George Braziller, 1956.

—. "Green Goddess of Realism." In *The Green Crow*, 73-86

—. "Kathleen Listens In." *The Tulane Drama Review* 5 (June 1961): 36-50.

—. *The Letters of Sean O'Casey.* Ed. David Krause. Vol 1: London: Cassell, 1975; vol. 2: London: Macmillan, 1980.

—. "Literature in Ireland." In *Blasts and Benedictions*, 170-181.

—. "O'Casey's Drama Bonfire." In *Blasts and Benedictions*, 138-141.

—-. "Shaw's Corner." In *Sunset and Evening Star*, 210-251.

—-. *Sunset and Evening Star.* London: Macmillan, 1954.

—-. "Tender Tears for Poor O'Casey." In *The Green Crow*, 177-190.

Pauli, Manfred. *Sean O'Casey: Drama-Poesie-Wirklichkeit.* Berlin (GDR): Henschel-verlag, 1977.

"Sean O'Casey Seen in London: Irish Dramatist's First Visit to England." *Evening Standard*, 5 March 1926, 4. Reprint. Ed. Edward H. Mikhail and John O'Riordan. *The Sting and the Twinkle: Conversations With Sean O'Casey.* London and Basingstoke: Macmillan, 1974.

Templeton, Joan. "Sean O'Casey and Expressionism." *Modern Drama* 14 (May 1971): 47-62.

Todorov, Tzvetan. *Introduction à la littérature fantastique.* Paris: Editions du Seuil, 1970.

Toliver, Harold E. *Pastoral Forms and Attitudes.* Berkeley: University of California Press, 1971.

Worth, Katharine. "O'Casey's Dramatic Symbolism." In *Sean O'Casey: Modern Judgements*, ed. Ronald Ayling, 183-191. London: Macmillan and Co. Ltd., 1969.

Donald E. Morse

"Fidelity to Failure": Time and the Fantastic in Samuel Beckett's Early Plays

One person's reality is another's fantasy, while the reality of one age may prove the fantasy of another. George P. Landow describes this symbiotic relationship between fantasy and reality:

> Fantasy and our conception of what is fantastic depend upon our view of reality: what we find improbable and unexpected follows from what we find probable and likely, and the fantastic will therefore necessarily vary with the individual and the age. Many of the basic assumptions which the Middle Ages or the eighteenth century made about society, human nature, the external world and the laws that govern it appear bizarre today, while many of our century's attitudes towards body and spirit, like its technological, artistic, and political creations, would appear as pure fantasy to earlier times. (107)

What is true for history is also true for literary texts. What many spectators find fantastic in Samuel Beckett's early plays is actually his view of reality, reflected in his startling, unremitting picture of life lived in time as "moments for nothing" (*Endgame* 83). This vision, found throughout his work, clearly focuses on what decades ago he termed "impotence": "I am working with impotence, ignorance," he declared then (quoted in Olsen 43). In a dialogue held forty years ago with Georges Duthuit on the Dutch painter, Bram van Velde, Beckett maintained that "he [van Velde] is the first to accept a certain situation and to consent to a certain act," which he went on to characterize as: "The situation . . . of him who is helpless, cannot act, in the event cannot paint, since he is obliged to paint. The act of him who, helpless, unable to act, acts, in the event paints, since he is obliged to paint" (Beckett *Three Dialogues* 19). Beckett sees his own situation as a writer partially reflected here:

> I know that all that is required now . . . is to make of . . . this admission, this fidelity to failure, a new occasion, a new term of relation, and of the act which, unable to act, obliged to act . . . makes, an expressive act, even if only of itself,

of its impossibility, of its obligation. (21)

But he sees his situation as more radically helpless than van Velde's, for he finds himself unable to draw any such "relation," to make such "an expressive act": "I know that my inability to do so places myself . . . in what I think is still called an unenviable situation, familiar to psychiatrists" (21). The result is that as his career progressed, his work, to those who did not share his vision of the helpless, impotent artist, became more and more "fantastic" as he himself became more and more "realistic" about the limits within which he had to work. Lance Olsen accurately characterizes Beckett's concerns as ". . . with self-destruction, with art-as-deconstructor, with the journey toward minimalism through the window of entropy and exhaustion" (43). Hence, plays appear with no dialogue, no action, no characters, until in "Breath," there is nothing recognizable as a play, not even a cry, only respiration. Olsen calls "Breath" "an aesthetically terminal remnant," and rightly concludes: "The essence of drama has been deformed" (49).

Beckett's work — formed or deformed — is remarkable for the intensity and integrity with which he confronted, pursued, and presented his vision of impotence. Only in his earliest play, *Waiting for Godot*, do we find any suggestion that there might be something to express and something with which to express it. The German round song which begins Act two is a good example of the kind of action possible within the play. According to Ruby Cohn, this song is "an old favorite of Beckett (who translated it from the original German)" (40)

> A dog came in the kitchen
> And stole a crust of bread.
> Then cook up with a ladle
> And beat him till he was dead.
>
> Then all the dogs came running
> And dug the dog a tomb
> And wrote upon the tombstone
> For the eyes of dogs to come:
>
> A dog came in the kitchen
> And stole a crust of bread.
> Then cook up with a ladle
> And beat him till he was dead.
>
> Then all the dogs came running
> And dug the dog a tomb.
>   (37a-b)

Cohn says that the song "exemplifies a Chinese-box structure through time and words: the dog's tombstone commemorates a dog who has been beaten to death and so on *ad infinitum"* (40). But seen in light of the whole play, the movement of the song suggests not so much a series of nesting boxes as it does a spiral circling around itself, which in turn mirrors the movement of the play where the same or identical actions are repeated with the same or identical characters who make use of the same or identical props. Each act begins with a pair of boots on the stage which looks exactly like the pair of boots on stage at the beginning of the other act; each act follows a similar pattern: the two tramps meet, greet, and talk to one another; Pozzo and Lucky arrive, encounter the tramps, and depart; night falls suddenly; and each act concludes with a small boy who arrives to announce — inevitably — that: "Mr. Godot . . . won't come this evening but surely to-morrow" (33b). As each day a dog rushes into the kitchen to be beaten, buried, and a tombstone erected with its story written upon it, so each "day" the tramps meet, pass the time in waiting, and having "waited long enough [they] will wait forever" (*Malone Dies* quoted in Deane "Joyce and Beckett" 62). "We are not saints," says Vladimir, "but we have kept our appointment" (*Godot* 51b). Yet he is also correct when he observes near the beginning of Act two: "things have changed here since yesterday" to which Estragon adds: "It's never the same pus from one second to the next" (*Godot* 39a). Thus in *Godot* the Heraclitean flux shifts from the river of time as the river of life, to the "pus" of time as the "pus" of life. Within that constricted view tiny distinctions between dogs, cooks, boys, or tramps performing similar actions, singing similar songs, saying similar or sometimes seemingly identical things become important as does an improbable tree with no leaves and one with "four or five" (*Godot* 37); between a blind and a seeing Pozzo; or between a speaking and a silent Lucky.

The opposing view, that there are no distinctions which become differences, is eloquently maintained by Pozzo:

> Have you not done tormenting me with your accused time! It's abominable! When! When! One day, is that not enough for you, one day he went dumb, one day I went blind, one day we'll go deaf, one day we were born, one day we shall die, the same day, the same second, is that not enough for you? (Calmer.) They give birth astride of the grave, the light gleams an instant, then it's night once more. (*Godot* 57b)

Ironically, Pozzo confuses the infinitely slow progress of time in which nothing happens with the infinitely fast progress of time where everything blurs together. Ihab Hassan puts it well when he says: *"In Beckett's work . . . time runs out at an infinitely slow pace. At the beginning and at the end, we still wait for Godot, but things become a little worse. . . . This is the world of entropy"* (188). But the term entropy applies more precisely to *Endgame* than to *Godot,* for in *Godot* waiting becomes a positive activity of the tramps which both the play's action and the German round song mirror. As Lancelot St. John Butler says:

Waiting is how we comport ourselves towards possibility, according to Heidegger, and for Vladimir and Estragon this is roughly the case too. . . . the tramps are authentically keeping their options open while waiting for possibility. Meanwhile it is essential that they do nothing that will preclude their genuine availability for possibility. In other words they must do nothing. Which is why nothing happens in the play. (54)

Or, as one wag put it, why nothing happens twice in the play.

So Vladimir and Estragon wait for "possibility" by doing nothing and in their waiting there is some hope. They are, as Vladimir says, "inexhaustible" (*Godot* 40a). Time for them is similar to the spiral where action repeats but not quite exactly as the spiral comes round to the same position but never in quite the same place. In that slight shift lies all the "possibility" there is.

In the plays that follow, possibility shrinks radically as the sense of powerlessness, of impotence continues to grow. Gone is the spiral of time with its modicum of hope, and in its place are images which increasingly constrict action: the traditional line stretching from the disappointing past through the agonizing present into the doomed future accurately describes time in *Endgame*, *All That Fall*, *Happy Days*, *Act Without Words I* and *II*, *a*nd the brief dramaticules. In other plays, however, time becomes, if it is possible, even more constricted: a series of concentric circles in *Krapp's Last Tape*, a closed circle in "Play," a Möbius strip in *Embers*. Whichever geometric form best exemplifies time in any particular play, however, the underlying reality of time for Beckett remains constant as "moments for nothing." It is this vacuity which drives the characters into immobility, with the possible exception of the tramps in *Waiting for Godot*, and leads readers and audiences to substitute other values, any other values, for Beckett's: to make his "reality" into the "fantastic" in order, perhaps, not to disturb their own "reality." Michael Levenson describes precisely this kind of shift in his review of the beautiful book of photographs, *The Beckett Country*:

> The book includes scores of landscapes (rocky beaches, mountain vistas, banks of clouds), included on the strength of any passing mention in Beckett's writing. David Davison, a gifted photographer, renders these landscapes beautifully, apparently without stopping to consider whether his canons of the beautiful have anything to do with Beckett's own. Where, one wonders, are the severed heads and the bloody torsos? What would blind Hamm make of the sunset? In which heap of sand would Winnie be buried up to her neck? Where are the ash bins, the tape machines, the harsh lights, the urns? (35)

All of Beckett's settings (with the possible exception of the two radio plays), many of his characters, much of the action, and most of the time in his plays violate our sense of reality, and in truth none can be photographed. For example, here are the settings for *Happy Days* and "Play" which, Levenson points out, are missing from *The Beckett Country:*

> *Expanse of scorched grass rising centre to low mound. Gentle slopes down to front and either side of stage. Back an abrupter fall to stage level. Maximum of simplicity and symmetry. Blazing Light.*
> *Very pompier trompe-l'oeil backcloth to represent unbroken plain and sky receding to meet in far distance.*
> *Embedded up to above her waist in exact centre of mound, WINNIE. (Happy Days 9)*

> *Front centre, touching one another, three identical grey urns . . . about one yard high. From each a head protrudes, the neck held fast in the urn's mouth. The heads are those, from left to right as seen from auditorium, of w2 [Second Woman], m [Man], and w1 [First Woman]. They face undeviatingly front throughout the play. Faces so lost to age and aspect as to seem almost part of urns. But no masks. ("Play" Cascando 45)*

In such plays we enter a world obviously very different from our own, one which does not reflect "consensus reality" (Hume 21), but Beckett's own, and which is not captured in a beautiful photograph of a sunset, beach, or bank of clouds. Similarly, in the mime *Act Without Words II*, there are two characters, each occupying his own sack, each responding to the same "goad," each filling his "time" according to his own personality and values, yet each, despite these differences, moving exactly the same distance horizontally across the bare stage from stage right to stage left — a stage which is not remotely familiar:

> NOTE: This mime should be played on a low and narrow platform at back of stage, violently lit in its entire length, the rest of the stage being in darkness. Frieze effect. (in *Krapp* 137)

The effect Beckett strives for is, again, not mimetic, but fantastic: as if the audience were looking at a frieze with the actors appearing in bold relief against the black background. The action itself Beckett terms an "argument" as in a philosophical demonstration of the futility of action within time. The two characters move on unconscious of their not getting anywhere, of their not accomplishing anything, of their impotence. As they proceed across the stage the audience has a sense of the futility of action and of the inexorable passing of time within which human beings act.

Rosemary Jackson accurately describes the estranging effect achieved by these several fantastic settings, characters, and actions, when she asserts:

> To introduce the fantastic is to replace familiarity, comfort . . . with estrangement, unease, the uncanny. It is to introduce dark areas, of something completely other and unseen, the spaces outside the limiting frame of the "human"

and "real," outside the control of the "word" and of the "look." (179)

Endgame also introduces considerable "unease" through the "dark areas" of Nagg and Nell in their dustbins, Hamm in his wheel chair, Clov in his kitchen, and, above all, through time winding down. The play's action itself is truly fantastic, in Jackson's sense of introducing "something completely other and unseen," as it focuses on those moments which immediately precede immobility, when "time will have a stop." Having progressed through the play, time has at last come to an end. Like a story which has a beginning, middle, and end, so Hamm's life story began with his "accursed progenitor" (9), moved through various stages until it and he arrived, finally, at immobility, at the impossibility of action.

Like all successful drama, *Endgame*'s verbal and visual imagery reinforce one another: Hamm, blind and imprisoned in his chair, gradually becomes fully immobile; and at last completely silent: "Old endgame lost of old, play and lose and have done with losing" (82); "Moments for nothing, now as always. Time was never and time is over, reckoning closed and story ended" (83). After he concludes his story, throws away his dog, and "covers his face with handkerchief, he lowers his arms to armrests, remains motionless" (84): curtain. Visually and verbally, the play is over, the story concluded, time ended.

For Clov, too, time runs out though he appears to be leaving at the end. His poignant line, "I say to myself that the earth is extinguished, though I never saw it lit" (81), suggests that he will continue to see and experience only "ashes" (44) in his physical, moral, emotional, and mental landscape. "Something . . . [for him, too, has taken] its course" (13), "reckoning closed and story ended" (83).

Endgame is an eschatological play about time moving toward those "last things" in Beckett's universe. Like the chess game — or any game — like the journey through life, like the living of a day, time progresses in a straight line through the knowable present on into the unknown future. While there is repetition in *Endgame*, as there is in *Godot* and in "Play," the repetition here is more background against which the play's action, which does move forward into the future, takes place. Nagg does die, Clov does get dressed for the road, the painkiller does run out, the story Hamm tells is finished, and the end is an end without the real possibility of additional action, unlike in *Godot.* Thus the fantastic setting, characters, and action, all work "to replace familiarity, comfort . . . with estrangement, unease" (Jackson 179).

Similarly, in *Act Without Words I*, a lone mime faces a Pavlovian world where he is expected to salivate and respond on cue, yet where he cannot possibly meet such expectations because the cues themselves appear arbitrary, and even contradictory. Events, orders, and rewards appear random, unpredictable, and finally, out of control. There is no discernible pattern, no reason why certain events occur before or after other events. It is as if the Pavlovian psychologist in charge of this particular experiment intended to drive his subject mad.

Perhaps for the mime in *Act Without Words I*, "there is no way, only a wavering," as Kafka once remarked, but if so then the wavering itself dissolves into isolated random points without meaning.

The mime's situation may be compared to the dog's in Kafka's wonderfully comic story, "Investigations of a Dog," in which the hero, a precocious dog, attempts through the use of reason, observation, and experimentation to predict what action on his part will result in bringing food down from the air. He concludes that:

> we find [our food] on the earth, but the earth needs our water to nourish it and only at that price provides us with our food, the emergence of which, however, and this should not be forgotten, can also be hastened by certain spells, songs, and ritual movements. (*Stories* 215)

The dog conducts his scientific experiments and makes his observations, but for him to assess accurately his situation he needs access to information about human beings, their actions, and their motives — information which is forever and completely denied to him by his very nature, his dogginess.

Like Kafka's dog, for the mime in *Act Without Words I* to respond "correctly" to a given stimulus, he would need to know what purpose or plan, if any, the manipulator of objects had. Without such knowledge he is left with the enormously frustrating task of attributing purpose and meaning to what must remain for him entirely random, often maliciously arranged events in the truly "fantastic" world in which he finds himself. Butler sees his situation as an illustration of what Heidegger meant by man being "thrown" into time (36-37). In the present, man first contemplates the past to discover where he has been: "From my 'state of mind' I look backwards, as it were, at my throwness into factity; from understanding I look forwards into my possibility" (36).

In the play, however, the first image is not of a person being thrown into existence, but, more precisely: "The man is flung *backwards* on stage from the right wing" (*Krapp* 125; emphasis added). For, unlike Heidegger, who sees man being first thrown into time, then looking backward, Beckett sees humanity flung backward almost at random into chaotic experience from which no reflection will yield knowledge reliable enough to become a basis for action. The mime does not even face the future willingly, but attempts to retreat into the wings only to be unceremoniously tossed back on stage in order that he may "get on with it" — whatever "it" may prove to be! And he must do it in "a desert" under "dazzling light" — as once more Beckett chooses a barren setting in a fantastic landscape, a visual image which accurately reflects his belief in human impotence, rather than possibility.

Like Kafka's dog, it is impossible for the mime to act with any real knowledge; hence, whenever he succeeds in making a few correct predictions, it is purely accidental and, ultimately, misleading for his chain of reasoning is based upon a faulty premise. What is worse, his desire to predict in the present by reasoning from the known past to the possible future — in order to be in a position to satisfy whatever demands are being made upon him — works to his own frustration and defeat. Beckett offers us an extraordinary, dramatic image of human inability to predict anything, to establish any cause and effect through a temporal sequence of events. As Thomas Postlewait observes:

> In terms of the temporal sequence there is no orderly principle of cause and effect that unifies memory and expectation. ... Time and space may be a priori conditions for understanding as Kant argues, but for Beckett's characters neither things next to each other nor one thing after another provides a modal basis for demonstrating interconnection. (480)

Time as a straight line leads straight to impotence.

As the settings of *Act Without Words I* and *II*, *Happy Days*, "Play," and *Endgame* are fantastic, so is the very time itself of *Krapp's Last Tape:* "A late evening in the future" (9), presumably when Krapp makes his "last tape" at age sixty-nine. Since the future is always a metaphor (Le Guin 149), Beckett uses Krapp's future as a fantastic device to reflect accurately the emptiness of his past and present life. At sixty-nine he listens to "that stupid bastard I took myself for thirty years ago" (24), when he believed he had "every reason to suspect he was at the ... (hesitates) ... crest of the wave — or thereabouts" (14); that recorded thirty-nine-year-old Krapp looks, in turn, back ten-to-twelve years earlier in disgust at "that young whelp" (16) who must be about twenty-seven or twenty-nine years old.

The very image of time in this play emphasizes impotence and the impossibility of humans accomplishing anything: rather than a straight line or even a "wavering," time is a series of concentric circles with the Krapp of about twenty-nine in the center, then Krapp of thirty-nine, followed by an outermost ring of Krapp at sixty-nine. In between are all forty of the Krapps represented by the "spools" (read "stools"?) of recorded tape piled up in his "den."

Krapp's project of recording a spool of tape each year is predicated on two false premises: first, that the year is a significant unit of time; and second, that he will realize the significance of events as they occur. As each year passes, Krapp uses his birthday to evaluate each year's events or, as he puts it, "separating the grain from the husks" (14). He then records these achievements "against the day when my work will be done and perhaps no place left in my memory, warm or cold, for the miracle that ... (*hesitates*) ... for the fire that set it alight" (20-21). But ironically, the older sixty-nine-year-old Krapp has no patience with the younger Krapp of thirty-nine whose aspirations he sees as pretentious and whose language he finds riddled with jargon and hard words. In fact, the eldest Krapp loses all interest in the very project itself: "Last fancies. (*Vehemently.*) Keep 'em under! ... Ah finish your booze now and get to your bed. Go on with this drivel in the morning. Or leave it at that. (*Pause.*) Leave it at that" (25-26).

In the past year, the event he enjoyed above all others was reveling in pronouncing the word, "Spooool! Happiest moment of the past million." Otherwise life, for him, has been reduced to "the sour cud and the iron stool" (25). Like Emil Jennings's clown in *The Blue Angel*, Krapp now waits only for death with little or no interest in his former years' activities. His earlier excretions, the "crap" of his life, all neatly packaged, labeled, and filed, surround him in his den, but hold no interest for him. Instead, he thinks how it might be to recall earlier memories of physical activities, not mental achievements:

> Lie propped up in the dark—and wander. Be again in the dingle on a Christmas Eve, gathering holly, the redberried. (*Pause.*) Be again on Croghan on a Sunday morning, in the haze, with the bitch, stop and listen to the bells. (*Pause.*) And so on. (*Pause.*) Be again, be again. (*Pause.*) All that old misery. (*Pause.*) Once wasn't enough for you. (26-27)

Like the dog in Kafka's story, Krapp built his plans, created his project, constructed his argument upon inaccurate assumptions: he thought he knew when young what would be valuable to him when old, but time proves his youthful ideas false. At the end he turns back to an earlier tape in which he said "farewell to love," but which also has a clear description of his lying "across [Bianca] . . . with my face in her breasts and my hand on her" (27). Gone are the claims of being "at the crest of the wave," of being engaged in meaningful, significant life work, and in their place are memories of physical events: sights, sounds, smells, and human contact. Thus this "piece of Protestant sentimentality" (Murray 111), concludes as it began with "moments for nothing," as Krapp in the future listens to and comments disparagingly upon Krapp of the present and upon Krapp of the past. Finally, the last Krapp abandons the project entirely, wrenching off the tape on which he is recording events in his sixty-ninth year, throwing it away in order to listen to moments from the earlier "farewell to love" incident. (Again, Beckett reinforces his verbal images with visual ones by having Krapp physically throw the tape away, as Hamm threw his dog away.) His youthful bravado, "No, I wouldn't want them back" (28), rings completely false. The future, Beckett's fantastic metaphor, mirrors Krapp's present wasted life which he throws away in posturing.

In "Play," every dramatic element, setting, character, action, and speech is fantastic, as are the visual and verbal images of time. The past here parallels the future in *Krapp's Last Tape* in providing a metaphor for the present empty lives of the three characters. Now dead, they find themselves trapped in Beckett's version of Dante's vision of hell where the damned are condemned to travel forever in an endless circle, continually reminded of the evil that led them to this infernal place and always faced with the knowledge that there is no exit, there is no hope: "Abandon All Hope, Ye Who Enter Here." Time is a closed, endlessly revolving circle. In contrast to Krapp, who is free to choose whatever tape he wishes to listen to and, if not free to "be again" then at least is free to recall again whatever portion of his "old misery" he desires, the three characters in "Play," like those in Dante's *Inferno*, are condemned to repeat the same action over and over, speak the same speeches over and over, and have the same thoughts over and over. Hell is the absence of hope signified by the impotence experienced through such endless repetition. Time for the three has stopped: nothing new happens, no events occur; no new emotions, ideas, or perceptions intrude; there is only endless, complete repetition of their "moments for nothing." As the voice in *Embers* says—and he could well be speaking of the characters in "Play"—"That's what hell will be like, small chat to the babbling of the Lethe about the good old days when we wished we were dead" (in *Krapp's Last Tape* 102).

In contrast, the most non-fantastic of Beckett's plays are those for radio where he goes to great pains to establish the realistic setting. For example, in *All That Fall*, the sounds are those of a rural setting, the characters are out of an Irish village, the action occurs in the present. Something happened before the play begins—a murder is committed; an action takes place in the present moving the characters toward the future in much the same way as the comic, improbable bulk of Maddy Rooney moves inexorably, but with considerable difficulty, to the railway station to meet blind Mr. Rooney. Her struggle to arrive takes on epic proportions and occupies all of the listener's attention as "something [there, too] is taking its course" (*All That Fall* in *Krapp's Last Tape* 33-60; *Endgame* 13). The play, a comic masterpiece, includes mystery, but no fantasy.

Embers, at first, appears fantastic because of the surface chaos, but actually is not. Eugene Kaelin in an essay, "Voices, in English, on the Air," declares that *Embers* is "as clear a presentation of schizophrenia as Beckett has devised" (*Unhappy Consciousness* 187). He continues:

> Henry has only one last ray of hope: to tell a story clearly so that others may understand who and what he is. But the alienation and self-entanglement of his inauthenticity is such, and the turbulence it creates so overwhelming, that he shall never find either the end or the significance of his tale, to which only the sea is a fitting background. (187)

But the surface chaos of the story, the "turbulence" of which Kaelin speaks, may also be accounted for by observing that while at first there appear to be several characters performing discrete actions, speaking their own lines each in his or her own time with various actions occurring within and without the main tale, there is, as Kaelin himself suggests, really only one tale, and only one time, the present moment of Henry's telling his story. All time in the play is his time. Thus time in *Embers* is not over, as in "Play," nor yet to come, as in *Krapp's Last Tape*, but occupies the very present, as in *All That Fall*. Within that present moment Henry creates his characters, through recall or through imagination, and brings them not into *their* conscious existence, but into existence in *his* consciousness. In other words, nothing in the play exists except what is in

Henry's head.

Because events occur only in the present and as Henry thinks of them, however, time is experienced neither as a repetitious circle nor as a continuing straight line. Instead time appears almost to double back upon itself, and so might best be represented by a Möbius strip—a figure which appears to have two sides but which in reality has only one, or which appears to have only one side but which in reality has two, exactly as the play appears to have many characters and to take place at several different times, but has only one character, Henry the narrator, and one time, the time of his telling of the tale.

Whether time is represented by a closed circle signifying a completed, unchanging, and unchangeable condition, by a series of concentric circles of diminishing and diminished meaning rippling out from a center, by a spiral of endlessly repeating actions in slightly changed positions, or by the more traditional line stretching from a beginning to the inevitable end—whatever the appropriate figure may be—characters in Beckett's plays are stuck in their time as a fly becomes stuck on what Langston Hughes once so poignantly called, "the sweet flypaper of life," and none is able to overcome its limitations. As Maddy Rooney says, "It is suicide to be abroad. But . . . what is it to be at home? A lingering dissolution" (*All That Fall* in *Krapp* 39). Hence the progression in Beckett from the options for action or inaction in *Waiting for Godot*, which remains his most optimistic and occasionally even hopeful play, to the other plays where characters are driven to immobility, as the author reminds us again and again that, "in [this] . . . universe, no man can shuffle off his mortal coil. We are beings who exist in time; death is inescapable" (Kearney 273)—as is impotence.

Beckett's early wrestling with the problem of time is itself a kind of lesson in intellectual impotence, for, as Jorges Luis Borges so eloquently reminds us, it is a problem which can never finally be solved:

> The real problem, the problem we have to grapple with, and of course the problem whose solution we'll never find, is the problem of time, of successive time, and therein, the problem of personal identity, which is but a part of the problem of time. (quoted in Knapp 124)

Beckett grappled with this problem within his life and work, never denying the starkness of his vision, the reality of his impotence. To do so most effectively, he used the fantastic to express what could not be expressed, and in the process created compelling, unforgettable images; each one testifying to his "unenviable situation," as he strictly maintained his "fidelity to failure." In so doing he, of all Irish dramatists, and perhaps of all Irish writers, best illustrates the truth in Rosemary Jackson's assertion that: "fantasy . . . is a literature of desire, which seeks that which is experienced as absence and loss" (3).

Works Cited

Beckett, Samuel. *Cascando and Other Short Dramatic Pieces.* New York: Grove Press, Inc., 1968.

—-. *Endgame: A Play in One Act.* New York: Grove Press, Inc., 1958.

—-. *Happy Days.* New York: Grove Press, Inc., 1961.

—-. *Krapp's Last Tape and Other Dramatic Pieces.* New York: Grove Press, Inc., 1960.

—-. *Waiting for Godot.* New York: Grove Press, Inc., 1954.

—- and Georges Duthuit. "Three Dialogues." In *Samuel Beckett: A Collection of Critical Essays*, ed. Martin Esslin, 16-22. Englewood Cliffs: Prentice-Hall, 1965.

Butler, Lancelot St. John. *Samuel Beckett and the Meaning of Being: A Study in Ontological Parable.* London: Macmillan, 1984.

Cohn, Ruby. *Just Play: Beckett's Theatre.* Princeton: Princeton University Press, 1980.

Deane, Seamus. "Joyce and Beckett." *Irish University Review* 14, No.1 (Spring 1984):57-68.

Hassan, Ihab. "Joyce-Beckett: A Scenario in Eight Scenes and a Voice." In *New Light on Joyce from the Dublin Symposium*, ed. Fritz Senn, 180- 194. Bloomington: Indiana University Press, 1972.

Hume, Kathryn. *Fantasy and Mimesis: Responses to Reality in Western Literature.* New York: Methuen, 1984.

Jackson, Rosemary. *Fantasy: The Literature of Subversion.* London: Methuen, 1981.

Kaelin, Eugene. *The Unhappy Consciousness: The Poetic Plight of Samuel Beckett.* Boston: D. Reidel Publishing Co., 1981.

Kafka, Franz. *Selected Stories of Franz Kafka.* Trans. Willa and Edwin Muir. New York: The Modern Library, 1952.

Kearney, Richard. "Beckett: The Demythologizing Intellect." In *The Irish Mind*, ed. Richard Kearney, 267-293. Dublin: The Wolfhound Press, 1985.

Knapp, Bettina L. "Borges: 'The Library of Babel'—The Archetypal Hexagonal Gallery." In *Archetype, Architecture, and the Writer*, 100-124. Bloomington: Indiana University Press, 1986.

Landow, George P. "And the World Became Strange: Realms of Literary Fantasy." In *The Aesthetics of Fantasy Literature and Art*, ed. Roger C. Schlobin, 105-142. Notre Dame: University of Notre Dame Press, 1982.

Le Guin, Ursula K. "Introduction to The Left Hand of Darkness." In *The Language of the Night*, ed. Susan Wood, 145-149. 1979. New York: Berkley,1982.

Levenson, Michael. "The Nayman of Noland." Rev. of *The Beckett Country: Samuel Beckett's Ireland*, by David Davison; *Four Dubliners*, by Richard Ellmann; *On Beckett: Essays and Criticism*, ed. by S. E. Gontarski; and *Beyond Minimalism: Beckett's Late Style in the Theatre*, by Enoch Brater. *The New Republic* 6 July 1987, 34-37.

Murray, Christopher. "Beckett Productions in Ireland: A Survey." *The Irish University Review* 14, No.1 (Spring 1984):103-125.

Olsen, Lance. *Ellipse of Uncertainty: An Introduction to Postmodern Fantasy.* Westport,CT: Greenwood Press, 1987.

Postlewait, Thomas. "Self-Performing Voices: Mind, Memory, and Time in Beckett's Drama." *Twentieth Century Literature* 24, No.4 (Winter 1987): 473-491.

Csilla Bertha

Thomas Murphy's Psychological Explorations

Bellemin Noël contends that "One could define fantastic literature as that in which the question of the unconscious emerges" (quoted in Jackson 62). Even if not all fantastic literature is concerned with the unconscious, the fantastic mode has proven to be exceptionally suitable for psychological exploration. While Kathryn Hume is right in asserting that "drama presents more complex problems" in producing fantastic effects than prose narrative, and "some kinds of fantasy are not easily reduced to a physical stage, human actors, and a three-hour time span" (163), drama nevertheless can fruitfully use fantastic means, especially when revealing psychological phenomena. Since the stage is a place where, Peter Brook reminds us, "the invisible can appear" (quoted in Murray 9), fantasy can offer powerful help in realizing this process, since one of its main functions is to "trace . . . the unsaid and unseen of culture," and — we may add — of the individual human soul: "that which has been silenced, made invisible, covered over or made 'absent'" (Jackson 4).

The use of the fantastic is a strong legacy of modern Irish drama, in part because the "creative confluence" (Kearney 9) of reality and fantasy has invigorated it since its beginnings. As the Hungarian playwright Arón Tamasi says: "The harmony of reality and fantasy is the gift of the most ancient poetic soul" (224), and the Irish are among those few peoples in Europe who were able to preserve this ancient poetic soul up to the present.[1] Hence most playwrights of the Irish Dramatic Movement deeply relied on the living folk imagination in which this poetic soul manifests itself.

Contemporary Irish playwrights continue the tradition of drawing on the fantastic. Among the several purposes for which they employ the fantastic are: investigating the folk imagination in the peasant play, using expressionistic staging, and exploring the psychology of character. In the still extant peasant play the fantastic is often used to depict the liability of people cherishing fantastic dreams, building up whole worlds out of words, of keeping alive fairy-tale figures in their consciousness, and of mistaking them for reality (for example, John B. Keane's *Sharon's Grave* 1960). Expressionistic stage-techniques may include nonimitative, symbolic, or stylized gestures, images, incantatory speeches, and projections of visions. Thus Tom Mac Intyre's plays create fantastic effects wholly through the mode of presentation rather than through the consciousness of the characters or in the plot (see, for instance, his staging of *The Great Hunger* 1983).

Most frequently, however, playwrights such as Brian Friel in *Philadelphia, Here I Come!* (1965), Thomas Kilroy in *Tea and Sex and Shakespeare* (1976), and Thomas Murphy in several of his plays use the fantastic as a means of revealing psychological events or processes, of making what is invisible inside human beings appear in the theater. Murphy's great strength is that he finds ways to project the invisible, often miraculous events of the human soul onto the stage. The miracles are usually very human miracles: something unexpected happens, some so-far unknown or unattained possibility or ability manifests itself, through which the characters can arrive at a better understanding and realization of their own needs and aspirations, and through which they become able to transcend the limitations of their own selves.

Murphy's world is one deserted by God in which man's plight is, in Christopher Murray's words, "tragic, dispossessed of not only paradisal inheritance but of all those absolutes which childhood experience intimates" (13-14). In this orphaned state his characters struggle to grow up and to grow toward self-recognition and self-realization. Yet no peaceful growth into adulthood seems possible. The miracle of the liberation of the self, of finding peace and love among and within themselves, or of discovering some creative activity, happens in or through an unexpected action of special significance. This action is often verbal, in accordance with the magic power that the Irish have always attributed to words; sometimes the action is physical, and if so, almost always it is violent. One of the most conspicuous features of Murphy's theater is the presence of violence: the accumulated, great repressed forces and tensions burst out through violence. His characters manage to become adults, to grow into independent and integrated personalities only through much suffering, violence, and sin.

Murphy's characters are torn by desires which are sometimes definite and conscious, sometimes vague and uncertain. Fantasy, as one of its main functions, helps to articulate and deal with these desires.

> In expressing desire, fantasy can operate in two ways (according to the different meanings of "express"); it can *tell of*, manifest or show desire (expression in the sense of portrayal, representation, manifestation, linguistic utterance, mention, description), or it can *expel* desire, when this desire is a disturbing element which threatens cultural order and continuity (expression in the sense of pressing out, squeezing, expulsion, getting rid of something by force). In many cases fantastic literature fulfills both functions at once, for desire can be "expelled" through having been "told of" and thus vicariously experienced by author and reader. (Jackson 3-4)

What Rosemary Jackson says about desire as a disturbing element threatening "cultural order and continuity" is, of course, true of the individual, too. The desires Murphy's characters struggle with are sometimes disturbing and threaten the integrity of the personality, making self- acceptance impossible; in other cases through desires the characters — consciously or unconsciously — move toward finding or regaining a lost wholeness and peace with themselves. In the course of this quest for integrity some characters in earlier plays clash primarily with their environment, while later they have to face themselves, come to terms with their past experiences, their memories, or their split personalities. In depicting the actions of the human soul, Murphy uses fantastic means to express desires in both meanings of the word "express" — to manifest and to expel — and sometimes even to fulfill them.

In a fairly early play, *A Crucial Week in the Life of a Grocer's Assistant* (1969), the dilemma whether to emigrate or stay at home — this crucial Irish question — is dramatized in the conscious as well as the unconscious struggle of the chief character, John Joe. The fantastic elements Murphy uses here culminate in Freudian kinds of dreams of unconscious fears and distorted desires, projected on stage. The elaborate, surrealistic dream scenes in Scene eight, for instance, reveal John Joe's confused state of mind: his fear of the authority figures, who merge into each other and appear as allies against him; and his repressed sexual desires mixed with shame (as Mona, his love, then a family friend, Agnes, appear one by one in his bed, scantily dressed to tempt or attack him, respectively, in the presence of others). But most of all these scenes dramatize his terror of the necessary split in his life if he emigrates, which is expressed in the authority figures' attempts to scalp him and collect his soul in a bag together with those of other emigrants.

This projection of fears and desires does not, however, lead to John Joe's finding a solution to his dilemma, not even to his seeing more clearly where he is. Although the struggle goes on in his soul, he first has to sort things out with his environment. So the liberating action, after all, goes on not so much within him as in his violent clash with the people around him. His act of rebellion brings about a fantastic effect: by shouting out the secrets of his family and those of the neighbors to the street he violently breaks the unwritten rules of provincial life. Doing so he also breaks the spell: once secrets — this good soil for gossip, hypocrisy, and the poisonous ruining of human relationships — come out into the open, they lose their dark force. John Joe's action and its result parallels that of the fantastic in general: "The fantastic is the sudden release of deeply repressed material," as it "reveals that which must be concealed so that one's internal and external experience may be comfortably known" (Olsen 21-22). Once John Joe is able to face his narrow-minded, petty surroundings, he becomes able to deal with them and find his place, not by accepting their dominance and adapting to it but by maintaining his own values and his independent personality. Now he does not need to go into exile any longer, and his decision to stay is not "forced" on him but is entirely his own choice. In a twofold, simultaneously external and internal action he both breaks the silence

isolating the people around him and allows his suppressed anger and disgust to
come to the surface; he becomes an autonomous personality. The magic power
of his publicly uttered words makes him an adult overnight, and this is a real
miracle.

In some of Murphy's other plays, although the external world is present,
the conflicts take place more definitely inside the characters. In order to
achieve self-realization they have to face not only their environment but also,
with greater difficulty, their own selves, their own conscious and unconscious
desires. The unconscious can hardly be projected onto the stage without
fantastic means; fantasy is the right medium for conveying it. As Rosemary
Jackson says:

> Fantasy in literature deals so blatantly and repeatedly with unconscious
> material that it seems rather absurd to try to understand its significance without
> some reference to psychoanalysis and psychoanalytic readings of texts. (6)

Several of Murphy's plays can be read — without violating them — as dramatiza-
tions of the struggle between the conscious and the unconscious, or at least
between two equally important halves of the one whole. One of the two
characters is the "double," fighting with, complementing, and sometimes coming to terms with the other. The function of this double is often similar to Jung's
shadow figure — the personification of all the evil, shameful, dark sides of the
personal unconscious, haunting, threatening, or destroying the ego if it is not
integrated into the whole self. Several of Murphy's characters, in their quest for
wholeness, have to undertake the difficult task of facing their shadow figures
and dealing with them.

The Morning after Optimism, a unique play from the point of view of the
fantastic in Murphy's oeuvre, is set, unlike the essential naturalism of the others,
in an entirely fantasylike environment: a forest reminiscent of *A Midsummer
Night's Dream*, with actions and some figures more allegorical than realistic.
One of the two couples, the down-to-earth, "fallen" Rosie, a whore, and James,
a pimp, after reminiscing about their past state of innocence encounter the
images of perfect innocence and purity, a fairy-tale young woman and a young
prince. These latter two embody the incorruptible ideal, the dreams and higher
aspirations of human beings. In the light of their purity the other two see
themselves and each other as all the more fallen, dark, hopelessly irredeemable.
The reaction of James and Rosie runs the whole gamut of possible human
responses: they run away from them (to escape from the haunting memories of
innocence); are constantly challenged by them; admire and chase them to unite
with them (to regain and reintegrate innocence in themselves, to find their
"hidden, real, beautiful self" [14]); and when that proves impossible, to bespoil
them by bringing them down to their own level in order not to have always to
confront the ideals against which they appear all the more faulty. At last, when
all attempts turn out to be futile, nothing else is left for them to do except to kill

the innocent couple; that is, kill the ideal in themselves in order to be able to accept their real selves.

The embodiment of all the unwanted, inferior, hidden dark features of the human being in a second figure — in a double — has been a strong tradition in literature (See, for example, Heine's "Der Doppelgänger," Stevenson's *Dr. Jekyll and Mr. Hyde*, Dostoyevski's *The Double* (Apter 48ff), Wilde's *The Picture of Dorian Grey*, and Babits's *Gólyakalifa*.) What makes Murphy's treatment so unusual is that he approaches the self from the point of view of the dark side. Jung maintains that one must face the fact that one is not identical with one's ideal self, and must accept and integrate one's "shadow" or dark side into oneself in order to have a whole, healthy personality:

> The shadow is a moral problem that challenges the whole ego-personality, for no one can become conscious of the shadow without considerable moral effort. To become conscious of it involves recognizing the dark aspects of the personality as present and real. This act is the essential condition for any kind of self-knowledge. ("Aion" 145)

Murphy in this play goes further: in his darker view of this fallen world, in which the ideal is so far from the real that it cannot be integrated into the whole, and in which the dirty, bespoiled, wicked is not only part but also the very essence of reality, he shows the fallen man and woman as real flesh-and-blood human beings and the ideal ones as only images of the others' dreams and desires, hence unreal illusions or self-deceptions. The humans must get rid of the ideal images in order to survive. There is no shadow without the sun; consequently if the sun is eliminated, there will not be a shadow. In the ensuing darkness the fallen, bespoiled people, no longer shocked by their own darkness, can accept themselves and each other.

By doubling the doubles — instead of the usual one pair of characters here there are two couples — the shadow phenomenon is complemented by the man-woman aspect of the split personality. The two men personify the woman's, while the two women embody the man's ideal of the other sex and the disappointing reality, respectively. As in W. B. Yeats's *The Only Jealousy of Emer* the woman's two main, archetypal aspects are embodied in two different persons: ideal beauty, innocence, and perfection are attributes of Anastasia exclusively, while only the very earthy elements of womanhood are found in Rosie; neither is complete alone. If there was no completeness attainable in Yeats's idealistic world, it is even farther away in Murphy's contemporary one. Yeats at least included Emer, who once, albeit imperfectly, united both the spiritual and the physical aspects in herself, while the other two female characters — Fand the fairy and Eithne Inguba — only embodied these features in their more polarized form. In Murphy's play no uniting third exists, and out of the two only the earthy survives; the ideal with hardly any vitality and no reality at all perishes.

One of the functions of the fantastic is to offer an escape from reality, and one of the forms this escape often takes is the pastoral (Hume 59ff). Escape into illusions and exile is also central to the Irish experience as well as to Irish literature. The fantastic in earlier Irish plays often served to create a dreamland, an imaginary world superior to the existing one, into which the imaginative or visionary characters escaped, as, for example, in Yeats and George Fitzmaurice (see Bertha "Myth and the Fantastic: The Example of Yeats," and Murray "Irish Drama and the Fantastic"). In Murphy's plays, however, the fantastic means are used to remind the characters that there is no escape, that exile is no solution. The fantastic dream scenes in *A Crucial Week in the Life of a Grocer's Assistant* may be thematically linked to exile, but offer no escape to the dreamer from his stifling dilemma. *The Morning After Optimism* has a pastoral setting yet is full of ironic inversions: the fantastic fairytale-like forest could be a place of escape from the real world, but instead becomes the medium in which the characters sober up from their lost illusions, grow up to be adults at last, and in which they get ready to re-enter reality. In this fantastic forest their desires for innocence are "expressed" in both of Jackson's senses of the word.

The fantastic means Murphy uses encourage several equally valid interpretations, of which this psychological interpretation is only one. Fintan O'-Toole suggests that "*The Morning After Optimism* does reflect Murphy's own psychology, but as with his theatre in general that psychological concern also reflects the inner history of his country" (74). He reminds us that in the sixties the Irish still maintained dreams about the possible return of the "innocence and bliss" of the Golden Age, that is of Gaelic culture and freedom (73). Thus in the ideal but rather lifeless couple the ideal state of the beautiful historical past flares up, while in the other two figures we encounter the prosaic present. The latter two, like the Irish in general, cannot reconcile themselves to the reality of the present, as long as they vainly dream about returning to the past and incorporating it in their lives; but they need the sobering experience of their failure as well as of their own violence in order to turn toward the present and the future in a more constructive and realistic way.

In *The Sanctuary Lamp* (1976) the values are much more mixed; no ideal is present, only versions of fallen humanity. Yet Harry and Francisco can easily be seen as two sides of the one whole, in conflict with each other. Harry is the more conscious, positive self while Francisco is the destructive, negating side. At the beginning of the play Harry is escaping from Francisco, who, in his turn, is openly identified with evil: "Evil, be thou my good! Evil, light my path!" (15). Harry is trying to find God, Francisco blatantly refuses Him. And Harry, in his superior moral position, tries to ignore Francisco, then physically confronts him (by hitting him), and wants to punish him; that is, he wants to get rid of his shadow by killing rather than embracing him. But finally, instead of eliminating him, Harry triumphs over him in a fantastic action: while Francisco is lecturing Harry that he should not be so selfrighteous ("Everyone to blame but you, Har?" 63), the latter suddenly gathers his long-vanished strength and lifts the pulpit with Francisco in it onto his shoulders. This is a great private victory for Harry, for by lifting the pulpit — an absurd manifestation of regaining his strength and manliness — he experiences a miracle lifting him up from his despair and impotent anger, which at the same time elevates the play's action from the level of "consensus reality"[2] into a different, fantastical sphere. This fantastic action reflects Harry's strength and capability now to take his darker self under his own control. Once he shows that he can do so, he can also accept the fact that he is not blameless, which in turn prepares him for his final reconciliation with Francisco.

Seeing the two men as two halves of one person helps in understanding the play's central feelings, such as anger, fear, despair, pain and loneliness, guilt and innocence; and questions such as revenge, death, and religion. Of the two men, Francisco always embodies the negative approach in their various activities and relationships. Thus he steals Harry's wife and eventually lets her die; he tries to seduce Maud, the young girl whom Harry protects more as a child than as a woman, drinks the altar wine, and so on. Maud herself relates to each of them differently: she tells her secrets only to Francisco, to the one who is closer to the hidden side of human experience. The three of them create a symmetrical tableau when they lay a confessional on the floor and, with Maudie in the middle, the two men go to sleep in the two compartments at her two sides. In matters of religion Francisco sharply attacks any inclination to maintain or regain faith, and yet Harry is able to establish his new, human religion with the help of Francisco's negation. The private tragedies of the three — the death of children, unfaithfulness and death of a wife, friend betraying friend, feelings of pain, guilt, the "compulsion to ... kill" (10) in revenge — are all set against the more general tragedy of human beings: their homelessness and loneliness in this godforsaken world, their unanswered yearning for the divine, and their failure to receive help and consolation from the Catholic church.

The two men approach the question of faith from two opposite directions, the positive and the negative, yet both approaches are based on religious images and concepts. The play is full of religious imagery, both in the language and in the objects on the stage: Francisco "preaches" and reveals his blasphemous vision from the pulpit, the sanctuary lamp itself is always center stage, and the characters use the wine, the confessional; but these images are treated in such a peculiarly twisted way that they carry both the Christian mystery and the mystery of the new religion these people build for themselves. Thus Harry does feel the presence of the spirit in the sanctuary lamp, watching him; he speaks to it, complains to it, makes a contract with it. So, on the one hand, he (and through him the audience) can feel the mystical presence, but on the other hand, he drags the presence down to his own level, to be his companion. Francisco, in his turn, passionately and violently attacks and mocks the church and the religious doctrines, rages against the priests, and blasphemously uses the religious images and biblical texts.

Apart from the fantastic action of lifting the pulpit, verbal fantasy also contributes to bringing the two complementary figures close together. Although their "religious" dreams, like everything else in themselves, are polar opposites, they still arrive at contemplating each other's visions. Maurice Levy's statement that "The fantastic is a compensation that man provides for himself, at the level of imagination . . . for what he has lost at the level of faith" (quoted in Jackson 18) is borne out in this play even at the level of the concrete situation. These miserable beings in this godforsaken world are trying to build up some new, human religion for themselves. Francisco in his "sermon" delivered from the pulpit, inverts the prophecy of the last judgment:

> I have a dream! I have a dream! The day is coming: The second coming: The final judgement: The not too distant future: Before that simple light of man: When Jesus, Man, total man, will call to his side the goats: Come ye blessed!— Yea, call to his side all those rakish, dissolute, suicidal, fornicating goats, taken in adultery, and what-have-you. And proclaim to the coonics: blush for shame, you blackguards, be off with you, you wretches, depart from me ye accursed complicated affliction! And that, my dear brother and sister, is my dream, my hope, my vision and my belief. (72)

After this inversion of religious teaching Francisco, this disbeliever, this fuming destroyer, is able to ask Harry, whom he has betrayed, to forgive him.

Harry's attitude is different; his fantastic vision is more positive, more attractive: it describes the human soul's need for uniting with other souls in love and support:

> HARRY The soul—y'know?—like a silhouette. And when you die it moves out into . . . slow-moving mists of space and time. Awake in oblivion, actually. And it moves out from the world to take its place in the silent outer wall of eternity. The wall that keeps all those moving mists of time and space together.
> FRANCISCO . . . So what's to be done with the new soul-silhouettes that arrive?
> HARRY Stack them softly, like clouds, in a corner of space, where they must wait for a time. Until they are needed. . . . And if a hole comes in one of the silhouettes already in that outer wall, a new one is called for, and implanted on the damaged one. And whose silhouette is the new one? The Father's. The father of the damaged one. Or the mother's sometimes. Or a brother's, or a sweetheart's. Loved ones. That's it. And one is implanted on the other. And the merging—y'know? Merging?—merging of the silhouettes is true union. Union forever of loved ones, actually. (76)

What these characters achieve is human, not divine forgiveness; nor is it inspired by the divine presence, yet it is not completely independent of it. It is true that Harry found only temporary refuge in the church instead of the home that he sought both physically and spiritually, and it is true that Francisco directed all his violent rage against the church and its representatives; still, all this movement toward reconciliation and forgiveness takes place in the church. Their ideas become clear through confrontation with Christian religious doctrines, and they define their own beliefs in Christian terms. The violence with which Francisco attacks the church reveals how deeply its teaching lies in him, requiring great force if he is to become free of it. This freedom is, however, not entirely unequivocal; it is rather similar to Stephen Dedalus's state of mind at the end of *A Portrait of the Artist as a Young Man* where he neither believes nor disbelieves. Harry's and Francisco's human religion is built upon Christian ideals of love, understanding, and forgiveness, without a divinity, but not without the irrational, or without the transcendental. Their visions, the religious concepts and images that constantly feature in their speeches, and the objects of the church ritual they use in their profane rituals bring about some mysterious effect: that of some profane mystery working against yet not without the divine presence.

Yet another way in which the double can become integrated into the self is dramatized in what is probably the most miraculous and most victorious resolution in Murphy's plays: that of *The Gigli Concert* (1983). Two desperate men — an Irish self-made businessman suffering a kind of nervous breakdown and an English quack psychologist, a "dynamatologist" — struggle with themselves and with each other in a varying relationship: trusting, hating, savagely attacking, then understanding each other (and/or themselves). At times each arrives at a strange identification with the other though in different forms. The nameless Irishman seeks healing from his breakdown, which manifests itself in arrogant, violent, destructive activities (especially in his otherwise beloved family) and, most of all, in his irrepressible desire to sing like Beniamino Gigli. J. P. W. King, the quack psychologist, surprised at having a patient at last, takes the challenge and tries whatever method he can think of, including a Freudian kind of psychoanalysis which turns out to be a parody. In the process he comes to identify himself with his patient, gradually takes over his obsession to sing like Gigli, and in the last scene the miraculous happens on the stage: in his most exhausted, most desperate, abandoned, chaotic state he actually does sing like Gigli.[3]

The play is often examined in its relation to the Faust legend (O'Toole 164ff; Mason 102), to which it has very strong references. J. P. W. corresponds basically to Faust, the Man to Mephistopheles — although they each share certain features of the other — and the two women correspond to the two versions of Goethe's Helena. Yet O'Toole is also very much right when he maintains that Murphy equates his characters with Goethe's in the sense that Jung interpreted the protagonists of Faust (167), that is, Faust and Mephistopheles are two parts of the same entity, of one whole, and represent the conflict of good and bad, spirit and matter, light and darkness. Jung believed that:

Faust, the inept, purblind philosopher, encounters the dark side of his being,

his sinister shadow. Mephistopheles . . . who in spite of his negating disposition,
represents the true spirit of life as against the arid scholar who hovers on the
brink of suicide. (*Memories* 262)

Murphy dramatizes the split personality striving to become again an integrated
whole through J. P. W. King and his evil, dark side, his shadow—this Mephistopheles figure, who will be the instrument of his revival. In his deepest despair
he suddenly finds his redemption.

This play, even more than Murphy's earlier ones, dramatizes obsessive
desires. They first have to be expressed, that is, manifested, faced, acknowledged, which happens when the Irish Man reveals his inner struggle to J. P. W.
King. In doing so he mixes up reality and fantasy; for example, he tells about
his childhood as if he himself were Beniamino Gigli. Then, as he gradually gives
his burden to the psychologist, he is able to return to reality and leaves his desire
and fantasy to the other. By thinking and speaking about it—a normal
psychological process—and by the other taking over his obsession—a fantastic
process—he can expel his desires. But, what is even more fantastic: the desires
survive, now in the psychologist, and at the end are even fulfilled.

The most perfect union between the ego and alter ego in Murphy's plays is
achieved by King in *The Gigli Concert*: he not only makes peace with his shadow
figure, but also incarnates him by taking over his dream, his obsession, realizing
it in himself. This union, this integration of the shadow liberates such energies
that, when turned into creativity, produces the unparalleled beauty of artistic
creation. Accepting and integrating the dark side of oneself is, however, a very
painful task. Metaphorically it can be described as going to hell. In the words
of a well-known Hungarian folk song: "Aki dudás akar lenni, pokolra kell annak
menni, ott kell annak megtanulni, hogyan kell a dudát fújni" ("He who wants to
become a piper, must first go to hell, there he has to learn how to play the pipe").
This metaphorical process is enacted concretely on the stage: J. P. W. King does
go to the deepest hell in his despairing, lonesome, abandoned, chaotic, meaningless life (the woman he longs for rejects him, the one who loves him is about
to die, his only patient left him, the group he belongs to forgot him long ago, his
only consolation lies in drinking). His whole life is like his office: dirty, chaotic,
dark, with blinds pulled down to keep the light out. He also descends to hell in
asking the help of the underworld dark powers: "Assist please. In exchange—"
(74). (In the critical moment some red light playing in the darkness also
enforces the suggestion of hell.) Once he has descended into hell, goes through
all his suffering, then he can ascend with an unbelievable creative power: he can
sing like Gigli.

Murphy's world is one where "body *is* . . . bruised to pleasure soul," where
"beauty [is] born out of its own despair," and "wisdom out of midnight oil"—to
borrow Yeats's words (244-245). Wholeness, "unity of being," and salvation,
both for the individual and for the nation, are achieved only through damnation,
suffering, and despair, yet even this way leads to only a qualified kind of

redemption. Still, miracles do happen in this world, usually in the most hopeless moments. These miracles connect violence with reconciliation, guilt with forgiveness, hopelessness with hope, damnation with salvation — not as cause and effect, or in a logical succession, but in a dialectical unity, in the way the Irish mind habitually operates, holding the traditional oppositions of reason together in "creative confluence." Tom Murphy uses fantastic means in his plays to help powerfully this creative confluence work. In so doing he hints at the "harmony of reality and fantasy" possible even in this "painfully orphaned" world.

Notes

1. For a more detailed discussion of the Irish attitude to the fantastic see: Bertha, "Myth and the Fantastic."

2. See Kathryn Hume's definition: *"Fantasy is any departure from consensus reality"* (21).

3. Several critics maintain that King does not really sing. Des Maxwell is certainly right when he asserts that it does not make much difference whether he does sing on the stage aloud or only "in his mind": "He sings like Gigli—'Che A Dio Spiegasti L'Ali.' Or is it, after many vodkas and Manorax, a sound in his mind, which we 'overhear'? Either way, it is a superb moment, and perhaps, either way, the necessary affirmation from despair" (57-66). Murphy, however, appears to leave little room for doubts when he writes in the stage directions: *"He cues in his imaginary orchestra and we get the orchestral introduction to 'Tu Che A Dio Spiegasti L'Ali,' and he sings the aria to its conclusion (Gigli's voice); triumphant, emotional ending. He is kneeling on one knee; glow of red light receding, as to its point of origin . . . and shaft of yellow light becoming less intense: light back to normal"* (75).

Works Cited

Apter, T. E. *Fantasy Literature*. Bloomington: Indiana University Press, 1982.

Hume, Kathryn. *Fantasy and Mimesis: Responses to Reality in Western Literature*. New York: Methuen, 1984.

Jackson, Rosemary. *Fantasy: The Literature of Subversion*. London: Methuen, 1981.

Jung, Carl Gustav. "Aion: Phenomenology of the Self (The Ego, the Shadow, the Syzygy: Anima/Animus)." In *The Portable Jung*, ed. Joseph Campbell, 139-162. New York: The Viking Press, Inc., 1971. 139-162.

—-. *Memories, Dreams, Reflections*. London: Fontana, 1983.

Kearney, Richard. *The Irish Mind*. Dublin: Wolfhound Press, 1985.

Mason, Patrick. "Directing the Gigli Concert: An Interview." *Irish University Review* 17, no. 1 (Spring 1987): 100-113.

Maxwell, Des. "New Lamps for Old: The Theatre of Tom Murphy." *Theatre Research International* 15 (1): 57-66.

Murphy, Thomas. *The Gigli Concert*. Dublin: The Gallery Press, 1984.

—-. *The Morning After Optimism*. Dublin: The Mercier Press, 1973.

—-. *The Sanctuary Lamp*. Dublin: Poolbeg Press, 1976.

Murray, Christopher. "Introduction: The Rough and Holy Theatre of Thomas Murphy." *Irish University Review* 17 (Spring 1987): 9-17.

Olsen, Lance. *Ellipse of Uncertainty: An Introduction to Postmodern Fantasy*. Westport, CT: Greenwood Press, 1987.

O'Toole, Fintan. *The Politics of Magic*. Dublin: Raven Arts Press, 1987.

Tamási, Aron. *Jégtörö gondolatok*. Budapest: Szépirodalmi Kiadó, 1982.

Yeats, William Butler. *The Collected Plays of W. B. Yeats*. London: Macmillan, 1960.

—-. *The Collected Poems of W. B. Yeats*. London: Macmillan, 1971.

Part IV

THE OCCULT, FANTASY, AND PHANTASMAGORIA IN SWIFT, JOYCE, AND YEATS

Almost every Irish writer, but especially Jonathan Swift, Edward John Morton Drax Plunkett, the eighteenth Baron Dunsany, James Joyce, and W. B. Yeats "had a lover's quarrel with [Ireland]" — to adapt Robert Frost's definition of a poet. That is, each had a lifelong, often difficult relationship with his native land: Swift hated it, believing himself exiled there, while Joyce, deliberately exiling himself from it, never left it in his writing. Yeats, although choosing Ireland for his subject, lived most of his life abroad. Of these four, only Dunsany deliberately chose to live and write there, but given his active life as soldier, adventurer, and sportsman, he was often in France or Africa; and given his identification with the Anglo-Irish ruling class, he was often treated, and he himself often acted, as an outsider. Dunsany's most famous battle wound, to cite only the most obvious example, occurred when he went to Dublin to see how he might help in putting down the Easter Rising of 1916 — the same Rising which Yeats would later memorialize. Yet out of their "quarrels" each wrote memorable literature in a multiplicity of genres utilizing the fantastic in a variety of ways.

Of all eighteenth-century writers writing in English, Swift created the best-known, most successful fantasy in *Gulliver's Travels*. In his detailed examination of the many forms of the fantastic in Swift, Colin Manlove observes that "Swift . . . liked writing fantasy for its own account," and after comparing and contrasting him with other fantasists, he concludes that Swift is a great skeptic and questioner. His work, if not himself, may, as Vivian Mercier believes, lie in an indirect line from the ancient Irish satirists, who hurled their powerful verbal satiric barbs at the enemy as they led the Irish into battle or when necessary, could rhyme rats to death to end a plague. Still, Manlove is surely correct in contending that of all Irish writers, Swift appears the odd man out in having virtually no connections with "the mythic and folk roots of [Irish] culture which play . . . such an important role in Lord Dunsany's, Joyce's, and Yeats's work."

Chess champion of all Ireland, dedicated family man as well as a man of letters, Lord Dunsany wrote novels, short stories, articles, introductions, and hundreds of plays—a few of which were produced by Yeats in the Abbey Theatre. His published work ran to over fifty-five volumes, yet today most of it is little known and little read. Vernon Hyles, in "The Geography of the Gods," accounts in part for this neglect by claiming that Dunsany, especially in his fiction, was ahead of the taste of his time in writing a kind of "protomagical realism" that anticipates and links him to Jorges Luis Borges, Gabriel García Márquez, and James Joyce. Comparing his work to the English writers C. S. Lewis and J. R. R. Tolkien, and the American H. P. Lovecraft, Hyles describes Dunsany's artistic strengths and weaknesses, concluding that "although Dunsany's words are beautiful . . . they are in the end easily shattered . . . by time."

Both Joyce and Yeats, the two giants of modern literature in English, drew extensively upon the fantastic, but in very different ways and for very different ends. Aladár Sarbu, discussing the "Circe" and "Penelope" chapters of *Ulysses*, contends that Joyce uses the fantastic "in a dogged attempt" to "probe into the . . . depths of the subconscious." "What we witness on the plane of the phantasmagoric," he concludes, "is the mind dramatized."

"The mind dramatized" might also stand as a succinct description of Yeats's *A Vision*, that strange volume, which the poet spent much of his last years revising and which Joseph Swann describes as "the utterance of a powerful mind driven to find, and thereby inexorably to transgress, the limits of its power in ordering the world." Here we encounter "the creative imagination taken to its limits," claims Swann, as Yeats attempts to account for what for him is reality. In so doing he creates the conditions that give rise to the modern fantastic, as in Richard Ellmann's words, he "struggles by imaginative passion to overcome the prosaic to revolutionize reality."

From myth and legend, from alchemy, from ghosts, through all the forms the fantastic takes in Irish literature and the arts, we return to consider the mysteries of the human mind, the place of human beings in the world, and the relation of humans to all the realms of the invisible. What Ellmann concluded of Yeats will serve equally for all four of these writers, as well as for all the other writers and artists considered earlier: "The great questions could be given only momentary answers, couched in passionate utterance." It should not surprise us, however, that these "momentary answers" call forth the fantastic, since, as Hume among others forcefully contends: "To answer questions about the nature of the universe without fantasy is practically impossible" and for an Irish writer almost inconceivable.

C. N. Manlove

Swift and Fantasy

Of all the writers of his age Jonathan Swift stands out as a fantasist. If there is any one fantasy we remember from the antifantastical period that lasted from about 1670 to 1790, it is *Gulliver's Travels*. Yet Swift was an even more rigorous satirist than Alexander Pope, determined to try to change this world, not just to lash it. Pope's *Dunciad* is an exhibition of folly, leaving us to admire while the poet demolishes fools and exposes Dulness; Swift's *Gulliver's Travels* will not let us stay complacently outside. And yet the whole of the *Travels* is set in fantastic worlds that often have no evident link with our own. Therein lie both Swift's method of paradox and a certain duality in himself.

Swift's fantasy has often been seen only as it subserves satiric purpose, but it is clear that Swift also liked writing fantasy on its own account. How else, for instance, could we have the elaborate description in his poem "Baucis and Philemon" of the transformation of a peasant cottage to a church after the hospitality of its owners to two wandering saints? It certainly goes far beyond the detail in its more serious Ovidian original (*Metamorphosis* 8:6ll-724). Swift lingers over the way the cottage roof grew higher, "the heavy Wall went clamb'ring after," the chimney widened, grew taller and became a spire, the kettle was raised and hung upside down to become the church bell, and how

> The groaning Chair began to crawll
> Like a huge Insect up the Wall,
> There stuck, and to a Pulpitt grew,
> But kept it's Matter and it's Hue.
> And mindful of it's antient State,
> Still Groans while tatling Gossips prate.
> (lines 105-110)

It is this zestful side of Swift's fantasy which is to be found also in the elaborate accounts in *Gulliver's Travels* of Gulliver's day-to-day adventures among the Lilliputians and the Brobdingnagians — accounts of how the people of Lilliput fed, clothed, and housed the giant Gulliver, and were mystified by the "strange" objects in his possession; of how Gulliver captured the entire fleet of the enemy state of Blefuscu by wading over, tying all its capital ships together, and towing them back to Lilliput; or of how among the giants of Brobdingnag Gulliver was made a sort of portable doll's house in which to live; or of how in the Brobdingnagian library he had to walk from side to side to read the pages of a book. Such episodes, which form the staple of the appeal of *Gulliver's Travels* to children, are often omitted from critical accounts of the work, which tend to concern themselves much more with its clearly satiric elements,[1] and their particular manifestation in Book four, where Gulliver is among the rational horses, the Houyhnhnms: yet even Book four has its elements of "pure" fantasy, as in Gulliver's account of a female Houyhnhnm threading a needle with her pastern, or the picture of the Houyhnhnms sitting in their circle of mangers at the dinner table.

We should not be too quickly sentimental about this and credit Swift with a Rabelaisian love of life and creativity. Swift owes much in *Gulliver's Travels* to the tradition of Menippean satire and in particular to Rabelais, with his use of giants to shift perspective on human life, but he is without Rebelais's love of variety for its own sake,[2] nor does his imagination start off in any direction it chooses. The element of control in Swift is strong. Each item always plays its part in a larger design. If Gulliver is a giant among small people, it has to be described how they reduce him to their purposes, how they maintain him, how he serves them in a military capacity or entertains them as a would-be-favorite. Swift might, for instance, have given us the account in *Gargantua and Pantagruel* of how Pantagruel sheltered a whole army from a rain shower with his tongue, but he would not have described Panurge's adventures among the new worlds he finds inside Pantagruel's mouth, or the Asimovian "fantastic voyage" by which a stomach illness of Pantagruel's is cured by his swallowing several men enclosed in special copper spheres from which they emerge to clear his duodenal obstruction before being vomited up again (Book 2 chap. 32, 33). And in Swift each journey of Gulliver's is strictly limited, and he remains more or less in one place, while in Rabelais both the protagonists and the plots wander in whatever direction they please. Swift is, too, extraordinarily cool and matter-of-fact even in his most wondrous accounts: indeed he is often at pains to minimize the role of human feeling in his work. The only area in which this is not the case is that where he describes episodes involving disgusting experiences with vermin, excrement, insects, or disease, when the narrative takes on a degree of direct register of response it does not elsewhere so readily manifest. A further difference between Swift's work and that of Rabelais is that Swift is concerned to portray the everyday practical matters of how one might survive as a giant among tiny men, or vice versa; or of a man faced with horses where the sole diet and food they can offer him is milk and saltless oats. Throughout *Gulliver's Travels* there are accounts of Gulliver's practical difficulties in the worlds he visits — how he is to be fed, clothed, and housed when a giant, how he is to be given adequate protection when a relative manikin. Swift enters into Gulliver's situation to the extent of imagining how if he were very "small," wasps and flies would be the size of birds or more to him, a monkey might treat him like its baby, a rat try to devour him, or an eagle bear him off. The general satiric force of such a predicament is the portrayal of man at the mercy of the beasts; but this does not qualify Swift's interest in exploring the practical means by which Gulliver's environment might be adapted to him: the method the Lilliputians hit upon to transport him, the technique by which he enters their capital city without damaging it, the way by which the Brobdingnagians construct a living room in a box for him, or Gulliver's own use of loose strands of the "giant" Queen's hair out of which to fashion a seat for a chair. Such accommodations between the perspectives of a Pantagruel and a Panurge are only incidentally to be found in Rabelais. We might wish to attribute this concern with practical details to satire by the *Travels* of Daniel Defoe's *Robinson Crusoe*,[3] in which an obsessive absorption in the everyday practical matters of survival is continually evident: but if we look at other of Swift's satires we find the same industrious survey of a particular situation under every head, from the exhaustive examination of the advantages to be derived from the preservation of nominal Christianity to the practical benefits to be gained from the systematic rearing of children as food. Three features of Swift's fantasy emerge from this: his sheer empiricism and practicality, his curiosity, and his comprehensiveness. All three features put him very close to the cast of mind of the scientist, testing a hypothesis from every angle to see how it stands up. The moments appearing the most favorable in *Gulliver's Travels* come when Gulliver is describing the sensible and seemingly practical Brobdingnagians, or the farmer Lord Munodi in Balnibarbi, whose sane methods of husbandry have been abolished by the projectors of Lagado, the kind of scientists who try to impose their ideas on phenomena rather than reconcile "mind" with "things." And yet it is typical of Swift that no sooner have we said that, than we realize that this same scientific cast of mind is found expressed in fantasies, where mental categories are most certainly imposed on things.

The forms of Swift's use of fantasy are varied. It is true that stories about giants and flying islands may seem more evidently fantastic than a meditation on a broomstick which makes likenesses between man and a sweeping brush, or an argument against abolishing Christianity which proposes that we should keep up a purely nominal Christian faith for the sake of public order. But each of the works in which these appear is on its own terms a fantasy. Each is founded on the notion of the imagination attempting to construct a little world with its own laws.[4] From this perspective a world in which it can be argued that the one route to Ireland's salvation is to be found through a state-regulated sale of poor Irish infants as a luxury food item is no less fantastic than a world where horses rule a rational utopia with degenerate humans as their slaves. Again, the poem "A Beautiful Young Nymph Going to Bed," which describes the undressing of a raddled whore step by step is, however sordid its contents, in its own way a fantasy: Swift portrays, through the removal of all the apparatus that props and strives to beautify Corinna's body, almost an inversion of the fantastic account of Belinda at her toilet in Pope's *The Rape of the Lock* (where beauty is made more beautiful). The account develops a life and logic of its own. It becomes, in its way, a metaphor of the dissolution of self and identity into the formless chaos from which they emerged: Corinna's night and morning are almost escha tological. If most fantasies involve a fantastic "making," this one is a fantastic unmaking:

> Returning at the Midnight Hour;
> Four Stories climbing to her Bow'r;
> Then, seated on a three-legg'd Chair,
> Takes off her artificial Hair:
> Now, picking out a Crystal Eye,
> She wipes it clean, and lays it by.
> Her Eye-Brows from a Mouse's Hyde,
> Stuck on with Art on either Side,
> Pulls off with Care, and first displays 'em,
> Then in a Play-Book smoothly lays 'em.
> Now dextrously her Plumpers draws,
> That serve to fill her hollow Jaws.
> Untwists a Wire; and from her Gums,
> A Set of Teeth completely comes.
> Pulls out the Rags contriv'd to prop
> Her flabby Dugs and down they drop.
>   (lines 7-22

By the end of the passage Corinna has disappeared as the subject of each sentence's account of what is done.

Thus all these different works can be seen as fantasies. And they have at least one other central feature in common: they often portray some form of inversion. This technique is one also domiciled in satire, as for example in Erasmus's *Praise of Folly* or Pope's use of mock-heroic in which the little is portrayed as grand. In that sense, then, satire may be said to use the techniques of fantasy.[5] At any rate, in Swift we find man literally turned upside down in "A Meditation Upon a Broom- Stick" (1703). *Gulliver's Travels* is of course full of inversions: Swift's version of mock-heroic or little-made-big, and vice versa, is again literally conveyed within the picture of Gulliver first as giant among little men, and then the other way round; then in the third book we have all practical enterprises appropriated by people so given over to mind and theory that they are in a way mad; and in the fourth a race of horses, servants of European man and Renaissance symbols of the passions, have become masters of a republic founded on reason. Swift's scatological poems, exploring in nauseous detail the supposedly physical truths about women, can be seen in part as an inversion of the standard praises of female beauty. Even the supposedly realistic poem "A Description of the Morning" can be seen, in its grimy empiricism, as an inversion of neoclassical *aubade*, a consistently imagined reversal of a standardized *topos* (see Savage 171 – 94).

Inversions are also to be seen in Swift's literalizations of metaphor, which form one of his fantastic techniques.[6] Thus in *The Battle of the Books* the contest of preference between ancient and modern authors is portrayed in terms of an actual war in a library, with books attacking one another as knights and men-at-arms. It is almost the technique used in allegory or in emblem books, except that for Swift it is deliberately absurd. Swift derives inspiration from divine afflatus or wind and can speak of the proponents of inspired truths as people possessed of torsion of the guts which, when released in the form of fart, belch, or excrement, produce ineffable enthusiasm in their eager followers (*A Tale of a Tub*, *The Mechanical Operation of the Spirit*). Wit can be described in terms of whether it is weighty or light and frothy: hence Swift argues that the theater is divided into pit, boxes, circle, and upper gallery, so that the heavier forms of wit "may fall plum into the Jaws of certain Cricticks," while, for example, the "whining Passions and little starved Conceits, are gently wafted up by their own extreme Levity to the middle Region, and there fix and are frozen by the frigid Understandings of the Inhabitants" (*A Tale of a Tub*, 1:296). Swift's choice of this technique shows how close his method can be to that of the metaphysical conceit as used by John Donne (see also Leavis 78). But there is one central difference between Swift and the metaphysical poets: where they yoke disparate contexts together to further spiritual meanings, Swift is constantly to be found lowering the spiritual to the physical, particularly in his frequent references to the mind operating mechanically or by material processes.[7]

Nevertheless there are other uses of fantasy in Swift which go beyond these terms. *Gulliver's Travels*, for instance, is in one way a fantasy to the extent that it is a lie. Swift exploits the custom of contemporary travel writers to protest their narratives as a true record or based on personal experience. Such was the prefatory claim of Defoe's *Robinson Crusoe*: "The editor believes the thing to be a just history of fact; neither is there any appearance of fiction in it." Thus, too, Gulliver: "Gentle Reader, I have given Thee a faithful History of my Travels . . . wherein I have not been so studious of Ornament as of Truth." Within the story, Gulliver himself need not be a liar – "Splendide Mendax" though he is editorially subtitled in the 1735 edition of the *Travels*.[8] Unless he is to be believed to have invented his entire history, unless we are to suppose that he has flown in the face of the detestation of lying he conceived from his knowledge of the Houyhnhnms, he is telling what he thinks happened to him (which still leaves the possibility that his descriptions may be the inventions of a madman). But Swift as writer, presenting false worlds which Gulliver maintains to be real, is a liar. Or is he? How false are those worlds? No more certainly so, to ordinary people in the early eighteenth century, than some of those which other travel writers invented or embroidered.[9] And even if they do not thus exist in the physical world, do not Lilliput, Brobdingnag, or Laputa exist in the metaphysical one, as landscapes of the spirit? And certainly they exist within the fiction, while we read. Swift would enjoy such upsets of certainty. It is he who has the Houyhnhnms, impossible creatures of a fabulous land, declare that in speaking of his voyage to their country from England, Gulliver is speaking of places and events that cannot be, is saying *"the Thing which was not."* The Houyhnhnms, we are to be told, can only with difficulty be brought to understand the concepts of lying and false representation, "For he [Gulliver's Houyhnhnm master] argued thus; That the Use of Speech was to make us understand one another, and to receive Information of Facts; now if any one *said the Thing which was not*, these Ends were defeated" (4:207).

What drives Gulliver mad in Book four is not only his guilty horror at his association with the Yahoos, which removes one area of certainty about what he is, but his growing knowledge that the European reality which he has so long assumed is now questioned as fantastic. Thus he becomes drawn, as in no other of his voyages, to remain in the land of the Houyhnhnms, and when forced to return home still tries to turn his English house into a little Houyhnhnmland. One reality has driven out another, and even though surrounded by his family and by other men and women, Gulliver sees them as Yahoos, and his own horses as cousins to the Houyhnhnms. Swift will not let us rest with the assurance that Gulliver's madness is only delusion: insane — and proud — though he may be, his vision of humanity still has the possibility of some truth.

Clothing is a recurrent metaphor relevant to an understanding of Swift's use of fantasy. On the one hand there is the plain sense or truth and on the other hand the fable or metaphor in which it must be dressed (like language, which is in humanist terms the dress of thought) so that it may be the more vividly felt. Seen this way, the satiric portions of *Gulliver's Travels* are put over in the clothes of the fabulous travel story. Clothes can be a form of falsehood, a concealment rather than a furthering of the truth, as when Gulliver tries to use his clothes as a way of keeping the Houyhnhnms from realizing his physical affinities with the Yahoos. Equally, clothes may be one with the truth itself. Swift chooses a plain suit of clothes to represent the true Christian faith left by their father to the brothers in *A Tale of a Tub*; it is they who turn the clothes into pieces of falsehood by covering them with ornaments which their father's will expressly forbade. The idea of undressing, of stripping, of laying bare, of exposure, recurs in Swift's work; and typically he varies what is revealed by the removal of clothes all the way from truth to falsehood. Clothes, like Swift's metaphors made literal, invite the same question as fantasy: are they mere screens, or even forms of delusion or lying, or might they be the truth itself, as Swift can turn his supposed fantasies into sudden realities (as in *Gulliver's Travels*, where we shift between fantasy and direct satire in fantasy), or are they á la Carlyle of *Sartor Resartus*, the potentially ultimate truth of life, "what is Man himself but a *Micro-Coat*, or rather a compleat Suit of Cloaths with all its Trimmings?" (A *Tale of a Tub*, 2:304).[10]

Swift of course has much to say of madness, inspiration, and delusion throughout his writings. Nowhere perhaps is the subject more fully canvased than in the celebrated "Digression Concerning Madness" in *A Tale of a Tub* (9:350-352), where the narrator no sooner seems to praise honest realism than he condemns it for seeing life in all its ugliness; and no sooner does he praise imagination for beautifying life like nature, which always tries to put its best foot forward, than he seems to condemn it for obscuring the truth with false lights and varnish. Most accounts of Swift see him only as the mocking satirist here, removing one seat after another and watching his readership fall variously to the floor. Others have seen Swift as simply attacking the fantasy-making imagination.[11] But it is quite possible that Swift felt pulled here and in all his work toward realism and toward fantasy. Certainly while there is much in *Gulliver's Travels* that is realistic in that it uses a fantastic realm the more surely to lay bare, strip, and expose (in the sense of reason in the "Digression Concerning Madness") our own world, there is also much fantasy for its own sake, much invention of the sorts of adventures Gulliver might have when placed in such strange circumstances. (It is a paradox, perhaps one that pleased Swift, that the less fantastic *Gulliver's Travels* becomes, as the satiric impulse almost uniformly increases over the four books, so it deals with more fantastic situations, not with giants and midgets, but with flying islands and rational horses.)

A similar ambiguity concerning fantasy and reality is evident in Swift's scatological poems, where he exposes the filthy realities that give the lie to the purities that their lovers attribute to women: his remedy is still in the end to cover up the sordid details he has revealed, so that the illusion may be preserved. The wretched Cassinus in "Cassinus and Peter" and Strephon in "The Lady's Dressing Room" have both partly lost their wits at the discovery of the animal facts behind the outward beauty of their beloveds. They are both satirized: Cassinus, of filthy appearance and habit himself, for his fastidiousness, Strephon for his obsessive prying; and there is the sense, as in other poems of this class, that such disgust is inevitable where the woman is regarded as pure in physical terms only, rather than in moral and spiritual ones. The poems to Stella, praising the constant beauties of her spirit despite the changes of her body, are a telling contrast (see also Probyn: 88-89). Nevertheless the very opposition between the scatological poems and those to Stella suggests a dualism in Swift between body and mind. The real horror that Swift perhaps felt through Cassinus is only masked by portraying the latter as an obsessed fool. When in "Strephon and Chloe" Strephon finds out the reality of Chloe's animal needs, they proceed to the opposite extreme from their former platonic relationship, and wallow and excrete together: a rude remedy to which Swift can only offer the moral with which he ends the poem, namely that the woman should continue to delude the man even more after marriage than before it.

But what has fantasy to do with excretion? The point is that Swift's fantasy cannot be separated from the terms fancy, imagination, delusion, fiction, and lying. It is for him an expression of a faculty of the mind, a product of a mode of seeing. This may not be the least reason for the fact that almost everyone of his fantasies is not presented directly but through the subjective medium of a narrator — a Gulliver, a proposer, a hack. Clearly his sort of fantasy has little connection with that of a C. S. Lewis or a J. R. R. Tolkien. There is nothing supernatural in Swift's fantasy; and in particular no implied sense that any of the worlds he creates could come from an origin beyond his own head. Lewis, George MacDonald, and Tolkien might propose that the fantastic worlds they create are ultimately derived from a divine source or partake in a divine truth, but Swift would never have suggested such a thing. Further, while many modern fantasies are filled with desire for the beautiful and the wonderful, Swift's are by contrast scattered with episodes of disgust at the loathsome, from Gulliver's reaction to the spectacle of cancers and lice on the giant Brobdingnagians to the hideous prospect of dining on babies in *A Modest Proposal*.

In a way, Swift's fantasies could be said to invert desire. Indeed one might go further with this idea of repugnance and say that where modern fantasies tend to unite things, Swift's fantasy divides. Gulliver is variously severed from humanity on each of his voyages, exists only as a freak within the worlds he visits, and returns to his own world progressively more alienated — to the point where he cannot bear even to be in the company of his own family. (It is a paradox that he is never left alone, but is continually surrounded by changing groups of people.) And where a Lewis of *Out of the Silent Planet* or Tolkien in *The Lord of the Rings* seeks to show the interdependence of the different races in their fantasies, Swift leaves them separated in their different lands, or as polar opposites in the forms of Yahoos and Houyhnhnms. In *A Modest Proposal* the proposer is coldly separated from human feeling for the Irish, a mind reducing them to mere bodies; in *An Argument Against Christianity* the proposer has divided nominal from real Christianity; in *A Tale of a Tub* both the brothers and the various madmen cut themselves off from plain sense; in the scatological poems the mental vision and physical facts concerning women are at variance; in every area madness and dissociation of mind from body seem pervasive. To some extent this may be attributed to the fact that Swift is writing satire where modern fantasies are often more panegyric in aim; or to put it more broadly, that the one is tragic and the other comic; but there are many modern fantasies from Poe to Calvino which, while working subversively like Swift's and while often portraying a split between conscious and unconscious levels of mind, do so to suggest that those opposites should be brought together and integrated.[12]

Where the worlds of modern fantasy are each founded on their own self-consistent rules so that we can give them temporary reality while we read of them, Swift's fantastic worlds have no rules as such, or if they do, they are continually violated, so that the fiction is repeatedly being punctured and has only a maimed existence. For Swift nothing is unquestioned, and the result is that the being of all things is contingent and uncertain. He will never let us settle on any one view or opinion. His fantasies are a means of probing being — the ontology of all things, including ourselves. This ontological emphasis comes through his constant explorations of lying, delusion, and ornament: what is the true nature of a thing? The paradox is that this question is asked through fantasy which is filled with extraordinary solidity: almost every word strikes us with the force of a material object:

> *Temperance, Industry, Exercise* and *Cleanliness*, are the Lessons equally en-
> joyned to the young ones of both Sexes: And my Master thought it monstrous
> in us to give the Females a different Kind of Education from the Males, except
> in some Articles of Domestick Management: whereby, as he truly observed,
> one Half of our Natives were good for nothing but bringing Children into the
> World: And to trust the Care of their Children to such useless Animals, he said
> was yet a greater Instance of Brutality. (*Gulliver's Travels* 4:235)

This constant pricking of the fictional in Swift's work, this continual under-mining, has further ramifications. In most modern (and postromantic) fantasy, if the central character goes from the real into a fantastic world, the real world is largely forgotten while the character is there. Alice becomes wholly immersed in Wonderland, Kingsley's Tom in *The Water-Babies* forgets his earlier life as a sweep when he becomes a creature of the stream. C. S. Lewis's Ransom is caught up entirely in the new worlds of Malacandra and Perelandra that he visits: he does not, unlike his antagonists, attempt to impose the mores of one world upon another. The contrast here would be Mark Twain's *A Connecticut Yankee in King Arthur's Court* where the title really says it all.[13] But in *A Tale of a Tub*, the tale of the strange coat is continually interrupted, and the status of the work both as fiction and as book is always being questioned. Gulliver, when he visits Lilliput or Brobdingnag or Laputa, is still, coarsely enough, Gulliver, marked out by his size or his mental habits. In all his voyages he makes continual comparisons between the worlds he finds and his own European civilization. Not that this apparent retention of his former self makes us any more certain of who he is. He is both Gulliver from Europe and Gulliver within Brobdingnag, a hybrid. In the fourth book, among the Houyhnhnms, he tries to escape this middle state and identify himself entirely with the Houyhnhnms while rejecting European society and indeed humanity altogether. But here his human form and habits, from which he cannot escape, throw him back toward the Yahoo in the eyes of the Houyhnhnms. Thus in the book where Gulliver most identifies with the inhabitants, Swift makes him most unlike them in aspect. Where in the other books Gulliver to greater or lesser degree chose to keep his distance, here he is forced to. He never entirely enters the fictional worlds he encounters, and their reality is always being worn away by his own. And that their reality is contingent is further suggested in the way that, despite his (changing) memory of his European world, he scarcely ever refers while he is in any one of the fantastic realms to any of the others that he has visited.

A further feature which marks the fantastic in Swift is his largely discursive approach.[14] He does not tell a story that has a direction. The only fable he embarks on in *A Tale of a Tub* is given no independent life, but is continually interrupted. In *Gulliver's Travels* each voyage simply describes Gulliver's arrival in one of four different lands and gives a series of observations, experiences, and reflections that occurred to him; there is no central objective. In Laputa he is picked up by a flying island, observes the people, their odd manners, and their science, before leaving for a "fixed" island below, where he explores methods of farming and tours an academy of projectors; then he leaves the island and visits two more strange realms, that of the wizard who can call up great figures from the past and the country of the Struldbruggs, where he can explore the supposed benefits of immense longevity; thereafter he returns to England via Japan and Holland. The mode is simply that of a list of more or less isolated items. We are not allowed to rest with him in one context or assumption before being shifted to another; nor, apart from little incidental narratives, are we able to lose ourselves for long in an adventure he experiences. Just as he is not immersed in the worlds he visits, neither are we as readers in the fiction in which he takes part. Just as Swift would not give the palm to either illusion or realism, so we are not allowed either to become absorbed in the fantasy or to escape from the satire.

There is finally nothing alien in Swift's fantasies except man himself. The societies Gulliver encounters are, apart from the last, made up of human beings, of whatever relative size, age, or mental disposition; and in the last book there is a satiric inversion of our society, with horses in charge of degenerate man. All these societies are at the same or a simpler (and more natural) level of technological sophistication than European man. They are not faerian, nor is any of their countries a truly other world. Swift gives no account of alien landscapes: his protagonist is continually involved with different *societies*. His interest is much more in the fantastic situation, the collision of different beings and attitudes, than in the fantastic individual: the grotesquely geriatric Struldbruggs of Luggnagg, for example, are portrayed not for their own sake but for the way they explode Gulliver's, and man's, illusions concerning the desirability of long life. Swift's object in all his satires is less to introduce us to the strange, than to reveal the strange and the potentially terrible in ourselves.

Often Swift's fantasy asks us: what is fantastic? In *An Argument Against Abolishing Christianity* the proposer recommends the retention of Christianity in name only, so as to provide a useful subject on which wits and freethinkers can exercise their contempt, soldiers their blasphemy, and potential insurrectionists their spleen; other purposes which such a nominal faith may serve are the retention of a healthy stock of unpampered and undebauched humanity in the form of parsons, the provision of topics to keep the vulgar amused or to put children to sleep, and the maintenance of an established church which will keep popery at bay. No suggestion is being made, says this proposer, that we should keep any *real* Christianity: to do that would be to upset all life, private and public, at one blow. The nominal faith he proposes will be no inconvenience: Sundays do not halt gaming and whoring; nor does being in church halt flirtation or even the conduct of business; and where else would the pleasure be in doing wrong but in having someone there to tell you so? These reasons sound preposterous.

As reasons for keeping Christianity they are preposterous. But then it may occur to us that the proposal is not a proposal at all. It can be seen as a description of the current state of affairs. Real belief in Christianity has already sunk to the level of only nominal belief, and Christianity is already being used for the purposes the proposer puts forward as recommendations. People now use Christianity to exercise their wits or to vent their blasphemy; people now ignore the sabbath or go to church for form's sake alone; people see the church in the light of their hatred of Roman Catholicism, not for itself. What looks like a proposal for a future state is a present reality. What looks like fantasy is fact.

The method is taken to the limit in *A Modest Proposal*. There, after we have been shocked out of any early assumptions of the charitableness of the proposer toward the Irish poor into an awareness of the hideous truth of his proposal, we are even then not allowed to remain in any position of detachment from the proposer. For he asks us (and Swift through him), what other remedy, given English and Irish rapacity and intransigence, is available given the wretched condition of Ireland? No other proposal has made any headway. No other proposal offers so much to the Irish. At one stroke they will have produce of their own which will bring wealth to them and their country, a lessening of the population of useless (and papist) mouths, and an increase of happiness both national and domestic. If one were to ask the poor Irish themselves whether they would welcome this proposal of selling their children as meat at one year old, they would with one accord assent – as they would gladly wish that they themselves had been so treated, and so rid of the world. Furthermore, if we are horrified at the idea of eating babies, we are asked whether the Irish, reduced as they are (and the theme of the capacity for human devolution and degeneration runs through all Swift's writings; see Seidel 201- 225), are to be considered other than animals that may be fairly slaughtered as with cattle: we recall that the Houyhnhnms in *Gulliver's Travels* are not condemned for thinking of exterminating the degenerate humans-become-Yahoos.[15] In this sense the constant likening of the Irish to cattle by the proposer begs the question, a question which goes far beyond our conventional horror. That this proposal is the only answer in the circumstances constitutes the force of the satire. But more to the point, we are not allowed to dismiss it simply as a horrible fantasy. In this way we can be forced some distance along the road to acceptance even while kicking and struggling against the process.

Much, though not all, of Swift's fantasy exists when there is a separation between the self and reality. Gulliver meets little people and giants because like most Europeans he has lost touch with himself, a fact symbolized in his being cast away on four unknown territories on the globe, far from home, suggesting the unvisited region of the mind. Gulliver is nothing if not determinedly conscious and rational: the peoples he meets, rational though they may often be, challenge his own mental categories, suggest an area of the mind – and an image-making, fantastical one at that – which he has not explored. The Gulliver who tells the story has finally entered that part of the mind and become mad.

That is why, while he completely believes in the reality of the lands he describes, they may still be his inventions. The modest proposer conducts his proposal in bureaucratic, Eichmann-like detachment from the plans he puts forward; and we the readers find his proposal fantastic for only as long as we are able to stand back from it. The flying island of the Laputans, severed from the earth, is an image of dualism of mind and body and likewise of its inhabitants, who have so given themselves over to speculation that they have lost all touch with the world. The literalized metaphors show fiction divorced from reality, living a life of its own.

Although Swift's fantasy does show some recurrent characteristics, it is plain that both the visions that produce it and the forms that it takes are various. It exists to amuse, to parody, to subvert, to castigate, to disgust; it exists as lie, as fiction, as truth, as conceit, or as world. It even continually questions its own nature as fantasy. Indeed it would be fair to settle for its variety as its most constant and pervasive feature, were it not possible to sharpen the point a little further. The plain fact is that Swift will not stay with any world or view in his work, whether serious or comic: no sooner have we seen something in one guise than it shifts to another, denudes itself, or further ornaments itself. There is in Swift's fantasy a peculiar mixture of changeability and solidity. The solidity arises in large part from an obstinate exclusion of the spiritual as such from Swift's work: there is no sense, as there is in Sir Thomas Browne or in the Cambridge Platonists, of a divine medium in which all creation exists and toward the realization of which it must strive. Rather it is just such figures that Swift mocks. His way is often to turn the spiritual to the physical, to deny any binding or pervasive agent in creation, just as he lets his own works slip from any unified philosophy or perceived ground of being. (Unlike much modern fantasy, it may be added, his work gives little place to the plastic agency of water.) Put like this he sounds a materialist, but it is precisely the uncertainty in what seems most solid that he exploits by his continual reversals. In one book of *Gulliver's Travels* the hero is realized, in every minute detail of the experience, as a giant in a land of little people: in the very next book Swift turns what seemed absolute to the relative, for in Brobdingnag Gulliver is a mite beside the gigantic inhabitants of that country; and they themselves speak of their own race as a degeneration from originals far greater even than they. Swift presents us with a world that shivers and breaks as we read, and defies us to put it together again — if we can.

What then of Swift in relation to Ireland and Irish writers? Most evidently we are aware of Swift's separateness from Ireland. His main literary debts are to the classics and to English and European culture: in particular, to Erasmus, More, and Rabelais.[16] He himself hated having to be in Ireland, and detested both the land and its natives:[17] he was a reluctant member of the Anglo-Irish ruling class. His literary descendants, so far as his work as a fantasist is concerned, despite the enthusiasm of Yeats,[18] are mainly to be found outside Ireland: in Carlyle, whose *Sartor Resartus* owes much to *A Tale of a Tub*; in Kafka; in Aldous Huxley; even the more specifically fantastic — Lewis Carroll's *Alice* books, Samuel Butler's *Erewhon*, E. A. Abbott's *Flatland*, C. S. Lewis's *Out of the Silent Planet*, or T. H. White's *Mistress Masham's Repose*. Some Irish literary forebears and followers of Swift have been traced:[19] but it is perhaps better in such a case to try to show what Swift has or has not in common with other Irish writers than to attempt to establish definite links. One writer with the kind of comprehensive knowledge really required for such a task has already done something of this, linking Swift's harshness of satire, his macabre and grotesque humor, his use of parody, and his linguistic subversiveness, to habits in Irish literature (Mercier 67, 79-80, 95-98, 178, 188, 190).

For the amateur in such a context, the scope for wild generalizations and strained likenesses is of course immense. One could for instance say that the Irish comic genius, from the stories of leprechauns onward, has a special bent toward putting the ludicrously small or trivial beside the large, or even turning it into the large. (Perhaps it comes from Ireland's special sense of its large neighbor England; but apart from the fact that both are islands, one might well ask whether, say, Polish literature has registered the same idiom given its neighborhood to Russia.) At any rate we have in Sterne's *Tristram Shandy* a vast novel and much erudition devoted to the gestation and babyhood of the obscure Tristram, surrounded by his eccentric relatives. Goldsmith's *The Deserted Village* is, arguably, something of a fantasy of national disaster built out of Goldsmith's possible experience of the depopulation suffered by one uncertain hamlet. In Sheridan Le Fanu's "Green Tea," it is merely from an addiction to green tea that the vicar suffers his visions of the sermon-interrupting familiar in the shape of a monkey. Joyce in *Ulysses* makes a single and ordinary day in Dublin into a huge modern epic. Yeats finds a "terrible beauty" in a few revolutionaries in a post office. Samuel Beckett makes a play out of two tramps sitting beneath a tree saying nothing of apparent consequence. The aim is frequently to exploit disproportion: certainly to invert things, turn them upside down, so that we are no longer sure what is true. Sterne inverts the conventions of the novel; Oscar Wilde is forever turning people's ideas on their heads, lamenting "The Decay of the Lying," arguing for "The Critic as Artist," or declaring that literature has nothing to do with morality. Joyce explores multiple forms of mutually opposed narration in *Ulysses*. In George Bernard Shaw's plays conventional assumptions about class, history, politics, and love are constantly upended. An apparently pathetic parricide becomes the cynosure of the whole community in J. M. Synge's *The Playboy of the Western World*. The leftover characters from one of the narrator's scripts in Flann O'Brien's *At Swim-Two-Birds* come to life and cannot be removed until the script is burnt. It can be said that Irish literature is sometimes, like Swift's, centrifugal in character: as Yeats put it in another context, "Things fall apart; the centre cannot hold." The presentation of truth through a series of centers or masks is fairly common, as in the work of Sterne, Yeats, or Joyce.[20] Where English fiction may imply a discoverable meaning or central judgment, Irish literature is perhaps more elusive; even, perhaps, more interested in portraying madness than in discovering sense. Perhaps, too, Irish literature is unique in the way that it often seeks as in Swift's work to drag the reader in, to break down the barriers between fiction and fact. Both Sterne and Joyce, for example, give us novels which attempt to mirror the triviality of life, and in so doing pull against our preconceptions.[21]

But beyond this — and this is already "enough! or too much" — we begin to sense divergences. Irish literature is often highly local in character: we know a good deal about the house and garden in *Tristram Shandy*, or Coole and Innisfree from Yeats, or Dublin from Joyce or O'Casey, or the Aran Islands from Synge or O'Flaherty, while in Beckett's plays the inhabited space is minutely explored. Frequently we stay in that one place. Swift's Gulliver, however, is a traveler to many lands; and Swift's satire is applicable most often to man in general rather than Irishmen in particular. At the same time, it could be said that though the Irish delight, as does folktale, in the comic potentialities of the small beside the large, they have usually a special sympathy for the small, even a sense that it contains some grandeur. Sterne has an affection for Tristram and the inhabitants of his little world, as does Joyce for the half-heroic Bloom in his tiny but inflated time and space. One of the strongest moments in Shaw's *Saint Joan* is the scene where Joan, full of the sense of her own insignificance, nevertheless rouses the Dauphin to action. Yeats feels the heroic among the ordinary people who became rebels in 1916; and similarly with Synge's "playboy." Swift's object, by contrast, is usually to belittle pride, not elevate humility, to render small rather than to glorify. While there is a strong satiric tradition in Irish culture (Mercier 105-209), it has perhaps never been quite so piercing, bitter and wide-ranging as it is in Swift: and it is arguable that the panegyric or lyric streams have greater place in Irish tradition. And we have to consider one other factor in Irish tradition from which Swift's work seems divorced, and that is the sense of the mythic and folk roots of their culture. This is far stronger and more present in Ireland and Irish culture than in that of the English or Scots. For all the power of the church, the native Irish have never forgotten the gods of the Tuatha De Danaan, or the Fianna, or the great heroes of the past. That sense of a grand — or sometimes even a comic or vulgar — past, which is from time to time recreated in the deeds of present-day men, is very strong in them. It may produce paralysis or cultural stasis as Stephen Dedalus in Joyce's *Portrait of the Artist* thinks, but it also makes the meanest or most obscure deed or work able to glow with a meaning and presence rooted in a mystic continuity. This is what was expressed in the Irish Renaissance; this is what Yeats meant by Byzantium, or a terrible beauty being born; or what Dunsany describes in the reawakening at the end of *The King of Elfland's Daughter*. In that sense all true Irish literature will be what is commonly called fantasy. But Swift is no evident part of this: the only references to the past he makes are to the classical past, and that not to dignify but to belittle modern man.

Many of these generalizations are only of broad value. For instance there are many English works that turn things on their heads, such as the metaphysical poems of Donne, the work of Blake or Byron, D. H. Lawrence or T. S. Eliot; or for fantasy, the *Alice* books, Butler's *Erewhon*, or E. A. Abbott's *Flatland*. Many English works also are highly local—the poems of John Clare, Elizabeth Gaskell's *North and South*, the Wessex novels of Thomas Hardy. And as for making the small great, we have the romantics who could see the world in a grain of sand, or a baby as a "seer blest"; or children's literature, from the stories of Hans Christian Andersen about tiny things to those of Mary Norton about tiny people. But it has to be said that the Irish predilection for this theme comes from no revolutionary insight or sentiment, but from an age-old disposition, almost a collective or archetypal belief. And while the generalizations made about Irish literature are not unique to them, they are more common perhaps to them than to any other nation. The main point here is clear: if Swift's work shares in certain of the recurrent features of Irish literature, it does not on the whole share in the culture from which those features emerge. In that, as in so much else of his work, Swift remains elusive to the last.

Notes

1. John Traugott is, however, at some pains to argue that in Books 1 and 2 the charming of children is not accidental, for what Swift portrays is a child's game of power, but this is then projected as a critique of the child's games adults play (127-150).

2. Jenny Mezciems remarks how "Swift introduces sudden uncomfortable limits on fantasy where Rabelais gives it free rein" (254). Compare also Traugott (105-106) and Max Byrd saying that Swift has none of Rabelais's "gaiety" (520).

3. On *Robinson Crusoe* as likely stimulus for *Gulliver's Travels*, and for a comparison of the two, see Nigel Dennis (122-133) and Mezciems (248, 274, 276-277).

4. Compare J. R. R. Tolkien's idea of the "Secondary World" of the subcreative fantasist in his *Tree and Leaf* (43-44).

5. Compare Eric S. Rabkin: "Satire is inherently fantastic. Not only does it depend on narrative worlds that reverse the perspectives of the world outside the narrative, but the style usually depends on irony (stating the reverse of the truth as though it were truth)" (146).

6. For comment on this technique of Swift's, see Maurice J. Quinlan (516-521), and Byrd (526-527).

7. Thus we have a likening of the mind to a field watered by different vapors which produce their own crops (*A Tale of a Tub* 9:346), or a description of the brain as an assemblage of clawed animalcules (*The Mechanical Operation of the Spirit* 2:407), or the idea of coming to a mean between extreme political views by having those so opposed have half of their brain cases sawn through and exchanged for those of their contraries (*Gulliver's Travels* 3:161-162).

8. The source of this phrase is Horace, *Odes* 3:11, where it is a noble lie designed to protect another. For further commentary on Gulliver's attitude toward lying, see Robert M. Philmus (62-79), who sees Gulliver as failing to see that fiction can better convey truth

than the kind of literalism he attempts; or Everett Zimmerman who says that, while for Gulliver "fiction is falsehood," he nevertheless produces fiction, or is a splendid lier, "in order to fulfil a higher moral commitment" (122-123).

9. Percy G. Adams doubts whether any but "certain simple souls took it literally" (228). Compare, however, Lord Mondobbo writing in 1776 on the convincingness of the *Travels: "And accordingly, I have been informed, that they imposed upon many when they were first published" (3:195-196). See also W. B. Carnochan on the apparent reality of the voyages (117-120).*

10. In this same section of *A Tale of a Tub* Swift takes the word "invested," used in scholastic contexts to describe the relation of the Primum Mobile to the fixed stars, of the stars to the air and of the air to the earth, as a starting point from which to picture the earth as a suit of clothes; thence he moves to a view of clothes by themselves as venerable, since they provide the image of creation; and finally he asks whether it is not men that move and speak, but the clothes which cover them, which also provide the sole distinctions among them: thus, "if certain Ermins and Furs be placed in a certain Position, we stile them a Judge and so on" (2:304). Here, too, clothes are played with as both truth and falsehood.

11. For example Miriam K. Starkman (34-37); Irvin Ehrenpreis (222-223); Byrd (517, 526-527, 530). The view is specifically attacked in Denis Donoghue (5-10).

12. For a full account of such fantasies see Rosemary Jackson.

13. Twain's book is actually indebted to *Gulliver's Travels*, according to Liela Goldman (14-17), though I have not seen this article.

14. See also Jean-Paul Foster: "Discourse is an apt concept to describe Swift's satires. . . . The framework, however discreet it may be, is always argumentative, in contradistinction to narrative or dramatic structures" (178). I am grateful to Professor Alastair Fowler for drawing this article to my attention.

15. And beyond that is Swift's own detestation of Irish beggars and the shiftless poor generally: see the remarks assembled in Oliver W. Ferguson (473-479), particularly the quotation from Swift's "Letter to the Archbishop of Dublin, Concerning the Weavers" (1728) wondering of the Irish, "whether these animals which come in my way with two legs and human faces, clad and erect, be of the same species with what I have seen very like them in England" (quoted on 478). Ferguson remarks, "In their conception of the Irish as beasts, Swift and the projector are one. The crucial difference is economic; Swift's is moral" (479). For further exploration of this argument, see Donald T. Torchiana (195-212).

16. On *Gulliver's Travels* in relation to the work of Erasmus, More, and Rabelais, see Mezciems.

17. On this see Beckett (151-165). Beckett notes that Swift's "concern for Ireland sprang from the fact that he was compelled to live there," and that in Ireland he felt himself a reluctant exile surrounded by a race of "savages" (153-163).

18. On Yeats's fascination with Swift—mainly for his character, his political work, and his poetry rather than for his fantasy, see Michael Steinman (103-151).

19. Vivian Mercier, especially 190-209. Of particular interest is Mercier's claim that no other work in English is so close as *Gulliver's Travels* to the Early Irish immram, or voyage story (188; see also 16-18); and his suggestion (29, 188) that despite his ignorance of and contempt for Gaelic, "some Gaelic student of Swift's acquaintance" might have

supplied him with a literal translation of *The Death of Fergus*, the early comic epic of the *lucorpain* (leprechauns) which, apart from the interplay of big and little people, has several episodes similar to some in *Gulliver's Travels*, Books 1 and 2 (Mercier 17-31).

20. On Sterne's indebtedness to Swift (primarily to *A Tale of a Tub*), see Byrd. On that of Joyce to Swift, see James S. Atherton (114-123); Carnochan (170-174); and Michael Patrich Gillespie (178-190). None of these shows more debt on Joyce's part to Swift's work as fantasy: the emphasis is mainly linguistic.

21. For other recurrent features in Irish writing, see Bernard O'Donoghue (33-40), who notes "minute observation of detail in objects," "extreme and often unhelpful specificity," and pedantry. These, he says, add up to an ignoring of obvious realities which shows a disposition toward the purely mental (and thus, one may infer, the fantastic).

Works Cited

Adams, Percy G. *Travellers and Travel Liars, 1660-1800*. Berkeley: University of California Press, 1962.

Atherton, James S. *The Books at the Wake: A Study of Literary Allusions in Joyce's Finnegans Wake*. London: Faber and Faber, 1959.

Beckett, J. C. "Swift and the Anglo-Irish Tradition." In *The Character of Swift's Satire*, ed. Claude Rawson. 151-165. Newark, DE: University of Delaware Press, 1983.

Byrd, Max. "Sterne and Swift: Augustan Continuities." In *Johnson and His Age*, ed. James Engell. *Harvard English Studies* 12. Cambridge, MA: Harvard University Press, 1984.

Carnochan, W. B. *Lemuel Gulliver's Mirror for Men*. Berkeley: University of California Press, 1968.

Dennis, Nigel. *Jonathan Swift: A Short Character*. London: Weldenfeld & Nicolson, 1964.

Donoghue, Denis. *Jonathan Swift: A Critical Introduction*. Cambridge: Cambridge University Press, 1971.

Ehrenpreis, Irvin. *Swift: The Man, His Works, and the Age*. 3 vols. Vol. 1, *Mr. Swift and His Contemporaries*. London: Methuen; Cambridge: Harvard University Press, 1962-1983.

Ferguson, Oliver W. "Swift's *Saeva Indignatio* and *A Modest Proposal*." *Philological Quarterly* 38 (1959): 473-479.

Foster, Jean-Paul. "Swift: The Satirical Use of Framing Fictions." In *The Structure of Text*, ed. Udo Fries. *SPELL: Swiss Papers in English Language and Literature* 3. Tübingen: Günter Narr Verlag, 1987.

Gillespie, Michael Patrick. "A Swift Reading of *Ulysses*." *Texas Studies on Literature and Language* 27 (1985): 178-190.

Goldman, Liela. "A Giant among Pigmies." *Mark Twain Journal* 21, No. 4 (Fall 1983): 14-17.

Jackson, Rosemary. *Fantasy: The Literature of Subversion*. London: Methuen, 1981.

Leavis, F. R. *The Common Pursuit*. London: Chatto and Windus, 1952.

Mercier, Vivian. *The Irish Comic Tradition*. Oxford: The Clarendon Press, 1962.

Mezciems, Jenny. "Swift's Praise of Gulliver: Some Renaissance Background to the *Travels*." In *The Character of Swift's Satire*, ed. Claude Rawson. Newark, DE: University of Delaware Press, 1983.

Monboddo, Lord. *Of the Origin and Progress of Language*, 1776; 2nd ed. 1786. Reprint: *Swift: The Critical Heritage*, ed. Kathleen Williams. London: Routledge and Kegan Paul, 1970.

O'Donoghue, Bernard. "Irish Humour and Verbal Logic." *Critical Quarterly* 24 (1982): 33-40.

Philmus, Robert M. "Swift, Gulliver, and 'The Thing Which Was Not.'" *ELH: A Journal of English Literary History* 38 (1971): 62-79.

Probyn, Clive T. *Jonathan Swift, Gulliver's Travels: A Critical Study*. Penguin Masterstudies Series. Harmondsworth: Penguin Books, 1987.

Quinlan, Maurice J. "Swift's Use of Literalization as a Rhetorical Device." *PMLA* 82 (1967): 516-521.

Rabkin, Eric S. *The Fantastic in Literature*. Princeton: Princeton University Press, 1976.

Savage, Roger. "Swift's Fallen City: A Description of the Morning." In *The World of Jonathan Swift: Essays for the Tercentenary*, ed. Brian Vickers, 171-194. Oxford: Basil Blackwell, 1868.

Seidel, Michael. *Satiric Inheritance: Rabelais to Sterne*. Princeton: Princeton University Press, 1979.

Starkman, Miriam K. *Swift's Satire on Learning in 'A Tale of a Tub.'* Princeton: Princeton University Press, 1950.

Steinman, Michael. *Yeats's Heroic Figures: Wilde, Parnell, Swift, Casement*. London: Macmillan, 1983.

Swift, Jonathan. *The Writings of Jonathan Swift; Critical Edition*. Eds. Robert A. Greenberg and William B. Piper. New York: W. W. Norton & Co., 1973.

Tolkien, J. R. R. *Tree and Leaf*. London: Allen and Unwin, 1964.

Torchiana, Donald T. "Jonathan Swift, the Irish, and the Yahoos: The Case Reconsidered." *Philological Quarterly* 54 (1975): 195-212.

Traugott, John. "The Yahoo in the Doll's House: *Gulliver's Travels* the Children's Classic." In *English Satire and the Satiric Tradition*, ed. Claude Rawson, asst. Jenny Mezciems, 127-150. Oxford: Basil Blackwell, 1984.

Zimmerman, Everett. *Swift's Narrative Satires: Author and Authority*. Ithaca: Cornell University Press, 1983.

Lord Dunsany:
The Geography of the Gods

C. S. Lewis urged his friend J. R. R. Tolkien to attempt two things in *The Lord of the Rings:* a sense of reality located firmly in the background and a mythical system of values (Carpenter 38). Concerning the first, after long talks and arguments with Lewis, Tolkien eventually came to the conclusion that the writer of fantasy becomes a "sub-creator" (the primary creator being God), a term which embraces both the making of a believable and self-consistent world and "a quality of strangeness and wonder in the expression derived from the image" (Carpenter 130). Again as Tolkien put it, "Anyone can say the green sun, but to make a secondary world inside which the green sun will be credible will probably require labor and thought, and will certainly demand a special skill, a kind of elvish craft" (Carpenter 71-72).

Because of its antithesis to the real world, fantasy is the most difficult secondary world to create in such a way that it has the inner consistency of reality (which is Tolkien's primary strength). This unlikeness makes fantasy not an inferior art but one of the most potent, in fact the most nearly pure form of fiction. Fantasy made by humans then aspires to the elvish condition of enchantment, and this delight in making, in creating another universe is a primal urge (Carpenter 52). Yet again, Tolkien says, "We make in our measures and in our derivative mode, because we are made; and not only made, but made in the image and likeness of a maker" (Carpenter 19). So, if both Tolkien and Lord Dunsany fulfill well the primal urge of subcreation, then why does Middle Earth continue to exist even in the form of Saturday morning television cartoons — and Zaccarath, the Dubious Land, Zretazoola, and Babbulkund fade into the mists?

Colin Manlove contends, and I agree, that the wonder Dunsany celebrates lacks vitality (134). In the end, his books are beautiful and moving, but they do not move us deeply as do Tolkien's because they do not face evil and pain, central Christian issues for Tolkien as well as Lewis.

Moreover, Dunsany has no interest in any connection with the real world or in human character. He considered that to write about the familiar was a regrettable necessity for those who had not the imagination to conjure something beautiful from the air (Amory 46). He said himself of his earliest stories: "I did not feel in the least as though I were inventing but rather as though I wrote the history of lands that I had known in forgotten wanderings" (Amory 46). Nevertheless he thought at this stage that the history of lands known in remembered wanderings was poor stuff to work into fiction and drew nothing consciously from firsthand experience; later he realized what had inspired many stories, often a strange or beautiful sight half-forgotten, and, as for character, he had a remarkable lack of curiosity about people and their motives and did not think to try and understand them. Unusually self-centered, he saw the world almost entirely in terms of himself and his reactions, but at the same time he was not in the least given to self-analysis. When people came into his plays and stories, they remained less important than the language they spoke, the land they lived in, and the situation that surrounded them.

Which leads to the second criticism of Lord Dunsany: that he is simply a poetically gifted Adam going about the process of inventing names. It is certainly true that he has become the old master of neocognomina. His twentieth-century disciple, H. P. Lovecraft, worshiped him for his skill, a skill which Lovecraft himself honed but was unable to master, often resorting to the nameless things and thingless names, the beasts too horrible to describe, the gods unnamable and inscrutable that haunt his fictive world (for instance *At the Mountains of Madness*, *Dagon*, and *The Dunwich Horror*). He always considered Dunsany the greatest master of dreams, although he discovered the Irish writer somewhat tardily in 1919 (Levy 32). But he professed a great joy at entering his master's subtly decadent universe, where life and the world were presented to the reader as being merely fragile dreams of archaic Gods. That unreal atmosphere, that sublimation of the emotions, that antiquated aestheticism that characterizes *The Gods of Pegana* (1905), *The Sword of Welleran* (1908), or *The Book of Wonder* (1912) flattered his taste for poetic reverie, and at the same time the astonishingly precise and fantastically beautiful drawings of S. H. Sime, Dunsany's lifelong friend and illustrator, stimulated his imagination. In 1923 Lovecraft wrote:

> Dunsany has influenced me more than anyone else except Poe—his rich language, his cosmic point of view, his remote dream-world, and his exquisite sense of the fantastic all appeal to me more than anything else in modern literature. My first encounter with him—in the Autumn of 1919—gave an immense impetus to my writing; perhaps the greatest it has ever had. (Levy 33)

The gods and people who animate Lovecraft's mythical universe run the gamut from the indescribable horror of Dagon to others as physically repulsive but somehow less dangerous, such as Umr-at-Tawil, dean of the great old ones and direct servant of Yog-Sothoth; Tsathoggua, the Toad-God, pot-bellied, hairy, and swarthy, settled on earth since its creation and originating from the planet Cykranosh; the gigantic Ghatanothoa, imprisoned since his rebellion in the crypts of the fortress constructed by the "crustaceans" of Yoggoth at the summit of Mount Yaddith-Gho; and Shub-Niggurath, wife of Yog-Sothoth, the Black Goat of the Woods, of whom it is said in the mythical *Necronomicon* that she will proliferate hideously throughout the world.

Such are the actors in a drama that, having the cosmos for its stage, unfolds in Lovecraft's tales. It is a drama where humans appear to have no role other than to act as victim — terrorized, mutilated, tossed from one corner of the universe to another. Indeed, the old legends themselves have set down in fable man's destiny; and Lovecraft, who as a child played at building altars in honor of pagan deities, knew it well. Lovecraft's idol, Dunsany, had on his part often conceived divinities with exotic names, such as Mana-Yood-Sushai, the god who created the gods; Slid whose soul is in the sea; Mung the God of Death; and Loharneth-Lahai, God of Fantasy who spends eternity in dream. Yet these slightly decadent gods of the Irish writer simply do not have the odious and fascinating presence of those invented by Lovecraft. They belong instead to a completely subcreated world of fantasy where the imagination of poets of the "Yellow Nineties" readily took refuge. Lovecraft's gods, in contrast, are fantastic because they are manifested in daily reality, outside the author's every belief, every adherence to a dogma or a church. Surging from the depths of dreams, they settle into the waking world, mingle and mate with humans, and inflict a thousand experiments upon them. Yet somehow the Great Old Ones heed humans, for it is through human adoration that they can hope to liberate themselves and return to the earth in all their glory.

In the earlier works, the strengths of Lord Dunsany are style and mythopoesis. At his best, in *The Gods of Pegana* for example, he can evoke the fantasy world even when describing London because his is a language that conjures rather than asserts. Like the poet, his diction is impeccable, his syntax varied, and his cadences perfectly timed. These tales and sketches are mythopoeic as well, for they ornately record the creation of the gods by Mana-Yood-Sushai and the drumming of Skarl that measures time. In many ways a continuation of *The Gods of Pegana*, *Time and the Gods* (1906) expands the cosmology of Pegana, and the powers of fate and chance begin to play a significant role much as they do in Dunsany's later dramatic works. The tales are concerned with man and his reactions to the gods instead of the actions of the gods themselves, and as a result, the entire book has a semiallegorical feel. The two books together might be thought of as a kind of bible since they pose a beginning and an apocalypse.

Dunsany continued to develop into more than just a stylist. *The King of Elfland's Daughter* (1924) is a remarkably polished work of high fantasy; like all of the stories and sketches it is full of splendid descriptions, but it also contains wit and irony, unexpected actions and reactions, and sprinklings of real humor. *The Charwoman's Shadow* (1926) is a blend of bumbling farce and high magic, satiric and philosophic at the same time. As always, too, there are wonderful set pieces. The journey of the shadows into the "chill of Space" and Ramon's dance with his shadow are two memorable scenes.

Is Manlove then correct when he characterizes Dunsany as a "writer of fantasy who . . . fails to make the wonder . . . [he] celebrates vital" — a writer whose "work is often delightful, beautiful or exciting, but in the end it lacks the fibre of reality" (127)? Yes and no. Manlove rightly says that Dunsany's work lacks "the fibre of reality," but if we place it within the new tradition of magical realism, then that lack becomes a plus rather than a minus.

The term magical realism, as applied to fiction, has a certain currency since the award of the 1982 Nobel Prize for Literature to García Márquez, but before that it was anything but well known. The term had been used in art to characterize some painters, most notably Giorgio De Chirico (Young 1). It was first used in its present sense by Angel Flores in 1954 to characterize the work of Borges and writers who followed him (Young 1), but its use was controversial, and in 1973 Gregory Rabessa, García Márquez's translator, felt moved to protest its use be cause he felt it gave too much credence to "realism" as a norm (Young 1).

Whatever its limitations — and all such terms have them — magical realism and what it implies are extremely useful in defining a category of fiction that can be distinguished from traditional realistic and naturalistic fiction on the one hand, and from recognized categories of the fantastic on the other: ghost story, science fiction, Gothic novel, and fairy tale. Dunsany exists in this in-between area along with John Collier, Charles Beaumont, Charles Finney, Vladimir Nabokov, Octavio Paz, Italo Calvino, Robert Coover, Donald Barthelme, and R. A. Lafferty.

One way to understand magical realism and thus to appreciate more fully a Dunsany play such as *The Glittering Gate*, or *The Gods of the Mountain*, or *A Night at an Inn* (the first two published in *Five Plays* [1914], the third appearing in several volumes especially *Plays of Gods and Men* [1917]), is as a kind of pleasant joke on realism, suggesting as it does a new kind of fiction, produced in reaction to the confining assumptions of realism, a hybrid that somehow manages to combine the truthful and verifiable aspects of realism with the magical effects we associate with myth, folktale, tall story, and that being inside all of us — our childhood self — who loves the spell that narrative casts even when it is perfectly implausible.

Encouraged by William Butler Yeats, Dunsany wrote his first play in less than four hours (Amory 130). The idea came from a picture of the great golden gate of heaven, set in green marble. A burglar condemned for his sins tries eternally to break in, and Lord Dunsany introduced another burglar so that they could talk to one another. The first burglar opens an endless supply of beer bottles that are always empty; the other continuously attacks the gate with his burglar tools. When it finally yields at the end of the play, the two discover only "Stars, Blooming Great Stars" (quoted in Amory 135). There is bitterness in the final line as "cruel and violent" laughter echoes around them, and one of the sinners reflects, "That's like them. That's very like them. Yes they'd do that" (quoted in Amory 136).

Like many of his tales, *The Gods of the Mountain* has an Eastern flavor and setting. It concerns beggars who pass themselves off as gods — the seven green gods — with success until the gods themselves come from the mountain to take revenge, turning the beggars to stone. In his early books, the gods are often ineffective and vulnerable, but typically in the plays they are invincible and terrible. This shift results because the plays had to concern themselves mainly with humans, with whom the gods are contrasted. Doubters at the end of *The Gods of the Mountain* are silenced and the petrified beggars are worshiped as they had wished to be in life.

A Night at an Inn tells the lurid tale of robbers pursued by Indian priests because they have stolen the ruby eye of their idol. The priests are neatly disposed of by the Toff, the leader of the band of robbers, but then the blind idol appears groping for its stolen eye. The eight human characters end up dead while the god places its missing ruby in its head. One playgoer summed up the effect of Dunsany's work as follows: "What a creepy-crawly thing" (quoted in Amory 147).

A crucial feature of magical realism and of Dunsany's whole body of work lies in its duality, what Flores called an "easy or uneasy amalgamation" (quoted in Young 2). What this suggests is that the most distinctive aspects of magical realism lie at the point where two different realities intersect, perhaps to collide, perhaps to merge. Familiar dichotomies — life and death, waking and sleeping, child and adult, civilized and savage — are much at home here, though rarely with their differences resolved. What matters is that the domination of any one way of looking at things is, at least temporarily, placed in jeopardy. Normal notions about time, place, identity, matter, and the like are challenged, suspended, lured away from certitude. The results are much like the exhilarating feeling we receive from Dunsany's *Time and the Gods*, where Time, the servant of the gods and thus relative, turns out to be a scourge even they must fear, for long after the great cities have been destroyed, they too will fall either in god-time or in man-time. There is the sense that two kinds of truth are being woven together in a way that — to use a word that always applies to Dunsany — delights us, expands us. Our real waking moments are often spent out of touch with our imaginations; when something puts us back in touch, without cutting us off from our wakefulness, we feel more at home in both worlds.

Sometimes, both in postmodern magical realism and in Dunsany, the intersecting is on a large scale, a colliding of cultures or civilizations, one primitive and thus in touch with magic, the other civilized and presumably committed to science and wary of illusion and superstition. It is important to recognize this collision in cultural terms because its very scale helps us to understand that magical realism is not so much a challenge to the conventions of literary realism as it is to the basic assumptions of modern positivistic thought. Magical realism's inquiries drive deep, questioning the political and metaphysical definitions of the real by which most of us live. Perhaps this is one reason why both South America and Ireland have been such fertile grounds for this kind of fiction. Native and colonial cultures have collided there again and again. The primitive and the modern still coexist. Peasants, whom we tend to see as both wiser and more credulous than ourselves, still constitute a large segment of the population of each region. Political extremes and turmoil have helped to nourish a skepticism about the values of the industrial revolution. In writers such as Borges and Dunsany, García Márquez and Joyce, reality is capable of turning sharp corners and surprising us, a maneuver behind which we sense a biting critique of the vanity of Western civilization and an understanding of cultural relativity.

There are doubtless people among whom genuine magic still survives — Native Americans, Irish peasants, eccentric professors, clowns, and conjurers — and that is enough of an opening for the wedge of doubt Dunsany employed. A complementary factor may be found in the way in which modern civilization seems magical to outsiders, so there is a relativity to reality, and that relativity, which is after all a scientific term used since Einstein, should remind us that science itself has moved from the positivist and materialist views that support realism to a set of skeptical and pluralistic attitudes matching both Dunsany's and the new mode of fiction known as magical realism.

The intersections, then, in a good Dunsany play or in a García Márquez novel or a Borges short story are multiple. Indeed, we need to remember that a collision of cultures may be metaphorical as when the coexistence of childhood and adulthood is suddenly revealed, or when the interpenetration of life and death is exposed. Juxtaposing past and present, near and far, exposes the vulnerability of our norms for time and space. When we finish *A Night at an Inn*, we cannot say which is the real and which is the magical, where fact leaves off and fancy begins. Todorov has rightly said that in works of Dunsany's ilk the reader must hesitate. That "hesitation" is produced by an irreducible element — a man with wings, blind idols retrieving their jeweled eyes, or monoliths turning beggars into stone — something that cannot be explained by hallucination or neurosis or anything from that large body of modern orthodoxy called psychology. These are phenomena beyond our ken and must be taken as a given, the "realism" in the term, but since they cannot be explained they are "magical." Of course we know as we read *A Night at an Inn* that it is fictitious. But we like to go into even an illusory labyrinth with something analogous to Ariadne's ball of twine to help us get out. In science fiction, the way out is that science will eventually be able to account for everything the universe may confront us with; we rise to the challenge of verification. In a ghost story, we simply suspend our disbelief. Some stories, like those of Isaac Bashevis Singer, are associated with a traditional body of religious belief, and that connection constitutes a kind of validation that makes possible a certain detachment; in other words, none of these examples makes a reader hesitate.

Dunsany's work resist, as do good magical realism stories, our contemporary faith in the idea that things anomalous and unsettling, beyond the grasp of "proof," can generally be accounted for as aberrations of the human mind.

If the reaction to literary realism can be said to have taken one important direction through the internalization of the fictional as in Joyce – a turning inward to a more faithful representation of subjectivity, of the shifting but ever-present screen between ourselves and things beyond us called consciousness – then magical realism can be recognized as a divergent tendency toward a different treatment of the external, the world outside consciousness. The distinction between stories that explain themselves and stories that do not sounds easier to make than in practice is actually the case. That is because the presence of explanation in a story can be a subtle and arguable matter. Perhaps it is not only that Dunsany makes us hesitate between possibilities, but also that he makes us value that hesitation. Not only does he withhold answers, but also he teaches us to enjoy the questions.

There is the Dunsany play or story that offers one fantastic premise and then adheres to logic and natural law. For example, in *Time and the Gods* the "magical" comes first and then the "realism" ensues. A second type is the play or story which begins naturally and with familiar events and details, and then moves toward the extraordinary as in *If* (1921), which begins amazingly, to those familiar with the exotic nature of Dunsany's plays, with a prosaic scene in which a happily married man misses his train. Magical realism accommodates stories of more or less pure fantasy, and it includes works which are only slightly tinged with strangeness. We may have to work hard when applying magical realism's use of the terms amalgamation, intersection, collision, hesitation, externalization, and explanation to Charles Beaumont or George Effinger or John Barth, but they fit Dunsany easily.

Lord Dunsany wrote of a friend's work that:

> Of pure poetry there are two kinds, that which mirrors the beauty of the world in which our bodies are, and that which builds the more mysterious kingdoms where geography ends and fairyland begins, with gods and heroes at war, and the sirens singing still, and Alph going down to the darkness of Xanadu. (quoted in Amory 87)

The same can be said of the entire body of his own stories, tales, and plays. Like J. R. R. Tolkien, he felt compelled to create mystical and magical kingdoms; however, he lacked a certain knowledge gained by Tolkien, C. S. Lewis, and Charles Williams through their own interaction which centered upon their Christian worldview. Thus, although Dunsany's words are beautiful, gossamer, fascinating, and wonderful (in its original Mary Shelley meaning of "full of wonder"), they are in the end easily shattered and fragmented by time.

Dunsany's genius for the naming of names was a uniquely poetic gift. He possessed the ability of stating a thing perfectly; his prose teems with brilliant images, the perfect mix of understatement and hyperbole, all within impeccable diction, but his supreme gift was in the coining of magical and evocative names, a gift of transcendent importance to sustaining an illusion of reality in a story set in imaginary worlds. But these are stylistic devices of the poet, and many would rightly suggest that they are form lacking substance. Dunsany lacks the depth of meaning of that other Irish wordsmith, Joyce, but so do many whom we continue to read and write about. What keeps Dunsany consistently in the background of twentieth-century fiction is what may also prove to be most valuable in his plays for it is what we now mean by magical realism as the term applies to Italo Calvino, García Márquez, Donald Barthelme, and others. Although Dunsany is not the father of magical realism, he is its distant uncle, for much of what we admire in that postmodern reaction to realism and naturalism is already present in many of his works, especially in the plays.

Works Cited

Amory, Mark. *Lord Dunsany: A Biography*. London: Collins, 1976.

Carpenter, Humphrey. *The Inklings*. New York: Ballantine Books, 1978.

Dunsany, Lord [Edward John Morton Drax Plunkett]. *The Charwoman's Shadow*. London and New York: Putnam, 1926.

—-. *Five Plays*. London: Grant Richards, 1914.

—-. *The Gods of Pegana*. London: Elkin Mathews, 1905.

—-. *The King of Elfland's Daughter*. London and New York: Putnam, 1924.

—-. *Plays of Far and Near*. London and New York: Putnam, 1922.

—-. *Plays of Men and Gods*. Dublin: Talbot, 1917.

—-. *Time and the Gods*. London: Heinemann, 1906.

Levy, Maurice. *Lovecraft: A Study in the Fantastic*. Detroit: Wayne State University Press, 1988.

Manlove, C. N. *The Impulse of Fantasy Literature*. Kent, OH: The Kent State University Press, 1983.

Tymn, Marshall, Kenneth Zahorski, and Robert H. Boyer. *Fantasy Literature*. New York: R. R. Bowker, 1979.

Young, David and Kenneth Holloman. *Magical Realist Fiction*. New York: Longman Inc., 1984.

Aladár Sarbu

The Fantastic in James Joyce's *Ulysses*: Representational Strategies in "Circe" and "Penelope"

Fiction is traditionally synonymous with narration. Story and plot, these most ancient narrative devices, are for most people the principal attractions of reading even today. But story and plot were not the conventions of the craft that the modern novelist *par excellence* held in highest regard. With the shift of attention from external to internal reality in the second half of the nineteenth century, the atmosphere of the mind – to use Henry James's felicitous phrase – became immensely more important than the hero's creative engagement with the world. Action in novels became thinner and slower, and at times it came to a standstill as the story was reduced to a series of tableaux. The less the novel narrated, the more it represented. *Kinesis* dissolved into *stasis*.

This is not meant to imply that the modern novel succeeded in abolishing plot and story. Even in *Ulysses*, there is a steady evolution toward a conventional climax – the meeting of Bloom and Stephen in Bella Cohen's brothel – followed by an equally conventional denouement in which Bloom returns to Molly and the marital bed, and Molly, before she falls asleep, reviews the day's (and many earlier days') events. Yet this plot is anything but interesting, and it is extremely slight for the enormous wealth of life it has to carry. It cannot even fulfill its traditional function of imposing unity on the material. As the coherence and unity that plots lend to narratives are always reflections of the novelist's faith in the intrinsic coherence and order of reality, the subordinate position to which plot is relegated in *Ulysses* is the low watermark of such a faith. But a work of art cannot do without at least a semblance of unity – craftsmanship for the modern novelist is still an important consideration – so something else than plot must be found to do the job. There are several extrinsic devices employed to this effect in *Ulysses*, none so obvious as time – objective time, the time of the clock. When Molly's long interior monologue ends in that final, triumphant *yes* in the middle of the night, with the prospect of another day starting soon, the reader cannot help feeling that the chronicle of 16 June 1904 has been wound up in the most natural way.

But *Ulysses* has far more unity than can be attained by compressing its action and what that action is subservient to, the innumerable manifestations of human life, into a natural temporal frame. Its symbols, leitmotifs, allusions, analogies (Homeric and otherwise) are all effective agents in controlling the mass of detail that fills its pages. They come into play in pictures of the mental world of the characters — Bloom, Stephen, and Molly in the first place. Each of these characters in a block of unity within the overall scheme, each of them has the vitality — Bloom and Molly in abundance, Stephen less so — necessary to come through as a credible human being. But one personality, the author's, so pervasive in earlier phases of fiction and so often the source of both interest and unity, is conspicuously absent. There are times — or rather episodes — when we feel that we are taken by the hand by an old-fashioned storyteller and commentator, but the gesture never goes beyond a faint squeeze, and the narrator never becomes a distinct personality of the novel. Impersonality as a creative principle, defined with such precision by Stephen Dedalus in *A Portrait of the Artist as a Young Man* ("The artist, like the God of the creation, remains within or behind or beyond or above his handiwork, invisible, refined out of existence" 215), is observed also in *Ulysses*, even though the multiplicity of points of view makes us forgetful of the fact. For all the occasional deviations, the basic representational strategy of the novel, the one that gives rise to the other strategies, is authorial neutrality, which ultimately comes down to objectivity. And it is this that determines the representational strategies of both "Circe" and "Penelope."

Static and uneventful at the important level of plot, devoid of any visible sign of the author's personality, packed full with an enormous quantity of trivia, *Ulysses* stood a good chance of becoming an insufferably boring novel. While planning and writing it, Joyce was clearly troubled by this prospect and sought to forestall it. His richest resource, as was only fitting, was language. Owing to the style changing from episode to episode, *Ulysses* is so varied and so full of surprises that this alone should gratify the natural curiosity about "what will happen next," with which readers habitually come to fiction. Joyce knew very well what he was doing. When Harriet Shaw Weaver, his generous supporter through the difficult years of writing the book, was dismayed by the changing styles of the episodes and, after the completion of "Sirens," expressed her preference for the initial style, Joyce replied that "in the compass of one day to compress these wanderings and clothe them in the form of this day is for me possible by such variation which, I beg you to believe, is *not capricious* (6 August 1919, *Letters* 1:129, emphasis added). Few people doubt that he succeeded, succeeded perhaps too well, in realizing this aim. Umberto Eco sums up the prevalent view when he writes that stream of consciousness in *Ulysses* "has all the appearances of the most decisive, naturalistic, realistic reduction, and yet it achieves a life-language identification that is derived from symbolist poetics" (36).

It would be wrong, however, to regard Joyce's use of styles as only a dazzling display of his mastery of the English language for the mundane purpose of making interesting a book which is not intrinsically interesting. And indeed, he hints at there being something more to style here than is commonly believed. The variation, he writes, "is not capricious." I take this to mean that there are specific considerations governing his choice of style for each of the episodes. "Oxen of the Sun" may have suggested "the futility of all styles" to T. S. Eliot, but as Wolfgang Iser claims, style is not merely parody here. The subject being embryonic development, by tracing the evolution of the language the parodies meet a basic requirement of the subject (200-202).

If so, style beyond a point ceases to be linguistic clothing and becomes technique. The variation which is certainly not capricious is one of the strategies with which Joyce goes to work on his novel. My concern is the way in which the exigencies of the subject are served by the particular varieties of style and technique in the two episodes conjoined in my title.

This conjunction of "Circe" and "Penelope," appearances to the contrary notwithstanding, is not capricious either. Both probe into the same depths of consciousness, both come up with the same feelings, and both are informed by the same vision of how literature would concern itself with the inner life. In the manner of representation, however, they are poles apart. The (elusive) goal of capturing reality by reducing to a minimum the distance that separates art and life is pursued with the same stubbornness as before. This intent is so evident in "Penelope" that it needs little demonstrating. "Circe," on the other hand, seems to be a far cry from any such endeavors. On the face of it, it subverts the aesthetic premises which underly *Ulysses*, and takes temporary leave of the restraints that realism and naturalism impose on the imagination by allowing that imagination to dwell in the realm of fantasy. This, however, is no more than appearance, and "Circe," like the companion piece with which I have joined it, is a dogged attempt to represent the mind.

In any discussion of technique, the two episodes are useful foils for each other. In addition to the shared objectives, the very place they occupy in the pattern of the novel justifies the joint consideration. The last episode is as much of a culmination—the reunion of Bloom and Molly—as is the fifteenth. Both take place at a time of day in a situation in which the control of the conscious mind over the subconscious (superego *versus* id, if you will) is weak. Although "Penelope" is pure free association, the ultimate stream of consciousness, it presents fewer difficulties to the uninitiated (as my experience with students reading *Ulysses* for the first time shows) than does "Circe." It is still *waking reality* and not *dream*, and one can, with a modicum of critical assistance, establish from it the prehistory of the heroine, which makes subsequent readings pleasurable. Indeed, the past exists as present, and indeterminancy is the rule here, but not to the extent of making Molly disappear "behind the richness of her own life," as Iser would have us believe (225). That richness is a richness of human relations and situations (Mulvey, Gardner, Boylan, Bloom, Stephen,

Major Tweedy, Mrs. Rubio, Rudy and Milly, Dublin and Gibraltar, and so on), each of which actuates responses which in the final analysis define Molly as a complex personality, not just some vaguely conceived universal woman, as she is sometimes depicted. In many of its essential features her world is the same as Bloom's, whose prehistory, for obvious reasons, includes a good deal of hers; and when not — childhood and early youth — it runs in the same grooves. At crucial moments (her married life, her adulterous affair with Boylan, the loss of Rudy, fantasies of Stephen as lover) what matters is not so much the characters and events already familiar from "Circe" and before, but her view and judgment of them, which puts the finishing touches to the nearly completed portraits.

This "string of veritable psychological peaches," as Carl Jung called the episode (? August 1932, *Letters* 3:253) fulfills the twofold task of presenting a character and a microcosm, the latter being mirrored in the consciousness of the former. In other words, there is as much of this world on the last thirty-odd pages of the novel as that consciousness can emcompass. The single point of view is consistently adhered to, and even the occasional reminders of the objective temporal frame (the whistling of the train, St. George's clock striking the hour) within which Molly's mind freely traverses the gulf between past and present, are part of that consciousness. There is every reason to see this particular chapter as a further advance in the direction pointed to by *Portrait*.

In that book, Stephen's theorizing notwithstanding, the god of the creation does not quite withdraw from his handiwork. Owing to the third person singular (and what I regard as inseparable from the third person singular: the careful articulation of the thought, perception, and speech of the hero) we never immerse ourselves in Stephen's world as we do in Molly's. With the third person, there always remains a sense of mediation between the reader and the fictional reality. By shifting the point of view and employing a primary first-person narrator, Joyce achieves the greatest possible verisimilitude in "Penelope." This chapter records the myriad impressions as they are born and extinguished, and even traces a pattern, much in the manner recommended by Virginia Woolf. Those eight long sentences, revolving round what Joyce considered the cardinal points of a woman's body, and describing a figure eight, come closer to capturing the moment than anything else before in the history of fiction. The principal interest of the episode, however, is not philosophical but psychological. It was hailed and is still regarded as the first complete literary representation of what had for a long time been surmised, then verified about the human personality and the human mind. "I suppose the devil's grandmother knows so much about the psychology of a woman. I didn't" wrote Jung (? August 1932, *Letters* 3:253). Caution, however, is in order where the psychological implications are concerned, as there is a danger of being sidetracked by them, particularly if we read the monologue as Molly's self-administered psychotherapy. But the psychoanalytical approach may be helpful in establishing the relation of the reader to the text. In a recent study dealing with analogous situations in psychoanalysis and literature, Donald M. Kartiganer likens the role of such famous secondary first-person narrators as Ishmael in *Moby Dick* and Marlow in *Heart of Darkness* to that of the psychoanalyst. Like him, they read their patients (Ahab and Kurtz), and make a meaningful story out of an incoherent and baffling text (16-17). As there is no such secondary first-person narrator in "Penelope," the piecing together of the odds and ends of a rich and varied life in Molly's capacious memory must be undertaken by the reader. So, in part to repeat what has just been said, by creating a direct "interface" between reader and fiction, "Penelope" goes a long way further than does *Portrait* in investing literature with the status and ontological autonomy of an objet d'art.

Yet if Joyce's goal was to "refine himself out of existence," he did not fully succeed. Not because he lacked the ability to succeed, but — as in some other ambitious experiments in this novel, most notably in "Wandering Rocks" — his medium was simply inadequate for the task. He turns the mind inside out, and mind here includes both the conscious and the subconscious (perhaps it is better to speak of preconscious) domains. The subconscious operates at a preverbal level, so to represent it by means of language is tantamount to depriving it of its most distinct characteristic, which is only in part counterbalanced by symbolization (Humphrey 71). The "I" of the primary first-person narrator is called upon to ensure the maximum objectivity that language is capable of, but the goal is not quite realized, because the medium is expected to perform what it cannot. But what about "Circe," which is distinguished by the total absence of the "I," primary or secondary? Its form, the dramatic, is after all the most impersonal, therefore most perfect, of literary forms on Stephen Dedalus's scale of values. Before any more questions of this nature are asked, let us remember that the dramatic form does not mean that the episode is a play. Despite the fact that it incorporates elements from a wide range of dramatic art, from mystery to pantomime (Gose 148-150), the essential functions of drama are not observed, and the stage directions read more like narrative underpinnings than actual instructions about setting and action (Iser 215). The characters, weary or fuddled with drink, are in no state to adhere to the norms of behavior by which, with varying degrees of success, they try to live during the day. What was surpressed then, will be released now.

As to the technique of the episode, the free play that the implied author's imagination is allowed to have is of even greater significance than the dramatic form, although it would be unjustified to treat the two as separate entities. Whereas the realistic assumptions of the novel are not seriously challenged in any of the other episodes, those assumptions are shattered here. Labels like "Walpurgisnacht" (Gilbert 320), "crazy drama" (Duff 53), "ridiculous fantasy" (Iser 216) express sympathy for the confusion the ordinary reader may feel when first confronted with the text; at the same time they suggest a bemused sort of admiration for the cheek and the mastery with which Joyce pulls it off. The admiration is certainly justified, but the readiness with which it is expressed is backed (or not even backed) by generalizations in which some of the more pertinent features of this tour de force are overlooked. Attention is often

focused on Bloom only, and Stephen is lost sight of. Concern with the phantasmagoric is overwhelming with regard to the action, less so when the stage
directions are discussed. There is also a tendency to regard all manifestations
of the fantastic as projections of the minds of Bloom and Stephen. There are
plenty of reasons for a reconsideration of "Circe" with a view to finding, as we
hopefully did with "Penelope," the connection between the rationale for the
technique and the governing principle of *Ulysses*.

While the bulk — and that is a very considerable bulk — of "Circe" is in the
domain of fantasy, there is also a solid ground level without which the fantasy
would collapse. Bloom, running after Stephen, is out of breath when he arrives
in nighttown, is questioned by the policemen, talks with one of the prostitutes,
goes inside Bella Cohen's brothel, is witness to the brawl that Stephen occasions,
takes care of his money, and rescues him when he is knocked down by a drunken
soldier. Thin as this narrative plane is, it is firm enough to support the elaborate
fantasies enacted upon it. It stands in the same relation to the fantasies as does
the plot of the whole novel to the whole of the theme. What the outline cannot
suggest, however, is the bending of even this apparent factual narrative to the
exigencies of the theme. Fatigue and absinthe may in part account for the
upwelling of Bloom's and Stephen's subconscious, but this we are prepared to
accept without demur as both are free agents, authors of their own thoughts and
actions. The degradation of Bloom in the brothel, for instance, originates not
in Bella's imperious conduct, but in Bloom's personality, thus the connection
between action and agent is clear. Nighttown is not a projection, yet right at the
beginning it appears more like an expressionist painting with touches of surrealism and cubism than a factual, realistic description. The same is true of
accounts of the jerky action. The vision that informs this residual narrative part
is evidently that of the implied narrator who identifies himself with his heroes
to the extent of entering into their states of mind, and even of suspending the
cherished authorial principle of impersonality:

> Snakes of river fog creep slowly. From drains, clefts, cesspools, middens arise on
> all sides stagnant fumes. A glow leaps in the south beyond the seaward reaches
> of the river. The navvy, staggering forward, cleaves the crowd and lurches toward
> the tramsiding. On the farther side under the railway bridge Bloom appears,
> flushed, panting, cramming bread and chocolate into a sidepocket. From
> Gillen's hairdresser's window a composite portrait shows him gallant Nelson's
> image. A concave mirror at the side presents to him lovelorn longlost lugubru
> Booloohoom. Grave Gladstone sees him level, Bloom for Bloom. He passes,
> struck by the stare of truculent Wellington, but in the convex mirror grin unstruck
> the bonham eyes and fatchuck cheekchops of jollypoldy the rixdix doldy.
> (354:138-149)

"*Jollypoldy the rixdix doldy*" is lifting the anchors from moorings provided
by language. These chains, however, are loosened long before the passage is

concluded. The creeping snakes of river fog and the leaping glow already indicate the narrator's desire to go beyond the merely objective and factual, and have the description tinted in his own colors, which are at the same time the colors Bloom would use to paint the scene. As he enters somewhat later than the passage opens, there can be no doubt whose vision the words convey. The tendency to make language the primary reality of the episode culminates with the Distant Voices crying, "Dublin's burning! On fire, on fire!" (488:4660), and the subsequent evocation of the apocalypse of the city à la Hieronymus Bosch, where the vision is not pinned down to any particular consciousness, either (488 – 489:4660-4697). Naming is creating in these instances, and the writer is indeed the god of creation within his handiwork.

But there is another side to this adjustment of vision. As the action and the accompanying stage directions move into sheer fantasy, the implied narrator shifts his angle away from the principal agent to the secondary characters springing from the consciousness of that agent. The effect of the shift is a certain measure of irony and distance. When, after his apotheosis, the trajectory of Bloom's first series of transformations enters its declining curve, "Several shopkeepers from upper and lower Dorset Street throw *objects of little or no commercial value*, hambones, condensed milk tins, *unsaleable cabbage*, stale bread, sheep's tails, odd pieces of fat" (402:162-165). This irony is of a piece with the irony permeating the dialogues through the discrepancies between social status and stylistic register; Biddy the Clap speaks more elevated language than does, say, Edward the Seventh.

But what is of chief concern is the second level of action in "Circe," recognizably a case of the fantastic in Joyce. We should, in the first place, see these occurrences in some sort of perspective, as they are not all of the same importance and magnitude. The two dominant points of view being Bloom's and Stephen's, the forms that they take (alderman, emperor, Christ, beast, cardinal) are basic. Next in order are the apparitions that people their fantasy world (Molly, Rudolph and Lipoti Virag, Rudy; Stephen's father and mother). Clearly, the numerous minor figures that Bloom and Stephen come into contact with during their wanderings, and who now reappear, constitute a third group. A fourth can be made up of those who play little or no substantial part in the lives of the two main characters, yet are important as projections of complexes and fixations (the society ladies, Tennyson, Edward the Seventh). The last ragbag may be reserved for those forms and shadows which personify objects and abstract concepts (the nymph, the waterfall, the halcyon days, the hue and cry). Joyce's most common device for providing a more or less organic transition from the narrative to the fantasy level is to take his cue from something uttered at the former level. Bloom's apotheosis, for instance, starts with his "lewd" reply to a request for a "swaggerroot" by Zoe: "The mouth can be better engaged than with a cylinder of rank weed." This is countered by Zoe's "Make a stump speech out of it" (389-390:1347-1354). Bloom takes the advice and, metamorphosed into a workman-orator, immediately proceeds with the proposed stump speech, after which he changes into personae which can be associated with stump speeches (alderman, Lord Mayor, emperor). These transformations have a self-perpetuating quality, as once they have started in actuality, they are kept going at the fantasy level by an inherent logic, which is not easy to recognize at first, as it is not necessarily sequential or, rather, causal.

If we say that the projections of Bloom's mind are in fact fantasies, we state only half the truth. For there can be no doubt that his reincarnations at an ever higher social level (in this particular instance) are intended to objectify a still very strong urge to rise in the world; it is also obvious that his trial is the expression of anxieties he either does not want to acknowledge or is not conscious of during the day; his treatment by Bella/Bello brings to light what is shameful and hidden in his past, but for all that, the changes cannot be arranged in a sequence of neat, interlocking cases. The impression that one has is that Bloom and Stephen pass through these metamorphoses in an apparently haphazard, random fashion. Whatever we may think of it in another context, this is still the best clue to the way the fantastic is controlled or organized in the episode: in a random and haphazard way, that is, in the same manner as the meandering thoughts of Molly three chapters later. Which means that free association is the name for the underlying pattern of the phantasmagoric in "Circe," too, and which again confirms the fundamental similarity of themes in the two chapters.

The concern of this essay, however, is the difference in approach and not the similarity in theme. Joyce left until the end of the book his most perfect representation of the mind, which is at the same time his most realistic representation. The mind is uncovered also in "Circe," but the principal goal there is not verisimilitude but the creation of vivid and captivating pictures of the data and processes that fill the consciousness of the heroes. The limitations inherent in language, which in the last episode Joyce cannot but accept, are here transcended; and what is more, they are transcended by means of language. The method of "Penelope" is eminently suited to *stasis*, a condition in which the body rests, while the mind roams freely. (Imagine how impenetrable stream of consciousness would be on this vast scale if Molly had more external stimuli to react to than just the train and the church clock.) What is merely recorded there, is converted into action here. But action is possible only because a secondary level has been provided, at which anything can happen.

Representation in "Circe" thus becomes a series of enacted thoughts, half-thoughts, anxieties, and complexes. What we witness on the plane of the phantasmagoric is the mind dramatized. The question now is, to what end does Joyce resort to the phantasmagoric in a novel which is at least as much in the realistic as it is in the symbolist tradition? Part of the answer has to do with the literary climate whose influence he could not escape. The decade which saw the publication of two of the most notable experimental works of literature in English, *Ulysses* and *The Waste Land*, also saw the consolidation of avant garde achievements in the arts, and an increasing fascination with the psychology of

Freud by writers and scholars alike. Joyce was aware of both phenomena. If stream of consciousness in his novel often reads like symbolist poetry (Wilson 205), some of the episodes, most notably "Aeolus," display the spatial and temporal ambiguities of cubism (Loss 48, 51-52). (One wonders where in this order of things "Wandering Rocks" would be placed.) It has also been known for some time that "Circe" has affinities with expressionism and surrealism (Egri 171). André Breton did not like Joyce, but, unwittingly, in "Manifesto of Surrealism" (1924) he threw the most illuminating light on the strange happenings in "Circe." Exhilarated by the prospect of the new finally gaining ascendancy over the outmoded, he declares that:

> The imagination is perhaps on the point of reasserting itself, of reclaiming its rights. If the depths of our mind contain within it strange forces capable of augmenting those on the surface, or of waging a victorious battle against them, there is every reason to seize them—first to seize them, then, if need be, to submit it to the control of our reason. (Breton 10)

Freud and the avant garde both contributed vital elements to this perplexing picture of nighttown adventures. But does that mean that Joyce was swept off his feet by these powerful influences? Not quite. He took from them what they offered without any commitment regarding their application. The Freudian argument, for instance, which suggests that what we see is how Bloom is purged of his anxieties and "gathers enough strength to confront the existential problem in his life" (Gose 151), misses the point. The anxieties are there, but a purging of the kind suggested would require a healer as well, somebody on the premises to respond to what is released from the hero's mind; but no such analyst is present. Iser opines that what emerges in nighttown is not a symptom of repression or "a way around the censorship imposed by the superego," but "an attempt to realize the potential of a character which in everyday life can never be anything more than partially realized" (Iser 217). If this were the case, "Circe" should be read as a kind of wish fulfillment. But then Bloom would not be subjected to so much humiliation, as the thing uppermost in his mind would be the forbidden pleasure and not the shame attendant upon it. It is not, as Iser believes, that Bloom responds to situations which bring out his whole personality; on the contrary, it is his personality which produces the situations in which his character is revealed. The same is true of Stephen: the evocation of his mother is brought about by his sense of guilt and not by anything in the situation inside the brothel.

My point of departure for the foregoing discussion was that Joyce was trying to make his work interesting by means of stylistic diversity. Although we would need a systematic study of the whole novel to unravel the full implications of his statement that the choice of styles for the individual chapters was not capricious, these two episodes certainly bear out the claim that there is a close connection between the two. "Penelope" expands to the outermost limits the frontiers of literary realism, and the result is an objective representation of extreme subjectivity, which has fascinated lovers of literature and professional psychologists alike, but has also met with a lot of hostile criticism. Erich Auerbach, for his part, preferred the more moderate doses of stream of consciousness as administered by Virginia Woolf. "The mirroring of Mrs. Ramsey's consciousness is much more easily comprehensible than the sort of thing we get in such cases from other authors (James Joyce, for example)" (475). With "Circe" these objections do not hold, as here the reader has to find his bearings not in a mass of trivia embedded in a frightening amount of words, but in a series of highly entertaining scenes — pictures if you like — whose artistic affinities are now easily recognizable. Of course, the reader must do his homework, but that homework is light, as most of what he needs to know of Freudianism and avant garde art is now part of our culture. Once those hurdles are cleared, he can sit down and abandon himself to the fun of witnessing the capers and frolics of this select company of Dubliners.

With the surge of interest in fictional worlds other than the one which directly reflects the world of the senses, with the growing popularity of science fiction and fantasy, and, paradoxically, with the opening up of the canon of which *Ulysses* is now an integral part, a new state of affairs may come about, in which what once was formulated as wishful thinking rather than the actual case, may become a reality. "Granted that the plain reader has the flexibility of mind and sophistication necessary to enter into the absinth-poisoned [*sic*] brain of Stephen and Bloom," wrote Charles Duff in 1932, "it is by no means difficult to follow" (53). My own arguments are offered in support of that claim.

Works Cited

Auerbach, Erich. *Mimesis: The Representation of Reality in Western Literature*. 1946 Trans. Willard Trask. 1946; Garden City: Doubleday and Company, Inc., 1957.

Breton, André. *Manifestoes of Surrealism*. 1924 Trans. Richard Seaver and H. R. Lane. 1924. Ann Arbor: University of Michigan Press, 1969.

Duff, Charles. *James Joyce and the Plain Reader*. 1932 Folcroft, PA: The Folcroft Press Inc., 1969.

Eco, Umberto. *The Aesthetics of Chiasmos: The Middle Ages of James Joyce*. 1966 Tulsa, OK: University of Tulsa, 1982.

Egri, Péter. *James Joyce és Thomas Mann. Dekadencia és modernség*. Budapest: Akadémiai Kiadó, 1967.

Gilbert, Stuart. *James Joyce's Ulysses*. 1930 New York: Vintage Books, 1955.

Gose, E. B., Jr. *The Transformation Process in Joyce's Ulysses*. Toronto: University of Toronto Press, 1980.

Humphrey, R. *Stream of Consciousness in the Modern Novel: A Study of James Joyce, Virginia Woolf, Dorothy Richardson, William Faulkner et al.* 1954 Berkeley: University of California Press, 1968.

Iser, Wolfgang. *The Implied Reader: Patterns of Communication in Prose Fiction from Bunyan to Beckett*. 1972 Baltimore and London: The Johns Hopkins University Press, 1974.

Joyce, James. *A Portrait of the Artist as a Young Man*. 1916 Ed. Chester G. Anderson. New York: The Viking Press, 1968.

—-. *Ulysses*. 1922 Ed. W. Gabler. New York: Vintage Press, 1986.

—-. *Letters of James Joyce*. 3 vols. Vol. 1, ed. Stuart Gilbert, 1957; vol. 3, ed. Richard Ellmann, 1966. New York: The Viking Press, 1957-1966.

Kartiganer, D. M. "Freud's Reading Process: the Divided Protagonist." In *The Psychoanalytic Study of Literature*, eds. J. Reppen and M. Charney. Hillside, New Jersey and London: The Analytic Press, 1985.

Loss, A. K. *Joyce's Visible Art: The Work of Joyce and the Visual Arts, 1904-1922*. Ann Arbor, Michigan: UMI Research Press, 1984.

Wilson, Edmund. *Axel's Castle: A Study of the Imaginative Literature of 1870-1930*. 1931 New York: Norton, 1984.

Joseph Swann

The Displacement of the Real:
From Coleridgean Fancy to
Yeats's *Vision* and Beyond

Louis MacNeice drily observed of W. B. Yeats's *A Vision* that it was "the most ingenious, the most elaborate, and the most arid of his writings"; Yeats, he went on to say,

> . . . attached great importance to it. Although from one angle a romantic individualist, even an anarchist, he had always had a desire to docket the universe. He did not fancy himself beating his wings in a void. (112)

More recent critics have seen little reason to reverse MacNeice's judgment. Although some eminent scholars have used Yeats's system to expound his work—notably Helen Vendler in her reading of the later plays—a sense of puzzlement remains, an embarrassment almost, as to why a major poet should burden himself and his readers with so difficult a text. The reason Mac Neice gives, hovering between the romantic introspection of the period and the need for law, but allowing, too, for romantic self-importance, is perceptive and persuasive as far as it goes. *A Vision* is the utterance of a powerful mind drive to find, and thereby inexorably to transgress, the limits of its power in ordering the world.

Yeats evidently felt the need for an explanation, a general theory of his experienced universe, that would be continuous with his poetry; aided by his "instructors" who, out of the reaches of some common unconscious, dictated the pages of his book through the medium of his wife, he set out to provide such an explanation. The instructors themselves very early established their *caveat*: "We have come to give you metaphors for poetry" (*A Vision* 8); metaphors, that is, for the world, or what Yeats, in his own *caveat*, called "stylistic arrangements of experience" (25). But the question remains why a poet should need such a thoroughgoing arrangement, and why the arrangement should take on the form, or style, which it did.

For to the modern mind this phrase of Yeats's would be an acceptable definition of poetry itself, one which emphasizes the continuity between poem and world: a poem is not a radical departure from, it is simply an "arrangement," a more pointed arrangement of experience. It is—though this is not the way Yeats's generation thought of it—the play, in a world of words, of the words that make that world. To Yeats's generation, poem and world were separate; ever since Kant, or even Luther, there had been an elemental divide between word and thing. Yeats's *A Vision* was an attempt to build across that divide. Its primary importance lies not in the details of its system—an idiosyncratic mix, often wayward, sometimes profound, of the various philosophical, mystical, and cabbalistic traditions in which Yeats had always been interested—but in the part it played in a general poetic undertaking to make the world of things articulate, to subject it once again to law, and in particular to the mind which made that law.

Here the details are important, for it was the point of view of the knowing subject that Yeats's *A Vision* set out to colonize the void. Like Coleridge, and like the dominant philosophical tradition of the twentieth century, Yeats saw in the act of knowing the principle which constitutes the world. Although *A Vision* was by no means a work of orthodox philosophy, it was in its very unorthodoxy instrumental in opening the way toward that revolution in the approach to language which has characterized our own day; a revolution based on an understanding of language as the medium in which the world is known and therefore, in the contours of knowledge, comes to be (Gadamer 426).

This understanding is already making itself felt in Yeats's last poems. A reading of the "Death" poems will show to what extent the poet was, at the end of his life, moving away from his late romantic antecedents toward an attitude to language which has, among other things, nurtured the modern fantastic. Yeats had, in his later work, brought together again what Coleridge had so strictly separated, the imagination and the fancy which implements it. Doing so he had made room for a play of language back into the world; and that playfulness, disregarding, and indeed revoking the inherited cultural antinomies of Western thought, has reestablished the fantastic as continuous with the world in which we live. The unreal is no longer divorced from the real. The nonfantastic text, Christine Brooke-Rose can assert, is a "displaced form of the fantastic" (*A Rhetoric of the Unreal* 65); or, as she later puts it, the text of our universe "merely [shows] the real, in its unique 'idiocy,' as the fantastic, which it is" (388). The revolution here is complete; but this most modern of revolutions can only be understood in terms of an earlier change, for it was the romantic movement which constituted the imagination as the supreme arbiter, not yet of the fantastic, but first of the poetic, and then of the accepted, real world.

Coleridge, the most overtly philosophical of the English romantics, provided the etymology and the critical discourse on which this change was founded. He observes in the *Biographia Literaria* that the Greek term *phantasia* would best be translated by the Latin *imagination;* but he needed something more robust:

> Repeated meditations led me first to suspect . . . that fancy and imagination were two distinct and widely different faculties, instead of being, according to the general belief, either two names with one meaning, or at the furthest the lower and higher degree of one and the same power. (4:50)

He insists on this distinction, and the language in which he does so reveals his reason. The imagination is the "shaping or modifying power," the fancy the "aggregative and accosiative power" (12:160). The fancy has "no other counters to play with but fixities and definites," it is "no other than a mode of memory" or "mechanical memory" and, like the ordinary memory, "it must receive all its materials ready made from the law of association" (13:167; 5:60). Coleridge goes into the Aristotelian doctrine of association at some length, being all the time at pains to separate the "passive fancy," which supplies thought with its objects, from the active and properly creative force of the imagination (5:59-60; 8:77). This alone is the truly spirited principle:

> The imagination, then, I consider either as primary or secondary. The primary imagination I hold to be the living power and prime agent of all human perception, and as a repetition in the finite mind of the eternal act of creation in the infinite I AM. (13:167)

Fancy, so important to the modern mind, was put firmly aside in order to concentrate on a power which formed and unified the world in language, for only thus could the Kantian disjunction of *noumena* from *phenomena* be overcome, and the consequent departure from the world of God, the principle of meaning, be reversed.

Coleridge's distincion was seminal. Like William Blake he had established the imagination at the centre of his universe, but that universe was in one sense broader than Blake's. If Blake could write that: "Natural objects always did and now do weaken, deaden & obliterate Imagination in Me" (821), Coleridge's remarks embraced those objects too. The interpretive force of the imagination gave being not only to the truths of poetry but also to the realities of the world; for Coleridge was writing not only as a poet, but also as a philosopher and a divine. Breadth and lucidity, however, had their price, and it was a price paid the more dearly as the romantic age progressed. For in his eagerness to establish a principle of meaning to man, Coleridge had virtually dematerialized meaning: what was made by the imagination must be as spiritual as the imagination, and fancy was reduced to the mechanical provision of data for the imagination to mold and name.

Romanticism is a thing of many paradoxes, and one of the most poignant lies in the rigor of Coleridge's mind. For his separation of the powers of the imagination helped bring about one-sidedness in the development of romantic thought which instigated both the modernist dilemma and the postmodernist response to that dilemma; yet that same rigor provides the instrument with which both modernism and postmodernism may be overcome. Coleridge set in train the dichotomy between matter and spirit, world and word, which his own distinction between the powers of fancy and imagination, once the balance had been slightly shifted, would aptly and succinctly reverse. Again, and this is not unconnected, Blake's poetic imagination is firmly grounded in this world, but his occasional comments suggest a separation between art and world of a sort that was to become the stock-in-trade of later nineteenth-century romanticism. Blake however, like Shelley in the *Defence of Poetry*, was combating the scientific rationalism of the day; Coleridge was both leaning on and combating German idealism—a different, and more radical, adversary.

The later poets of the nineteenth century, faced with the loss of God on the one hand, and on the other with the loss of the material world to the progressive positivists, could think of salvaging language as the vehicle of meaning only by projecting it into an inviolate realm beyond both economics and technocracy. "Words alone are certain good," wrote the young Yeats; but words alone, he went on to say, "die a pearly brotherhood" (*Collected Poems* 7, 8). It was a pearliness born of the Coleridgean imagination, which had eradicated from the interpretive faculty all that had to do with the particularity, the irreplaceable otherness, and that *is* the materiality of its object.

Wordsworth had a healthier instinct than Coleridge when he doubted the complete separation of the two faculties; and Keats, in a different context, accused Coleridge of what was, here too, the central weakness of his thought: a lack of "negative capability" (Keats 101-104). Coleridge conceived of meaning as something positive and complete—he was, it will be remembered, a Unitarian—and he thus quite naturally ordered the cognitive functions in a strict hierarchy, power being synonymous with activity, and being ascribed, therefore, solely and entirely to the imagination. It is the other side of the romantic paradox that, for us, the power to associate, and the displacement inherent in association, with its random juxtaposition and its purely individual givennesses, is so crucial to language: that this is indeed the endpoint of the interpretive process and not just its beginning, as well as being the logical basis for the literature of the fantastic.[1] The terms of Coleridge's distinction seem as valid now as they did two hundred years ago; it is the relative value he gave them, and above all their emphatic separation, that nowadays seems so questionable.

Coleridge's practice as a poet, however, puts things in a different light. One might indeed be forgiven for thinking him the most fanciful of all the English romantics; for if the images of "Kubla Khan" or "The Rime of the Ancient Mariner" are the fruit of fancy, then to this faculty must be accorded much of the power of those poems. The dark symbolism of the "Mariner"'s spectral ship and her spectral crew, the tumbling chasms of "Kubla Khan," cannot ultimately be separated from the opaqueness of figures which enter the poem from other contexts, be they dreams or nightmares or whatever, and pull away again toward those other contexts where they are more properly at home. "All the images," Coleridge tells us in his preface to "Kubla Khan," "rose up before him as *things*," as the "fixities and definites," that is to say, of fancy. And it is their self-sufficiency as things, their inpenetrability to any accrued meaning, that gives the poem its force. Out of them the poet builds, but they disrupt and dislodge his building. The genius of the poem lies in the fact that the poet makes of both moments — the building and the disruption — his imaginative theme. "Kubla Khan" belongs to those early works of romanticism which hold intact the concerns of both the romantic and the modernist generations, stating in clear terms not only the problem of meaning, but also, in outline at least, the solution which is belatedly beginning to surface in our own world.

The Khan conceives a garden of delights, a paradise complete with sacred river and encircling walls, and in it he decrees a "stately pleasure-dome," the symbol of attained meaning. Nature, however, is not as univocally happy as he would have her be, and the exclamatory "But oh! that deep romantic chasm . . ." with which the second stanza opens, introduces the series of tumultuous images — the dancing rocks, the measureless caverns, the cedar forests, the lifeless ocean — which break the upward flow of the creative mind. Both as metaphor and as metonymy, both as created image and as collected fantasm, these figures assert the willfulness of all figures and all words. The pleasure-dome can never be unequivocal because meaning can never simply be made; that out of which it is made refuses such simplicity, and the making becomes a loss. The dome is reduced to a shadow, floating "midway on the waves," the embodiment of a very Platonic irony. But Coleridge goes a good way beyond Plato:

> It was a miracle of rare device,
> A sunny pleasure-dome with caves of ice!
> ("Kubla Khan" 35-36)

A wanton humor is transposing and thematizing that irony.

In the final stanza of "Kubla Khan" the pleasure-dome becomes a hypothesis, built now by the poet, but built "in air" on the basis of a forgotten song. The song remains forgotten — a typically Coleridgean device — and the hypothesis therefore unfulfilled. But, if this were not so, we are told, the poet's own voice would be such that "all who heard should see them there": should see, that is, both dome and ice. The status of linguistic meaning is thus defined as both generative of the world of things and discontinuous with it; furthermore it is dependent in its origins on memory: on association, that is to say, and on fancy. The already complex argument is taken a step further in the closing lines of the poem, where a doubly hypothetical audience addresses an incantation to the poet's hypothetical speech. In this twice-removed sphere of fanciful imagining, the poet is shaman, fed on the food of paradise, attaining in a material union the consummation which had eluded the Khan. But he attains it because, and in the measure in which, the poem's language has been removed from the dichotomy of sign and thing which governed Coleridge's theoretical considerations and has become one in which the elements are continuous:

> Weave a circle round him thrice,
> And close your eyes with holy dread.
> ("Kubla Khan" 51-52)

Irony has turned through paradox into identity. The sign, cut off from its logical roots in a universe where it is the sign of something else, has become that something else. The images that rose up before the poet as things have taken on the power, and the alienness, of things. For words have power here as words being sung to, but not assimilating, matter. We are back in a universe of enchantment and myth before meaning was separated from materiality and had to be regained. And meaning here *is* material, not in the crude sense of the Khan's attempted hypostasization of it in his dome, but in the sense in which matter is energy and energy is the force of otherness, the darkness at the center of things. The poet's chant, playing out into its hypothetical world, shares in that energy; the poet's hypothetical act of total speech, which would reify his imagined world, does not. Such power is not in language. The unreal addresses the unreal in these lines, but it does so on its own terms; and in these terms, which have been established unequivocally by the poem, that address is very real. Interpretation, the fruit of the imagination on which Coleridge set such store, has been left behind for a world in which sign plays on sign, generating in that play the tension between opposing forces which is the hallmark of what we call reality.

Coleridge gave his poem a curious setting. He relates in the preface how he had fallen asleep reading from "Purchas's Pilgrimage," and in his sleep

> he has the most vivid confidence, that he could not have composed less than from two to three hundred lines. . . . On awaking he appeared to himself to have a distinct recollection of the whole ("Kubla Khan" Preface)

but he was "unfortunately called out by a person on business from Porlock," and on returning to his room could remember only the lines of the poem he has left us. Although Todorov expressly excludes poetry from the genre of the fantastic (29ff), Coleridge seems here to fulfill his most stringent requirements, for the reader really does not know how to take this text. Is the poem we have the relict of the dream, or is the dream part of the poem, or is the uncertainty itself the real meaning? There is a mirroring quality about these propositions which allows all three at once. Of set purpose, the author dislocates the reader's suppositions, and his instrument in doing so is fancy. Dream and fancy belong to Coleridgean fancy, not to the imagination, and the break in memory, repeated at the center of the poem, serves not only to effect the abrupt changes in context which characterize this work, but also in doing so illustrates the origin as well as the ending of the interpretive process in an immediate encounter: an encounter which is both that of memory and of the forgetting which inaugurates new knowledge. When Coleridge presents his poem as an awakening from vision and dream, this may be read either as fancy waking to the imagination, or as the imagination waking to fancy. Either way, the movement that began with fancy ends there too. Far from being the "living power and prime agent of all human perception," the imagination visibly ceases, after a certain point in the poem, to play any role at all.

In the intellectual complexity of his argument Coleridge stands on his own among the English romantics. His great contemporaries, however, all share a sophistication in their approach to language that would have forbidden the simple reduction of word to meaning which took hold of later romanticism, leading not only to the modernist response to that movement but also to a good deal of subsequent literary theory, up to and including the deconstructionism of our own day.

Yeats was born into the late romantic world, and his early poetry is informed by the dream of a meaning purified from all contact with materiality, reflecting only the sadness of the heart so purified: a meaning beyond earthly speech. Both the happy shepherd and his sad companion in the first two of Yeats's *Collected Poems* speak their story to an "echo-harbouring shell," and in both cases the story fades away and dies in narcissistic beauty:

> But the sad dweller by the sea-ways lone
> Changed all he sang to inarticulate moan
> Among her wildering whorls, forgetting him.
> *(Collected Poems* 9)

It is a different inarticulateness, a different forgetting, and a different transcendence at work here from that of "Kubla Khan," but it was the logical conclusion of Coleridge's theory of the imagination without his poetry, or indeed of Keats's poetry bereft of the irony which informs it. Yeats was saved from the full rigor of this logic not least by being born into the Irish tradition, whose oral, myth-centered ethos ran entirely counter to the dichotomies which at that time governed the intellectual climate of Europe. Where meaning has never been thought of as existing more fully than in the remembered word, and where the story is integral with life, words will have a wider function and a more palpable being than in cultures dominated by the individual interpreting voice. Born of a Protestant line, Yeats found somewhere in the Catholic, pagan past of Ireland the system he needed, not explicitly to overcome the modernist dilemma, for he seems never to have experienced the full force of that crisis, but to rejoin on his own terms the poem with the world. This is what he is doing in *A Vision*.

In the looseness of its coordination and its eclecticism, Yeats's *A Vision* is not unlike the *Biographia Literaria*; it is, however, more of a system, and its principles derive more closely from Yeats's poetic practice. Both are works of the interpreting mind seeking to unify poetic and secular experience on the basis of the creative imagination. For Coleridge, however, the imagination was an individual perceptive faculty, borne aloft by the divine will. Yeats, living in a world without God, paid greater attention to the will and the emotions of men, and their interaction with the mind to form the universe of letters and events in which he lived. That universe lacked coherent interpretation, for the century which had elapsed between the *Biographia* and the beginnings of *A Vision* in October 1917 (four days, Yeats tells us, after his marriage), had seen the demise of the entire mental and social orders that Coleridge could still have taken for granted. Kant had been succeeded by Nietzsche; it was the time of the Great War, the Russian Revolution, and of Irish independence. Romantic Ireland, indeed the whole fabric of what the Victorians had meant by romanticism, was dead and gone. And Yeats, recently married, must have felt more mastery of his personal world than he had felt before.

Poetically, Yeats had, by the 1920s, left far behind him the transcendental ideals of the *fin de siècle*. His work had established itself as a continuing discourse on the relation of the human mind and heart with reality, and that relation had revealed itself in increasingly clear terms as the interplay of structures of perception governed by the movement of the affections. The growth of images out of casual associations and their dissolution into higher associative complexes, the movement of the mind from the encounter of the senses through interpretation to the encounter of knowing, is evident in such poems as "The Wild Swans at Coole," "The Second Coming," "Leda and the Swan," "Among School Children," and the poetic epilogue to *A Vision*, "All Souls' Night."[2] All of these come from the period when Yeats was working on *A Vision*, and all of them thematize in their own way the processes of knowing, whether we call these association and analogy, metonymy and metaphor, or fancy and imagination. When Yeats set out to order his experience into a more universal system, it was on these same structures that he built.

The key to Yeats's *A Vision* is the cone or vortex. Always a double cone, it is arranged either end to end as a chiasmus, or overlapping, the apex of one cone touching the base of the other, and vice versa, to form a double helix: a figure which Robert Graves in *The White Goddess* — also a universal poetic system — sees as an archetype of the life force (103), and which modern science has established as the pattern of DNA, the substance that determines the generic makeup of the cell. Like these other vortices, Yeats's cones are thoroughly interpretive in nature, but their pattern is more directly heuristic. The opening chapters of *A Vision* proper cite Empedocles, Heraclitus, and Plato as the most ancient sources of this figure; of these the most relevant for our concerns is Plato. Here Yeats writes:

The first gyres clearly described by philosophy are those in the *Timaeus* which are made by the circuits of "the Other" (creators of all particular things), of the planets as they ascend or descend above or below the equator. They are opposite in nature to that circle of the fixed stars which constitutes "the Same" and confers upon us the knowledge of Universals. (*A Vision* 68)

But the Other and the Same are the objects produced by the associative and the analogical moments of the knowing process respectively: knowing begins with an encounter with something that is randomly *other*, something which is then assimilated to the already known by a process of likening and abstraction, only to reassert itself at this higher level as once more radically unknown. It is the pattern of *eros* and *thanatos*, and this lies at the heart of language. It is visible in the movements of fancy and imagination in "Kubla Khan," where meaning and loss of meaning go hand in hand, as they frequently do in Yeats's own poems. And it is visible in *A Vision*, not only as the process Yeats expounds, but also, more crucially, as one that determines the course of his exposition.

Through the intellectual movements of the modern era, from Luther to the twentieth century, there runs a single strand of awareness, that of discontinuity. Yeats was immune to it (as was William Carlos Williams), and no document is greater proof of that immunity than *A Vision*. Where Williams's ability to bridge over the crisis of modernism stemmed from an intellectual holism close to that of Hindu thought, Yeats's stemmed from a more analytic awareness of man's linguistic interaction with the world. Emotion and will, as well as intellect, had a constitutive role to play in this process, the world being wrought in the flow of affective forces through the senses and above all through the mind. Spirit and matter were for Yeats (as they had been three hundred years earlier for Shakespeare) inseparable. Thus the first "gyres" of *A Vision* depict the movement of the "*Four Faculties: Will* and *Mask, Creative Mind* and *Body of Fate*" in the generation of reality (73). Yeats explains what he means in a way that prompts the reader's sense of perils ahead:

It will be enough until I have explained the geometrical diagrams in detail to describe *Will* and *Mask* as the will and its object, or the Is and the Ought (or that which should be), *Creative Mind* and *Body of Fate* as thought and its object, or the Knower and the Known, and to say that the first two are lunar or antithetical or natural, the second two solar or *primary* or reasonable. (73)

This is already pressing on the limits of understanding. Once one has adopted the vocabulary, however, the value of Yeats's complex argument becomes apparent. There is a perfect balance in his system between the forces of the subject and those of its objects, between potentiality (or energy or materiality) and that actuality which transpires when energies meet and break. Just as Yeats's mature poetry never separates deeds from words and history from the mind which makes it (see for instance, "Long-Legged Fly," *Collected*

Poems 381-382), so his intellectual formulation of the poetic awareness is a continuum where opposition and identity, discord and concord are treated on equal terms. "'There is a place at the bottom of the graves,'" he says, quoting Blake with approval, "'where contraries are equally true'" (*A Vision* 72). This itself is closer to Eastern thought than to the traditional antinomianism of the West, and it suggests that *A Vision* may have something to do with the rapprochement between those two traditions which is beginning to take place in our own day.

The acuteness of Yeats's insight into the status of reality is evident when he combines the dimensions of time and space in the symbolism of a line and a plane respectively, intersecting at right angles to form the cone which is his principal model. (One is reminded of the four dimensions of Einsteinian physics.) The heuristic quality of the model is emphasized when Yeats ascribes subjectivity to the line, objectivity to the plane. The line is the dynamic element here and the plane the static; moreover, subjectivity is called "*antithetical . . .* because it is achieved and defended by continual conflict with its opposite," and objectivity is "*primary*" because it "brings us back to the mass where we begin" (71-72).

There is still a great deal of direct value here; but the model is becoming very complex, and when Yeats at the beginning of what is only the fifth section of the first part of Book One, speaking of the Four Faculties, tells us that: "These pairs of opposites whirl in contrary directions" (74), one may be forgiven for wondering where this might all be leading. When he goes on to couple his superimposed vortices with the twenty-eight divisions of the lunar month or Great Wheel, and notes that: "This wheel is every completed movement of thought or life, twenty-eight incarnations, a single incarnation, a single judgment or act of thought (81)," one realizes that the model has become self-replicating. No longer encountering any experience other than itself (although it is at all times a model of such encounter), it is developing an uncanny life of its own. It is self-perpetuating: it has become its own purpose — almost a definition of life, in fact. Reality has tipped over into irreality; the system has subsumed its object, becoming itself what it systematizes. In doing so it has laid important conceptual foundations for the literature of the fantastic and established some claim to be itself a document of that literature.

The creative imagination has been taken here to its limits. Yeats's system was to be a total explanation of the world he lived in; history, the cosmos, the minds and hearts of men. It is as purely interpretive a construct — as purely imaginative, then, in the Coleridgean sense — as could well be conceived; and yet within it, interpretation has become so rarefied and so intense as to pass into a realm which is not that of interpretation at all, but of fancy, of metonymy. For, taken to the end of its gyre, where all contact with the breaking force of experience, the not-yet-organized world of things, has been lost, the creative imagination, interpreting only itself, can produce only models that are like itself, or like each other, but not like anything outside itself. There is indeed no "thing" outside it any more. The elements of a perfect imagination are left floating in loose associative clusters in the mind, fantastic images in a detached, fantastic world, members of a set that *is* its own reality, for it has forgotten its relationship to any other. And Yeats's system has been saved, albeit not quite in the manner he purports to want.

Taken to its limits his model vindicates itself, not discursively, as an explanation of the universe, but simply by surviving as a model. What it explains is not any recognizable world, but the way in which the human faculties operate in the creation of all and any possible worlds. This is something like what Coleridge has set out to do, only Yeats's model goes much further; so far, indeed, as to lose touch with any dimension of experience and thought which might impinge on and negate it. Yeats's more tangible mistake, if it was a mistake, was to pretend, at least to his readers, that it reflected an ontological order distinct from the logical order of reflection. He seems sometimes to have known, sometimes to have forgotten, that all his cones and gyres were only one: the gyre explanation growing out of and returning to that which is to be explained — but increasingly failing to get there. "Some will ask," he writes in "Introduction to 'A Vision,'" "whether I believe in the actual existence of my circuits of sun and moon," and he replies that:

> if sometimes, overwhelmed by miracle as all men must be when in the midst of
> it, I have taken such periods literally, my reason has soon recovered; and now
> ... I regard them as stylistic arrangements of experience. ... They have helped
> me to hold in a single thought reality and justice. (25)

Yeats's *Vision* holds in a single bond reality and law; for the double helix, separating itself from that objectivity which forms one of its members, and thereby according to its own logic breaking down, does not in fact break down but reconstitues itself on a different level, in a different context, but with exactly the same logic as before. Reality has thereby been displaced; from being ontological it has become a thing of logic, of law; and law, in the same moment, has taken on a new dimension of reality. The paradox of the complete loss of the initial level of fanciful, associative discourse in *A Vision* — and this is coterminous with our primary level of reality — is its reappearance at the level of explanation. Instead of being directed at some "other" object, external to itself, this is directed now only toward the mind which apprehends it. And the mind apprehends it, not as explanation, but as at once pattern and thing. The gyre of fancy and imagination, transmuted in this paradox, is still intact; for what was purely imaginative has become purely fanciful, fantastic. And paradox, too, is a helical figure.

In its intricate, self-commenting, self-replicating manner, Yeats's "principal symbol" is akin to the Julia sets of modern mathematics, patterns of total symmetry which come into being when a simple feedback mechanism is repeated in a sequence of astronomical magnitude (see Peitgen and Richter

4-18). The mechanism itself, like Yeats's cones, is perfectly symmetrical; but, repeated to a sufficient degree, it generates numbers which tend, as one might predict, either toward an uncontrollable chaos or toward zero, or however, as one would not so readily expect, toward the pattern named after the French mathematician Julia. Represented graphically, this is a matrix which remains constant in shape at all levels of magnification: a hierarchically ordered sequence of self-reflecting contexts. And this is very much what Yeats's gyres become in the course of *A Vision*. Explanation generates that which no longer relates to an explained, symmetry generates the asymmetry of a theory whose only reason of being is itself; and this, in turn, is perfectly symmetrical, perfectly self-propagating. Logically the process should, and can only, repeat itself as an unending play between separation and identity. The two terms of the heuristic act. It is perhaps no coincidence that the Julia sets are unlike anything we know except the structures — at certain levels of explanation — of corals and crystals and living cells: patterns we see through a microscope as fundamental to life. It has been suggested that life itself may take place at the frontiers of chaos (Peitgen and Richter 17). If Yeats's vortices are to be trusted, this is at all events the locus of knowledge.

At this frontier, reality is both constituted and reconstituted. It is constituted in the play of imagination and fancy which Yeats's initial helix (and Coleridge's "Kubla Khan") describes. It is reconstituted in the continuum between theory and reality established in the course of *A Vision*, when the concept of materiality that grounds a discrete order of objectivity is transformed into a concept of energy: the energy that is present in the coiling and uncoiling of the helix, or, to put it another way, the energy that is stored in each separate contextual level and released in the passage from one level to the next. For the "objective" levels of Yeats's cosmology become, as his model progresses, simply different contexts of enquiry, governed always by the same internal laws, and by a single overriding law, that of contextual limitation. It is this, in *A Vision*, that replaces the concept of reality, and it is on that displacement that the genre of the fantastic is built.

The fantastic is the natural offspring of the reunion between the world and the language that utters it. All is now language, and *yet* there is a meaning to the term "reality" within that language. Once the epistemological order has subsumed the ontological, the old ontological distinction between the real and the unreal has been made redundant; the knowing process that grounds them is identical, and it is the realization of the hegemonic quality of that process that has led to the sort of assertion that Brooke-Rose has made, that the real and the unreal are now continuous. In the enthusiasm of this insight one might be tempted to suggest, as she does, that the real is really no more than a backwater of the unreal, but this is an exaggeration. For the distinction that has been removed at one level of discourse has been reinstated at another. Reality and unreality have different contexts, for we live in different contexts and have different uses for the meanings we make. The real and the unreal may reflect each other in every respect, both in their heuristic structure and in the breaking of that structure, but they lie at different points in the spectrum of knowing. Even in its ambivalence — for Todorov its key characteristic — the unreal is not radically different from the real; for even when it flouts the law of contextual limitations it reinforces the principle on which that law, and with it the real, are founded; namely that reality *is* a matter of context and nothing more. At the level of the real we simply cannot afford too much ambivalence — that is all.

Ambivalence is certainly present in Yeats's *A Vision*, not only in the removal from the familiar ordering of word to thing, but also in the whole apparatus of accounts with which Yeats surrounds and mystifies, but finally demythologizes his book. For Yeats goes to great lengths, indeed Coleridgean lengths, to confuse the reader about his status and genesis. In one of the several prefaces he appends to the *A Vision* proper, the "Stories of Michael Robartes and his Friends: An Extract from a Record made by his Pupils," he ascribes the Great Wheel to a certain Giraldus. Robartes, himself a fictional figure, and one who is uncertainly reported at that, tells the intriguing story of Giraldus's book:

> My mistress had found it in a wall cupboard where it had been left by the last tenant, an unfrocked priest who had joined a troupe of gypsies and disappeared, and she had torn out the middle pages to light our fire. (38-40)

Yeats too has his "person from Porlock." But, as always, he is more thorough than Coleridge, for the real story of his system's origins is that of its dictation, through the medium of his wife, by the "instructors," spirits whose word he followed, however difficult it might become. Perhaps *A Vision* is Yeats's most humorous book; perhaps, as a piece of fantastic writing, it may be able to reclaim a place in our serious consideration. At all events critical response to this notion certainly vindicates Todorov's stipulation about the literature of the unreal when he writes that "L'hésitation du lecteur est donc la première condition du fantastique" (36).

Typically, it was in "All Souls' Night," the poem he wrote as epilogue to *A Vision* that Yeats most directly expressed the cycle of life and death, of language and loss of language, on which his *A Vision* is based:

> Such thought—such thought have I that hold it tight
> Till meditation master all its parts,
> Nothing can stay my glance
> Until that glance run in the world's despite
> To where the damned have howled away their hearts,
> And where the blessed dance;
> Such thought, that in it bound
> I need no other thing,

Wound in mind's wandering
As mummies in the mummy-cloth are wound.
                    (*CP* 259)

The hegemony and continuity of *A Vision*, and of course, too, its helical
structure, are here, as well as some honest — even perhaps too honest — thoughts
about the origins of the book and its possible reception. Yeats's claims to
universal insight were not modest. The image of the mind comprehending life
and death and finding its own life in the tension between those opposites, is one
that is dear to Yeats. But it is rather on the mind in its approach to and encounter
with reality that the poem, like *A Vision* itself, concentrates. Only in Yeats's
"death" poems does this give way to something else: to a sense of moving in the
linguistic world which *A Vision* has established, a world that is real on its own
terms, as the achieved utterance of "Kubla Khan" is real, or as, in Yeats's own
lifetime, Wallace Stevens's dense universe of words was fast becoming.

"Cuchulain Comforted" is such a poem. Like "Kubla Khan" it deals in a
world of displaced images, but the manner of their displacement is now different. The battle between language and reality is over; the poem moves in a
world beyond the grave, and it moves with the placidity of its Dantesque tercets,
the achieved rhythm of a universe conscious of no break between itself and its
myth.

Cuchulain, the warrior-hero, moves unselfconsciously among the Shrouds
and obeys them, despite the fact that they are "'Convicted cowards all, by
kindred slain' / 'Or driven from home and left to die in fear.'" At their command
he takes up a shroud and begins to sew, for:

> 'Your life can grow much sweeter if you will
>
> 'Obey our ancient rule and make a shroud;
> Mainly because of what we only know
> The rattle of those arms makes us afraid.
>
> 'We thread the needles' eyes, and all we do
> All must together do.'
>   (*CP* 395)

This poem, too, envisages a communion between opposites: a community of
adverse spirits founded in the ritual enactment of a sign or myth. The Shrouds
sew shrouds; they recreate themselves in common action. What those selves
are, however, we cannot know; for although the language of the poem is very
lucid, it indicates in its lucidity that certain things lie beyond it. It is contextually
limited, and yet it breaks its context, foregrounding its limitation in the slight
dislocations of its logic. The Shrouds "stared . . . and were gone"; they "came
and were gone": their place is elsewhere, and Cuchulain, who is among the dead,

is not yet of them.

In pursuit of their common purpose, the Shrouds bid him listen to their song:

> They sang, but had nor human tunes nor words,
> Though all was done in common as before;
>
> They had changed their throats and had the throats of birds.
> *(CP* 396).

The hero is being initiated into the language community of death, a world where deeds and song are one, a universe of self-reflecting, self-breaking otherness. Even now he is the first to pass over this border, and his passage is his "comfort," though more specifically that comfort is the song itself, whose nature we cannot know, but only that it *is*, and that it is unlike any human song. Beyond the border of death there is this other border, where the strange inhabitants of that country, the Shrouds whose name and being is the proper epiphany of death, become stranger still, changing their throats for the throats of birds. But birds belong to fluidity and air and the darkness of psychic displacement, and air at least is the proper dimension of speech. Symbol and context, sign and world, merge and identify; but as they do so, and each time they do so, the context breaks and shifts, just as it does in *A Vision*.

All of this gives only suggestions of sense; but that *is* the sense of the poem: that in a universe where language, action, and being are one, we can no longer speak of meanings, but must change our own discourse and speak of sign acting upon sign to engender the tension that holds speech in place. Context and the breaking of context, reality and the experience of words, are in this language world a single continuum; and it is a world of relative stasis. The images of the poem move round each other rather than toward any consummation that might be distilled out of the poem. And again in this it models *A Vision*. We interpret, but the interpretation leads us back into the elements of disjointed speech: not "where the ladders start" but where they end is now our critical location, in language whose irreducibility is its identity, but whose identity is newly accessible.

Yeats has achieved his reality: he is where Coleridge was and where Wallace Stevens had already started from. Creative imagination has rejoined fancy, for there is something strictly fantastic about the Shrouds and their twofold transformation. They move in a world that we are able to value only as linguistic fact — and that is what Todorov means by the fantastic. The poem fulfills what *A Vision* explosively defined: a new myth of word breaking on word to release the energy that is synonymous with being. Yeats's "death" poems are the first fruits of a finally demythologized ontology in which the romantic ghost of his youth was laid to rest and the true task of romanticism accomplished: to work in a world understood to exist as world only in the contours, but the very material contours, of signs. Achieving this, *A Vision* set the stage not only for the directness of modern poetry, but also for that "gaiety of language" that is the modern fantastic.

Notes

1. See Keats's letter of 21st December 1817 to George and Thomas Keats in *Poetical Works* (101-104).

2. Roman Jakobson established the generative role of association and analogy in what he called the metonymic and metaphoric poles of language respectively (69-96). I use the term metonymy in his sense (of continguity, synechdoche) rather than in the traditional sense which, as Harold Bloom has observed, is closer to that of metaphor (11).

3. For further discussion of this theme see Swann (236- 245).

4. See H. O. Peitgen and P. H. Richter (4-18).

5. See Peitgen and Richter (17).

Works Cited

Blake, William. *Poetry and Prose*. 1927 Ed. Geoffrey Keynes. London: Nonesuch Press, 1967.

Bloom, Harold et al. *Deconstruction and Criticism*. New York: Seabury, 1979.

Brooke-Rose, Christine. *A Rhetoric of the Unreal*. Cambridge: Cambridge University Press, 1981.

Coleridge, S. T. *Biographia Literaria*. Everyman Edition. London: Dent, 1956.

—. *The Portable Coleridge*. Ed. I. A. Rich ards. New York: Viking, 1950.

Jakobson, Roman and Morris Halle. *Fundamentals of Language*. The Hague/Paris: Mouton, 1971.

Keats, John. *The Poetical Works and Other Writings of John Keats*. Ed. H. Buxton Forman. New York: Scribner, 1939.

MacNiece, Louis. *The Poetry of W. B. Yeats*. Oxford, Oxford University Press, 1941; London: Faber and Faber, 1967.

Peitgen, H. O. and P. H. Richter. *The Beauty of Fractals: Images of Complex Dynamical Systems*. New York: Springer Verlag, 1986.

Swann, Joseph. "'Where all the ladders start': Language and Experience in Yeats's Later Poetry." In *Studies in Anglo-Irish Literature*, ed. Heinz Kosok. Bonn: Bouvier, 1982.

Todorov, Tzvetan. *Introduction à la littérature fantastique*. Paris: Seuil, 1970.

Vendler, Helen. *Yeats's VISION and the Later Plays*. Cambridge, MA: Harvard University Press, 1963.

Yeats, William Butler. *The Collected Poems*. London: Macmillan, 1950.

Yeats, William Butler. *A Vision*. London: Macmillan, 1937.

Donald E. Morse and
Csilla Bertha

Afterword: Looking Backward, Looking Ahead: The Study of the Fantastic in Irish Literature and the Arts

In any collection such as this one, there must be far more writers and artists excluded than included. The ones selected are broadly representative of Irish literature and the arts as well as of the variety of uses to which the fantastic has been put. Irish literature and art are exceptionally rich in the fantastic. Yet fantasy in its most pure form is as rare in Ireland as it is elsewhere, and, therefore, most of the essays in this volume explore works of art and literature that are not obviously or exclusively fantastic. This exploration is indebted to recent theoreticians of the fantastic as a mode of presentation who examine such works and discuss the role fantastic elements can play, and how such elements may modify the scope of the text.

The theoreticians most widely quoted by the authors of essays in this collection, Kathryn Hume (*Fantasy and Mimesis: Responses to Reality in Western Literature* 1984) and Rosemary Jackson (*Fantasy: the Literature of Subversion* 1981), map the territory of the fantastic. Jackson is especially clear on psychology, while Hume, having the advantage of Jackson's work before her, traces the evolution of the idea of the fantastic through not only literary theory, but also philosophy, psychology, and history.

Building on both Jackson and Hume, Lance Olsen in *The Ellipse of Uncertainty* (1987), extends the theoretical discussion to include postmodern literature. Following Jackson's thesis of the subversive nature of the fantastic, Olsen declares: "The fantastic confronts civilization with the very forces it must repress in order for it to remain whole, functioning and successful. Fantasy presents a culture with that which it cannot stand" (22).

This thesis could be illustrated in the treatment of the ongoing crisis in contemporary Irish culture which resides in the senseless brutality of the Northern Ireland "troubles." In contemporary Irish drama, for example, Tom Paulin emphasized the tragic nature of the Northern Irish situation by rewriting Sophocles' *Antigone* in *The Riot Act* (1985). In fiction Benedict Keily convincingly records in his richly drawn novel *Nothing Ever Happens in Carmincross* (1985), the all-pervasive horror of the endless, meaninglessly savage bombings, killings, and maimings, while the film *Cal* (1984) graphically shows how people become trapped within this world, unable to keep and hold onto love, relationships, jobs, or security. No one is immune and no one escapes. Only the gunman with his sense of self-righteous brutality or pure thuggery keeps going, and he in his turn will also come to a firey end. Yet it remained for John Morrow to mix together elements of the fantastic in characters and plot with a macabre sense of humor, to drive home the terrible, often repressed truth of just how impossible the situation in the North really is, and of exactly who benefits from keeping that pot on the boil.

In the short story "The Humours of Ballyturdeen" (*Northern Myths* 1979), Morrow's hero is a washing-machine repairman who leaves town to answer a call for repairs out in No Man's Land "attuned to every nuance of change which spelt danger" (14). On his way he reflects on the omnipresent dangers of the city where he lives:

> Behind him lay the homely, smoking ruin of Belfast; there he knew where he was, or where he shouldn't be, at any given time, in his head a tracery of invisible battle-lines created by polarisation (git out or be brunt [*sic*] out, ya taig/prod basters); a city of vast pigeon-holes . . . in which he had become attuned to every nuance of change that spelt danger: the mid-day stillness that might herald a sudden swarming from side-streets like maddened bees from a smoked hive, as some hunger-striker gasped his or her last; the abrupt acceleration of a police Land Rover for no apparent reason; the look on the face of a search paratrooper that told him not to remark pleasantly on the state of the weather or England's position in the World Cup. (14)

As in all of Morrow's fiction, this story is told in an exact replication of both Belfast dialects, both "prod" (Protestant-pro-Unionist) and "taig" (Roman Catholic-Irish Nationalist), and includes beside the inherently dangerous landscape, the unexpected but welcome sexual encounters, and a surprising central event—in this case a rogue washing machine which performs at the end of its electric cord tether. The repairman has both the wit and the will to survive under these circumstances in this world once familiar from street ballads eulogizing those who were "poor but never gave in."

Not so the "punter" in Morrow's comic, highly fantastic—especially for those who do not live in contemporary Belfast—novel, *The Confessions of Proinsias O'Toole* (1977): amoral at best, the "punter" will do anything no matter how despicable or reprehensible, if he is paid. Taking what most outsiders would agree is this desperate situation in Belfast and using elements of the fantastic Morrow creates a wildly improbable, hugely comic exposé of opportunism and of those who prey on the unfortunate victims of the chaos. In this war zone, only the punter—the person willing to sell anything for a price—succeeds, and his success is short lived indeed. As the narrator says at the end about *all* the characters in the book: "All the fut sodgers perished, of course" (163). "Of course," they always do. Morrow thus exposes what the "culture . .

cannot stand," which apparently is neither the senseless brutality nor the extensive murder and mayhem, since both are widely acknowledged in the culture, but the cynical opportunism which takes advantage of even the most desperate human conditions purely for financial gain. Typically for an Irish writer, Morrow's language carries fantasy not only in its poetic flight but also in its humor and irony. As Brian Friel contends in his play *Translations*: "Certain cultures expend on their vocabularies and syntax acquisitive energies and ostentations entirely lacking in their material lives. . . . [Irish] is a rich language . . . full of the mythologies of fantasy and hope and self-deception. . . . It is our response to mud cabins and a diet of potatoes; our only method of replying to . . . inevitabilities" (42).

Such humor and irony — always a strong feature of Irish thinking and literature — frequently accompany the fantastic in modern literature in general, but rather than becoming a means of escape, they become a means of fighting against meaninglessness and chaos — even, or perhaps especially, in contemporary Belfast. As Richard Alan Schwartz affirms:

> Contemporary writers mine the fantastic for this vitality as a way of combating the bleak aspects of our age. Black humor, which frequently uses elements of the fantastic, acknowledges the negative facts of our existence but, without seriously trying to effect a change in the facts themselves, generates vigor and energy from them. The vigor and energy become the reply to our absurd plight. (29)

Within the absurd world of contemporary Belfast John Morrow is one of the authors best able to mine this kind of black comic vision.

The fantastic may also be used to maintain the ideal as well as to subvert it, as in the example of W. B. Yeats, who gave shape to his romantic ideal of legendary Ireland, and of the noble heroic human quest for unity and wholeness in many of his early plays, but mocked the same ideals in some later plays, such as *The Herne's Egg* (1938) or *The Death of Cuchulain* (1939), which introduce the fantastic in a harshly comic, sometimes grotesque context. Denis Johnston, however, far more radically subverted Yeats's — and many of his contemporaries' — romantic ideals and dreams about Ireland using fantastic means: such as, shifts of time and scenes, metamorphoses, and several devices of expressionistic stagecraft to highlight his satiric vision in *The Old Lady Says 'No!'* (1926).

There is a quintessentially Irish genre which includes such works as James Stephen's *The Crock of Gold* (1912), Eimar O'Duffy's *King Goshawk and the Birds* (1926), Brinsley MacNamara's *The Various Lives of Marcus Igoe* (1929), and above all Flann O'Brien's *At Swim-Two-Birds* (1939). (Miles Orvell calls O'Brien "an acknowledged father of fictional anarchy [whose] . . . statue is being ordered for the Gallery of Anti-Mimetic Fiction" [522]). In this genre the fantastic in various measures is combined — in Denis Donoghue's words — "nonchalantly" with "pedantry, inconsequence and verbiage" (1171). Or, occasionally, fantasy may remain pure as in Sheridan Le Fanu's Gothic tales or in Pat O'Shea's recent novel *The Hounds of the Morrigan* (1985). The latter fairy-tale-like novel, starting out as a charming, lighthearted story about nice innocent young children, uses all the classical devices of fantasy such as metamorphoses, enchantments, and various forms of charms and magic, in order to show the struggle between good and evil on different levels of existence, and to depict the human condition: fragile but also heroic in the midst of all the forces of nature.

Virtually all theoreticians of the fantastic, including Hume, Jackson, and Olsen, focus almost exclusively on fiction. So, valuable as their studies are, they leave gaps which need to be filled. In this collection Christopher Murray, for example, demonstrates how Hume's theory of fantastic fiction may be adapted to drama. Several other essays on Irish drama also break new critical ground by applying various theoretical aspects of studies on the fantastic to Irish playwrights and their works. Other important issues in drama which could add to our understanding of the use of the fantastic on the Irish stage include: Austin Clark's use of poetic fantasies, George Fitzmaurice's depiction of the dreamer and the fantasist on the stage, Michael J. Molloy's evocation of a past Ireland, Denis Johnston's expressionistic technique in the satires, or Brian Friel's, Thomas Kilroy's, Frank McGuinness's, and Tom Mac Intyre's more contemporary fantastic devices.

There is also a need to attend to poetry and the fantastic. Only one full-length study of fantasy tropes in poetry from Chaucer to the present time exists: Vernon R. Hyles and Patrick D. Murphy, *The Poetic Fantastic* (1990), and there is no comparable study of Irish poetry. The discussion of theory, therefore, needs to be extended beyond the confines of prose fiction to include all literary genres and then to include all artistic genres. Péter Egri's discussion of John Field's music and Hilary Pyle's of Jack B. Yeats's painting point the way toward possible studies of other Irish artists.

And there is much to be gained from the study of the fantastic in Irish literature and the arts. In *The Feast of Fools* (1969) Harvey Cox might have been glossing the works of O'Casey, Synge, Joyce or Yeats or a host of lesser known Irish writers and artists when he complained that:

> we have terribly damaged the inner experience of Western man. We have pressed him so hard toward useful work and rational calculation he has all but forgotten the joy of ecstatic celebration, antic play, and free imagination. (10)

In short: we in the West have neglected the fantastic, and in forgetting that which is "more real than reality" we have become like the mermaid of Irish legend forcibly held in captivity against our nature and against our wishes. The study of the fantastic in Irish literature and the arts offers a way out of this predicament, for what Northrop Frye suggests of all works of the imagination is especially true of the fantastic: "The work of imagination presents us with a vision, not of personal greatness of the poet, but of something impersonal and far greater; the vision of a decisive act of spiritual freedom, the vision of the recreation of man." Such a vision may begin by acknowledging human mortality. Yet, in Irish fantasy the focus is rarely, if ever, on the bleakness of this prospect but on life lived fully with this knowledge. Samuel Beckett and Lord Dunsany are exceptions: Beckett because he sees little that is not blasted and bleak, and Dunsany because he refuses to confront evil and pain directly or indirectly. But other writers do employ the fantastic for exactly that purpose: to face evil and pain, but in ways that extend rather than overwhelm or bury common humanity. Sophocles, delving deeply into the evil, pain, and mortality in the myth of Oedipus, has his protagonist affirm at the very end of his life, after all his incredible suffering:

> And yet one word
> Frees us of all the weight and pain of life:
> That word is love.
>   (Sophocles 162)

Similarly many of the Irish writers and artrists discussed in this volume utilize the fantastic to commit what can be described as a decisive act of spiritual freedom by focusing directly on that word, "the word known to all men" of which Joyce spoke in *Ulysses*: love, the word spoken throughout the day and on into the night by Leopold and Molly Bloom, but the word, "the only true thing in life" yet to be heard by Stephen Dedalus; the word Pegeen withdraws from Christy Mahon in *The Playboy of the Western World*; the word Emer experiences so deeply and so tragically in *The Only Jealousy of Emer*. The word Yeats traced again and again in the visible and invisible worlds until at last he located it "in the foul rag-and-bone shop of the heart" (*CP* 336). Love which, like the fantastic, proves to be again and again in literature and in life "more real than reality."

Works Cited

Cox, Harvey. *The Feast of Fools: A Theological Essay on Festivity and Fantasy.* Cambridge, MA: Harvard University Press, 1969.

Donoghue, Denis. "In the Celtic Twilight." Rev. of *No Laughing Matter*, by Anthony Cronin. *Times Literary Supplement*, 27 October-2 November 1989; 1171-1172.

Friel, Brian. *Translations.* London: Faber and Faber, 1984.

Frye, Northrup. *The Educated Imagination.* Bloomington, IN: Indiana University Press, 1964,

Hume, Kathryn. *Fantasy and Mimesis: Responses to Reality in Western Literature.* New York: Methuen, 1984.

Hyles, Vernon R. and Patrick D. Murphy. *The Poetic Fantastic*. Westport, CT: Greenwood Press, 1990.

Jackson, Rosemary. *Fantasy: The Literature of Subversion*. New York: Methuen, 1981.

Morrow, John. *The Confessions of Proinsias O' Toole*. Belfast: Blackstaff Press, 1977.

—-. *Northern Myths and Other Stories*. Belfast: Blackstaff Press, 1979.

Olsen, Lance. *Ellipse of Uncertainty: An Introduction to Postmodern Fantasy*. Westport, CT: Greenwood Press, 1987.

Orvill, Miles D. Rev. of Rudiger Imoff. *Alive Alive O! Flann O'Brien's At Swim-Two-Birds*. Totawan, NJ: Barnes and Noble Books, 1986, *Journal of Modern Literature* 13, nos.3/4 (Nov. 1986):522.

Schwartz, Richard Allen. "The Fantastic in Contemporary Fiction." In *The Scope of the Fantastic—Theory, Technique, Major Authors*, ed. Robert A. Collins and Howard D. Pearce. Westport, CT: Greenwood Press, 1985.

Sophocles. "Oedipus at Colonus." Trans. Robert Fitzgerald. In *The Oedipus Cycle: an English Version*. New York: Harcourt, Brace & World, 1949.

Yeats, William Butler. *Collected Poems*. New York: Macmillan, 1956.

Select Bibliography on the Fantastic

Aldiss, Brian W. "Was Zilla Right? Fantasy and Truth." *Journal of the Fantastic in the Arts* 1.1 (1988): 7-23

Apter, T. E. *Fantasy Literature*. Bloomington: Indiana University Press, 1982.

Brooke-Rose, Christine. *A Rhetoric of the Unreal*. Cambridge: Cambridge University Press, 1981.

Collins, Robert A. and Howard D. Pearce, ed. *The Scope of the Fantastic — Theory, Technique, Major Authors Selected Essays from the First International Conference on the Fantastic in Literature and Film*. Westport, CT: Greenwood Press, 1985.

Cook, Elizabeth. *The Ordinary and the Fabulous: An Introduction to Myths, Legends, and Fairy Tales*. 1969 Second Edition. Cambridge: Cambridge University Press, 1976.

Cox, Harvey. *The Feast of Fools: A Theological Essay on Festivity and Fantasy*. Cambridge, MA: Harvard University Press, 1969.

Coyle, William, ed. *Aspects of Fantasy: Selected Essays from the Second International Conference on the Fantastic in Literature and Film*. Westport,CT: Greenwood Press, 1986.

Hume, Kathryn. *Fantasy and Mimesis: Responses to Reality in Western Literature*. New York: Methuen, 1984.

Hyles, Vernon R. and Patrick D. Murphy. *The Poetic Fantastic*. Westport, CT: Greenwood Press, 1990.

Irwin, William. *The Game of the Impossible: A Rhetoric of Fantasy*. Urbana: University of Illinois Press, 1976.

Jackson, Rosemary. *Fantasy: The Literature of Subversion*. London: Methuen, 1981.

Johnson, Toni O'Brien. *Synge: The Medieval and the Grotesque*. Gerrards Cross, Bucks.: Colin Smythe; Totowa: Barnes & Noble, 1982.

Kroeber, Karl. *Romantic Fantasy and Science Fiction*. New Haven: Yale University Press, 1988.

Landow, George P. "And the World Became Strange: Realms of Literary Fantasy." In *The Aesthetics of Fantasy Literature and Art*., ed. Roger C.

Schlobin. Notre Dame, IN: University of Notre Dame Press, 1982.

Lanford, Michele, ed. *The Contours of the Fantastic: Selected Essays from the Eighth International Conference on the Fantastic in the Arts*. Westport, CT: Greenwood Press, 1990.

Lewis, C. S. *Of Other Worlds: Essays and Stories*. 1966. Ed. Walter Hooper. New York: Harcourt Brace Javanovich, 1975.

Manlove, Colin N. *The Impulse of Fantasy in Literature*. Kent: The Kent State University Press, 1977.

—-. "The Elusiveness of Fantasy." *Fantasy Review*. 9, 74 (April 1986): 13-14; 49-50.

—-. *Modern Fantasy: Five Studies*. Cambridge: Cambridge University Press, 1975.

Martin, Augustine. "Fable and Fantasy." In *The Genius of Irish Prose, ed. Augustine Martin, 110-120. Dublin: The Mercier Press, 1985.*

Mercier, Vivian. *The Irish Comic Tradition*. Oxford: The Clarendon Press, 1962.

Morse, Donald E. *The Fantastic in World Literature and the Arts: Selected Essays from the Fifth International Conference on the Fantastic in the Arts*. Westport, CT: Greenwood Press, 1987.

Olsen, Lance. *Ellipse of Uncertainty: An Introduction to Postmodern Fantasy*. Westport, CT: Greenwood Press, 1987.

Palumbo, Donald. *Spectrum of the Fantastic: Selected Essays from the Sixth International Conference on the Fantastic in the Arts*. Westport, CT: Greenwood Press, 1988.

Rabkin, Eric S. *The Fantastic in Literature*. Princeton: Princeton University Press, 1976.

Schlobin, Roger C. *The Aesthetics of Fantasy Literature and Art*. Notre Dame: University of Notre Dame Press, 1982.

Scholes, Robert. *Fabulation and Metafiction*. Urbana: University of Illinois Press, 1979.

Swinfen, Ann. *In Defense of Fantasy: A Study of the Genre in English and American Literature Since 1945*. London: Routledge and Kegan Paul, 1984.

Todorov, Tzvetan. *Introduction à la littérature fantastique*. Paris: Editions du Seuil, 1970. *The Fantastic: A Structuralist Approach to a Literary Genre*. Translated by Richard Howard. Cleveland: Case Western Reserve University Press, 1973; Ithaca: Cornell University Press, 1975.

Tolkien, J. R. R. *Tree and Leaf*. Boston: Houghton Mifflin Company, 1965.

The Journal of the Fantastic in the Arts. Carl B. Yoke, ed.

Index

About the Editors and Contributors

CSILLA BERTHA, co-editor, teaches English and Irish literature at Lajos Kossuth University Debrecen, Hungary. She is the accredited representative of the International Association for the Study of Anglo-Irish Literature for Hungary, a member of the Bibliography Committee for the *Irish University Review* and was a founding member of and serves on the Advisory Board for the International Centre for the Study of Literatures in English at Graz, Austria. Her publications include *A drámairó Yeats* ("Yeats the Playwright," 1988), numerous articles, both in English and in Hungarian, on Irish drama, W. B. Yeats, J. M. Synge, Brien Friel, Thomas Murphy, and J. B. Keane, on the Hungarian painter, Csontváry, on the fantastic in literature and the arts, and on parallels between Irish and Hungarian literature. She has lectured on Irish literature in Austria (1988), West Germany (1989), Canada (1989), and the United States 1990). She has presented at many conferences of IASAIL since 1984 and at several conferences of the International Association for the Fantastic in the Arts. She held a Rockefeller fellowship at the Bellagio study center in 1991.

PÉTER EGRI is Professor of English and American Literature at Lóránt Eötvös University in Budapest where he has developed a series of courses on the interrelations among literature, painting and music. He has been an IREX Fellow at Harvard and an ACLS Fellow at the University of California-Berkeley. Among his many books are ones on Hemingway, Joyce, Mann, Proust, Kafka, Chekov and O'Neill, as well as *Dream, Vision and Reality: On Modern European Fiction* (1969), *Avantgardism and Modernity* (1972), *The Reality of Poetry* (1975), *Fault Lines: Trends in European Drama at the Turn of the Century* (1983), and most recently, *Literature, Painting and Music: An Interdisciplinary Approach to Comparative Literature* (1988).

VERNON HYLES teaches fantasy and English literature at Auburn University. Together with Patrick D. Murphy he edited *The Poetic Fantastic*, Greenwood Press, 1990 the only full length study of fantasy tropes in poetry.

His *Reader's Guide to George Effinger* (Starmont House) was published in 1988. The author of numerous published scholarly articles and poems, he has also had several of his plays produced.

TONI O'BRIEN JOHNSON holds advanced degrees from Trinity College, Dublin (MA) and the Université de Lausanne (Doctorat ès Lettres) where she currently teaches. Her publications include *Synge: The Medieval and the Grotesque* (1982), numerous essays on Samuel Beckett, J. M. Synge, Elizabeth Bowen, James Joyce, and Medieval Irish poetics, translations, abstracts and reviews. She has been a Visiting Professor at the University of Calgary, on the faculty of the Yeats International Summer School, and a frequent presenter at international conferences of the Canadian Association for Irish Studies and the International Association for the Study of Anglo-Irish Literature.

JÜRGEN KAMM, Lecturer in English at Wuppertal University, Germany, studied English language and literature, history and philosophy in Wuppertal and at Cambridge. He is the co-author of a two-volume study of the English novel about World War II. His other publications include essays on the works of Thomas Moore, Oscar Wilde, G. B. Shaw, Liam O'Flaherty, Frank O'Connor, Adian Higgins, and Michael MacLaverty.

BETTINA KNAPP, Professor of French, Hunter College in New York, teaches courses in French, World and American literature, and in Jungian criticism. A prolific literary critic she has also published translations, interviews, biographies, collections of criticism, and edited anthologies. Her many books include single author studies of: Louis Gouvet (1957), Jean Genet (1968, 1975), Antonin Artaud (1969), Jean Cocteau (1970), Jean Racine (1971), Georges Duhamel (1972), Celine (1974), Maurice Materlinck (1975), Anaïs Nin (1978), Fernard Crommelynck (1978), Emile Zola (1980), Edgar Allan Poe (1984), Stephen Crane (1987), and Emily Dickinson (1989); her contributions to Jungian criticism include: *Dream and Image* (1979), *Prometheus Syndrome (1979), Theatre and Alchemy* (1980), *Archetype, Dance and the Writer* (1983), *A Jungian Approach to Literature* (1984), *Word, Image and Psyche* (1985), *Archetype, Architecture and the Writer* (1986), and *Machine, Metaphor and the Writer* (1989). She has been invited to lecture around the world including in Paris, Budapest, and Jerusalem.

COLIN MANLOVE, Reader in English Literature at the University of Edinburgh has interests in all areas of literature, but particularly in fantasy and science fiction. He is the author of *Modern Fantasy: Five Studies*; *Literature and Reality 1660-1800; The Gap in Shakespeare: The Motif of Division from Richard II to The Tempest; The Impulse of Fantasy Literature; Science Fiction: Ten Explorations*; *C. S. Lewis: His Literary Achievement*; and *Critical Thinking: A Guide to Interpreting Literary Text*. In 1989 he received the International Association for the Study of the Fantastic in the Arts' Distinguished Scholarship Award. His latest book is on Christian fantasy from Dante to the present day.

DONALD E. MORSE, Co-Editor, is Professor of English and Rhetoric at Oakland University in Michigan, Conference Coordinator for The International-al Association for the Fantastic in the Arts, and Fulbright Professor of American Studies at the University of Debrecen, Hungary (1987-1989 and 1991-1993). Among his numerous publications are *A Reader's Guide to Kurt Vonnegut* (1991), essays on W. H. Auden, J. P. Donleavy, James Joyce, Csaba Lászlóffy. and Vonnegut, articles on satire, fantasy and belief, the American Dream, management training, adult developmental psychology, and several on the teaching of intelligence, literature, writing, and fantasy,. He is the editor of *The Choices of Fiction* (1974), and *The Fantastic in World Literature and the Arts* (Greenwood Press, 1987). An international lecturer on a wide variety of topics, he has been on three lecture tours sponsored by the United States Information Service: to Austria (1985 and 1988) and to Germany (1989). He was a founding member of and serves on the Advisory Board for the International Centre for the Study of Literatures in English at Graz, Austria. He is a frequent presenter at conferences of The International Association for the Fantastic in the Arts and at many conferences of the International Association for the Study of Anglo-Irish Literature. In 1989 he delivered the Opening Plenary Lecture at IASAIL international conference in Debrecen. In 1991 he was awarded a Rockefeller fellowship to the Bellagio study center..

MAUREEN MURPHY, Dean of Students at Hofstra University, is Past President of the American Conference for Irish Studies, member of the Execu-tive Committee and Bibliographer of IASAIL, a member of the Executive Council of the American Irish Historical Society, and has been on the faculty of the Yeats International Summer School. Her publications include articles on Irish history, literature, folklore, and the Irish language, and she is editor of *A Guide to Irish Studies in the United States* (1979, 1982, 1987) and *Maire MacNeill's Maire Rue: Lady of Leamaneh* as well as co-editor of *Irish Literature: A Reader* (1987) and *James Joyce: A Centenary Tribute* (Greenwood Press, 1988). Her current project is a book-length study of the Irish servant girl in America.

CHRISTOPHER MURRAY teaches drama in the Department of English, University College, Dublin. Editor of the *Irish University Review*, he has pub-lished extensively on Irish theater and drama. His most recent work is (with Masaru Sekine) *Yeats and the Noh* (Colin Smythe, 1989).

HILARY PYLE, Irish writer, art critic, and art historian, is the author of biographies of the poet, James Stephens, and of the painter, Jack B. Yeats. (The last in a revised edition 1989.) Her latest work is a double biography of the Dublin poet and satirist, Susan L. Mitchell, and her mother Kate Cullen.

ANTHONY VALENTINE ROCHE, Lecturer in Anglo-Irish Literature at University College-Dublin, has also taught at the University of California-Santa Barbara and Auburn University. Currently he is Associate Director of the Yeats International Summer School and Irish editor of the *Irish Literary Supplement*. His many essays on Irish literature have appeared in *Genre*, *The James Joyce Quarterly*, the *Irish University Review*, *Hermathena*, and he has contributed essays to several collections, including *A J. M. Synge Literary Companion* (Greenwood Press 1989).

ALADÁR SARBU, Professor of English at Lóránt Eötvös University in Budapest, is the author of numerous books on the English working class novel, Joseph Conrad, Henry James. He has also published a novel, essays, studies, and a number of short stories. He has edited an anthology of essays by English left-wing radicals of the 1930s. His most recent book is *The Reality of Appearance: Emerson, Hawthorne, and Melville*.

JOSEPH SWANN, Lecturer in English and American Studies, University of Wuppertal, Germany, studied philosophy and German in Rome, Oxford, Canterbury, and London. He has published numerous essays on modern poetry, Commonwealth writing, and Irish literature, as well as original poetry. He is a frequent presenter at conferences of the International Association for the Study of Anglo-Irish Literature.

**Contributions to the Study of
Science Fiction and Fantasy**

Welsh Celtic Myth in Modern Fantasy
C. W. Sullivan III

When World Views Collide: A Study in Imagination and Evolution
John J. Pierce

From Satire to Subversion: The Fantasies of James Branch Cabell
James Riemer

The Shape of the Fantastic: Selected Essays from the Seventh International
Conference on the Fantastic in the Arts
Olena H. Saciuk, editor

The Poetic Fantastic: Studies in an Evolving Genre
Patrick D. Murphy and Vernon Hyles, editors

In the Image of God: Theme, Characterization, and Landscape in the
Fiction of Orson Scott Card
Michael R. Collings

Contours of the Fantastic: Selected Essays from the Eighth International
Conference on the Fantastic in the Arts
Michele K. Langford, editor

The Connecticut Yankee in the Twentieth Century: Travel to the Past
in Science Fiction
Bud Foote

The Reclamation of a Queen: Guinevere in Modern Fantasy
Barbara Ann Gordon-Wise

Seven Masters of Supernatural Fiction
Edward Wagenknecht

Out of the Night and Into the Dream: A Thematic Study of the Fiction
of J. G. Ballard
Gregory Stephenson

	DATE DUE		